Programming Solutions Handbook
for IBM Microcomputers

Other McGraw-Hill Books of Interest

ISBN	AUTHOR	TITLE
0-07-006551-9	Bosler	*CLIST Programming*
0-07-044129-4	Murphy	*Assembler for COBOL Programmers: MVS, VM*
0-07-006533-0	Bookman	*COBOL II for Programmers*
0-07-046271-2	McGrew, McDaniel	*In-House Publishing in a Mainframe Environment*
0-07-051265-5	Ranade et al.	*DB2: Concepts, Programming, and Design*
0-07-054594-4	Sanchez, Canton	*IBM Microcomputers: A Programmer's Handbook*
0-07-002467-7	Aronson, Aronson	*SAS System: A Programmer's Guide*
0-07-002673-4	Azevedo	*ISPF: The Strategic Dialog Manager*
0-07-007248-5	Brathwaite	*Analysis, Design, and Implementation of Data Dictionaries*
0-07-009816-6	Carathanassis	*Expert MVS/XA, JCL: A Guide to Advanced Techniques*
0-07-015231-4	D'Alleyrand	*Image Storage and Retrieval Systems*
0-07-016188-7	Dayton	*Integrating Digital Services*
0-07-017606-X	Donofrio	*CICS: Debugging, Dump Reading, and Problem Determination*
0-07-018966-8	Eddolls	*VM Performance Management*
0-07-033571-0	Kavanagh	*VS COBOL II for COBOL Programmers*
0-07-040666-9	Martyn, Hartley	*DB2/SQL: A Professional Programmer's Guide*
0-07-050054-1	Piggott	*CICS: A Practical Guide for System Fine Tuning*
0-07-050686-8	Prasad	*IBM Mainframes: Architecture and Design*
0-07-051144-6	Ranade, Sackett	*Introduction to SNA Networking: Using VTAM/NCP*
0-07-051143-8	Ranade, Sackett	*Advanced SNA: A Professional's Guide to VTAM/NCP*

Database Experts Series

ISBN	AUTHOR	TITLE
0-07-020631-7	Hoechst et al.	*Guide to Oracle*
0-07-033637-7	Kageyama	*CICS Handbook*
0-07-016604-8	DeVita	*The Database Experts' Guide to FOCUS*
0-07-055170-7	IMI Systems, Inc.	*DB2 and SQL/DS: A User's Reference*
0-07-023267-9	Larson	*The Database Experts' Guide to DATABASE 2*
0-07-039002-9	Lusardi	*Database Experts' Guide to SQL*
0-07-048550-X	Parsons	*The Database Experts' Guide to IDEAL*

Communications Series

ISBN	AUTHOR	TITLE
0-07-055327-0	Schlar	*Inside X.25: A Manager's Guide*
0-07-005075-9	Berson	*APPC: Introduction to LU6.2*
0-07-034242-3	Kessler	*ISDN: Concepts, Facilities, and Services*
0-07-071136-4	Wipfler	*Distributed Processing in CICS*
0-07-002394-8	Arnell, Davis	*Handbook of Effective Disaster/Recovery Planning*
0-07-009783-6	Cap Gemini America	*DB2 Applications Development Handbook*
0-07-009792-5	Cap Gemini America	*Computer Systems Conversion*

Programming Solutions Handbook for IBM Microcomputers

Julio Sanchez
Northern Montana College

Maria P. Canton
Skipanon Software Co.

McGraw-Hill, Inc.
New York   St. Louis   San Francisco   Auckland   Bogotá
Caracas   Hamburg   Lisbon   London   Madrid
Mexico   Milan   Montreal   New Delhi   Paris
San Juan   São Paulo   Singapore
Sydney   Tokyo   Toronto

Library of Congress Cataloging-in-Publication Data

Sanchez, Julio.
    Programming solutions handbook for IBM microcomputers / by
    Julio Sanchez and Maria P. Canton.
        p.   cm.
      ISBN 0-07-054605-3
      1. IBM micorcomputers—Programming.   2. Subroutines (Computer
    programs)   I. Canton, Maria P.   II. Title
    QA76.8.I259193S26   1991
    005.265—dc20   90-24112
                                                                        CIP

1 2 3 4 5 6 7 8 9 0   DOC/DOC   9 6 5 4 3 2 1

P/N   054605-3
PART OF
ISBN   0-07-054597-9

*The sponsoring editor for this book was Theron Shreve, the editing
supervisor was David E. Fogarty, and the production supervisor was
Pamela A. Pelton.*

Printed and bound by R. R. Donnelley & Sons Company.

Several trademarks appear in this book. The companies listed here
are the owners of the trademarks following their names: Compaq
Computer Corporation (Compaq); Hewlett-Packard Company (Hewlett-
Packard); Intel Corporation (Intel); International Business Machines
Corporation (IBM); Microsoft Corporation (Microsoft, MS-DOS).

For information about our audio products, write us at:
Newbridge Book Clubs, 3000 Cindel Drive, Delran, NJ   08370

Contents

Preface

Human beings have no ancestral experience with digital logic and little instinctive understanding of machine intelligence. It is often easier to grasp the complications, assumptions, and sophisticated inferences of our mental processes than to develop a simple sequence of instructions for a programmable digital machine. This explains why most programming errors are not subtle failures of reasoning, but coarse omissions and misjudgments, which we often call "stupid mistakes." Frequently, the error can be related to our *natural assumption* that the machine was equipped with some form of human understanding.

Fortunately, computer programming is an acquired skill; the more programs we write, the easier it becomes. At the same time, programming creates its own equity. In each new task that we tackle as programmers we use not only the experiences gained in previous ones but also even sections of code developed for other chores, to the extent that we can sometimes create a new program by cutting and pasting bits and pieces of old ones. These routines, procedures, and code fragments become assets that we can use and reuse as the need arises.

For this reason our growth as programmers can often be measured by the size of our accumulated code libraries. As mechanics add useful devices and gadgets to their toolboxes, programmers add routines and code fragments to their libraries. These are the tools of the programmer's trade. But it would be quite awkward if tradespeople had to personally manufacture every tool used, or if programmers had to personally code every routine in their respective libraries. Luckily, we profit from the experience and work of others in our field and add their tools to our own collection. Undoubtedly we sometimes feel more familiar and comfortable with code that was personally created than with code created by others. But as we use, study, and modify the routines developed by other programmers we gain greater insight into their design and operation. After some time, it becomes difficult for us to tell which code in our library was personally developed and which is the work of others.

The principal usefulness of the *Programming Solutions Handbook* is as a practical problem solver for programmers and students. It is a programmer's cookbook; therefore, it includes a collection of routines to solve the most common problems encountered in a language. But, unlike a conventional cookbook, Programming Solutions also includes many singular, unusual, or interesting programming problems that are seldom treated in the literature. These uncommon subjects include coding an operating system, laser printer programming, graphics and animated games, event modeling, and computer simulations.

This book is unique in that many code samples are contained in complete programs which serve a useful purpose. Some of the programs are finished applications. The book includes a mini operating system, a printer spooler, a graphics dump to a Hewlett-

Packard laser printer, a serial communications program, a modem driver, two keyboard enhancement utilities, several mathematical conversion routines for programming the 80x87 coprocessor, an animated arcade game, and a resource scheduling simulation.

The reader should note that commercial software is usually developed by programming teams. In most projects one of these teams is a specialized program testing group. It is their task to ascertain and certify the program's correctness. Considerable time and resources are often spent in this phase of software development. However, the programs presented in this book were developed individually by the authors. Their purpose is not commercial, but to illustrate programming ideas, principles, and techniques. In addition, for reasons of space limitations, most of these programs contain very little, if any, error trapping. It is important for the reader to be aware of these facts and use the programs accordingly.

The authors would like to thank the friends and associates who provided advice, support, and assistance in this project. Jay Ranade, the series editor, was very helpful at every stage of this book. At McGraw-Hill, Theron Shreve, David Fogarty, Catherine Hertz, and Nancy Sileo were always available when we needed help. Dr. Martha Ann Dow, Vice-President for Academic Affairs at Northern Montana College, and Kevin Carlson, Assistant Vice-President for Academic Affairs in Great Falls, have made us feel their enthusiasm and support. Our thanks to Dr. Ron Talmage, Virgil Hawkinson, Susan Tanner, Wes Tucker, Roger Stone, Bob Cooper, and Sharon Lowman, also from Northern, for moral support and technical assistance. And a very special thanks to our friend Chet Harris for his continued encouragement.

Great Falls, Montana   Julio Sanchez
                                                                  Maria P. Canton

Abbreviations and Conventions

μs	microsecond	APA	all-points addressable
Bd	Baud rate	bps	bits per second
CDA	Color Display Adapter	CGA	Color Graphics Adapter
cps	characters per second	CRC	cycle redundancy check
CTS	clear-to-send	DOS	Disk Operating System
DSR	data set ready	DTR	data terminal ready
EGA	Enhanced Graphics Adapter	EIA	Electronic Industries Association
FAT	file allocation table	FCB	file control block
HMI	horizontal motion index	Hz	hertz
in	inch	I/O	input/output
K	kilobyte	kHz	kilohertz
LAN	local area networks	LSB	least significant bit
Mbytes	megabytes	MCGA	Multicolor Graphics Array
MDA	Monochrome Display Adapter	MHz	megahertz
MSB	most significant bit	NDP	Numeric Data Processor
NMI	nonmaskable interrupt	NPX	Numeric Processor Extension
ns	nanosecond	PCjr	PC Junior
PGS	Professional Graphics System	POST	Power-On Seft-Test
PS/2	Personal System/2	RAM	random-access memory
ROM	read-only memory	s	second
tpi	tracks per inch	TSR	terminate-and-stay resident
UART	Universal Asynchronous Receiver and Transmitter	VGA	Video Graphics Array
		VMI	vertical motion index
W	watt		

Typographical symbols in tables and figures:

->	Pointer, as in ES:BX -> video buffer
⇒ ⇐ ⇔	Direction of data flow

Number Systems:

Hexadecimal numbers are postfixed with the uppercase letter H, for example, 7E23H. Binary numbers are postfixed with the uppercase letter B, for example, 00011001B. Numbers written without the H or B postifix are in decimal notation.

1

Models, Conventions, and Interfacing

1.0 Program Design and Coding

Large scale software projects, developed according to engineering principles, usually take place in three stages: design, implementation, and testing. In the design stage an indefinite list of abstract requirements is transformed into detailed and unambiguous specifications that concretely determine the individual tasks to be performed by the software. A well-designed software project follows hierarchical principles so that program execution can proceed from the top down. In addition, the design stage identifies the individual modules that perform the logical functions of the program. Finally, the program designers provide the implementation specialists with detailed graphs of data structures and flowcharts of the program's logic.

A typical design specification document includes the following elements:

1. A hierarchical list of program specifications along with the technical standards of precision and performance that will allow an objective evaluation of the finished product.

2. A definition of the program modules, describing systems, routines, procedures, or other divisions of execution. This document is used in the detailed planning of the implementation stage.

3. A description of the data structures and a list of the mathematical formulas used in the program.

4. A drawing or graph for each major screen display or hardcopy form.

5. Flowcharts and other diagrams of the program's logic.

When program development is performed by small groups or individual programmers, there is an unfortunate tendency to devote minimum time and resources to the design and testing stages. It is often assumed that *programming is coding* and that program design and testing are merely incidental stages in the real chore of writing code. Even flowcharts are deemed academic drills of little practical consequence. These misconceptions regarding the importance of following rigorous methods of program design and testing account for the poor quality of many software products.

1.0.1 To Code or to Copy

Coding cannot take place until the programmer(s) have some idea of the tasks to be performed by the software. Ideally, the coder will have available a detailed and rigorous set of documents resulting from a good program design. At worst, the coding stage begins with a bare notion of these tasks. However, whether the program has been well thought out or not, the implementation stage of program development always consists of defining, designing, coding, and interfacing routines that perform the program's assignments. For example, the design documents for a serial communications program could tell the coders that the software is to include the following elements:

1. A routine to initialize the serial port to certain fixed parameters.
2. A routine to monitor the serial port registers for received characters.
3. A routine to transmit characters through the serial lines.
4. A routine to monitor the keyboard for characters typed by the user.
5. A routine to display characters on the system's CRT screen.

The person(s) responsible for implementing the program code must decide whether to code or to copy each individual routine. Coding routines has the advantage of creating a product that is specifically suited to the task, while copying them from another program or from a book such as this one is frequently easier and faster than developing new code. Occasionally the decision to code or to copy is an easy one. For example, if the programmers have at hand a routine that performs the required processing to the precision and performance standards specified for the program, there would be little justification in spending time and effort in developing a new one. Developing new routines to perform identical tasks as existing ones is as futile as reinventing the wheel.

But often the choice of whether to code or to copy is not as easy; the routines at hand may not meet the program's performance standards or the processing may not exactly match the requirements. For example, in the case of the serial communications software previously mentioned, the program specifications may mandate simultaneous data reception and transmission, while the available routines could have been designed to perform these functions alternatively.

In each particular case the degree of suitability of existing code to the requirements of the new program can vary from being perfectly matched to being totally unacceptable. In most cases, it is better for the programmers to have a code sample at hand, even if it is not exactly suited to the task, than to have to start from zero. Existing routines can often be enhanced, modified, or expanded to match new needs. There is no general solution to the dilemma of creating versus copying code.

1.0.2 Algorithms and Routines

One way to make the solution of programming problems usable in any system is to describe it in generic terms. By avoiding the specifics of a programming language we make the solution useful to programmers working in any system or environment. The term *algorithm* is frequently used to describe the sequence of steps or mathematical operations that will lead to the solution of a specific problem. Rigorously speaking, an algorithm can be a mathematical formula, a textual description, a routine in any real or imaginary programming language, or just a set of verbal instructions. In this book, in order to differentiate algorithms from routines, we will limit the concept of an algorithm to problem solution expressed in textual or mathematical form, and we will use the term *routine* to refer to problem solutions in computer code.

Often the best assistance that a programmer can hope for is a coded routine that performs the required tasks exactly and precisely or, if this is not available, an algorithm that describes the logical and processing steps that lead to the solution of a similar problem. In this book we list and describe both algorithms and routines. The algorithms are sometimes found independent of the code. On other occasions they are explained as part of the code listings. In every case we have tried to ensure that the programmer understands and is able to follow, step by step, the processing performed in the routines and code fragments. It is our belief that this understanding often leads to the solution of programming problems that do not exactly match those solved in the particular routines.

1.0.3 Language Choices

The programmer should have direct access to a collection of routines and code fragments and be able to incorporate these components into the code at hand so that thay become part of the program. Consequently, the language in which the routines are coded must be compatible with the language in use. The simplest solution is to have the program and routines in the same programming language — or even better, in the same implementation of the programming language. For example, a programmer working in Borland's Turbo Pascal version 5.5 could very easily use code fragments and subprograms coded in this same version of Turbo Pascal. To a lesser degree this programmer could use routines coded in other versions of the same implementation, in other implementations of the language, or in other programming languages compatible with Turbo Pascal version 5.5.

Therefore, the ideal collection of routines is one that lists code in all programming languages and is constantly updated to new language versions and implementations as they are released. But this solution is practically impossible, even if we limit the target system to a single machine type. For instance, there are half a dozen implementations of Pascal, C language, BASIC, Fortran, and Cobol that are compatible with the IBM microcomputers. Some of these implementations have had 10 or more versions and releases in the course of the last 5 years. Add another 10 or 12 computer languages of lesser renown and the task becomes enormous.

What criteria can be followed in order to boil down this list of languages to a more manageable number? Should we pick the more popular languages, the more technical ones, or the ones that are preferred professionally? Should the code be compatible only with the current version of the selected languages or also with previous versions? Another consideration that comes to mind in selecting programming languages for a book of routines is that many programmers specialize in a single language. Therefore, three-fourths of a book of routines in four different languages will be useless to most individuals. By the same token, the amount of material that can be covered in a given number of pages is inversely proportional to the number of languages used.

A solution to this dilemma would be to use assembly language instead of one or more high-level languages. There are three important advantages to this choice.

1. Assembly language is the most powerful of all programming media. There are no limits to this language, except the limits of the machine's hardware.

2. The code resulting from assembly language is more compact and efficient than the code generated by any high-level language.

3. All popular high-level languages provide means for interfacing with assembly language code, while communications between high-level languages is often difficult, or even impossible.

On the other hand, the main disadvantage of using assembly language is that the code is difficult to follow and understand by those not familiar with the language. However, in spite of this drawback, we have found no better choice.

1.0.4 The Big Picture

A programming problem is often solved with a code fragment or a routine that executes a certain task, but there are times when the programmer needs inspiration and ideas on how to tackle a large coding project. For example, a certain program could benefit from running under a small, customized operating system, instead of under the standard DOS. But the task of designing and coding an operating-system program, even a small one, can be an intimidating one. Most programmers have limited experience along these lines and only sketchy ideas of the functions and interrelations between the bootstrap, the command processor, the loader, and the error handler sections of an operating system. In this situation the assistance required by programmers and designers consists of not only routines and code sections but also the general blueprint of a disk operating system, including details of how each program module or processing group interacts with the other ones.

Thus, it is possible to expand the traditional levels of assistance offered by programming cookbooks, as follows:

1. Code fragments to illustrate processing details—for example, the code lines for initializing the segment registers at the start of a low-level language program.

2. Routines and procedures that perform specific functions, for example, a procedure to convert 16 binary digits in a central processing unit (CPU) register into five ASCII-hexadecimal digits in a buffer supplied by the caller.

3. Software floorplans for standard programs—for example, the logic and code for a disk operating system program.

At first sight the sheer volume of such a task may seem enormous, but on more careful observation we note that programs are collections of routines and code fragments. Therefore, the coded material can be classified, cross-referenced, and indexed so as to avoid repetition. For instance, if two illustrated programs require a binary-to-hexadecimal conversion routine, this code need only be listed in one of the programs. The second program can use the routine by merely referencing its location in the book. A second benefit derived from this approach is that, by developing the processing routines as solutions to real programming problems, we also demonstrate how these routines can be practically applied.

1.0.5 Using the Code

The code fragments, routines, and programs that appear in this book are coded in assembly language. Assembly language programmers can use this material directly by moving sections of code into their own programs or by expanding or modifying the complete programs.

Programmers working in high-level languages can also use the routines in their code by adopting a mixed-language environment. This is possible because most high-level languages provide means for interfacing with routines coded in assembler. For example, a program in Turbo Pascal can call an assembly language procedure. The Pascal program can pass values to the assembler code and receive values from it in much the same way as it interfaces with a Pascal procedure or function. The details of allocating and accessing data, of coding the assembler unit, and of the interfacing between languages depends on the specific language, implementation, and version being used. Some interface examples for the more popular IBM microcomputer high-level languages are provided starting in Section 1.3 of this chapter.

1.1 Coding Style

Assembly language code can range from undecipherable to excessively verbal and embellished. In this book we have aimed at creating code that is clean and direct, in which each important program section is clearly identified and commented so as to explain the purpose and function of the instructions without being repetitious or superfluous.

Regarding the actual programming, we have tried to be as straightforward as possible. In routines which could have been coded in any of several manners, we have often chosen the one that is most direct and easy to understand. The exception has been in time-critical areas of the code, in which performance was the most important consideration. Furthermore, we have tried not to favor any specific assembler or development system and have attempted to make the code compatible with all standard software.

1.1.1 Segment Models

Several assemblers and development systems released in the past few years attempt to simplify coding by providing easier ways of defining program segments. For example, the Microsoft Macro Assembler, starting with version 5.0, and the Borland Turbo Assembler recognize a special .MODEL directive. The use of this directive ensures that the resulting code conforms with one or more high-level language implementations. In the Microsoft system, the .MODEL directive is followed by a memory-size descriptor, which can be the operator name SMALL, MEDIUM, COMPACT, LARGE, or HUGE. In Borland's Turbo Assembler the .MODEL directive is followed by a compatibility codeword corresponding to a specific Borland version of a high-level language, for example, .MODEL TPASCAL.

The use of the .MODEL directive also implies the use of simplified segment definitions, which automatically ensures segment compatibility with the selected memory model or with a specific high-level language. This method of defining segments is particularly useful if the assembly language segments are to interface with high-level languages. By using these operators, the programmer automatically obtains the same segment structures of the high-level language without having to worry about segment names, align types, combine types, classes, or groups. However, as mentioned previously, this feature is available only in assemblers and systems of recent release, not in previous versions or implementations.

Consequently, the use of these operators renders the code incompatible with systems that use the operators in a different context, as well as with systems or versions that do not recognize the simplified segment directives. This consideration has compelled us to abstain from the use of the .MODEL and the simplified segment directives in this book. However, programmers who have available software that supports the simplified segment definition can easily modify the code listings to adapt to the newer system.

Our decision to define segments in the conventional manner also entailed the decision to define these segments in the simplest possible manner. This is quite feasible for code that is to be used directly as part of assembly language programs. But different implementations and versions of high-level languages impose on the assembly language routines with which they are to interface, numerous requirements in segment names, align types, combine types, classes, and groups. Therefore, note that the segment models described in the following sections are the general forms used in the code listed in this book. When the routines, procedures, or other fragments of code are interfaced in a mixed-language environment, the segments must often be modified to meet the requirements of the specific high-level language. The details of interfacing with various high-level languages are discussed starting with Section 1.3.

Stack Segment Model.   Our objective to create the simplest possible segment structures has sometimes led to minor dilemmas. For example, the linker provided with Microsoft's Macro Assembler automatically sets the stack pointer of an executable file, if the stack segment is given the *stack* combine type. This value set by the linker corresponds with an offset at the end of the stack segment, which is adequate for most programs. However, other linkers, like the one provided by Intel with their ASM86 development system, do not have this feature, and the code must initialize the stack pointer to the desired offset.

Since initializing the stack pointer requires a single instruction, we could have avoided conflict with non-Microsoft linkers by initializing the stack pointer manually in all our programs. The problem is that, in Microsoft systems, if the stack segment is not given the *stack* combine type, an error message will appear at link time. One solution that seems to work with Microsoft and non-Microsoft linkers is to define that stack segment with the *stack* combine type and, in addition, to initialize the stack pointer in the code. In Microsoft systems this initialization instruction is superfluous, since the stack pointer (SP) will be set automatically by the linker. In non-Microsoft systems the *stack* combine type serves no useful purpose, but the resulting source assembles and links correctly in both Microsoft and non-Microsoft development environments. The details of this solution can be seen in the coding template in Section 1.1.3. The stack segment model adopted for the programs and routines is this book is as follows:

```
STACK SEGMENT        stack

            DB       0400H DUP ('?')      ; Stack segment is 1K
STACK_TOP   EQU      THIS BYTE

STACK ENDS
```

Only executable files with the extension .EXE can have a stack segment. Command type files, with the extension .COM, cannot have a stack. When linking modules for .COM type files the error message regarding the stack segment is unavoidable and should be ignored.

Code Segment Model.   The model chosen for the code segment is, again, the simplest one possible. The reader is reminded that this segment will almost certainly have to be changed if the routine is to be called from a high-level language (see Sections 1.1.1 and 1.3). The code segment model is as follows:

```
CODE   SEGMENT
       ASSUME CS:CODE
       .
       .
CODE   END
```

In complete programs the start and end of the code segment must also contain the label at which execution is transferred by the loader and the initialization routines. This code is shown in the coding templates in Section 1.1.2.

Data Segment Model.   The data segment model is as follows:

```
DATA   SEGMENT
       .
       .
DATA   ENDS
```

If the data segment of the assembly language routine is to be accessed by a high-level language program, it may be necessary to change the segment's name, align type, combine type, class, and group to those compatible with the high-level language (see Section 1.3).

Models for Procedures.   Assembly language procedures for the Intel microprocessors used in the IBM microcomputers can be defined with the type specifiers NEAR or FAR. In procedures defined with the FAR specifier the procedure label references both the segment and the offset value of the address. In procedures defined with the NEAR specifier, the label references the offset value only. The CALL and RET instructions used in accessing and exiting procedures automatically adjust to the type specifiers present in the procedure's declaration.

This means that a CALL instruction that accesses a procedure defined with the FAR type uses the segment and offset of the procedure's label and pushes both the segment and the offset, of the return address on the stack. Conversely, the RET instruction in a procedure designated with the FAR type pops both elements, segment and offset, from the stack. On the other hand, NEAR procedures are accessed using only the offset part of the address, and RET instructions in these procedures pop from the stack only the offset element of the address.

Consequently, NEAR procedures must reside in the same segment as the calling code, while FAR procedures can reside in another segment. This means that NEAR procedures take up part of the caller's code segment. Since it is not possible to predict the caller's segment structure, or the cases in which it will have sufficient code space for the all the procedures used, we have found it preferable to define all procedures with the FAR type. One minor disadvantage of FAR procedures is that CALL and RET instructions take slightly longer to execute and use one additional word of stack space.

In order to take advantage of this expanded code space, procedures of the FAR type must be located in a segment different from that of the calling code. Otherwise, a 64K limit imposed on each segment will come into effect. No special provisions are necessary if the procedures declared to be of the FAR type and the calling code are located in different modules, that is, if they are stored in separate disk files. In this case the segment model used for procedures listed in this book is as follows:

```
P_CODE          SEGMENT
        ASSUME CS:P_CODE

ANY_NAME        PROC    FAR
     .
     .
     .
        RET             ; Return instruction in procedure
ANY_NAME        ENDP

P_CODE          ENDS
```

However, if a procedure of the FAR type and the code making the call are located in different segments of the same module, some assemblers will generate errors if the segment containing the procedure appear *after* the segment performing the CALL instruction. The problem is easily avoided by defining the segment with the procedures before the segment with the call, as follows:

```
P_CODE          SEGMENT

ANY_NAME        PROC    FAR
     .
```

```
            .
        RET                 ; Return instruction in procedure
ANY_NAME        ENDP


P_CODE          ENDS

CODE   SEGMENT
        ASSUME CS:CODE
START:
            .
            .
        CALL    ANY_NAME
            .
            .
CODE   ENDS
        END     START
```

1.1.2 Model for Comments and Banners

It would be difficult to overstress the importance of comments in assembly language code. Assembly language programs can be undecipherable, even to experts, if the code does not contain clear and detailed explanations of the logical reasons behind each instruction, operation, and routine. Since the language itself is unstructured, it is up to the programmer to design and organize the code in a consistent and reasonable manner. In addition to the comments, the code can be signaled in a way that will enable the reader to locate the important execution junctions.

In this book we have used graphical banners of various designs to mark the important sections of programs and routines and to pinpoint crucial junctions in the logic and execution, as follows:

1. Full banners are used to mark the start of the program, of the various segments, and of other major program divisions.

```
;**************************************************************
;**************************************************************
;                        SAMPLE.ASM
;**************************************************************
;**************************************************************
```

or

```
;**************************************************************
;                        code segment
;**************************************************************
```

2. Half banners are used to signal procedures and other second-level program divisions.

```
;*******************************|
;     binary-to-ASCII conversion  |
;*******************************|
```

3. Small banners are used to mark junctions in program execution.

```
;****************|
;    exit to DOS  |
;****************|
```

1.1.3 Coding Template

The following coding template is designed to assist in the development of assembly language code compatible with the routines and programs presented in this book.

```
;****************************************************************
;****************************************************************
;                          TEMPLATE.ASM
;****************************************************************
;****************************************************************
; Program title:
; Copyright (c) 199? by
; Developed by:
; Start date:
; Last modification:
;
; Description:
;
;****************************************************************
;                          stack segment
;****************************************************************
STACK SEGMENT stack

            DB      0400H DUP ('?'); Default stack is 1K
STACK_TOP   EQU     THIS BYTE

STACK ENDS
;****************************************************************
;                          data segment
;****************************************************************
DATA   SEGMENT
;
DATA   ENDS
```

```
;******************************************************************
;                      segment for procedures
;******************************************************************
; Note: This segment is used for FAR procedures coded in the same
; module as the main program.
;
P_CODE      SEGMENT
            ASSUME CS:P_CODE

P_CODE      ENDS
;
;******************************************************************
;                        code segment
;******************************************************************
;
CODE  SEGMENT
      ASSUME CS:CODE
START:
;
;*******************|
;  initialization   |
;*******************|
; Establish data and extra segment addressability
      MOV     AX,DATA        ; Address of DATA to AX
      MOV     DS,AX          ; and to DS
      ASSUME DS:DATA         ; Assume from here on
; Initialize stack. Note that this instruction is necessary for
; compatibility with non-Microsoft assemblers
      LEA     SP,SS:STACK_TOP ; Stack pointer to top of stack
;***********************************|
;              program code          |
;***********************************|
; Program instructions can be inserted at this point
;
;
;*******************|
;   exit to DOS     |
;*******************|
DOS_EXIT:
      MOV     AH,4CH         ; DOS service request code
      MOV     AL,0           ; No error code returned
      INT     21H            ; TO DOS
;
CODE  ENDS
      END     START          ; Reference to label at which
                             ; execution begins
```

1.2 Conventions

Individual programmers soon start developing their own personal preferences. In general, there is nothing objectionable about coding in a particular style, even though it may not adjust exactly to popular norms and conventions. But programming methods and styles that deviate from the standard norms, or that are unique or unconventional, have no place in a reference book — not only because these aberrations could result in confusion or lead to errors but also because readers often use the samples as a pattern by which to mold their own coding.

   We believe that clarity and consistency are the most important factors in creating reasonable code. To ensure that the processing will be in harmony throughout the book, we have adopted the conventions described in the following section.

1.2.1 PUSH and POP Sequence

Procedures generally restore machine registers to the state in which they were received, except those registers used to return information to the caller. In the header comments, procedures list the registers and data areas that are assumed to contain information passed to the procedure and the registers and data areas that are used to return information to the calling routine. The phrases "On entry:" and "On exit:" are used to highlight the registers and data areas used by the procedure. The following procedure header illustrates this point.

```
BIO_SET_CUR PROC   FAR
; Procedure to set the system cursor using BIOS service request
; number 2, of INT 10H
; On entry:
;                 DH = desired screen row for new cursor position
;                 DL = desired screen column for new cursor position
; On exit:
;           Nothing
        .
        .
```

Data and index registers are pushed on the stack in the following order:

```
                              AX
                              BX
                              CX
                              DX
                              SI
                              DI
```

   The pointer and segment registers, SP, BP, CS, DS, SS, and ES, as well as the flags register, are pushed and popped in the most convenient order for the purpose at hand.

1.2.2 Register Use

Machine registers are used according to their function in 8086/8088 assembly language, to preferred usage as recommended by Intel documentation, and to the more common programming practices. Accordingly, AX, BX, CX, and DX, and the corresponding half registers, are used as general-purpose data registers. CX is preferred as a counter, even if the encoding does not require the CX register. AX and DX are used to hold the low- and high-order words of a doubleword result, which is in agreement with the use of these registers in arithmetic operations. SI is generally used as a source index and DI as a destination index. BX is used as an index or pointer only if SI and DI are not available. SP and BP are almost exclusively reserved for stack and frame manipulations.

The ES Register.   Routines that use ES in string moves do not assume that ES equals DS and restore ES to its entry value. This allows the use of the ES register as a pointer to the video buffer with assurances that other processing will not alter this value. For the same reason, calls to BIOS and DOS services generally preserve the entry value of ES.

1.2.3 Error Handling

Many routines contain handlers that report to the caller the error conditions encountered during processing. In general, the routines listed in this book use the *carry flag set* to indicate error conditions. If the carry flag is clear, the processing has found no errors or does not implement error detections. Therefore, a carry clear condition can always be used to determine the continuation of normal processing, even if the called routine does not contain an error handler.

In routines that contain more detailed error handlers, the AH register holds the error code if the carry flag is set. Some error handlers return a diagnostic message to the caller. In these cases the segment and offset of the returned message depends on register use by the particular program or routine that contains the handler.

1.2.4 Number Systems

Decimal, binary, and hexadecimal numbers are all frequently used in assembly language programs and routines. We have selected the most meaningful numerical base for every number listed in the text or the code. Therefore, memory addresses, interrupt vectors, and ports are referenced in hexadecimal numbers, as is customary. Masks and bit maps appear in binary, because, in these cases, the information or action is relative to each individual bit. However, we have used decimals in all cases in which there is no authentic reason for using numbers in the hexadecimal or binary systems. For example, we can see no reason for listing the services in BIOS and DOS interrupts in hexadecimal numbers, although they often appear in this manner in the literature.

1.3 Interfacing with High-Level Languages

The power of high-level languages is increased considerably when it is possible for the programmer to revert to assembly language to perform those manipulations that the high-level language does not permit. Programming in a mixed-language environment can bring the best of both worlds, that is, the ease and convenience of the high-level language together with the power, efficiency, and hardware control of assembler. The obvious drawback is that much high-level language programming is done in order to avoid the difficulties and complications of assembly language. Adopting the assembler as a second programming language defeats this original purpose.

A major difficulty in interfacing high-level language programs with assembler code is that there are no general standards or conventions applicable to all high-level languages. Different versions of the same language often vary in their interfacing methods and rules. In general, compiled high-level languages generate object files (extension .OBJ) which can interface with assembled files (also with the extension .OBJ) at link time, but there are notable exceptions. On the other hand, interpreted languages, like some popular implementations of BASIC, require that the assembly language code be stored in special binary files. Some versions of the BASIC language use the keywords BSAVE and BLOAD to create and load these special files.

We have mentioned that, because there are no general guidelines for interfacing high-level languages with assembly language, the interfacing rules vary from language to language, implementation to implementation, and even version to version. Furthermore, a detailed discussion of the problems and complications related to interfacing high-level languages with assembler code could easily fill an entire book, especially because this subject is often documented very sparsely in the manuals of many high-level language programs. For these reasons, instead of a general treatment that would be useful to no one, we have preferred to choose a few well known high-level languages and to provide concrete interface examples for each of them. We hope that most readers programming in high-level languages will find their language among those illustrated. In the worst case, the examples could serve as a general guide to interfacing assembler code with high-level languages, implementations, or versions not illustrated in the book.

1.3.1 Interfacing through Header Routines

There are two ways of making an assembly language routines, like the ones that appear in this book, interface with a high-level language. One method is to modify the routines themselves so that they will meet the interface requirements of the language in question. This method entails editing the code of each procedure. A second possibility is to provide an interface header routine that will serve to adapt the requirements of the calling language to the assembler code, and vice versa.

Although this approach allows coding the assembly language routines without taking into consideration the naming and calling conventions of any specific high-level language, it is not without drawbacks. First, since the assembly language routines are designed to receive the caller's data through the most convenient registers and pointers, it is not possible to develop a single header that works with all the routines. In fact, most routines will require a particular, customized header that will remove the parameters from the caller's stack and place them in the required machine registers and buffers. Second, the interface routines add an additional processing step, which introduces an unnecessary delay in execution.

The main advantage of using interface headers is a didactical one: from the header the reader can grasp the fundamental manipulations that make possible the communications between languages. This is so because the interface headers perform no processing on their own, and thus provide a model than can be easily adapted to routines with various requirements.

We have used both methods in the interface examples listed in this chapter. Some of the assembly language routines are interface headers to other routines. In this case the called routines are the ones that perform the processing. In other examples, in which the manipulations require very few instructions, the interface routines also perform the processing. By illustrating both interface methods we hope to provide the reader with sufficient information for using either option.

1.4 Interfacing with Quickbasic

Quickbasic is an implementation of the BASIC programming language, for use in the IBM microcomputers, developed and marketed by Microsoft Corporation. The Quickbasic programming environment includes an editor and an interactive interpreter, as well as separate compiler and linker software. Most of the information necessary for interfacing Quickbasic with assembly language code is not found in the Quickbasic manuals, but in a booklet titled Mixed-Language Programming Guide which is included in the documentation package for Microsoft Macro Assembler 5.0 and later versions. This booklet also includes interface information for the Microsoft implementations of the C, Pascal, and Fortran languages.

The methods described in the following examples do not constitute the only way to incorporate assembly language code onto a Quickbasic program but are the ones best suited to the majority of the assembly language routines listed in this book. The first example illustrates interfacing with a subroutine to which Quickbasic passes three parameters by value. The second example shows a subroutine that receives a parameter passed by reference and uses this address to change the value of a Quickbasic variable.

1.4.1 Passing Quickbasic Parameters by Value

The first interface example with Quickbasic is in the form of a subroutine that passes three parameters, by value, to an assembly language procedure. The example consists of two modules. The Quickbasic module (TESTQB.BAS) can be created in the Quickbasic environment, or with an ASCII text editor. This source file is compiled in DOS using the program named BC.EXE, which is part of the Quickbasic software. The assembly language module is created using any text editor and assembled with a DOS assembler compatible with the Microsoft system, preferably with the Microsoft Macro Assembler. The assembled file is named QBCALLS.OBJ. The two files, TESTQB.OBJ and QBCALLS.OBJ, are linked using the linker program in the Quickbasic software.

The following is a listing for the Quickbasic module in this interface example.

```
' ** Quickbasic 4.5 demonstration program for interfacing with
' ** an assembly language module. The assembly language procedure
' ** in this demo displays any number of asterisks at any screen
' ** position. The Quickbasic call passes the desired screen row
' ** and column, and the asterisk count, to the assembly language
' ** routine.
'
' ** This Quickbasic module is compiled and saved as TESTQB.BAS.
' ** The assembly language module is assembled as QBCALLS.OBJ.
' ** TESTQB.BAS is compiled using the Quickbasic DOS compiler
' ** program named BC.EXE. The resulting file, TESTQB.OBJ, is
' ** linked with the assembly language module named QBCALLS.OBJ.
' ** The final run file is named TESTQB.EXE.
'
DECLARE SUB SHOWS ALIAS "QB_SHOW_IT" (BYVAL ROW%, BYVAL COL%,
BYVAL CNT%)
'
CLS
PRINT "Test program for interfacing Quickbasic and assembly"
INPUT "Enter display row: "; ROW%
INPUT "Enter display column: "; COL%
INPUT "Enter asterisk count: "; CNT%
CALL SHOWS(ROW%, COL%, CNT%)
END
```

Note the following points in the Quickbasic module:

1. A DECLARE statement is generated automatically by Quickbasic only if there is a subroutine that was created interactively. In this case the programmer must manually enter the DECLARE statement, which should appear near the beginning of the BASIC source file.

2. The ALIAS keyword, which is part of the DECLARE statement, allows referencing a procedure in another module even if the procedure name does not meet the Quickbasic conventions. In this example, the procedure QB_SHOW_IT, which is a PUBLIC name in the assembly language module, is not a Quickbasic legal name. Also note that the aliasname QB_SHOW_IT must be enclosed in quotes.

3. Quickbasic normally passes parameters by near reference. In order to force Quickbasic to pass parameters by value, the BYVAL keyword is entered preceding each variable in the parameter list of the DECLARE statement. Passing parameters by value is the default method for Microsoft C and Pascal. Parameters passed by value are easier to recover by the assembly language module.

4. The assembly language routine named QB_SHOW_IT appears to the Quickbasic program as a subroutine named SHOWS. Quickbasic will access the assembly language procedure with the CALL SHOWS instruction.

The following is a listing for the assembly language module.

```
;*****************************************************************
;                         QBCALLS.ASM
;*****************************************************************
; Assembly language interface header routine for Quickbasic,
; starting with version 4.0
;
;
PUBLIC        QB_SHOW_IT
PUBLIC        LSHIFT
;
P_TEXT        SEGMENT WORD  PUBLIC 'CODE'
      ASSUME CS:P_TEXT
;*******************************|
;  Quickbasic interface routines |
;*******************************|
QB_SHOW_IT  PROC    FAR
; Quickbasic version 4.0 (and later) interface header to call the
; assembly language routine AST_DISPLAY (also in this module)
; Note: This procedure is called by the Quickbasic demo program
; named TESTQB.BAS
; On entry:
;       FROM:     TO:         FUNCTION:
;     [BP+10]    -> DH        Screen row at which to set cursor
;     [BP+8]     -> DL        Screen column at which to set cursor
;     [BP+6]     -> CX        Counter for asterisks to display
; On exit:
;     Nothing
;
      PUSH    BP            ; Save caller's BP
      MOV     BP,SP         ; Set pointer to stack frame
      PUSH    AX            ; Save caller's registers so that
      PUSH    BX            ; they can be used by header
      PUSH    CX
      PUSH    DX
      MOV     AX,[BP+10]    ; Get first passed parameter to AX
      MOV     DH,AL         ; Passed value is a byte, although
                            ; storage space is word-size
      MOV     AX,[BP+8]     ; Get second parameter passed by call
      MOV     DL,AL         ; into DL
      MOV     AX,[BP+6]     ; Get third parameter passed by BASIC
      MOV     CX,AX         ; and move to CX
      CALL    AST_DISPLAY   ; Call routine to display *
      POP     DX            ; Restore registers
      POP     CX
```

```
        POP     BX
        POP     AX
        POP     BP              ; Restore base pointer register
        RET     6               ; Return and repair stack
QB_SHOW_IT  ENDP
;
;
AST_DISPLAY PROC    NEAR
; On entry:
;               DH = cursor row
;               DL = cursor column
;               CX = count of asterisks to display
; On exit:
;       Nothing
;
        PUSH    CX              ; Save counter register
        MOV     AH,2            ; Service request number
        MOV     BH,0            ; Assume display page No. 0
        INT     10H
; Display CX characters at cursor
        POP     CX              ; Restore counter from stack
        MOV     AL,'*'          ; Character to display
        MOV     AH,10           ; Service request number
        MOV     BH,0            ; Display page zero
        INT     10H
        RET
AST_DISPLAY ENDP
;
P_TEXT      ENDS
        END
```

Note the following points in the assembly language module:

1. The module contains two procedures. The procedure named QB_SHOW_IT is of the FAR type. This is necessary in order to make the procedure accessible to Quickbasic. It is declared PUBLIC so that it will be visible to Quickbasic. The procedure named AST_DISPLAY is of type NEAR, therefore, it is internal to the assembly language module and cannot be called from Quickbasic.

2. The segment declaration line is as follows:

```
P_TEXT  SEGMENT WORD    PUBLIC  'CODE'
    ASSUME  CS:P_TEXT
```

This declaration conforms to the Microsoft segment structure for the medium and large memory models, listed in Table 1.1.

3. After the instruction PUSH BP executes, the entry parameters are located at stack offsets 10, 8, and 6, respectively. The first argument passed is at the highest offset in the stack. Each parameter takes up 2 bytes of stack space. The Quickbasic variables are word-size, since they were defined using the percent (%) symbol. Figure 1.1 shows the stack frame at the time of the Quickbasic call.

4. The instruction MOV BP,SP sets the base pointer (BP) register to the stack top. Now BP can be used to remove the passed parameters from their respective stack offsets. This is more convenient than using SP, which does not allow indexed addressing forms. BP is sometimes called a *framepointer* when used in this manner.

5. After the caller's general-purpose registers are saved, the interface header uses BP to remove the entry parameters from the stack and to place these parameters in the registers where the procedure AST_DISPLAY expects them. After the registers are loaded, the interface header calls the processing routine using the instruction CALL AST_DISPLAY.

6. As soon as the assembly language processing routine returns to the interface header, the code restores the machine registers from the stack (including BP) and returns to the Quickbasic module. Notice that the return instruction RET 6 also repairs the stack by adjusting to the number of word-size items passed in the call. This means that if the calling procedure had passed a single word-size item in the stack, the return instruction would be coded in the form RET 2. This same method of stack repair is used in other high-level languages, but not C language.

Table 1.1. *Segment Structures in Microsoft/IBM Memory Models*

MEMORY MODEL	SEGMENT TYPE	SEGMENT NAME	ALIGN TYPE	COMBINE TYPE	CLASS NAME	GROUP
Small	CODE	_TEXT	word	PUBLIC	'CODE'	
	DATA	_DATA	word	PUBLIC	'DATA'	DGROUP
		CONST	word	PUBLIC	'CONST'	DGROUP
		BSS	word	PUBLIC	'BSS'	DGROUP
	STACK	STACK	para	STACK	'STACK'	DGROUP
Compact	CODE	_TEXT	word	PUBLIC	'CODE'	
	DATA	_DATA	word	PUBLIC	'DATA'	DGROUP
		CONST	word	PUBLIC	'CONST'	DGROUP
		BSS	word	PUBLIC	'BSS'	DGROUP
		FAR_DATA	para	private	'FAR_DATA'	
		FAR_BSS	para	private	'FAR_BSS'	
	STACK	STACK	para	STACK	'STACK'	DGROUP
Medium	CODE	xx_TEXT	word	PUBLIC	'CODE'	
	DATA	_DATA	word	PUBLIC	'DATA'	DGROUP
		CONST	word	PUBLIC	'CONST'	DGROUP
		BSS	word	PUBLIC	'BSS'	DGROUP
	STACK	STACK	para	STACK	'STACK'	DGROUP
Large	CODE	xx_TEXT	word	PUBLIC	'CODE'	
	DATA	_DATA	word	PUBLIC	'DATA'	DGROUP
		CONST	word	PUBLIC	'CONST'	DGROUP
		BSS	word	PUBLIC	'BSS'	DGROUP
		FAR_DATA	para	private	'FAR_DATA'	
		FAR_BSS	para	private	'FAR_BSS'	
	STACK	STACK	para	STACK	'STACK'	DGROUP

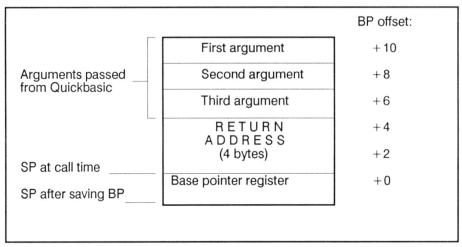

	BP offset:
First argument	+10
Second argument	+8
Third argument	+6
RETURN ADDRESS (4 bytes)	+4
	+2
Base pointer register	+0

Arguments passed from Quickbasic

SP at call time

SP after saving BP

Figure 1.1. *Stack Frame after Quickbasic FAR Call*

1.4.2 Passing Quickbasic Parameters by Reference

In the example of Section 1.4.1 we used the BYVAL operator in the DECLARE statement to override the Quickbasic default parameter passing mode, which is by near reference. In this way the assembly language procedure is able to obtain the present value of Quickbasic variables from the stack, but since the storage location of these variables is not known to the assembly code, the stored values of the variables are protected from undesirable alterations. In many cases this interface mode is safe and useful, but occasionally it may be preferable to have the assembly language code change the value of a Quickbasic variable. Note that changing the stored value of a variable is an expedient way to pass parameters back to Quickbasic.

The following is a listing for the Quickbasic module in this interface example.

```
' ** Quickbasic 4.5 demonstration program for interfacing with
' ** an assembly language module and for passing and returning
' ** parameters by near reference.

' ** This demo program calls an assembly language procedure named
' ** LSHIFT, which shifts left the bits of a Quickbasic integer
' ** variable named TARGET% and updates the variable by writing
' ** the result to its storage address.
'
' ** This Quickbasic module is saved as TESTQB1.BAS
' ** The assembly language module is part of QBCALLS.OBJ
' ** developed for the previous interface example.
' ** TESTQB1.BAS is compiled using the Quickbasic DOS compiler
, ** program named BC.EXE. The resulting file, TESTQB.OBJ, is
' ** linked with the assembly language module named QBCALLS.OBJ.
```

```
'** The final run file is named TESTQB1.EXE.
'
DECLARE SUB LSHIFT (TARGET%)
'
CLS
INPUT "Enter the value to shift left by 1 bit: "; TARGET%
CALL LSHIFT(TARGET%)
PRINT "The shifted value of the variable is: "; TARGET%
END
```

Note the following points in the Quickbasic module:

1. The DECLARE does not need the ALIAS operator, as in the previous example, since the name of this assembly language procedure is legal in Quickbasic. Note that the programmer must manually enter the DECLARE statement, as in the previous example.

2. In this example Quickbasic passes parameters by near reference, which is its default mode. Therefore, the BYVAL operator is not used in the parameter list.

The following is a listing for the assembly language module.

```
;****************************************************************
;                        QBCALLS1.ASM
;****************************************************************
; Assembly language interface header routine for Quickbasic,
; starting with version 4.0
;
PUBLIC  LSHIFT
;
P_TEXT  SEGMENT WORD    PUBLIC  'CODE'
        ASSUME  CS:P_TEXT
;******************************|
;  Quickbasic interface routine |
;******************************|
LSHIFT      PROC    FAR
; Procedure to shift left the bits in an integer passed by
; Quickbasic
; Note: This procedure is called by the Quickbasic demo program
; named TESTQB1.BAS
; On entry:
;    [BP+6] = offset address of passed variable
; On exit:
;
;    [BP+6] is updated with the shifted value
;
        PUSH    BP              ; Save caller's BP
```

```
        MOV     BP,SP           ; Set pointer to stack frame
        MOV     BX,[BP+6]       ; Value passed by near reference
                                ; which is Quickbasic default mode
        MOV     AX,[BX]         ; Load AX from variable's address
        SHL     AX,1            ; Shift left AX 1 bit
        MOV     [BX],AX         ; Restore result to the variable's
                                ; address
        POP     BP              ; Restore caller's BP
        RET     2               ; Return and repair stack
LSHIFT  ENDP
;
P_TEXT  ENDS
        END
```

In addition to the points noted in relation to the assembly language module in Section 1.4.1, note the following:

1. Since the variable TARGET% is passed by near reference, the value stored at BP + 6 is the variable's offset in the data segment. In this case, the assembly language module retrieves this value using BX as a pointer. In the previous example, in which the parameters were passed as values in the stack, these parameters were loaded directly into machine registers.

2. After the instruction SHL AX,1 has operated on the passed parameter, the result is placed back in the Quickbasic variable using the same pointer to the variable's address in memory. Quickbasic can now access the new value using the variable's original name.

1.5 Interfacing with Microsoft/IBM C Language

It has often been stated that, of all high-level languages, C language provides the easiest interface with assembly language routines. This is because a C language program calls an assembly language procedure in the same manner as it would a C language function. Variables, parameters, and addresses are passed to the assembly language routine on the stack. These values appear in the stack in opposite order to the program listing. A unique feature of the C language interface is that C automatically restores stack integrity. For this reason the assembly language routine can return with a simple RET or RETF instruction, and is not compelled to keep count of the parameters that were pushed on the stack by the call.

But not all implementations and versions of C follow identical interface conventions. In the Microsoft/IBM versions of C discussed in this chapter, the memory model adapted by the C language program determines the segment structure of the assembly language module. The Microsoft/IBM segment structures are listed in Table 1.1. In practice this means that if the C module was compiled using the small or compact model, the assembly language procedure should be defined using the NEAR directive. However, if the C module was compiled using the medium or large models, then the assembly language procedure should be defined with the FAR directive.

The Microsoft/IBM versions of the C language have two additional and distinctive interface requirements. One is that the these implementations of C language use the SI and DI machine registers to store the values of variables defined with the "register" keyword. For this reason, the assembly language procedure must be careful to preserve these registers. These implementations also assume that the processor's direction flag (DF) is clear when C language regains control. Therefore, if there is any possibility of this flag being changed during processing, the assembly language code should contain a CLD instruction before returning. In fact, it is a safe programming practice to include this instruction in the interface model, even though it may not always be necessary.

1.5.1 C Language Naming Conventions

The Microsoft/IBM C language compilers automatically add an underscore character (_) in front of every public name. For example, a C language reference to a procedure named RSHIFT will be compiled as a call to the procedure _RSHIFT. In coding the assembly language module, the programmer must take this peculiarity of the C compiler into account and add the required underscore character in front of the name of every assembly language element that is to be referenced in the C language module.

This convention applies not only to functions but also to data items that are globally visible in the C module. For example, if the C language module contains a variable named ODDNUM, which was declared globally, this variable will be visible to an assembly language module under the name _ODDNUM. The assembly language module can gain access to the variable by using the EXTRN statement. Accessing C language variables from assembly language modules is shown in the example of Section 1.5.2.

1.5.2 Passing C Parameters by Value

The interface example with Microsoft/IBM C language compilers is in the form of a C program that calls an assembly language routine. The caller passes an integer variable to the assembly language subroutine and the subroutine returns the value with all bits shifted right by one position. In addition, the assembly language routine modifies the value of a C variable named NUMB2. The example consists of two modules. The C language module (TESTC.C) is created using a standard editor and compiled using a Microsoft or IBM C language compiler. The assembly language module is created with an ASCII text editor and assembled with a DOS assembler compatible with the Microsoft system, preferably with the Microsoft Macro Assembler. The assembled file is named CCALLS.OBJ. Note that the examples refer to the Microsoft/IBM full-featured compilers, not the Microsoft QuickC programming environment.

The following is a listing for the C language module in this interface example.

```
/* Module name: TESTC.C                                          */



/* C Language module to show interfacing with assembly language*/
/* code. This sample assumes the use of Microsoft/IBM C        */
```

```
/* compilers excluding QuickC                                    */

#include <stdio.h>

extern int RSHIFT(int);

/* Variables visible to the assembly module must be declared */
/* globally in the C module.                                  */

int numb1, NUMB2;

main() {
     printf("Enter the variable numb1: ");
     scanf("%i", &numb1);
     printf("The shifted number is: %d\n", RSHIFT(numb1));
     printf("The variable NUMB2 has the value: %u\n", NUMB2);
}
```

Note the following points in the C language module:

1. The assembly language module is declared external to the C code with the *extern* C language keyword. The name in this declaration is not preceded with an underscore character, since it is automatically appended by the compiler.

2. Once declared external, the RSHIFT routine is called as if it were a C function.

3. The variables numb1 and NUMB2 are declared to be of *int* type. The value of numb1 is transferred by the C module to the assembly language module in the statement RSHIFT(numb1). The assembler module recovers the value of the variable numb1 from the stack. However, the assembly language module accesses the variable NUMB2 directly, using the variable's name. Note that the variable to be accessed by name is declared using capital letters. This is for compatibility with assembler programs that automatically convert names to uppercase.

The assembly language code is as follows:

```
;****************************************************************
;                          CCALLS.ASM
;****************************************************************
; C language-to-assembly language interface header routine for
; Microsoft/IBM C language compilers, excluding QuickC
PUBLIC         _RSHIFT
EXTRN          _NUMB2: WORD
_TEXT SEGMENT word    PUBLIC   'CODE'
     ASSUME  CS:_TEXT
;*****************************|
;  C language interface routine |
;*****************************|
```

```
_RSHIFT          PROC     NEAR
; Function to right-shift the bits in an integer passed by
; C language
; On entry:
;       [BP+4] = value of passed parameter
; On exit:
;       AX = right-shifted value returned to caller
        PUSH     BP              ; Save caller's BP
        MOV      BP,SP           ; Set pointer to stack frame
        MOV      AX,[BP+4]       ; Value passed by value
                                 ; which is C language default mode
        CALL     INTERNAL_P      ; Procedure to perform shift and
                                 ; to access C variable NUMB2
        CLD                      ; Clear direction flag
        POP      BP              ; Restore caller's BP
        RET                      ; Simple return. C repairs stack
_RSHIFT          ENDP
;
INTERNAL_P  PROC     NEAR
; Operational procedure
; On entry:
;       AX = value of variable numb1, to be shifted right
; On exit:
;       AX = shifted value
;       _NUMB2 = arbitrary new value assigned to C variable
        SHR      AX,1            ; Shift right AX 1 bit
                                 ; Return value is left in AX
        MOV      CX,12345        ; Arbitrary value to CX
        MOV      _NUMB2,CX       ; and to C variable NUMB2
        RET
INTERNAL_P  ENDP
_TEXT ENDS
        END
```

Note the following points of the assembly language module.

1. The procedure _RSHIFT is declared PUBLIC to make it visible to the C module at link time. An underscore character is affixed at the start of the procedure's name so that it matches the name used by the C compiler.

2. The segment structure is compatible with the Microsoft small memory model as shown in Table 1.1. The memory model of the C program is determined at link time by the library selected.

3. Procedures to be linked with C programs of the small or compact model must be declared with the NEAR operator, as the one in the example. If the C program used the medium or large models, then the assembly language procedure would have been declared using the FAR operator.

4. The _RSHIFT procedure in the assembly language module serves as an interface header routine, discussed in Section 1.3.1. The reader should note that this header will require modifications in order to adapt it to C programs using other memory models or with different specifications for the parameters passed and returned.

5. The structure of the stack frame at call time also depends on the adopted memory model. In this case, since the chosen model is small, the parameter passed is located at BP + 4 and the return address consists of only the offset component (2 bytes). This stack frame can be seen in Figure 1.2

   If the C language module conformed with the medium or large models, the stack frame would be similar to the one shown in Figure 1.1.

6. The variable declared as NUMB2 and initialized as "int" in the C language module is declared as EXTRN _NUMB2: WORD in the assembly language code. The underscore character is added in the assembly module because the C compiler appends this character at the beginning of the variable name. The variable is assigned a value in the INTERNAL_P procedure.

7. The routine clears the direction flag (CLD), restores the BP register (POP BP), and returns with a simple RET instruction. Note that the processing routine in this example does not use the SI or DI registers; hence they were not preserved. However, if SI or DI is used in processing, the entry value must be saved and restored by the assembler code.

1.5.3 Return Values in Microsoft/IBM C Compilers

In the Microsoft/IBM implementations of C for the IBM microcomputers parameters are returned to the calling routine in the AX register (as in the example of Section 1.5.2), or in the AX and the DX registers. Table 1.2 shows the return value conventions for different data types and pointers.

Another way of interchanging values between the modules is to access the C variables by name (as shown in the example of Section 1.5.2). This method requires that the assembly module use the same storage format as the C language. Since variable storage formats change in different implementations of the C language, this access technique must be adapted to each particular implementation of the language.

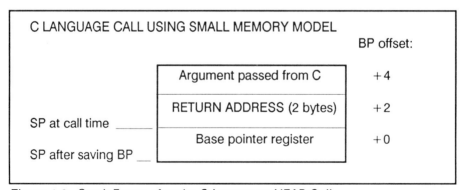

Figure 1.2. *Stack Frame after the C Language NEAR Call*

Table 1.2. *Microsoft/IBM C Language Returned Values*

DATA TYPE OR POINTER	REGISTER OR REGISTER PAIR
char short int unsigned char unsigned short insigned int	AX
long unsigned long	DX = high-order word AX = low-order word
struc or union float or double	AX = address value
near pointer	AX = offset value of address
far pointer	DX = segment value of address AX = offset value of address

1.6 Interfacing with Turbo Pascal

Borland Turbo Pascal allows linking of its modules with modules written in assembly language. However, the interface conventions and the required segment definitions are different from those of other Pascal compilers, including Microsoft Pascal. For this reason the interface examples in the following sections apply exclusively to Borland Turbo Pascal starting with version 5.0.

The fundamental interface rules for Turbo Pascal are as follows:

1. The assembly language procedure to be interfaced must be declared in the Pascal module using the *external* keyword.

2. The segment structure for the code and data segments in the assembler module must be as listed in Table 1.3.

3. Parameters passed by Turbo Pascal are passed by value or by reference, according to the variable type and size. Integer and real variables are pushed on the stack and so are arrays of less than 4 bytes. A pointer to the variable's address is passed for values larger than 4 bytes. Byte-size variables are passed as a word, with the high-order byte undefined. Table 1.4 shows the parameter passing conventions for Turbo Pascal, starting with version 5.0.

Table 1.3. *Segment Structures in Turbo Pascal 5.0*

SEGMENT TYPE	SEGMENT NAME	ALIGN TYPE	COMBINE TYPE	CLASS NAME	GROUP
CODE	CODE	word	PUBLIC	—	—
DATA	DATA	word	PUBLIC	—	—

Table 1.4. *Parameter Passing in Turbo Pascal*

VARIABLE TYPE	PASSED AS	PASSED BY	RETURNED IN
Integer	Byte Word Doubleword	Value	AX (AH undefined) AX DX-AX
Char	Byte	Value	AX (AH undefined)
Boolean	Byte	Value (0 or 1)	AX (AH undefined)
Enumerated	Byte	Value	AX (AH undefined)
Real	1 to 6 bytes	Value	DX-BX-AX
8087	10 bytes	Value	8087 ST(0)
Pointer	Doubleword	Reference	DX:AX
String	Doubleword	Reference	DX:AX
Arrays/records (< 4 bytes)	Byte Word Doubleword	Value	AX (AH undefined) AX DX-AX
arrays/records (> 4 bytes)	Doubleword	Reference	DX:AX

4. Turbo Pascal can interface with an assembly language procedure using a NEAR or FAR call. If the procedure was declared in the interface section of a unit, it is always accessed using a FAR call. On the other hand, if the procedure is declared in the program section, Turbo Pascal will assume that it is of NEAR type. The programmer can override this assumption using the $F+ compiler directive, which forces a FAR call to all procedures and functions. This last method is the one used in the example later in this section.

5. The name of the assembly language module that contains the procedures to be accessed by Turbo Pascal must be listed using the $L compiler directive. This declaration is found in the Turbo Pascal module of the sample program in this section. The declaration is necessary since the Turbo Pascal compiler also performs linking operations. If the module data is not made available at compile time, the Turbo Pascal system will not be able to generate an executable file.

The following sample program includes the listing of a Turbo Pascal program and an assembly language module. The Turbo Pascal program passes the variable num1 to the assembler code, which, in turn, shifts all bits right by one position and returns the shifted value in the AX register.

```
Program AL_INTERFACE (INPUT, OUTPUT);
  {$F+}
  {$L TPCALLS}

{ Turbo Pascal 5.0 demonstration program for interfacing with
  assembly language code. This file is named TESTTP.PAS }
```

```
function R_SHIFT (num1 : integer): integer; external;


var
    num1 : integer;


begin
    Write('Enter value: ');
    Readln (num1);
    Writeln ('The shifted value is: ', R_SHIFT (num1));
end.




;******************************************************************
;                          TPCALLS.ASM
;******************************************************************
; Turbo Pascal to assembly language interface routine
; This code is compatible with Turbo Pascal version 5.0 and later.
;
;
PUBLIC  R_SHIFT
;
CODE  SEGMENT byte     PUBLIC
      ASSUME  CS:CODE
;
;*****************************|
; Turbo Pascal interface routine |
;*****************************|
R_SHIFT        PROC   FAR
; Function to right-shift the bits in an integer passed by
; Turbo Pascal
; On entry:
;     [BP+6] = variable passed by Turbo Pascal
; On exit:
;     AX = shifted value of variable
;
      PUSH    BP             ; Save caller's BP
      MOV     BP,SP          ; Set pointer to stack frame
      MOV     AX,[BP+6]      ; Parameter is passed by value
      SHR     AX,1           ; Shift right AX 1 bit
      POP     BP             ; Restore caller's BP
      RET     2              ; Return and repair stack
R_SHIFT        ENDP
;
CODE  ENDS
      END
```

Note the following points in code:

1. The {$F +} assembler directive in the Turbo Pascal module forces all calls to be of FAR type. For this reason the assembly language procedure is declared FAR.

2. The assembly language module is assembled with the name TPCALLS.OBJ. This module name is referenced in the Turbo Pascal section using the statement {$L TPCALLS}.

3. The interfaced assembler routine is named R_SHIFT. This procedure is declared PUBLIC in the assembler module and external in the Turbo Pascal function decla-ration. Note that the word *procedure* has an unconventional meaning in the context of the Pascal language. To Pascal, a procedure is a function that returns no values. Or, in other words, a function is a procedure that returns a value. Therefore, in order for Turbo Pascal to receive a value from the assembler code, the assembler routine must be designated as a Turbo Pascal *function*.

4. The structure of the stack frame at call time depends on whether the interfaced procedure is of NEAR or FAR type. In this example the use of the {$F +} directive forces all procedures to be of the FAR type. Therefore, the parameter passed is located at BP + 6 and the return address consists of a segment and an offset (4 bytes). This stack frame can be seen in Figure 1.3.

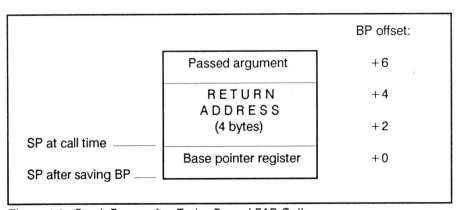

Figure 1.3. *Stack Frame after Turbo Pascal FAR Call*

2

A Library of Essential Routines

2.0 Fundamental Operations

The essential chore of most computer programs consists of performing fundamental input/output and data handling operations. The high-level language programmer has available a set of functions and keywords that execute these fundamental tasks without much complication. Thus, the programmer coding in BASIC uses keywords like INPUT, or PRINT, in order to communicate with the keyboard or the video display system. But, as we all know, there is no PRINT command built into the IBM microcomputer hardware. In reality, the BASIC PRINT keyword transfers execution to a software routine, almost certainly coded in assembly language, which contains a series of CPU instructions that perform the PRINT function.

Assembly language programmers are not as fortunate, in this respect, as their high-level language counterparts. In assembly language there are no powerful keywords that allow uncomplicated communications with input/output devices or the manipulation of elaborate data structures. This is, precisely, the objection most often raised against low-level programming. The next best option available to the low-level programmer is the use of BIOS or operating system services that simplify and standardize device interfacing. But most of the functions that can be obtained from these system services are not as powerful or versatile as those built into the high-level languages.

However, high-level language commands and functions are software blackboxes, which perform operations without revealing the processing steps involved in their execution. Therefore, the BASIC programmer using the PRINT keyword to display a screen message disregards whether the BASIC interpreter or compiler is accessing the video buffer directly, is using a DOS or a BIOS video service, or is directly controlling the display hardware. This mystery regarding the form of operation is not an important issue as long as the command performs as expected. But if a high-level language executes incorrectly, or cannot produce the results required by the programmer, its blackbox construction becomes an obstacle and a disadvantage.

2.0.1 Device Drivers

Routines to perform common input/output and data handling functions are a standard building block of every high-level language. These routines are sometimes called *device drivers*. The term is used, somewhat imprecisely, to denote the most elementary software elements that serve to isolate operating systems, programming languages, and application programs from the peculiarities of the hardware devices. It was the UNIX operating system that first used the idea of an installable device driver. To UNIX a device driver is a software element that can be attached to the UNIX kernel at any time. This concept was reproduced in DOS, starting with version 2.0, and in OS/2. Nevertheless, these DOS and OS/2 device drivers were conceived with specific devices in mind. These were, typically, interrupt-driven, character-stream devices that performed byte-oriented input and output and block storage devices such as disk or magnetic tape drives.

2.0.2 Primitive Routines

The term *primitive routine* is probably more suited than the term *device driver* to describe the fundamental, general-purpose services. The fundamental routines contained in this chapter perform the following operations:

1. Provide elementary input/output services by accessing, either directly or through system services, the corresponding hardware devices. The standard I/O devices include the video display, the keyboard, the parallel or printer port, the diskette and hard disk hardware, and the serial port.

2. Provide services to perform data manipulations and conversions that are frequently necessary for applications and system programs. These include binary, ASCII, and hexadecimal conversions. Floating point conversions are discussed in Chapter 8.

3. Provide auxiliary services often required by system and applications programs, such as machine and components identification and timing routines.

    The routines are distributed in the following modules:

	MODULE NAME	FUNCTION
1.	DAVIDEO.ASM	Direct-access video display routines
2.	BIOVIDEO.ASM	Video display using BIOS services
3.	KEYBRD.ASM	Keyboard input
4.	OUTPUT.ASM	Printer and serial port output services
5.	CONVERT.ASM	Data conversions and string operations
6.	DISKIO.ASM	Disk and diskette input and output routines
7.	AUXSERV.ASM	System ID and timing operations

2.1 Using a Routine Library

The seven modules listed in Section 2.0.2 can be collected in a library of fundamental routines. Most assembly language development systems provide a library manager that allows the creation, organization, and maintenance of routine libraries. The routines in a library operate as a collection of services that are made available to source program at link time. These routines are called by the program in the same manner as if they were internal procedures. The library may be formed of one or more independent modules, each of which is a separately assembled or compiled object file. Associating modules to form a library is one of the functions of the library manager program.

To the assembly language programmer the main advantage of creating and using a library of routines is one of expedience. All the routines in the library are automatically available to the source without special declarations. The disadvantage of collecting routines in a library is that all the routines in a module become part of the main program if one of them is referenced in the source. Consequently, all the routines in the module that are not used by the source will take up memory and disk space unnecessarily.

An alternative way of using the routines listed in this book is to use an editor to cut and paste the ones required by the program into the program code or into a separate source file. If the routines are moved to a separate file, this file must be assembled and then listed as an object module at link time. This method implies some text editing but has the advantage of not burdening the source with unused code. Since the only disadvantage of creating and using link-time libraries is one of memory and storage space, the decision must depend on the characteristics of each particular case.

2.2 The Direct-Access Video Display Module

The video display system in all IBM microcomputers is memory-mapped. In such an environment, alphanumeric display operations are performed by storing character codes and display attributes in an area of memory reserved for these operations. This is, in fact, the only character display technique possible in the IBM microcomputers. Programs that apparently do not use direct access to the video buffer, use BIOS and DOS services which access the buffer directly, because there is no other way of displaying alphanumeric characters in IBM systems.

One frequently mentioned disadvantage of programs that access the video buffer directly is the diminished portability that results from bypassing the BIOS software. In fact, direct-access display routines (see Table 2.1) can perform tests similar to those in the BIOS to adjust to the characteristics of the host system, thus ensuring portability of the code. However, there could still be difficulties related to the system cursor position when control is returned to software that uses BIOS display services. The following module, named DAVIDEO.ASM, contains the routines listed in Table 2.1.

Table 2.1. *Routines in the DAVIDEO Module*

ROUTINE NAME	FUNCTION
ES_TO_VIDEO	Set the ES segment register to the base address of the video buffer
CLEAR_SCREEN	Clear the video display screen
SET_DI_PTR	Set the DI register as a pointer into the video buffer based on the desired row and column coordinates
SHOW_BLOCK	Display a formatted block of text
SHOW_CX_CHARS	Display characters along a video row
SHOW_CX_VERT	Display characters along a video column

```
; Module name: DAVIDEO.ASM              Library: SOLUTION.LIB
; Created:
; Update:
;
;****************************************************************
;****************************************************************
;                       DAVIDEO.ASM
;****************************************************************
;****************************************************************
;
; Library module for video services using direct buffer access
;
;******************|
;        PUBLICS   |
;******************|
PUBLIC   ES_TO_VIDEO
PUBLIC   CLEAR_SCREEN
PUBLIC   SET_DI_PTR
PUBLIC   SHOW_BLOCK
PUBLIC   SHOW_CX_CHARS
PUBLIC   SHOW_CX_VERT
;
;
P_CODE   SEGMENT PUBLIC
         ASSUME   CS:P_CODE
;
;****************************************************************
ES_TO_VIDEO      PROC      FAR
; Set ES register to the base address of the video buffer
; according to the video mode stored in BIOS address 0040:0049
;
; On entry:
;          nothing
; On exit:
;          ES -> segment address of video buffer for alphanumeric
;                display
;          carry clear
;
         PUSH      AX                ; Save register
         PUSH      DS                ; Save segment
         MOV       AX,0040H          ; Segment base of data area
         MOV       DS,AX             ; To data segment
         MOV       AL,[0049H]        ; Current mode
         POP       DS                ; Restore segment
         CMP       AL,7              ; Code for monochrome card
         JE        SET_MONO_BASE     ; Set base for mono card
```

```
;********************|
;      color card    |
;********************|
        MOV     AX,0B800H       ; Color system base
        MOV     ES,AX           ; to ES
        POP     AX              ; Restore entry register
        CLC                     ; No error detection
        RET
;********************|
;  monochrome card   |
;********************|
SET_MONO_BASE:
        MOV     AX,0B000H       ; Video base in monochrome systems
        MOV     ES,AX           ; To ES
        POP     AX              ; Restore entry register
        CLC                     ; No error detection
        RET
ES_TO_VIDEO     ENDP
;****************************************************************
;
CLEAR_SCREEN    PROC    FAR
; Clear the video display with a block move
; On entry:
;           ES -> video buffer base address (ES_TO_VIDEO)
; On exit:
;           carry clear
        PUSH    AX              ; Save entry registers
        PUSH    CX
        PUSH    DI
        MOV     DI,0            ; Start at offset 0 in buffer
        MOV     AL,20H          ; Blank byte
        MOV     AH,7            ; Normal display attribute
        MOV     CX,2000         ; Repeat 2000 times
        CLD                     ; Forward direction in memory
        REP     STOSW           ; Store 2000 words in buffer
        POP     DI
        POP     CX
        POP     AX              ; Restore entry registers
        CLC                     ; No error detection
        RET
CLEAR_SCREEN    ENDP
;****************************************************************
;
SET_DI_PTR      PROC    FAR
; Set DI to the offset address in the video buffer that
; corresponds with a certain screen point, expressed as a row
```

```
; and column position
; On entry:
;          DH = screen row (0 to 24)
;          DL = screen column (0 to 79)
; On exit:
;  No error:
;          DI —> buffer offset (row * 160) + (column * 2)
;          carry clear
;  Error:
;         carry set. AX destroyed.
;
        CALL    TEST_RANGE      ; Local procedure
        PUSH    AX              ; Save accumulator
        PUSH    DX              ; and DX
        MOV     AL,160          ; Bytes per row
        MUL     DH              ; AX = 160 * DH
        MOV     DI,AX           ; Save partial result in DI
        MOV     AL,2            ; Bytes per column
        MUL     DL              ; AX = DL * 2
        ADD     DI,AX           ; Add in previous result
        POP     DX              ; Restore DX
        POP     AX              ; And accumulator
        CLC                     ; No error detection
        RET
SET_DI_PTR      ENDP
;*****************************************************************
;
SHOW_BLOCK      PROC    FAR
; Display a preformatted block message
;
; On entry:
;          SI —> start of block message
; Message format:
;       Offset:         Function:
;               0 —— Display row for start of message
;               1 —— Display column for start of message
;               2 —— Attribute for block
; Embedded codes:
;               00H = End of message
;               FFH = End of row
; On exit:
;         carry clear
;
        PUSH    AX                      ; Save entry registers
        PUSH    CX
        PUSH    DX
```

```
        MOV     DH,[SI]          ; Get row
        INC     SI               ; Point to start column byte
        MOV     DL,[SI]          ; Column
        MOV     CL,DL            ; Save start column in CL
        CALL    SET_DI_PTR       ; Set DI to offset in buffer
        INC     SI               ; Point to attribute byte
        MOV     AH,[SI]          ; To AH
        INC     SI
GET_AND_SHOW:
        MOV     AL,[SI]          ; Character
;********************|
;   test for control |
;     characters     |
;********************|
        CMP     AL,00H           ; Terminator
        JE      SHOW_END
        CMP     AL,0FFH          ; End of line
        JE      LINE_END
; Display it by storing character in video buffer
        CLD                      ; Forward direction
        STOSW                    ; Store word
        INC     DL               ; Next column
;********************|
;   bump pointer     |
;********************|
BUMP_PTRS:
        CALL    SET_DI_PTR
        INC     SI               ; Bump message pointer
        JMP     GET_AND_SHOW
;********************|
;   end of line      |
;********************|
LINE_END:
        INC     DH               ; Bump row pointer
        MOV     DL,CL            ; Reset column to start column
        JMP     BUMP_PTRS
;********************|
;   end of routine   |
;********************|
SHOW_END:
        POP     DX               ; Restore registers
        POP     CX
        POP     AX
        CLC                      ; No error detection
        RET
SHOW_BLOCK      ENDP
```

```
;******************************************************************
;
SHOW_CX_CHARS    PROC     FAR
; Display CX number of characters
; On entry:
;           AL = Character to display
;           AH = Attribute (if AH = 0 then attribute is not changed)
;           DH = screen row
;           DL = screen column
;           CX = number of characters to repeat
; On exit:
;           carry clear if no error
;           carry set if error. AX destroyed
         CALL    SET_DI_PTR
         JNC     OK_SHOW_CX       ; No error reported
         RET                      ; Error return
OK_SHOW_CX:
         CMP     AH,0             ; Test for attribute code
         JE      USE_BYTE_MOVE    ; Use installed attributes
;*******************|
;   attribute in AH |
;*******************|
         CLD                      ; Forward direction
         REP     STOSW            ; Store AX by [DI], bump twice
                                  ; and repeat
         CLC                      ; No error detection
         RET
;*******************|
;   current attribute |
;*******************|
USE_BYTE_MOVE:
         CLD                      ; Forward direction
         STOSB                    ; Store AL by [DI] and bump once
         INC     DI               ; Skip attribute byte
         LOOP    USE_BYTE_MOVE
         CLC                      ; No error detection
         RET
SHOW_CX_CHARS    ENDP
;******************************************************************
;
SHOW_CX_VERT     PROC     FAR
; Display CX number of characters vertically using current
; attribute
; On entry:
;           AL = character to display
;           DH = screen row
```

```
;           DL = screen column
;           CX = number of characters to repeat
; On exit:
;           carry clear
        CALL    SET_DI_PTR
        JNC     SET_VERTS           ; No error reported
        RET                         ; Error return
;********************|
;   attribute in AH  |
;********************|
SET_VERTS:
        CLD                         ; Forward
        STOSB                       ; Store AL by [DI] and bump once
        INC     DI                  ; Skip attribute
        ADD     DI,158              ; Bump to next row
        LOOP    SET_VERTS
        CLC                         ; No error detection
        RET
SHOW_CX_VERT    ENDP
;
;*****************************************************************
;                       internal procedures
;*****************************************************************
TEST_RANGE      PROC    NEAR
; Procedure to test that the screen address passed in the DH and
; DL registers is a valid one
; On entry:
;           DH = screen row (legal range is 0 to 24)
;           DL = screen column (legal range is 0 to 79)
; On exit:
;           carry set if error. AX destroyed. Returns to original
;           caller
;           nothing if no error
        CMP     DH,24               ; Test for valid input
        JG      BAD_CR              ; Invalid value
        CMP     DL,79               ; Maximum column value
        JG      BAD_CR              ; Invalid value
; Input is in legal range
        RET                         ; Return
BAD_CR:
        POP     AX                  ; Adjust stack
        STC                         ; Error flag on
        RET                         ; Return to original caller
TEST_RANGE      ENDP
P_CODE  ENDS
        END
```

Table 2.2. *Routines in the BIOVIDEO Module*

ROUTINE NAME	FUNCTION
BIO_CLEAR_SCR	Clear the video display screen
BIO_SET_MODE	Set video mode
BIO_GET_MODE	Obtain current video mode
BIO_SET_CUR	Set new cursor position
BIO_GET_CUR	Obtain current cursor position
BIO_CUR_OFF	Turn off system cursor
BIO_SHOW_ATR	Display character and attribute at the current cursor position
BIO_SHOW_CHR	Display character using current attribute at the current cursor position
BIO_SHOW_BLOK	Display a formatted block of text
BIO_SCROLL_UP	Scroll up a screen window
BIO_SCROLL_DN	Scroll down a screen window
BIO_SHOW_MESS	Display a message, terminated in a NULL byte, at the current cursor position
BIO_TTY	Display character or send control code using BIOS teletype service
DOS_STRING_OUT	Display a string of characters, terminated in a $ sign, using DOS service number 9 of INT 21H
BIO_CX_VERT	Display a number of characters along a video column

2.3 The BIOS and DOS Video Display Module

The BIOS services grouped under INT 10H provide a series of display functions available to the programmer. These services allow setting the video mode, manipulating the system cursor, and displaying characters and attributes in the alphanumeric modes. Although there are BIOS INT 10H services to perform elementary pixel operations, because of their unsatisfactory performance these services are seldom used in graphics programming. Chapter 9 is devoted to graphics routines and lists several graphics primitives to perform pixel operations.

Some services in this module are little more than an interface to those in the BIOS or DOS, while others perform some additional operations. The present module, named DAVIDEO.ASM, contains the routines listed in Table 2.2.

```
; Module name: BIOVIDEO.ASM              Library: SOLUTION.LIB
; Created:
; Update:
;
;****************************************************************
```

```
;******************************************************************
;                         BIOVIDEO.ASM
;******************************************************************
;******************************************************************
;
; Library module for video services using BIOS functions in
; INT 10H and DOS functions in INT 21H
;
;******************|
;       PUBLICS    |
;******************|
PUBLIC   BIO_CLEAR_SCR
PUBLIC   BIO_SET_MODE
PUBLIC   BIO_GET_MODE
PUBLIC   BIO_SET_CUR
PUBLIC   BIO_GET_CUR
PUBLIC   BIO_CUR_OFF
PUBLIC   BIO_SHOW_ATR
PUBLIC   BIO_SHOW_CHR
PUBLIC   BIO_SHOW_BLOK
PUBLIC   BIO_SCROLL_UP
PUBLIC   BIO_SCROLL_DN
PUBLIC   BIO_SHOW_MESS
PUBLIC   BIO_TTY
PUBLIC   DOS_STRING_OUT
PUBLIC   BIO_CX_VERT
;
;
P_CODE   SEGMENT PUBLIC
         ASSUME  CS:P_CODE
;
;******************************************************************
BIO_CLEAR_SCR    PROC    FAR
; Clear the video display using BIOS service number 6, INT 10H
; On entry:
;         nothing
; On exit:
;         carry clear
         PUSH    AX               ; Save entry registers
         PUSH    BX
         PUSH    CX
         PUSH    DX
         MOV     AH,6             ; Service request number
         MOV     AL,0             ; Code for blanking entire window
         MOV     BH,07            ; Normal attribute
         MOV     CX,0             ; Start at row #0, column #0
```

```
        MOV     DH,24           ; End at row #24
        MOV     DL,79           ; Column #79
        INT     10H             ; Transfer to BIOS
        POP     DX              ; Restore registers
        POP     CX
        POP     BX
        POP     AX
        CLC                     ; No error detection
        RET
BIO_CLEAR_SCR   ENDP
;********************************************************************
;
BIO_SET_MODE    PROC    FAR
; Set video display mode using BIOS service number 0 of INT 10H
;
; On entry:
;       AL = number of video mode to set
; On exit:
;       carry clear
;
        PUSH    AX              ; Save AX
        MOV     AH,0            ; BIOS service request number
        INT     10H
        POP     AX              ; Restore caller's register
        CLC                     ; No error detection
        RET
BIO_SET_MODE    ENDP
;********************************************************************
;
BIO_GET_MODE    PROC    FAR
; Obtain current video mode using BIOS service number 15 of
; INT 10H
; On entry:
;       nothing
; On exit:
;       AH = character columns on screen (40 or 80)
;       AL = active video mode
;       BH = active video page
;       carry clear
;
        MOV     AH,15           ; BIOS service request number
        INT     10H
        CLC                     ; No error detection
        RET
BIO_GET_MODE    ENDP
;********************************************************************
```

```
BIO_SET_CUR        PROC    FAR
; Set system cursor to a row and column coordinate
; On entry:
;          DH = screen row (range 0 to 24)
;          DL = screen column (range 0 to 79)
; On exit:
;          carry clear if no error
;
        CALL    TEST_RANGE      ; Local error handler
        PUSH    AX              ; Save entry registers
        PUSH    BX
        PUSH    DX
        MOV     AH,2            ; Service request number
        MOV     BH,0            ; Assume display page No. 0
        INT     10H
        POP     DX              ; Restore registers
        POP     BX
        POP     AX
        CLC                     ; No error
        RET
BIO_SET_CUR        ENDP
;****************************************************************
;
BIO_GET_CUR        PROC    FAR
; Read coordinates of current cursor position and start and
; end lines of cursor size
; On entry:
;          BH = active page number (normally 0)
; On exit:
;          CH = starting line of cursor size
;          CL = ending line of cursor size
;          DH = row number of current cursor position
;          DL = column number of current cursor position
;          carry clear
;
        PUSH    AX              ; Save entry registers
        MOV     AH,3            ; Service request number
        INT     10H
        POP     AX              ; Restore AX
        CLC                     ; No error
        RET
BIO_GET_CUR        ENDP
;****************************************************************
;
BIO_CUR_OFF        PROC    FAR
; Turn off cursor by setting the cursor address outside the
```

```
; current display page
        PUSH    AX              ; Save entry registers
        PUSH    BX
        PUSH    DX
        MOV     DH,25           ; y coordinate out of page
        MOV     DL,0
        MOV     AH,2            ; Service request number
        MOV     BH,0            ; Assume display page No. 0
        INT     10H
        POP     DX              ; Restore registers
        POP     BX
        POP     AX
        CLC                     ; No error
BIO_CUR_OFF     ENDP
;******************************************************************
;
BIO_SHOW_ATR    PROC    FAR
; Display character and attribute at current cursor position
; On entry:
;       AL = character
;       BL = attribute to use in displaying character
; On exit:
;       carry clear
;
        PUSH    AX              ; Save entry registers
        PUSH    BX
        PUSH    CX
        PUSH    DX
        MOV     AH,9            ; Service request number
        MOV     BH,0            ; Display page
        MOV     CX,1            ; Repetition factor
        INT     10H
        POP     DX              ; Restore caller's registers
        POP     CX
        POP     BX
        POP     AX
        CLC                     ; No error detection
        RET
BIO_SHOW_ATR    ENDP
;******************************************************************
BIO_SHOW_CHR    PROC    FAR
; Display the character in AL at the current cursor position
;
; On entry:
;       AL = character
; On exit:
```

```
;         carry clear
;
        PUSH    AX              ; Save caller's registers
        PUSH    BX
        PUSH    CX
        MOV     AH,10           ; Service request number
        MOV     BH,0            ; Display page No. 0
        MOV     CX,1            ; One character
        INT     10H
        POP     CX              ; Restore caller's registers
        POP     BX
        POP     AX
        CLC                     ; No error detection
        RET
BIO_SHOW_CHR    ENDP
;*******************************************************************
;
BIO_SCROLL_UP   PROC    FAR
; Scroll up video display window using BIOS service number 6
; of INT 10H
;
; On entry:
;         AL = number of lines to scroll
;         CH = y coordinate of upper left corner of window
;         CL = x coordinate of upper left corner of window
;         DH = y coordinate of lower right corner of window
;         DL = x coordinate of lower right corner of window
;
; CH/CL ->|————————————————————————————|
;         |                            |
;         |     screen area to be scrolled |
;         |                            |
;         |————————————————————————————|<- DH/DL
        MOV     AH,6            ; BIOS service request number
        INT     10H
        CLC                     ; No error detection
        RET
BIO_SCROLL_UP   ENDP
;*******************************************************************
BIO_SCROLL_DN   PROC    FAR
; Scroll down video display window using BIOS service number 7
; of INT 10H
;
; On entry:
;         AL = number of lines to scroll
;         CH = y coordinate of upper left corner of window
```

```
;            CL = x coordinate of upper left corner of window
;            DH = y coordinate of lower right corner of window
;            DL = x coordinate of lower right corner of window
;
; CH/CL ->|————————————————————————|
;         |                        |
;         |    screen area to be scrolled   |
;         |                        |
;         |————————————————————————|<- DH/DL
;
         MOV     AH,7          ; BIOS service request number
         INT     10H
         CLC                   ; No error detection
         RET
BIO_SCROLL_DN    ENDP
;**************************************************************
;
BIO_SHOW_BLOK    PROC    FAR
; Display a preformatted block message using BIOS service number 9
; of INT 10H
;
; On entry:
;         SI -> start of block message
; Message format:
;       Offset:            Function:
;              0 —— Display row for start of message
;              1 —— Display column for start of message
;              2 —— Attribute for block
; Embedded codes:
;              00H = End of message
;              FFH = End of row
; On exit:
;       carry clear
;
         MOV     DH,[SI]       ; Get row
         INC     SI            ; Point to start column byte
         MOV     DL,[SI]       ; Column
         MOV     CL,DL         ; Save start column in CL
         CALL    BIO_SET_CUR   ; Set cursor to message start
         INC     SI            ; Point to attribute byte
; Get attribute into BL
         MOV     BL,[SI]       ; SI -> attribute
         INC     SI
;
GET_AND_SHOW:
         MOV     AL,[SI]       ; Character
```

```
;*********************|
;   test for control  |
;      characters     |
;*********************|
        CMP     AL,00H          ; Terminator
        JE      SHOW_END
        CMP     AL,0FFH         ; End of line
        JE      LINE_END
; Display it
        CALL    BIO_SHOW_CHR
        INC     DL              ; Next column
;*********************|
;    bump cursor      |
;*********************|
BUMP_PTRS:
        CALL    BIO_SET_CUR
        INC     SI              ; Bump message pointer
        JMP     GET_AND_SHOW
;*******************|
;    end of line    |
;*******************|
LINE_END:
        INC     DH              ; Bump row pointer
        MOV     DL,CL           ; Reset column to start column
        JMP     BUMP_PTRS
SHOW_END:
        CLC                     ; No error detection
        RET
BIO_SHOW_BLOK   ENDP
;*****************************************************************
;
BIO_SHOW_MESS   PROC    FAR
; Display a string terminated in a NULL byte
;
; On entry:
;       SI -> message terminated in 00H
;
; On exit:
;       carry clear
;       SI points to message terminator
;       cursor bumped once for each character displayed
;
        PUSH    AX              ; Save caller's register
        PUSH    BX
SHOW_MS:
        MOV     AL,[SI]         ; Get character
```

```
          CMP      AL,0              ; Test for terminator
          JE       END_OF_MESS
          MOV      AH,14             ; BIOS service request number
                                     ; for ASCII teletype write
          MOV      BX,0              ; Display page
          INT      10H               ; BIOS service request
          INC      SI                ; Bump pointer
          JMP      SHOW_MS
END_OF_MESS:
          POP      BX                ; Restore caller's register
          POP      AX
          CLC                        ; No error detection
          RET
BIO_SHOW_MESS    ENDP
;*****************************************************************
;
BIO_TTY          PROC     FAR
; Display character or control code at cursor position using BIOS
; teletype service number 14, INT 10H
;
; On entry:
;         AL = character or control code
;               Recognized control codes are:
;                   07H = bell (beep speaker)
;                   08H = backspace
;                   0AH = line-feed
;                   0DH = carriage return
;
; On exit:
;         carry clear
;         cursor bumped to next position
;
          PUSH     AX                ; Save character
          PUSH     BX
          MOV      AH,14             ; BIOS service request number
                                     ; for ASCII teletype write
          MOV      BX,0              ; Display page
          INT      10H               ; BIOS service request
          POP      BX                ; Restore caller's registers
          POP      AX
          CLC                        ; No error detection
          RET
BIO_TTY          ENDP
;*****************************************************************
DOS_STRING_OUT PROC     FAR
; Display a string of characters terminated in a $ sign using
```

```
; DOS service number 9 of INT 21H
;
; On entry:
;       DX —> start of string
;
; On exit:
;       carry clear

        MOV     AH,9
        INT     21H
        CLC                     ; No error detection
        RET
DOS_STRING_OUT  ENDP
;*****************************************************************
;
BIO_CX_VERT     PROC    FAR
; Display CX number of characters and attributes vertically using
; a BIOS service
; On entry:
;       AL = character to display
;       AH = attribute (if AH = 0 then present attribute is
;            used)
;       DH = screen row
;       DL = screen column
;       CX = number of characters to repeat
; On exit:
;       carry clear
;
        CALL    BIO_SET_CUR
        CMP     AH,0            ; Test attribute unchanged code
        JE      KEEP_ATTR
CHANGE_ATTR:
        CALL    BIO_SHOW_ATR
        INC     DH              ; Next screen row
        CALL    BIO_SET_CUR     ; Move cursor
        LOOP    CHANGE_ATTR     ; Continue
        RET
KEEP_ATTR:
        CALL    BIO_SHOW_CHR
        INC     DH              ; Next screen row
        CALL    BIO_SET_CUR     ; Move cursor
        LOOP    KEEP_ATTR
        RET
BIO_CX_VERT     ENDP
;*****************************************************************
;                       internal procedures
```

```
;*******************************************************************
TEST_RANGE        PROC      NEAR
; Procedure to test that the screen address passed in the DH and
; DL registers is a valid one
; On entry:
;          DH = screen row (legal range is 0 to 24)
;          DL = screen column (legal range is 0 to 79)
; On exit:
;          carry set if error. AX destroyed. Returns to original
;          caller
;          nothing if no error
          CMP       DH,24             ; Test for valid input
          JG        BAD_CR            ; Invalid value
          CMP       DL,79             ; Maximum column value
          JG        BAD_CR            ; Invalid value
; Input is in legal range
          RET                         ; Return
BAD_CR:
          POP       AX                ; Adjust stack
          STC                         ; Error flag on
          RET                         ; Return to original caller
TEST_RANGE        ENDP
;
P_CODE   ENDS
          END
```

2.4 The Keyboard Module

For many programs the keyboard is the principal input device. User data and program controls are usually typed on the keyboard. Keyboard processing routines consist of character and string services and auxiliary keyboard operations. The following module includes standard services to obtain the keyboard status, to clear the keyboard buffer (flush), and to wait for a keystroke. In addition, the module includes two routines to obtain strings of characters typed by the user. One of these, named DOS_KBR_INPUT, uses DOS service number 10, of INT 21H, to obtain a line of input and place this line in a buffer designated by the caller. The procedure named KBR_INPUT is designed as a general-purpose keyboard input routine. KBR_INPUT recognizes the Enter, Backspace, and Escape keys and displays the characters typed by the user at a screen position selected by the caller.

The present module, named KEYBRD.ASM, contains the routines in Table 2.3.

Table 2.3. *Routines in the KEYBRD Module*

ROUTINE NAME	FUNCTION
KBR_STATUS	Check for keystroke in keyboard buffer
KBR_FLUSH	Clear old characters from keyboard buffer
KBR_WAIT	Wait for one keystroke
DOS_KBR_INPUT	Read a keyboard line using a DOS service
KBR_INPUT	General purpose keyboard input routine with input limit, control codes, and display address

```
; Module name: KEYBRD.ASM                    Library: SOLUTION.LIB
; Created:
; Update:
;
;******************************************************************
;******************************************************************
;                          KEYBRD.ASM
;******************************************************************
;******************************************************************
;
; Library module for keyboard services
;******************|
;       PUBLICS    |
;******************|
PUBLIC   KBR_STATUS
PUBLIC   KBR_FLUSH
PUBLIC   KBR_WAIT
PUBLIC   DOS_KBR_INPUT
PUBLIC   KBR_INPUT
;
;******************************************************************
;                             code
;******************************************************************
;
P_CODE   SEGMENT PUBLIC
         ASSUME   CS:P_CODE
;
;******************************************************************
KBR_STATUS   PROC     FAR
; On entry:
;         nothing
; On exit:
;         carry set if keystroke in buffer
```

```
        ;
                MOV     AH,1            ; BIOS service request numbers
                INT     16H
                JNZ     PRESSED
        ; No key waiting
                CLC
                RET
        PRESSED:
                STC
                RET
        KBR_STATUS  ENDP
        ;****************************************************************
        ;
        KBR_FLUSH   PROC    FAR
        ; Flush old characters from keyboard buffer
        ; On entry:
        ;       nothing
        ; On exit:
        ;       carry clear
        FLUSH_1:
                MOV     AH,1            ; BIOS service request number
                INT     16H
                JZ      NOCHAR          ; OK to exit, buffer clear
        ; Flush old character
                MOV     AH,0            ; BIOS service request number
                INT     16H
                JMP     FLUSH_1
        NOCHAR:
                CLC                     ; No error detection
                RET
        KBR_FLUSH   ENDP
        ;****************************************************************
        ;
        KBR_WAIT    PROC    FAR
        ; Wait for one keyboard character
        ; On entry:
        ;       nothing
        ; On exit:
        ;       AL = keyboard character
        ;       AH = keyboard scan code
        ;
                MOV     AH,0            ; Service request number
                INT     16H
                RET
        KBR_WAIT    ENDP
        ;****************************************************************
```

```
DOS_KBR_INPUT    PROC    FAR
;
; Read a line from the keyboard and place the input in a buffer
; designated by the caller
;
; Buffer structure:
;        Offset 0 = Maximum number of characters to input
;                   (provided by the caller)
;        Offset 1 = Character count actually input, excluding
;                   the CR (this area is filled by DOS)
; On entry:
;        DX -> buffer start
; On exit:
;        Caller's buffer contains keyboard input and CR
;
        MOV      AH,10
        INT      21H
        RET
DOS_KBR_INPUT    ENDP
;****************************************************************
;
KBR_INPUT        PROC    FAR
;
; General keyboard input routine with the following parameters:
; Control codes and exit codes:
;              0DH <Enter> .... Exit with carry clear
;              011BH <Esc> .... Exit with carry set
;              08H <Backspace>. Erase character and backspace
;                               cursor
;
; On entry:
;        DI -> storage buffer
;        SI -> Input format area:
;              Offset 0 = screen start row
;              Offset 1 = screen start column
;              Offset 2 = total characters allowed
; On exit:
;        Text is stored in buffer by DI
;              DI -> start of character buffer
;              CX = total characters input
;              carry clear
;
        PUSH     DX              ; Save entry DX
        MOV      DH,[SI]         ; Get display row
        INC      SI              ; Bump to offset 2
        MOV      DL,[SI]         ; Get display column
```

```
        CALL    SET_CUR             ; Local procedure
        INC     SI                  ; Bump to offset 3
        MOV     CL,[SI]             ; Set up counter
        MOV     CH,CL               ; Copy start value in CH
;
; Save entry value of buffer pointer in SI
        MOV     SI,DI
;
GET_KEY:
        CALL    KBR_WAIT            ; Get character
;*****************|
; input processing |
;*****************|
        CMP     AL,0DH              ; <Enter> key
        JNE     NOT_0DH
        JMP     KBR_EXIT_0          ; Take exit
NOT_0DH:
        CMP     AX,011BH            ; <Esc> key
        JNE     NOT_ESC
        JMP     KBR_EXIT_1          ; Take exit
NOT_ESC:
        CMP     AL,08H              ; <Backspace> key
        JNE     NOT_BAK
;
;*****************|
;      backspace    |
;*****************|
; Test for cursor at start of buffer
        CMP     CH,CL               ; Test present count with start
                                    ; value
        JE      GET_KEY             ; Ignore backspace at start
                                    ; position
; Execute backspace
        DEC     DI                  ; Buffer pointer
        DEC     DL                  ; Display column counter
        CALL    SET_CUR
        INC     CL                  ; Adjust maximum characters count
        MOV     AL,' '              ; Blank space
        CALL    SHOW_CHR            ; Display a blank
        MOV     [DI],AL             ; and put blank in buffer
        JMP     GET_KEY             ; Continue
;
;*****************|
; test for errors  |
;*****************|
NOT_BAK:
```

```
; Test for invalid input (less than 20H or more than 79H)
        CMP     AL,20H
        JL      GET_KEY             ; Illegal, too small
        CMP     AL,79H
        JG      GET_KEY             ; Illegal, too large
; Test for buffer full
        CMP     CL,0                ; CL is counter
        JNZ     DISPLAY_IT
        JMP     GET_KEY             ; Buffer is full
;*****************|
;    display      |
;    character    |
;*****************|
DISPLAY_IT:
        CALL    SHOW_CHR
; Store it in buffer
        MOV     [DI],AL
;*****************|
;  bump pointers  |
;*****************|
        INC     DI                  ; Bump buffer pointer
        INC     DL                  ; Bump display column
        CALL    SET_CUR
        DEC     CL                  ; Character counter
        JMP     GET_KEY             ; Continue
;
KBR_EXIT_0:
        PUSH    SI                  ; Save start of buffer
        SUB     DI,SI               ; Get total input
        MOV     CX,DI               ; into counter
        POP     DI                  ; Restore buffer start pointer
        CLC                         ; <Enter> key exit, no carry
        POP     DX                  ; Restore entry DX
        RET
KBR_EXIT_1:
        PUSH    SI                  ; Save start of buffer
        SUB     DI,SI               ; Get total input
        MOV     CX,DI               ; into counter
        POP     DI                  ; Restore buffer start pointer
        STC                         ; <Esc> key exit, carry set
        POP     DX                  ; Restore entry DX
        CLC                         ; No error detection
        RET
KBR_INPUT       ENDP
```

```
;*****************************************************************
;                        local procedures
;*****************************************************************
SET_CUR    PROC    NEAR
; Set system cursor to a row and column coordinate
; On entry:
;          DH = screen row (range 0 to 24)
;          DL = screen column (range 0 to 79)
; On exit:
;          carry clear if no error
;
           PUSH    AX                  ; Save entry registers
           PUSH    BX
           PUSH    DX
           MOV     AH,2                ; Service request number
           MOV     BH,0                ; Assume display page No. 0
           INT     10H
           POP     DX                  ; Restore registers
           POP     BX
           POP     AX
           RET
SET_CUR    ENDP
;*****************************************************************
;
SHOW_CHR   PROC    NEAR
; Display the character in AL at the current cursor position
; On entry:
;          AL = character
; On exit:
;          carry clear
;
           PUSH    AX                  ; Save caller's registers
           PUSH    BX
           PUSH    CX
           MOV     AH,10               ; Service request number
           MOV     BH,0                ; Display page zero
           MOV     CX,1                ; One character
           INT     10H
           POP     CX                  ; Restore caller's registers
           POP     BX
           POP     AX
           RET
SHOW_CHR   ENDP
;
P_CODE   ENDS
         END
```

Table 2.4. *Routines in the OUTPUT Module*

ROUTINE NAME	FUNCTION
SEND_PRN	Send one character to printer
STATUS_PRN	Obtain printer status
SET_PROTOCOL	Set communications protocol on the RS-232-C line
STATUS_RS232	Obtain serial line status
SEND_RS232	Send character through serial line
GET_RS232	Receive character through the serial line

2.5 The Printer and Serial Port Output Module

The printer and serial ports were optional attachments in the IBM microcomputers of the PC line but, because of their general usefulness, all models of the PS/2 line are equipped with these output devices. The services contained in this module are those required to provide a simple interface with the printer and the serial port. Both devices are discussed in more detail in separate chapters later in this book. The present module, named OUTPUT.ASM, contains the routines listed in Table 2.4.

```
; Module name: OUTPUT.ASM                      Library: SOLUTION.LIB
; Created:
; Update:
;**************************************************************
;**************************************************************
;                           OUTPUT.ASM
;**************************************************************
;**************************************************************
;
; Library module for printer and serial line operations
;*******************|
;       PUBLICS     |
;*******************|
PUBLIC   SEND_PRN
PUBLIC   STATUS_PRN
PUBLIC   SET_PROTOCOL
PUBLIC   STATUS_RS232
PUBLIC   SEND_RS232
PUBLIC   GET_RS232
;
;**************************************************************
;                            code
;**************************************************************
```

```
P_CODE   SEGMENT PUBLIC
         ASSUME  CS:P_CODE
;
;******************************************************************
;                         printer routines
;******************************************************************
SEND_PRN          PROC    FAR
; Test printer status and send character when printer ready
; On entry:
;          AL = character to send
;          DX = printer port (valid values are 0, 1, and 2)
; On exit:
;          carry clear if no error
;          carry set if print operation failed
;
;****************|
; initialize port |
;****************|
INIT_PORT:
        MOV     AH,1               ; Service request number
        INT     17H                ; Transfer to BIOS
        TEST    AH,80H             ; Test printer not-busy bit
        JNZ     NOT_BUSY
        TEST    AH,1               ; Time-out bit
        JNZ     STATUS_ERROR
        JMP     INIT_PORT          ; Repeat initialization and
                                   ; status check
;****************|
;    error exit    |
;****************|
STATUS_ERROR:
        STC                        ; Carry set to signal error
        RET
;****************|
;  send character  |
;****************|
NOT_BUSY:
        MOV     AH,0               ; Function request code
        INT     17H                ; Transfer to BIOS
        CLC                        ; No error in send operation
        RET
SEND_PRN          ENDP
;******************************************************************
;
STATUS_PRN        PROC       FAR
; Obtain printer status using BIOS service number of the specified
```

```
; port
; On entry:
;           DX = printer number (valid values are 0, 1, and 2)
; On exit:
;           AH = 7  6  5  4  3  2  1  0   printer status bit map
;                |  |  |  |  |  |  |  |
;                |  |  |  |  |  |  |  |__ time-out
;                |  |  |  |  |  |  |__|____ UNUSED
;                |  |  |  |  |  |_____ input/output error
;                |  |  |  |  |_____ printer selected
;                |  |  |  |_____ out of paper
;                |  |  |_____ acknowledge
;                |  |_____ printer not-busy
;          carry clear if valid status
;          carry set if invalid port request
; Test for invalid value in DX
        CMP     DX,2            ; 2 is maximum legal input
        JLE     OK_PORT_VAL     ; Input is valid
        STC                     ; Set carry to signal error
        RET
OK_PORT_VAL:
        MOV     DX,0            ; Port 0
        MOV     AH,1            ; Service request number
        INT     17H             ; Transfer to BIOS
        CLC                     ; Carry clear if no error
        RET
STATUS_PRN      ENDP
;


;****************************************************************
;                    serial port routines
;****************************************************************
;
SET_PROTOCOL    PROC    FAR
; Set communications protocol for the serial line
;
; On entry:
; BAUD RATE:
;           AL = 1 for 110 Bd        AL = 5 for 1200 Bd
;           AL = 2 for 150 Bd        AL = 6 for 2400 Bd
;           AL = 3 for 300 Bd        AL = 7 for 4800 Bd
;           AL = 4 for 600 Bd        AL = 8 for 9600 Bd
;
; PARITY:
;           BL = 1 for parity ODD    BL = 2 for no parity
;           BL = 3 for parity EVEN
```

```
; STOP BITS:
;            BH = 1 for 1 stop bit          BH = 2 for 2 stop bits
;
; WORD LENGTH:
;            DL = 1 for 7-bit words         DL = 2 for 8-bit words
;
; On exit:
;            carry clear if no error
;            carry set if invalid input values
;
          PUSH      AX                     ; Save caller's registers
          PUSH      BX
          PUSH      CX
          PUSH      DX
;******************|
;    baud rate     |
;******************|
; AL holds baud rate code. Valid range is 1 to 8
          CMP       AL,1                   ; Carry set if less than 1
          JL        BAD_VALUES             ; Error exit if less than 1
          CMP       AL,9                   ; or greater than 8
          JLE       OK_BAUD
;******************|
;    error exit    |
;******************|
BAD_VALUES:
          POP       DX                     ; Restore caller's register
          POP       CX
          POP       BX
          POP       AX
          STC                              ; Illegal baud rate code
          RET
; Input is in valid range.
OK_BAUD:
          SUB       AL,1                   ; To range 0 to 7
          MOV       CL,5                   ; Shift bit counter
          SHL       AL,CL                  ; Baud rate bits left 5 bits
;******************|
;      parity      |
;******************|
; BL holds parity code. Valid values is 1, 2, or 3
          CMP       BL,1                   ; Carry set if less than 1
          JL        BAD_PARITY             ; Error exit if less than 1
          CMP       BL,3                   ; or greater than 8
          JLE       OK_PARITY
BAD_PARITY:
```

```
        JMP       BAD_VALUES
OK_PARITY:
        MOV       CL,3             ; Shift bit counter
        SHL       BL,CL            ; Shift left 3 bits
        OR        AL,BL            ; OR with baud rate
;
;******************|
;    stop bits     |
;******************|
; BH holds stop bits code. Valid values are 1 and 2
        CMP       BH,1             ; Carry set if less than 1
        JL        BAD_STOP         ; Error exit if less than 1
        CMP       BH,2             ; or greater than 2
        JLE       OK_STOP
BAD_STOP:
        JMP       BAD_VALUES
OK_STOP:
        MOV       CL,2
        SHL       BH,CL            ; Shift digits
        OR        AL,BH            ; OR with stored parameters
;
;******************|
;   word length    |
;******************|
; DL holds word length code. Valid values are 1 and 2
        CMP       DL,1             ; Carry set if less than 1
        JL        BAD_WORD         ; Error exit if less than 1
        CMP       BH,2             ; or greater than 2
        JLE       OK_WORD
BAD_WORD:
        JMP       BAD_VALUES
OK_WORD:
        INC       DL               ; Bring to value 2 or 3
        OR        AL,DL            ; OR with stored parameters
;
;******************|
;   install new    |
;    protocol      |
;******************|
; AL holds bit code for BIOS service number 0, INT 14H
        MOV       DX,0             ; Always COMM1 card
        MOV       AH,0             ; Request code
        INT       14H              ; BIOS service
        CLC                        ; No error
        RET
SET_PROTOCOL    ENDP
```

```
;*****************************************************************

STATUS_RS232    PROC    FAR
; Obtain RS-232-C port status using BIOS service number of the
; specified  port
;
; On entry:
;          DX = RS-232-C port number (valid range is 0 to 3)
;               0 = COMM1, 1 = COMM2, etc.
; On exit:
;          AH = 7   6   5   4   3   2   1   0   RS-232-C line status bit map
;                |   |   |   |   |   |   |   |
;                |   |   |   |   |   |   |   |__ data ready
;                |   |   |   |   |   |   |_____ overrun error
;                |   |   |   |   |   |_____ parity error
;                |   |   |   |   |_____ framing error
;                |   |   |   |_____ break detect
;                |   |   |_____ transmission hold register
;                |   |                          empty
;                |   |_____ transmission shift register
;                |                              empty
;                |_____ time-out
;
;          AL = 7   6   5   4   3   2   1   0   modem status bit map
;                |   |   |   |   |   |   |   |
;                |   |   |   |   |   |   |   |__ delta clear to send
;                |   |   |   |   |   |   |_____ delta data set ready
;                |   |   |   |   |   |_____ trailing edge indicator
;                |   |   |   |   |_____ receive line signal detect
;                |   |   |   |_____ clear to send
;                |   |   |_____ data set ready
;                |   |_____ ring indicator
;                |_____ received line signal detect
;
;               carry clear if valid status
;               carry set if invalid port request
;
; Test for invalid value in DX
        CMP     DX,3            ; 3 is maximum legal input
        JLE     OK_RSPORT       ; Input is valid
        STC                     ; Set carry to signal error
        RET
;
OK_RSPORT:
        MOV     AH,3            ; Service request number
        INT     14H             ; Transfer to BIOS
```

```
            CLC                     ; Carry clear if no error
            RET
STATUS_RS232    ENDP
;****************************************************************
;
SEND_RS232      PROC    FAR
; Send character through RS-232-C port
; On entry:
;           AL = character to send
;           DX = RS-232-C port number (valid range is 0 to 3)
;               0 = COMM1, 1 = COMM2, etc.
; On exit:
;           AH = line status bit map (as in STATUS_RS232)
;               time-out bit set if character not sent
;           carry clear
;
;
        MOV     AH,1            ; Service request number
        INT     14H             ; Transfer to BIOS
        CLC                     ; Carry clear if no error
        RET
SEND_RS232      ENDP
;****************************************************************
;
GET_RS232       PROC    FAR
; Wait for a character and receive it through the RS-232-C port
; On entry:
;           DX = RS-232-C port number (valid range is 0 to 3)
;               0 = COMM1, 1 = COMM2, etc.
; On exit:
;           AL = character received
;           AH = line status bit map (as in STATUS_RS232)
;               time-out bit set if character not sent
;           carry clear
;
; Note: The routine waits until character is received
        MOV     AH,2            ; Service request number
        INT     14H             ; Transfer to BIOS
        CLC                     ; Carry clear if no error
        RET
GET_RS232       ENDP
;
;
P_CODE  ENDS
        END
```

Table 2.5. *Routines in the CONVERT Module*

ROUTINE NAME	FUNCTION
BIN_TO_ASC	Binary in the DX register to an ASCII decimal
ASC_TO_BIN	5-digit ASCII number in a user buffer to a binary in the DX register
BIN_TO_ASCHEX	16-bit binary in the DX register to an ASCII hexadecimal number
BIN_TO_ASCBIN	8-bit binary in the DL register to an ASCII binary number

2.6 The Conversions Module

We are members of a culture that has adopted the decimal system of numbers as its conventional mathematical language. To communicate with computers, which are binary machines, we often need routines that transform decimal numbers into binary and vice versa. The hexadecimal system of numbers is a useful shorthand for binary numbers, for this reason, conversion routines involving hexadecimal numbers are also frequently required.

The present module, named CONVERT.ASM, contains the routines listed in Table 2.5.

```
; Module name: CONVERT.ASM              Library: SOLUTION.LIB
; Created:
; Update:
;
;****************************************************************
;****************************************************************
;                          CONVERT.ASM
;****************************************************************
;****************************************************************
;
; Library module for numeric conversions
;
;*****************|
;      PUBLICS    |
;*****************|
PUBLIC   BIN_TO_ASC
PUBLIC   ASC_TO_BIN
PUBLIC   BIN_TO_ASCHEX
PUBLIC   BIN_TO_ASCBIN
;
P_CODE   SEGMENT PUBLIC
         ASSUME  CS:P_CODE
```

```
;********************************************************************
BIN_TO_ASC        PROC     FAR
;
; Convert a 16-bit binary in the DX register to an ASCII decimal
; number
;
; On entry:
;           DX = binary source
;           DI -> 5-byte output buffer
; On exit:
;           DI -> start of 5-byte buffer holding the ASCII decimal
;                   number
;           carry clear
;
        PUSH     DI              ; Save start of buffer
        CALL     CLEAR_5         ; Clear user's buffer
; DI -> last byte in user's buffer
        MOV      CX,0            ; Clear counter
BINA0:  PUSH     CX              ; Save count
        MOV      AX,DX           ; Add in numerator
        MOV      DX,0            ; Clear top half
        MOV      CX,10           ; Enter decimal divisor
        DIV      CX              ; Perform division AX/CX
        XCHG     AX,DX           ; Get quotient
        ADD      AL,30H          ; Make digit ASCII
        MOV      [DI],AL         ; Store digit in buffer
        DEC      DI              ; Bump destination pointer
        POP      CX              ; Restore counter
        INC      CX              ; Count the digit
        CMP      DX,0            ; Test for end of binary
        JNZ      BINA0           ; Continue if not end
;
        POP      DI              ; Restore pointer to start of
                                 ; buffer
        CLC                      ; No error detection
        RET
BIN_TO_ASC        ENDP
;********************************************************************
;
ASC_TO_BIN        PROC     FAR
;
; Convert an ASCII number to binary
; On entry:
;           BX -> start of 5-digit ASCII buffer
; On exit:
;           DX = binary number (range 0 to 65535)
```

```
;          carry clear
          MOV     DX,0               ; Clear binary output
ASC0:     MOV     AL,[BX]            ; Get ASCII digit
          INC     BX                 ; Bump pointer to next digit
          SUB     AL,30H             ; ASCII to decimal
          JL      EXASC              ; Exit if invalid ASCII
          CMP     AL,9               ; Test for highest value
          JG      EXASC              ; Exit if larger than 9
          CBW                        ; Extend to AX
          PUSH    AX                 ; Save digit in stack
          MOV     AX,DX              ; Move into output register
          MOV     CX,10              ; Decimal multiplier
          MUL     CX                 ; Perform AX = AX * 10
          MOV     DX,AX              ; Move product to output register
          POP     AX                 ; Restore decimal digit
          ADD     DX,AX              ; Add in digit
          JMP     ASC0               ; Continue
EXASC:    CLC                        ; No error detection
          RET
ASC_TO_BIN        ENDP
;*******************************************************************
;
BIN_TO_ASCHEX     PROC    FAR
; Convert a 16-bit binary in the DX register to an ASCII
; hexadecimal number
; On entry:
;          DX = binary source
;          DI -> 5-byte output buffer
; On exit:
;          DI -> start of 5-byte buffer. The last character
;                in the buffer is the letter H
;          carry clear
;
          PUSH    DI                 ; Save user's buffer pointer
          PUSH    DI                 ; twice
          CALL    CLEAR_5
          MOV     BYTE PTR[DI],'H'    ; Place H in buffer
          POP     DI                 ; Restore buffer pointer
          MOV     CX,4               ; Count 4 digits
HEX_CVR:
          PUSH    CX                 ; Save counter
          MOV     CL,4               ; 4 digits
          ROL     DX,CL              ; Rotate source left
          MOV     AL,DL              ; Move digit into AL
          AND     AL,00001111B       ; Clear high-order nibble
          DAA                        ; Adjust AL if A through F
```

```
          ADD      AL,11110000B      ; and bump the carry
          ADC      AL,40H            ; Convert hex to ASCII
          MOV      [DI],AL           ; Store in buffer
          INC      DI                ; Bump buffer pointer
          POP      CX                ; Restore digit counter
          LOOP     HEX_CVR           ; Continue with next digit
; Converted number is now in buffer
          POP      DI                ; Restore caller's pointer
          CLC                        ; No error detection
          RET
BIN_TO_ASCHEX    ENDP
;****************************************************************
;
BIN_TO_ASCBIN    PROC     FAR
; Convert a 8-bit binary number in DL into 8 ASCII binary digits
; On entry:
;          DL = 8-bit binary number
;          DI -> 9-byte output buffer
; On exit:
;          DI -> start of 9-byte buffer. The last character
;                in the buffer is the letter B
;          carry clear
;
          PUSH     DI                ; Save user's buffer pointer
          PUSH     DI                ; twice
          MOV      CX,9              ; 9 digits to clear
CLEAR_9:
          MOV      BYTE PTR [DI],20H    ; Clear digit
          INC      DI                ; Bump pointer
          LOOP     CLEAR_9           ; Repeat for 9 digits
          DEC      DI                ; Adjust buffer pointer to last
                                     ; digit
          MOV      BYTE PTR[DI],'B'     ; Place B in buffer
          POP      DI                ; Start of buffer
          MOV      CX,8              ; Count 8 digits
; DL has binary value to convert to ASCII
BIN_CVR:
          TEST     DL,10000000B      ; Test high-order bit of DL
          JNZ      SET_1             ; Bit is set
          MOV      BYTE PTR[DI],'0'
          JMP      NEXT_BIN
SET_1:
          MOV      BYTE PTR[DI],'1'
NEXT_BIN:
          INC      DI                ; Bump pointer
          SAL      DL,1              ; Shift bits left once
```

```
        LOOP     BIN_CVR
; Converted number is now in buffer
        POP      DI                  ; Restore caller's pointer
        CLC                          ; No error detection
        RET
BIN_TO_ASCBIN    ENDP
;*******************************************************************
;                      local procedures
;*******************************************************************
CLEAR_5          PROC    NEAR
; On entry:
;        DS:DI -> start of a 5-byte user buffer
; On exit:
;        DS:DI -> last byte in the 5-byte buffer
        MOV      CX,5                ; 5 digits to clear
CLEAR_BUF:
        MOV      BYTE PTR [DI],20H       ; Clear digit
        INC      DI                  ; Bump pointer
        LOOP     CLEAR_BUF           ; Repeat for 5 digits
        DEC      DI                  ; Adjust buffer pointer to last
                                     ; digit
        RET
CLEAR_5          ENDP
;*******************************************************************
;
P_CODE  ENDS
        END
```

Table 2.6. *Routines in the DISKIO Module*

ROUTINE NAME	FUNCTION
SET_DTA	Set DOS disk transfer area
GET_FIRST	Find first matching filename
GET_NEXT	Find next matching filename
OPEN_CREATE	Input filename, open or create file, and obtain file handle
CLOSE_FILE	Close file using file handle
READ_128	Read 128 bytes from an open file into a user buffer
WRITE_128	Transfer 128 bytes from a user buffer into an open file and obtain file handle
CLOSE_FILE	Close file using file handle
READ_128	Read 128 bytes from an open file into a user buffer
WRITE_128	Transfer 128 bytes from a user buffer into an open file

2.7 The Disk Input/Output Module

Diskette and hard disk drives are the most used data storage devices in the IBM microcomputers. Disk system routines can be classified in the following groups:

1. Primitive routines that operate on the hardware elements, for example, the device drivers contained in the BIOS.
2. Routines that manipulate internal data structures used by system software, for example, the DOS routines that create and maintain the file allocation table and the disk directories.
3. Routines for handling user files and data.

The first two groups of routines, which are of a highly specialized nature, are usually part of the operating system programs. Chapter 3 of this book, which is devoted to the design and coding of operating system software, lists some disk primitives. The disk routines in the present section belong to the third group. These are the routines generally required at the application level.

The present module, named DISKIO.ASM, contains the routines listed in Table 2.6.

```
; Module name: DISKIO.ASM                    Library: SOLUTION.LIB
; Created:
; Update:
;
;********************************************************************
;********************************************************************
;                           DISKIO.ASM
;********************************************************************
;********************************************************************
;
;
; Library module for disk operations
;
;******************|
;       PUBLICS    |
;******************|
PUBLIC   SET_DTA
PUBLIC   GET_FIRST
PUBLIC   GET_NEXT
PUBLIC   OPEN_CREATE
PUBLIC   CLOSE_FILE
PUBLIC   OPEN_FILE
PUBLIC   READ_128
PUBLIC   WRITE_128
;
;******************|
;      EXTERNALS   |
;******************|
```

```
;****************************************************************
;                              code
;****************************************************************
;
P_CODE   SEGMENT PUBLIC
         ASSUME  CS:P_CODE
;
;****************************************************************
SET_DTA          PROC    FAR
; Set memory area to be used by DOS as disk transfer area
; On entry:
;          DX -> 128-byte buffer to be used as DTA
;
; On exit:
;          carry clear
;
         MOV     AH,26            ; DOS service request
         INT     21H
         RET
SET_DTA          ENDP
;****************************************************************
;
GET_FIRST        PROC    FAR
; Define file or path name and find first matching filename in
; the current or the specified directory, if there is one
;
; Note: This procedure should be used in conjunction with the
; procedure GET_NEXT in processing filenames that can contain
; the DOS global characters "*" and "?"
;
; On entry:
;          DX -> Buffer formatted for DOS service number 10
;              Offset 0 = maximum characters to input
;              Offset 1 = characters actually input, excluding CR
; On exit:
;          Current DTA filled as follows:
;              Bytes 0 to 20   = reserved for DOS
;              Byte 21         = attribute of matched file
;              Bytes 22 and 23 = file time
;              Bytes 24 and 25 = file date
;              Bytes 26 and 27 = LSW of file size
;              Bytes 28 and 29 = MSW of file size
;              Bytes 30 to 42  = FILENAME AND EXTENSION in the
;                                form of an ASCIIZ string
;          carry clear if function was successful
;          carry set if function failed
```

```
;            AX = error code as follows:
;                 02H = invalid path
;                 12H = no matching directory entry found
;
;****************|
; buffered input |
; from keyboard  |
;****************|
        MOV     AH,10           ; DOS service request number
        PUSH    DX              ; Save buffer start address
        PUSH    DX              ; twice
        INT     21H             ; To DOS
; Filename now in buffer. Set a NULL byte in buffer to create an
; ASCIIZ string for the PATH or FILENAME
        POP     DI              ; Recover buffer start
        INC     DI              ; To input count byte
        MOV     AL,[DI]         ; No. of characters in buffer
        MOV     AH,0            ; Prepare for addition
        ADD     DI,AX           ; DX -> CR byte
        INC     DI              ; One more
        MOV     BYTE PTR [DI],0H
                                ; Set NULL-byte terminator
;****************|
; search for first|
;     match       |
;****************|
        POP     DX              ; Recover buffer start
        ADD     DX,2            ; Index to start of file or path
                                ; name
        MOV     AH,78           ; DOS service request number
                                ; to find first match
        MOV     CX,0            ; Normal attribute for file
        INT     21H
; Carry flag is set if no matched filename found
; If no carry, matched filename can be found as an ASCIIZ string
; in the current DTA + 30. This filename can be used to open the
; file or to obtain the file handle
        RET
GET_FIRST       ENDP
;**************************************************************
;
GET_NEXT        PROC    FAR
; This procedure assumes a previous, successful call to the
; procedure GET_FIRST. It finds the next matching filename that
; matches the filespec, if it exists
```

```
;  On entry:
;          The DTA must contain information from a successful
;          GET_FIRST call
;
;  On exit:
;          carry clear if operation successful
;          Current DTA filled as follows:
;                  Bytes 0 to 20   = reserved for DOS
;                  Byte 21         = attribute of matched file
;                  Bytes 22 and 23 = file time
;                  Bytes 24 and 25 = file date
;                  Bytes 26 and 27 = LSW of file size
;                  Bytes 28 and 29 = MSW of file size
;                  Bytes 30 to 42  = FILENAME AND EXTENSION in the
;                                    form an ASCIIZ string
;          carry set if operation failed - no match found
;
        MOV     AH,79           ; DOS service request number
                                ; for next match search
        INT     21H
;
; Carry flag is set if no next matched filename found
; If no carry, matched filename can be found as an ASCIIZ string
; in the current DTA + 30. This filename can be used to open the
; file or to obtain the file handle
        RET
;
GET_NEXT        ENDP
;
;****************************************************************
;
OPEN_CREATE     PROC    FAR
;
; Use DOS buffered keyboard input service to input a filename,
; to open file, and to return a 16-bit file handle that can be
; used for further file access
; The routine's action depends on the setting of the BL register
;
; On entry:
;          DX -> Buffer formatted as for DOS service number 10
;                  Offset 0 = maximum characters to input
;                  Offset 1 = characters actually input,
;                             excluding CR
;          BL = 0 - Open file
;          BL = 1 - Create new file
; On exit:
```

```
;           carry clear if file open - operation successful
;              AX = 16-bit file handle
;           carry set if operation failed
;              AX = error code as follows:
;                   1 = invalid function
;                   2 = file not found
;
; Note: This procedure assumes that DOS service number 26
;       has been previously used to set the DTA address
;
;****************|
; buffered input |
; from keyboard   |
;****************|
        PUSH    BX              ; Save exit/create switch
        MOV     AH,10           ; DOS service request number
        PUSH    DX              ; Save buffer start address
        PUSH    DX              ; twice
        INT     21H             ; To DOS
; Filename now in buffer. Set a NULL byte in buffer to
; create an ASCIIZ string for the PATH or FILENAME
        POP     DI              ; Recover buffer start
        INC     DI              ; To input count byte
        MOV     AL,[DI]         ; No. of characters in buffer
        MOV     AH,0            ; Prepare for addition
        ADD     DI,AX           ; DX -> CR byte
        INC     DI              ; One more
        MOV     BYTE PTR [DI],0H
                                ; Set NULL-byte terminator
; Recover buffer address and exit/create switch
        POP     DX              ; Buffer start
        ADD     DX,2            ; Index to path or filename
        POP     BX              ; Open/create switch
        CMP     BL,0            ; Test for open switch
        JE      OPEN_F
        JMP     CREATE_F
;
;****************|
;      open       |
;****************|
OPEN_F:
; This routine opens a file for read-write access if the filename
; is contained in the form of an ASCIIZ string pointed by DX
        MOV     AH,61           ; DOS service request number
                                ; to open file (handle mode)
        MOV     AL,2            ; Read-write access
```

```
        INT     21H
; Carry set if open failed
; If carry clear, file is open and AX = file handle
; BL (in stack) holds exit/create switch
        RET
;*****************|
;    create       |
;*****************|
CREATE_F:
        MOV     CX,0            ; Normal access
        MOV     AH,60           ; DOS service request
        INT     21H
; If carry clear, AX = handle for new file
; If carry set, create function failed
        RET
OPEN_CREATE   ENDP
;****************************************************************
;
CLOSE_FILE      PROC    FAR
; Close file using file handle
; On entry:
;          BX = file handle
; On exit:
;          carry clear if operation successful - file closed
;          carry set if operation failed - invalid handle or file
;          not open
;
        MOV     AH,62           ; DOS service request
        INT     21H
        RET
CLOSE_FILE      ENDP
;****************************************************************
;
READ_128        PROC    FAR
; Read 128 bytes from an open file into buffer using the file
; handle. This procedure assumes that the file has been
; previously opened or created using the procedure OPEN_CREATE
;
; On entry:
;          BX =  file handle
;          DX -> 128 bytes user buffer
;
; On exit:
;          carry clear if operation successful
;            AX = number of bytes read into buffer
;            AX = 0 if end of file
```

```
;           carry set if operation failed
;              AX = error code
;                 5 = access denied
;                 6 = invalid handle or file not open
;
        PUSH    CX              ; Save entry CX
        MOV     AH,63           ; DOS service request
        MOV     CX,128          ; No. of bytes to read
        INT     21H
        POP     CX              ; Restore
        RET
;
READ_128        ENDP
;****************************************************************
;
WRITE_128       PROC    FAR
; Transfer 128 bytes from buffer into disk file using file handle
; This procedure assumes that the file has been previously open or
; created
; On entry:
;           BX =  file handle
;           DX -> 128 bytes buffer area
;
; On exit:
;         carry clear if operation successful
;           AX = number of bytes written into buffer
;           AX = 0 if disk full
;         carry set if operation failed
;           AX = error code
;                 5 = access denied
;                 6 = invalid handle or file not open
;
        PUSH    CX              ; Save entry CX
        MOV     AH,64           ; DOS service request
        MOV     CX,128          ; No. of bytes to write
        INT     21H
        POP     CX              ; Restore CX
        RET
;
WRITE_128       ENDP
;****************************************************************
;
OPEN_FILE       PROC    FAR
; Open file using an ASCIIZ string for the filename
; On entry:
;           DX -> buffer containing ASCIIZ string for filename
```

```
; On exit:
;          if carry clear file was opened successfully
;          AX = file handle
;          if carry set open operation failed
;          AX = error code
;               1 = invalid function
;               2 = file not found
;               3 = path not found
;               4 = no available handle
;               5 = access denied
;              12 = invalid access code
;
;
          MOV       AH,61           ; DOS service request number
                                    ; to open file (handle mode)
          MOV       AL,2            ; Read/write access
          INT       21H
          RET
OPEN_FILE        ENDP
;
P_CODE    ENDS
          END
```

Table 2.7. *Routines in the AUXSERV Module*

ROUTINE NAME	FUNCTION
TIMER_ON	Read and store system timer in a code segment variable
TIMER_OFF	Read and store system timer in another code segment variable
SHOW_TIMER	Compare variables stored by TIMER_ON with variable stored by TIMER_OFF and display elapsed clock cycles at cursor position
SYS_PARAMS	Determine and return machine type, video hardware, screen columns, video mode, and active display page
EQUIPMENT	Determine and return standard and optional devices installed in a system, viz. printers, serial ports, diskette drives, math coprocessor, mouse, and memory
SOUND	Produce a speaker sound according to the frequency and duration passed by the caller
MILLI_TIME	Time event in millisecond intervals
RANDON_NUM	Generate a pseudo-random number within a range passed by the caller

2.8 The Auxiliary Services Module

A final category of routines serves as a catch-all for those useful functions that cannot be fitted into the previous modules. The auxiliary services module includes a routine to identify the system and the video hardware and timing routines. The programmer can add other services to this module.

The present module, named AUXSERV.ASM, contains the routines listed in Table 2.7.

```
; Module name: AUXSERV.ASM                    Library: SOLUTION.LIB
; Created:
; Update:
;
;*****************************************************************
;*****************************************************************
;                         AUXSERV.ASM
;*****************************************************************
;*****************************************************************
;
; Library module for auxiliary routines
;
;*******************|
;      PUBLICS      |
;*******************|
PUBLIC   TIMER_ON
PUBLIC   TIMER_OFF
PUBLIC   SHOW_TIMER
PUBLIC   SYS_PARAMS
PUBLIC   EQUIPMENT
PUBLIC   SOUND
PUBLIC   MILLI_TIME
PUBLIC   RANDOM_NUM
;
P_CODE   SEGMENT PUBLIC
         ASSUME  CS:P_CODE
;
;*****************************************************************
; IMPORTANT:
;          In order to avoid affecting the system, the timing
; routines do not reset the clock. This may cause a reading to be
; invalid as a result of counter overflow. For this reason, timing
; operations should be repeated at least twice, so as to discard
; the possibility of a timer overflow error.
;
;******************** program timing routines ********************
; This code section contains routines that can be used to time
```

```
; program execution in clock cycles. Timing is measured from the
; call to the procedure TIMER_ON to the call to the procedure
; TIMER_OFF. The auxiliary procedure SHOW_TIMER displays, at the
; cursor position, the number of clock cycles elapsed.
;
; Note: All internal data is stored in the code segment so as to
;       simplify interfacing with user software
;
START_COUNT     DW      0H          ; Counter value at start
END_COUNT       DW      0H          ; Counter at end
;
DEC_TIME        DB      0DH,0AH,'Clock Cycles:'
TIME_DIGITS     DB      '     $'
;
;
;*****************************************************************
TIMER_ON        PROC    FAR
; Read system timer and store low-order word of timer count
;
; On entry:
;       nothing
; On exit:
;       CS:START_COUNT = low-order word of system timer counter
;
        MOV     AH,0
        INT     1AH
        MOV     CS:START_COUNT,DX
        RET
TIMER_ON        ENDP
;*****************************************************************
;
TIMER_OFF       PROC    FAR
; Read system timer and store low-order word of timer count
;
; On entry:
;       nothing
; On exit:
;       CS:END_COUNT = low-order word of system timer counter
;
        MOV     AH,0                ; Read clock service request
        INT     1AH                 ; To time-of-day service
; Save counter low-order word in program storage
        MOV     CS:END_COUNT,DX
        RET
TIMER_OFF       ENDP
;*****************************************************************
```

```
SHOW_TIMER        PROC    FAR
;
; This procedure subtracts the timer counts stored by the
; TIMER_ON and TIMER_OFF procedures, converts the binary result
; to ASCII decimal, and displays it at the cursor position
;
; On entry:
;           nothing
; On exit:
;           elapsed clock cycles between the previous TIMER-ON and
;           TIMER-OFF calls is displayed at the current cursor
;           position.
;
        MOV     DX,CS:END_COUNT         ; Count at end
        MOV     AX,CS:START_COUNT       ; At start
        SUB     DX,AX                   ; End minus start
        LEA     DI,CS:TIME_DIGITS       ; ASCII output buffer
; Use BIN_TO_ASC local procedure for conversion
        PUSH    DS                      ; Save entry DS
        PUSH    CS
        POP     DS                      ; Pass code segment as data
        CALL    BIN_TO_ASC
; Use DOS service number 9 to display time string
; Note: DS is still set to CS
        MOV     AH,9                    ; DOS service request code
        LEA     DX,CS:DEC_TIME          ; Buffer
        INT     21H
        POP     DS                      ; Restore DS
        RET
SHOW_TIMER        ENDP
;****************************************************************
;
;************************************|
;  routine to obtain system hardware |
;************************************|
; Hardware elements identified:
;       1. Systems
;               a. PC line: PC, XT, AT, PC Convertible or PCjr
;               b. PS/2 line: Model 25/30, Model 50/60, or
;                             Model 70/80
;
;       2. PC line video display card or system:
;               a. Monochrome card
;               b. Color graphics adapter (CGA)
;               c. Enhanced graphics adapter (EGA)
;               d. No display card
```

```
;                       e. PCjr
;
;               3. PS/2 line video display options:
;                       a. Multicolor Graphics Array (MCGA) with analog
;                          monochrome display
;                       b. MCGA with analog coloer diplay
;                       c. Video Graphics Array (VGA) with analog
;                          monochrome display
;                       d. VGA with analog color display
;
;               4. Active display page
;
;               5. Active video mode
;
;               6. Number of screen columns in alphanumeric modes
;
; Code segment temporary storage for system identification codes
SYS_CODE        DB        0
;
SYS_PARAMS      PROC      FAR
;
; Procedure to obtain system identification parameters
;
; On entry:
;           nothing
; On exit:
;           CL = Machine line and type, as follows:
;                PC line (low-order bit is clear):
;                0 = Personal Computer    2 = PC XT
;                4 = PCjr                 6 = PC AT
;                8 = PC convertible
;                PS/2 line (low-order bit is set):
;                1 = Model 25/30          3 = Model 50/60
;                5 = Model 70/80
;           CH = Video hardware
;                PC line (high-order bit clear):
;                0 = MDA                  1 = CGA
;                2 = EGA                  3 = invalid code
;                PS/2 line (high-order bit set):
;                128 = VGA monochrome     129 = VGA color
;                130 = MCGA monochrome    131 = MCGA color
;           AH = number of screen columns in alphanumeric modes
;           AL = current video mode
;           BH = active display page (0 based)
```

```
;*******************|
;   clear storage   |
;*******************|
         MOV      CS:SYS_CODE,0     ; Could have garbage
;****************|
;  test for PS/2 |
;****************|
; Use service number 26 of INT 10H to determine whether system
; is a PC or a PS/2 line machine
         MOV      AH,26             ; BIOS service request number
         MOV      AL,0              ; Read display combinations
         INT      10H
; AL = 1AH if system is a machine of the PS/2 line
; AL not equal 1AH if system is a machine of the PC line
         CMP      AL,26             ; Is it a PS/2 system?
         JNE      MACHINE_TYPE      ; Hardware is not PS/2
                                    ; bit 0 is clear on default
;*****************|
;     PS/2 line   |
;*****************|
; Test for a value in BL less than 7 to discard non-PS/2 options
         CMP      BL,7
         JL       MACHINE_TYPE      ; Non-PS/2 display system
         OR       CS:SYS_CODE,00000001B   ; Set bit number 0
;****************|
;  machine type  |
;****************|
MACHINE_TYPE:
;          7  6  5  4  3  2  1  0  SYS_CODE bit map
;          |  |  |  |  |  |  |  |
;          |  |  |  |  |  |  |  |____ MACHINE LINE
;          |  |  |  |  |  |  |         0 = PC line   1 = PS/2 line
;          |  |  |  |  |__|__|____ MACHINE TYPE
;          |  |  |  |         PC line            PS/2 line
;          |  |  |  |         000 = PC           000 = Model 25/30
;          |  |  |  |         001 = PC XT        001 = Model 50/60
;          |  |  |  |         010 = PCjr         010 = Model 70/80
;          |  |  |  |         011 = PC AT
;          |  |  |  |         100 = PC Convertible
;          |  |  |__|____ VIDEO HARDWARE
;          |  |         PC line            PS/2 line
;          |  |         00 = MDA           00 = VGA monochrome
;          |  |         01 = CGA           01 = VGA color
;          |  |         10 = EGA           10 = MCGA monochrome
;          |  |         11 = invalid code 11 = MCGA color
;          |__|____ NOT USED
```

```
; Obtain machine identification code from address F000:FFFEH
; PC systems:
;
;          FFH ...... Personal Computer
;          FEH ...... PC XT
;          FBH ...... PC XT with BIOS dated 01/10/86 or later
;          FDH ...... PCjr
;          FCH ...... PC AT or Model 50/60
;          F9H ...... PC Convertible
; PS/2 systems:
;          FAH ...... Model 25/30
;          F8H ...... Model 70/80
;
         MOV     AX,0F000H        ; Base
         MOV     ES,AX            ; To extra segment
         MOV     AL,ES:[0FFFEH]   ; Machine ID byte to AL
; Select bit mask for bits 1, 2, and 3 according to machine ID
; code
         CMP     AL,0FFH          ; Personal computer
         JNE     TEST_FE
         JMP     VIDEO_HW         ; xxxx000x code is default setting
                                  ; for bits 1, 2, and 3
;
TEST_FE:
         CMP     AL,0FEH          ; PC XT
         JNE     TEST_FB
         OR      CS:SYS_CODE,00000010B
         JMP     VIDEO_HW         ; Machine code is xxxx001x
TEST_FB:
         CMP     AL,0FBH          ; PC XT with BIOS dated 01/10/86
         JNE     TEST_FD
         OR      CS:SYS_CODE,00000010B
         JMP     VIDEO_HW         ; Machine code is xxxx001x
TEST_FD:
         CMP     AL,0FDH          ; PCjr
         JNE     TEST_FC
         OR      CS:SYS_CODE,00000100B
         JMP     VIDEO_HW         ; Machine code is xxxx010x
TEST_FC:
         CMP     AL,0FCH          ; PC AT
         JNE     TEST_F9
         OR      CS:SYS_CODE,00000110B
         JMP     VIDEO_HW         ; Machine code is xxxx011x
TEST_F9:
         CMP     AL,0F9H          ; PC Convertible
         JNE     TEST_FA
```

```
            OR        CS:SYS_CODE,00001000B
            JMP       VIDEO_HW          ; Machine code is xxxx100x
      TEST_FA:
            CMP       AL,0FAH           ; Model 25/30
            JNE       TEST_F8
            JMP       VIDEO_HW          ; Machine code is xxxx000x
      TEST_F8:
            CMP       AL,0F8H           ; Model 70/80
            JNE       BAD_TYPE          ; Machine type cannot be
                                        ; determined
            OR        CS:SYS_CODE,00000100B
            JMP       VIDEO_HW          ; Machine code is xxxx010x
;********************|
; machine type error |
;********************|
BAD_TYPE:
            STC                         ; Carry flag to signal error
            RET
;********************|
;       PS/2         |
;   video hardware   |
;********************|
VIDEO_HW:
; Value returned by service number 26, INT 10H
;               BL = 6H if professional graphics system
;               BL = 7H if VGA monochrome
;               BL = 8H if VGA color
;               BL = 0BH if MCGA monochrome
;               BL = 0CH if MCGA color
;               BL = any other value if a nonstandard PS/2 system
;
            CMP       BL,06H            ; Test for professional graphics
                                        ; system
            JNE       TEST_VGA
            OR        CS:SYS_CODE,00110000B
            JMP       VIDEO_PAGE        ; Machine code is xx11xxxx
      TEST_VGA:
            CMP       BL,07H            ; Test for VGA monochrome
            JNE       TEST_VGA_C
            JMP       VIDEO_PAGE        ; Machine code is xx00xxxx
                                        ; default setting
      TEST_VGA_C:
            CMP       BL,08H            ; Test for VGA color
            JNE       TEST_MCGA
            OR        CS:SYS_CODE,00010000B
            JMP       VIDEO_PAGE        ; Machine code is xx01xxxx
```

```
TEST_MCGA:
        CMP     BL,0BH              ; Test for MCGA monochrome
        JNE     TEST_MCGA_C
        OR      CS:SYS_CODE,00100000B
        JMP     VIDEO_PAGE          ; Machine code is xx10xxxx
TEST_MCGA_C:
        CMP     BL,0CH              ; Test for MCGA color
        JNE     PC_VIDEO
        OR      CS:SYS_CODE,00110000B
        JMP     VIDEO_PAGE          ; Machine code is xx11xxxx
;*********************|
;  PC video hardware  |
;*********************|
PC_VIDEO:
; Obtain IBM equipment list word from address 0040:0010H
; Codes:
; Bit: 7  6  5  4  3  2  1  0
;      x  x  1  1  x  x  x  x___  Monochrome card
;      x  x  1  0  x  x  x  x___  CGA (80 x 25 mode)
;      x  x  0  1  x  x  x  x___  CGA (40 x 25 mode)
;
; Note: The data output by service request number 15 of BIOS
;       INT 10 does not differentiate between the CGA and the
;       EGA. Neither does the equipment list word. The presence
;       of a EGA card must be determined using BIOS service
;       number 18 of INT 10H
;
; Set ES to base address of ROM BIOS data area
        MOV     AX,0040H            ; Base
        MOV     ES,AX
        MOV     AX,ES:[0010H]       ; Equipment word to AX
        AND     AX,00110000B        ; Mask off all other bits
;*******************|
;       MDA         |
;*******************|
        CMP     AL,00110000B        ; Test for MDA card
        JNE     TEST_CGA
        JMP     VIDEO_PAGE          ; Machine code is xx00xxxx
                                    ; default setting
;*******************|
;       CGA         |
;*******************|
TEST_CGA:
        CMP     AL,00100000B        ; First CGA code
        JNE     TEST_CGA2
IS_CGA:
```

```
            OR      CS:SYS_CODE,00010000B
            JMP     VIDEO_PAGE          ; Machine code is xx01xxxx
TEST_CGA2:
            CMP     AL,00010000B        ; Second CGA code
            JE      IS_CGA
;*******************|
;         EGA       |
;*******************|
            MOV     AH,18               ; BIOS service request number
            MOV     BL,16               ; Return EGA information
            INT     10H
; Test for no EGA in system
            CMP     BL,16
            JE      NOT_EGA
; Must be the EGA
            OR      CS:SYS_CODE,00100000B
            JMP     VIDEO_PAGE          ; Machine code is xx10xxxx
; No video card identified in system
NOT_EGA:
            OR      CS:SYS_CODE,00110000B
                                        ; Machine code is xx11xxxx

;*******************|
;     video mode    |
;   page and columns |
;*******************|
VIDEO_PAGE:
; Use service request number 15 of BIOS INT 10H to obtain
; current display page, mode, and screen columns, as follows:
;  AH = number of screen columns in alphanumeric modes
;  AL = current video mode
;  BH = active display page (0 based)
            MOV     AH,15               ; Request code number
            INT     10H
;*******************|
; set return codes  |
;*******************|
            MOV     CL,CS:SYS_CODE      ; Bit map to CL
            AND     CL,00001111B        ; Clear 4 high-order bits
            MOV     CH,CS:SYS_CODE      ; Bit map to CH
            SHR     CH,1                ; Shift right 4 times
            SHR     CH,1
            SHR     CH,1
            SHR     CH,1
; Test low-order bit in CL for PC or PS/2 lines
            TEST    CL,00000001B        ; Set for PS/2
            JZ      EXIT_SYS_P          ; Not PS/2. End processing
```

```
; System is a PS/2 machine, set high-order bit in CH
        OR      CH,10000000B
EXIT_SYS_P:
        CLC                     ; No error detection
        RET
SYS_PARAMS      ENDP
;****************************************************************
;
EQUIPMENT       PROC    FAR
; Determine optional and standard devices present in system
; This procedure uses the BIOS service provided by INT 11H
; and INT 12H
; On entry:
;          Nothing
; On exit:
;          AH = number of printer ports
;          AL = number of serial ports
;          BH = number of diskette drives
;          BL = 1 if math coprocessor installed
;          CH = 1 if pointing device (mouse) installed
;          DX = number of 64K memory blocks
;
        INT     11H     ; BIOS service request
; INT 11H returns AX configured as follows:
;                       7 6 5 4 3 2 1 0  AH bit map
;                       | | | | | | | |__ RESERVED
;                       | | | | |_|_|____ serial ports
;                       | | | |_____ RESERVED
;                       | | |_____ internal modem
;                       |_|_____ printers
;                       7 6 5 4 3 2 1 0  AL bit map;
;                       | | | | | | | |__ IPL diskette
;                       | | | | | | |____ math coprocessor
;                       | | | | | |_____ PS/2 pointing device
;                       | | | | |_____ RESERVED
;                       | | |_|_____ Video hardware
;                       | |               01 = 40 x 25 color
;                       | |               10 = 80 x 25 color
;                       | |               11 = 80 x 25 monochrome
;                       |_|_____ diskette drives
;                                         00 = 1 drive
;                                         01 = 2 drives
;*********************|
;   test for printers |
;*********************|
        MOV     DX,AX              ; Bit pattern to DX
```

```
            PUSH    DX              ; Save bit map
            AND     DH,11000000B    ; Mask off unwanted bits
            MOV     CL,6            ; Positions to shift right
            SHR     DH,CL           ; Value is now in binary
            MOV     AH,DH           ; And move to return register
            POP     DX              ; Restore bit map
;*********************|
; test for serial ports|
;*********************|
            AND     DH,00001110B    ; Mask off unwanted bits
            SHR     DH,1            ; Value is now in binary
            MOV     AL,DH           ; And move to return register
;*********************|
;  test for diskettes  |
;*********************|
            PUSH    DX              ; Save bit map
            AND     DL,11000000B    ; Mask off unwanted bits
            MOV     CL,6            ; Positions to shift right
            SHR     DL,CL           ; Value is now in binary
            MOV     BH,DL           ; And move to return register
            INC     BH              ; Adjust to range 1 to 4
            POP     DX              ; Restore bit map
;*********************|
;      test for 8087   |
;*********************|
            PUSH    DX              ; Save bit map
            AND     DL,00000010B    ; Mask off unwanted bits
            SHR     DL,1            ; Value is now in binary
            MOV     BL,DL           ; And move to return register
            POP     DX              ; Restore bit map
;*********************|
;    test for mouse    |
;*********************|
            AND     DL,00000100B    ; Mask off unwanted bits
            SHR     DL,1
            SHR     DL,1            ; Value is now in binary
            MOV     CH,DL           ; And move to return register
;*********************|
;    get memory size   |
;*********************|
; BIOS INT 12H returns the number of contiguous 1K memory blocks
            PUSH    AX              ; Save return registers
            PUSH    BX
            PUSH    CX
            INT     12H
            MOV     DX,AX           ; Move memory to return register
```

```
        POP     CX              ; Restore registers
        POP     BX
        POP     AX
        MOV     CL,0            ; Clear nonmeaningful register
        CLC                     ; No errors detected
        RET
EQUIPMENT       ENDP
;****************************************************************
;
MILLI_TIME      PROC    FAR
; Timer in 1/1000-s intervals
; On entry:
;       BX = time delay in ms
;
READ_COUNTER:
; Read timer channel 0 at port 40H
        MOV     AL,00000110B    ; 0 0 0 0 0 1 1 0
                                ; __ __ ____ _
                                ; |  |    |  |__ binary mode
                                ; |  |    |_____ mode 3
                                ; |  |_____ latch for read
                                ; |_____ channel 0
        OUT     43H,AL          ; To counter command port
        JMP     SHORT $+2       ; I/O delay
; Read LSB then MSB
        IN      AL,40H
        JMP     SHORT $+2
        MOV     DL,AL
        IN      AL,40H
        JMP     SHORT $+2
        MOV     DH,AL
; DX holds timer counter value
;******************|
;    count 1 ms    |
;******************|
        SUB     DX,1190         ; 1-ms delay
ONE_MS:
        MOV     AL,06H          ; Latch for read code
        OUT     43H,AL          ; To counter command port
        JMP     SHORT $+2       ; I/O delay
; Read LSB then MSB
        IN      AL,40H          ; Port for channel 0
        JMP     SHORT $+2
        MOV     CL,AL           ; LOB to DL
        IN      AL,40H          ; Read HOB
        JMP     SHORT $+2
```

```
        MOV     CH,AL              ; HOB to DH
; CX holds timer counter value
; DX holds terminal count for 1-ms delay
        CMP     CX,DX              ; Compare counts
        JA      ONE_MS             ; Wait until DX < CX
;******************|
;   repeat BX ms   |
;******************|
        DEC     BX                 ; ms counter
        NOP
        JNZ     READ_COUNTER       ; Continue if count not finished
        RET
MILLI_TIME      ENDP
;
;*****************************************************************
;
SOUND           PROC    FAR
;
; On entry:
;           BX = Frequency of tone (in hertz)
;                Human audible range is 20 to 20,000 Hz
;           CX = duration of sound in ms
;                1000 ms = 1 s
;
;*********************|
;  calculate divisor  |
;*********************|
; Formula for calculating divisor word
;            1,193,180
;         ----------------  =   divisor word
;         desired frequency
; Note: 1,193,180 = 1234DCH
;
        MOV     AX,34DCH           ; High part of numerator
        MOV     DX,12H             ; Low part of numerator
        DIV     BX                 ; Divide numerator by frequency
                                   ; Quotient is in AX
        MOV     BX,AX              ; Divisor word to BX
; Set port 61H (8255 port PB) for timer 2 gate and for speaker
; direct control
        IN      AL,61H             ; Read current port status
        JMP     SHORT $+2
        OR      AL,00000011B       ; xxxx xx11 bit pattern
        OUT     61H,AL             ; To port
        JMP     SHORT $+2
; Program timer channel 2
```

```
          MOV       AL,10110110B      ; 1011 0110
                                      ; xxxx xxx0 = binary
                                      ; xxxx 011x = mode 3 (IBM mode)
                                      ; xx11 xxxx = LSB and MSB
                                      ; 10xx xxxx = timer channel 2
          OUT       43H,AL            ; To 8253 command register
          JMP       SHORT $+2
; Place frequency of BX Hz as channel 2 frequency divisor
; Address of timer channel 2 = 42H
          MOV       AL,BL             ; LSB
          OUT       42H,AL            ; To timer channel 2
          JMP       SHORT $+2
          MOV       AL,BH             ; MSB
          OUT       42H,AL
          JMP       SHORT $+2
; Use TIME_DELAY procedure to wait the number of 1/18th second
; intervals passed in CX
          MOV       BX,CX             ; DX has delay in 18th second
                                      ; units
          CALL      MILLI_TIME
; Turn off speaker
; Reset bits 0 and 1 of port 61H to turn off the speaker
          IN        AL,61H
          JMP       SHORT $+2
          AND       AL,0FCH           ; xxxx xx00 bit pattern
          OUT       61H,AL
          RET
SOUND              ENDP
;****************************************************************
;
RANDOM_NUM         PROC     FAR
; Random number generator using channel 0 of the system timer
; On entry:
;         BX = high value of range desired, for example, to
;              obtain a random number in the range 0 to 100
;              BX will hold the value 100
;              Lowest allowable range is 0 to 4
; On exit:
;         DX = random number in range
;
; Note: This random number generator will give a valid random
;       seed if it is not read at regular intervals. Otherwise the
;       values may be nonrandom
;       The random number is generated using the shift register
;       algorithm
;
```

```
; Read timer channel 0 at port 40H
        MOV     AL,00000110B   ; 0 0 0 0 0 1 1 0
                               ;  ___ ___ _____ _
                               ; |   |   |     |__ binary mode
                               ; |   |   |_____ mode 3
                               ; |   |_____ latch for read
                               ; |_____ channel 0
        OUT     43H,AL         ; To counter command port
        JMP     SHORT $+2      ; I/O delay
; Read LSB then MSB
        IN      AL,40H         ; Read LSB
        JMP     SHORT $+2
        MOV     DL,AL
        IN      AL,40H         ; Read MSB
        JMP     SHORT $+2
        MOV     DH,AL          ; Save in DH
; DX = value in timer latch
;*********************|
;   manipulate seed  |
;*********************|
; Shift register algorithm
RESCALE:
        MOV     AX,DX          ; Copy value in AX
        MOV     CL,3           ; Shift right 3 digits
        SAR     AX,CL
        ADD     AX,DX          ; Add with no carry
        MOV     CL,4           ; Value to shift left
        SAL     AX,CL          ; Shift left
        ADD     AX,DX          ; Add again
;********************|
;   scale to range   |
;********************|
; Dividing by the upper limit of the range will generate a
; remainder less than this limit
        MOV     DX,0           ; Use value in AX
        DIV     BX             ; Remainder is in DX
        RET
RANDOM_NUM      ENDP
;
;****************************************************************
;                    local procedures
;****************************************************************
BIN_TO_ASC      PROC    NEAR
; Convert a 16-bit binary in the DX register to an ASCII decimal
; number
; On entry:
```

```
;              DX = binary source
;              DI -> 5-byte output buffer
; On exit:
;              DI -> start of 5-byte buffer holding the ASCII decimal
;                    number
;
         PUSH    DI                  ; Save start of buffer
         CALL    CLEAR_5             ; Clear user's buffer
; DI -> last byte in user's buffer
         MOV     CX,0                ; Clear counter
BINA0:   PUSH    CX                  ; Save count
         MOV     AX,DX               ; Add in numerator
         MOV     DX,0                ; Clear top half
         MOV     CX,10               ; Enter decimal divisor
         DIV     CX                  ; Perform division AX/CX
         XCHG    AX,DX               ; Get quotient
         ADD     AL,30H              ; Make digit ASCII
         MOV     [DI],AL             ; Store digit in buffer
         DEC     DI                  ; Bump destination pointer
         POP     CX                  ; Restore counter
         INC     CX                  ; Count the digit
         CMP     DX,0                ; Test for end of binary
         JNZ     BINA0               ; Continue if not end
         POP     DI                  ; Restore pointer to start of
                                     ; buffer
         RET
BIN_TO_ASC       ENDP
;****************************************************************
CLEAR_5          PROC    NEAR
; On entry:
;          DS:DI -> start of a 5-byte user buffer
; On exit:
;          DS:DI -> last byte in the 5-byte buffer
         MOV     CX,5                ; 5 digits to clear
CLEAR_BUF:
         MOV     BYTE PTR [DI],20H      ; Clear digit
         INC     DI                  ; Bump pointer
         LOOP    CLEAR_BUF           ; Repeat for 5 digits
         DEC     DI                  ; Adjust buffer pointer to last
                                     ; digit
         RET
CLEAR_5          ENDP
;
P_CODE   ENDS
         END
```

3

Developing an Operating-System Program

3.0 System Software

An operating system is an executive program that serves as an intermediary between the user and the hardware. The most frequently used operating system for IBM microcomputers is MS DOS, developed and marketed by Microsoft Corporation. This program is also sold by IBM, under a Microsoft license, with the name PC DOS or IBM DOS. Other operating-system programs used in IBM microcomputers are OS/2, which was jointly developed by Microsoft and IBM, and Concurrent DOS, by Digital Research Corporation.

In IBM microcomputers the disk operating system is not the only system-level program. All machines are furnished with a lower-level interface called the *Basic Input/Output System* (BIOS). An additional software layer can be inserted between the disk operating system and the user. This layer consists of programs, sometimes called *operating-system shells*, which are designed to simplify the use of the operating system and to provide additional functions and user services. Microsoft Corporation markets several programs, under the name *Windows*, which serve as user shells for MS DOS. In addition, MS DOS version 4.0 includes its own shell.

3.0.1 System Development

The present chapter is not devoted to the discussion of existing operating systems for IBM microcomputers, such as MS DOS or OS/2, but rather to the fundamentals of designing and coding an operating-system program for these machines. Note that the development of a full-featured operating system, like those mentioned above, is generally considered one of the most technical tasks in software development. The job can require dozens of program designers, programmers, and testers, in addition to management and support personnel.

For this reason, the development cycle of an operating-system program is frequently measured in years, even when abundant human and technical resources are available. Consequently, it is practically impossible to discuss the subject at length within the limits of a single chapter of the present book. By the same token, it is inconceivable that a rigorous, full-featured operating system could be developed within the space constraints of one chapter. To make the task feasible we have had to reduce it to its barest fundamentals, to make assumptions regarding system hardware, and to enlist the aid of DOS in creating the software. The resulting sample operating system, which we have called MINIOS, can hardly be compared to any commercial product.

But the interest in developing operating systems is not limited to the creation of programs that will compete with MS DOS, OS/2, or similar software. Following the design and coding of an operating-system program enables the reader to better understand the purpose and operation of existing commercial products. Additionally, a compact, customized operating system can provide a convenient environment for copy protection purposes, for running dedicated or embedded systems, or for experimentation and research.

3.0.2 The IBM Microcomputer BIOS

All IBM microcomputers contain a version of the BIOS program, stored in a read-only memory (ROM) chip in the computer's motherboard. The presence of this BIOS software considerably simplifies the coding of an operating system. BIOS stores system controls, addresses, initialization parameters, and other useful data at certain fixed addresses. It creates an interrupt vector table that is required by the hardware. It tests and initializes the system hardware and brings the machine to an operational status. Finally, the BIOS provides a set of services, accessible through interrupts, that enable the programmer to readily access the system's input and output devices.

After its initialization functions are performed, BIOS tests for the presence of a formatted diskette in the first drive. If a diskette is found, BIOS loads code from it into memory and transfers execution to the loaded program. This BIOS function, called the *bootstrap loader*, is used by operating systems to gain control of the machine. In the case of IBM microcomputers, the machine has been pre-tested and initialized and contains a set of operational input/output drivers in the form of programmer services.

The original version of BIOS took up approximately 40K, starting at physical address F0000H. IBM provided listings of the BIOS code in their Technical Reference Manuals up to the introduction of the PS/2 line (1987). Other companies, such as Phoenix Technologies, have developed codes that perform functions analogous to those of the IBM BIOS. These versions of the BIOS are used in many IBM-compatible microcomputers.

3.0.3 System Memory Space

Figure 3.1 shows the memory structure of an IBM microcomputer after BIOS has executed.

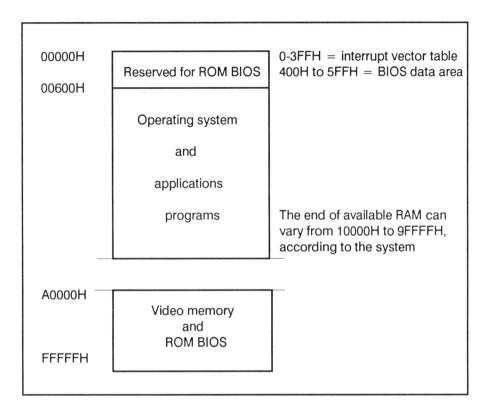

Figure 3.1. *Memory Structure after BIOS Execution*

The space from the beginning of RAM to address 3FFH is taken up by the interrupt vector table. This table is part of the reserved space of the Intel 8086/8088 family of processors. Each entry in the table consists of two words. The first word holds the segment address and the second one, the offset of 256 possible vectors. This makes a total of 1024 bytes which must be reserved for this purpose. Following the vector table IBM sets aside an area of 512 bytes, extending from 400H to 5FFH, which is used for storing system parameters. This area is sometimes known as the *BIOS data area*. In order to preserve system integrity and to ensure that the BIOS will remain operational, both the interrupt vector table and the BIOS data area must be protected from unintentional changes .

Another memory area that must be preserved from unintentional modifications is the video memory space, starting at address A0000H. Note that the BIOS code is automatically protected since it resides in a ROM chip. In conclusion, systems and applications must not access or reside in addresses below 600H or above 9FFFFH. However, the memory area within these limits is fair game for system and application software. The end of this usable random-access memory (RAM) space varies in different systems, from a minimum of 64K in the original IBM Personal Computers, to a maximum of 640K in a fully furnished system. Subtracting 1536 bytes (600H) from the available memory space leaves from 64,000 to 653,824 bytes for the operating system code, the loaded applications, and the user's memory space.

3.0.4 The MS DOS Addiction

MS DOS has been by far the prevalent operating system for the IBM microcomputers, which explains why programmers who work in this environment often take it for granted. We are so used to MS DOS services, structures, and concepts that we think of them as part of the machine. This is particularly true for disk and diskette operation and data structures. For example, the letter-based drive designations, filenames, paths, directories, EXE, COM, and batch file types, file allocation tables (FATs), file control blocks (FCBs), and other MS DOS notions and data structures are often perceived as much a part of the IBM microcomputer as the interrupt vector table or the BIOS services and data areas.

In tackling the design and coding of a new operating system program it is necessary to overcome the MS DOS habit. The programmer must remember that the logical structures of MS DOS, however useful, are particular to this software. The new system need not adopt these concepts or terminology. By the same token, the operating system designer is not committed to use letter drives, FATs, directories, filenames, and other typical components of MS DOS. In fact, it is doubtful whether it would be legal to code an MS DOS clone, and it would certainly be of little practical use.

3.1 The Elements of an Operating System

The components of an operating system vary according to its purpose and complexity. Large computer environments support several users as well as the simultaneous execution of more than one program. In this case, one of the main functions of the operating system program is to share the equipment among users by allocating slices of processing time. On the other hand, operating systems for personal computers usually support a single user executing just one program. In the first case the operating system must include multiprogramming and scheduling services that are not required in a single-user, single-task environment. There are presently available multitasking and multiuser operating systems for IBM microcomputers, such as OS/2, UNIX, and ZENIX. However, for practical reasons, the present discussion is restricted to single-user, single-task operating systems, such as MS DOS. After following the complexities of designing and coding the simplest of operating systems, the reader will realize that the discussion of a multitasking, multiuser program could easily fill several volumes.

If we assume an IBM microcomputer in which the BIOS has initialized the system hardware, and remains resident, the minimum tasks to be performed by a conventional single-user, single-task operating system can be listed as follows:

1. *Bootstrap*. The operating system must install itself in a legal memory space and assume control of the CPU.

2. *System initialization*. The operating system must initialize the processor registers as well as other necessary hardware components, create its own data and parameter tables, and take over the interrupt vectors that it will use.

3. *Command processor*. The operating system must provide an interface in order to process and execute the user's commands.

4. *Program loader*. The operating system must be able to load executable files into a legal memory space and transfer execution to these files.

5. *Memory and resource management*. The operating system must allocate memory and other system resources to applications program so as to preserve itself and other system software.

In addition, an operating system can provide technical services to users and programmers. For example, MS DOS provides many programmer services via interrupts 21H to 27H. Most of these are related to disk operations and input/output processing. Although programmer services are not strictly necessary in an operating system, most programs include them.

3.1.1 The BIOS Bootstrap

When the BIOS initialization and testing routines conclude satisfactorily and the machine is found to be in operating order, the BIOS code checks the first diskette drive for the presence of a formatted diskette. If a diskette is detected, BIOS then proceeds to load diskette side 0, track number 0, sector number 1, to the memory address 7C00H and transfer execution to this code. This process is known as the *bootstrapping*, in analogy with the image of lifting oneself by the bootstraps.

The operating system gains control of the machine as soon as execution is transferred to the code loaded at 7C00. Since BIOS loads a single disk sector (512 bytes) to this arbitrary address, one of the first functions of this code must be to continue loading the operating system program from its disk storage. The BIOS load address, 7C00H, seems to have no special meaning, except that it is low enough to exist in a system equipped with barely 32K of user memory. The installed operating system can later overwrite the code originally placed at 7C00H.

3.1.2 Kernel Initialization

We have seen in Section 3.0.2 that the bootstrap code, loaded by BIOS at 7C00H, proceeds to load the operating system itself into a safe memory address. One of the first functions performed by this core of operating system code, often referred to as the *kernel*, is to initialize the processor registers, thus creating a usable stack as well as an operational data area. The kernel may also store controls and data values required by the operating system, forming its own parameter tables, somewhat similar to those maintained by BIOS from 400H to 5FFH. In some cases the operating system may initialize or reinitialize hardware components to suit its own needs. For example, an operating system designed to provide copy protection may take control of the disk hardware and reset it in its own way. Finally, the kernel code may initialize certain interrupt vectors to its own entry points, so that other programs may access the system without concern for physical addresses.

3.1.3 The Command Processor

The typical operating system serves as an interface between the user and the electronic and electromechanical components of the computing machine. This is usually done through commands entered by the user and recognized by the operating system code. Typical operating-system commands serve to format storage media (usually disks and diskettes), to copy stored data to other media or devices, to diagnose system problems or operational errors, and to access input and output devices.

In order to perform these functions, the operating-system code must be able to monitor and process user input, usually entered from the keyboard or other input devices. For example, the MS DOS command processor receives input in the form of text strings, such as the command COPY *.* A: B:. Other operating systems allow selection from menus or the use of a mouse or other pointing device. In each case the code will process the command and direct execution to the corresponding routine or subprogram.

One convenient way to provide system commands without increasing the resident image of the operating system itself is to make these commands execute as independent programs. The programs are coded and stored as conventional disk files. MS DOS refers to them as external commands, to differentiate from the functions that are part of the operating system kernel code. For instance, the MS DOS services named DISKCOPY and DISKCOMP are independent programs that are stored as such in the diskette or hard disk device.

3.1.4 The Program Loader

It is difficult to imagine an operating system that contains, within its code, all the functions and services that a user may require. For this reason, virtually all operating systems provide means for loading and transferring execution to other programs, often developed independently. Although this function can be considered as one of the system commands, because of its peculiar nature, program loading is often treated as a separate operation.

A typical program loader includes the following functions: (1) locate the desired program in the storage device, (2) transfer the program's code to a safe memory area, (3) initialize processor registers and other data areas to facilitate program execution, (4) pass system data to the loaded code, and (5) transfer execution to the program.

3.1.5 Management of System Resources

The management of some system resources, particularly memory, is critical to the subsistence of the operating system itself and of other indispensable code and data. As can be seen in Table 3.1, not all the memory space is available for operating system and application programs. Furthermore, the amount of usable memory can vary from system to system. For the sake of its own subsistence, the operating system must administer these critical resources accordingly.

However, one peculiarity of programs executing under the real mode of the processors of the Intel iAPX 86/88 family is that these programs have no inherent restrictions in regard to addressing or controlling system elements. This means that, in spite of any precaution taken by the operating system, a program running in 8086/88 real mode owns the entire machine. It can access any memory address, output or input from any port, and execute all CPU instructions in all available addressing modes. Consequently, the best management techniques on the part of the operating system are sometimes offset by a badly behaved application.

3.2 Coding an Operating System

The sample operating system program developed in the following sections of this chapter contains the five fundamental elements described in Section 3.1. However, for reasons of space, the sample program has been reduced to the minimal functions that are required in an operational system. Furthermore, some of these functions are trivial and serve barely as a code skeleton. The reader can add meat to these skeletons as needed. Although the MINIOS operating system is entirely self-supporting, we use DOS software to develop the component programs and to create the MINIOS system diskette.

The name MINIOS was chosen to indicate that the operating system has been reduced to its minimum expression. The following software elements form the MINIOS system:

1. The MINIBOOT.BIN file is the bootstrap loader that receives execution from BIOS and proceeds to install MINIOS in memory.

2. The MINIOS.SYS file is the operating system kernel.

3. The TESTEF.COM file is a sample executable program that resides in the system diskette. One of the operating-system commands loads and transfers execution to this trivial demonstration.

In addition to its component parts, the MINIOS system requires two additional utilities:

1. MAKEOS.EXE is a program developed under MS DOS. It is used in creating the operating system diskette from the MINIBOOT.BIN and the MINIOS.SYS files.

2. MAKEEF.EXE is a second utility program, also developed under MS DOS. MAKEEF is used in moving an MS DOS program of the COM type to the MINIOS system diskette. The file moved by the MAKEEF utility holds the executable code that is loaded by MINIOS. The text uses a demonstration program named TESTEF.COM as an example, but the reader can create its own executable files, within the listed restrictions.

All the files and programs of the MINIOS system were created using the Microsoft assembly language development software furnished with the Microsoft Macro Assembler system. These are the MASM macro assembler, the LINK linker, and EXE2BIN conversion utility. However, these files can also be created using other compatible development environments.

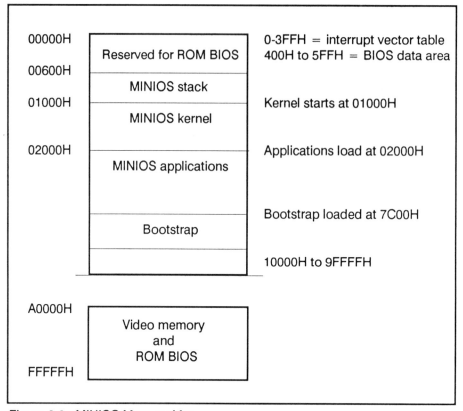

Figure 3.2. *MINIOS Memory Map*

3.2.1 MINIOS Memory Map

An operating system for the Intel 8086/8088 microprocessors can relocate executable code; however, the kernel itself must reside in a fixed physical address. This requires a few decisions and manipulations that are seldom necessary while programming in a segment-relocatable environment. The first decision to be made is to find a satisfactory residence address of the system kernel. We have determined (see Section 3.0.3) that the available memory space should be not lower than address 600H and not higher than A0000H. Because the original IBM PC could be purchased with as little as 64K of RAM, it is necessary to reduce the upper limit of available memory to the address 10000H.

Considering these limits we have chosen, somewhat arbitrarily, the addresses for the various elements of the MINIOS program that are listed in Figure 3.2.

The start of the MINIOS kernel is located at 1000H. The space between the end of the BIOS data area (600H) and the entry point of MINIOS (1000H) is used for the stack. These 2560 bytes provide more than enough stack space for the system. The applications area starts at 2000H. This leaves 4096 bytes for the kernel, that is, from memory location 1000H to 2000H. The actual code of the MINIOS kernel takes up approximately 1300 bytes. Note that the bootstrap code is automatically loaded by the BIOS at 7C00H, but once the bootstrap has executed, this memory can be reused, since the bootstrap is not reentrant.

3.2.2 The MINIBOOT File

The BIOS contains a bootstrap loader that reads the disk sector at side number 0, track number 0, sector number 1, to the memory address 7C00H and transfers execution to this code. An operating system gains control of the machine by placing its own code in this diskette space, which is often called the *boot record*. DEBUG or SYMDEB can be used to inspect and disassemble the boot record of an operating system. The command to load the boot record at the start of the data segment is entered as follows:

L DS:0000 0 0 1

Once loaded, the code can be disassembled with the command

U DS:0000

or displayed with the command

D DS:0000

In an MS DOS data or system diskette the start of the boot record contains a jump instruction to the remainder of the code area. This jump is not required, nor are the termination codes at the sector end.

The following source file contains the code for the bootstrap of the MINIOS system.

```
;**************************************************************
;**************************************************************
;                      MINIBOOT.ASM
;**************************************************************
;**************************************************************
; Bootstrap routine for the MINIOS operating system
;
;
; The bootstrap routine is contained in a file named MINIBOOT.BIN
; and transferred to head 0, track 0, sector 1, drive 1 onto a
; data-formatted diskette by the MAKEOS program
;
; The BIOS bootstrap loader places the code contained in the
; MINIBOOT file at logical address 0000:7C00H and transfers
; control to its first instruction
;
; MINIBOOT operation:
```

```
; 1. Initialize a temporary stack
; 2. Initialize the CS register so it can be used to access data
; 3. Display a message informing of MINIBOOT's execution
; 4. Load the MINIOS kernel from disk into address 1000H
; 5. Transfer execution to the MINIOS kernel code
;
; Steps in creating MINIBOOT.BIN
; 1. Assemble MINIBOOT.ASM into MINIBOOT.OBJ
; 2. Link MINIBOOT.OBJ into MINIBOOT.EXE
; 3. EXE2BIN MINIBOOT.EXE into MINIBOOT.BIN
;
;**************************** code ****************************
CODE    SEGMENT
        ASSUME  CS:CODE


;********************************|
;        bootstrap code          |
;********************************|
;********************|
;   create a stack   |
;********************|
        CLI                       ; Interrupts off
        XOR     AX,AX             ; Clear AX
        MOV     SS,AX             ; Create stack segment
        MOV     SP,7C00H          ; Stack pointer to code start
                                  ; Stack will grow downward
        STI                       ; Interrupts on
; Now stack is usable
;********************|
;   set DS segment   |
;********************|
        MOV     AX,7C0H           ; Hard code for CS and DS segment
        MOV     DS,AX             ; to DS
        ASSUME  DS:CODE
;
;********************|
;   display message  |
;********************|
; Now LEA can be used to calculate message offsets
        LEA     SI,MESS_1
        CALL    DISPLAY
;********************|
;  load MINIOS kernel |
;********************|
; The diskette in drive A contains the kernel of the MINIOS
; system stored in DOS logical sector number 2. The BIOS location
```

```
; for this sector is:
;        drive = 0
;        head = 0
;        track = 0
;        sector = 3
LOAD_MINIOS:
        MOV       AX,0H             ; Segment base from AX
        MOV       ES,AX             ; to ES
        MOV       BX,1000H          ; Offset to BX
        MOV       AH,2              ; BIOS service request
        MOV       AL,3              ; Transfer 3 sectors
; The present MINIOS kernel takes up less than 1536 bytes
; If the kernel is expanded, the value in AL may need adjustment
        MOV       DX,0              ; Head 0 and drive 0
        MOV       CH,0              ; Track 0
        MOV       CL,3              ; BIOS sector 3
        INT       13H
;*********************|
;  transfer execution |
;     to MINIOS        |
;*********************|
; Code assumes no error during transfer
        MOV       CX,1000H
        JMP       CX
;
; ****************** Auxiliary procedures ********************
DISPLAY           PROC    NEAR
;
READ_MS:
        MOV       AL,[SI]           ; Get ASCII character
        CMP       AL,0              ; Test for end of message
        JE        EXIT_DIS          ; End of text message, exit
        MOV       AH,0EH            ; Write in teletype-mode code
        MOV       BH,0              ; Display page 0
        INT       10H               ; BIOS service
        INC       SI                ; Bump pointer to message
        JMP       READ_MS
EXIT_DIS:
        RET
DISPLAY           ENDP
;
;************************* text message *******************
;
MESS_1  DB        'Bootstrap routine for MINIOS',0AH,0DH,00H
;
;*********************** disk buffer ***********************
```

```
; No space is assigned to the buffer in order to reduce the size
; of the bootstrap file. The code can assume sufficient free
; memory past this label
DISK_BUF          DB         0H
CODE     ENDS
         END
```

3.2.3 The MINIOS Kernel

The MINIOS operating system resides in the file MINIOS.SYS. This program, which is also called the MINIOS kernel, is loaded from the diskette file into memory address 1000H by the MINIBOOT code. The last operation performed by the MINIBOOT bootstrap is to transfer execution to the kernel at 1000H. MINIOS installs its own start address at the vector for interrupt 60H. This makes it possible for an application to return to the operating system without knowledge of its location in memory. One advantage of this method is that other versions of the operating system can reside elsewhere in memory without creating problems for previous applications.

The MINIOS kernel executes by displaying a menu of four commands. This menu appears on the screen as follows:

```
              MINIOS operating system kernel
              MENU OF SYSTEM OPERATIONS
                1. Machine type    2. Equipment
                3. Memory size     4. Load program
              Select operation desired:
```

Three of the four commands execute procedures in the SOLUTION.LIB library (see Chapter 2). Command number 4, load program, assumes that the system diskette contains executable code in a special format and located at a certain sector address. The details of the load command are found in Section 3.2.4. The loaded programs reside at 2000H. The program MAKEEF.EXE, discussed in Section 3.3.2, is used to move an MS DOS program to the system diskette so it can be executed using MINIOS command number 4.

```
;****************************************************************
;****************************************************************
;                           MINIOS.ASM
;****************************************************************
;****************************************************************
;
; Kernel for the MINIOS operating system
;
; The operating system kernel is contained in the file MINIOS.SYS
; This file is transferred to a data formatted diskette by the
; MAKEOS program
```

```
; The bootstrap loader routine in the file MINIBOOT.BIN loads the
; kernel, contained in the file MINIOS.SYS, to address 0000:1000H
; and transfers execution to this code
;
; MINIOS kernel segment structure:
;       SS is set to 0000H by bootstrap loader MINIBOOT.BIN
;       SP is set to 1000H by the kernel initialization. This
;           allows a stack space of 2560 bytes, extending down
;           from 1000H to 600H
;       CS:IP are set by the jump instruction in the bootstrap
;       DS is set to the segment base 100H during the kernel
;           initialization
;
; Steps in creating MINIOS.SYS
; 1. Assemble MINIOS.ASM into MINIOS.OBJ
; 2. Link MINIOS.OBJ into MINIOS.EXE
; 3. EXE2BIN MINIOS.EXE into MINIOS.SYS
;
;*************************** code ***************************
CODE    SEGMENT
        ASSUME  CS:CODE
;
;*********************|
;  kernel entry point |
;*********************|
; set up kernel stack
        MOV     SP,1000H            ; Stack can grow down to 600H
                                    ; without running into system
                                    ; data

;*********************|
;   set up kernel DS  |
;*********************|
        MOV     AX,100H             ; Hard code for data segment
        MOV     DS,AX               ; to DS
        ASSUME  DS:CODE
;*********************|
; install MINIOS kernel|
; interrupt at INT 60H |
;*********************|
; Take over interrupt vector at 0000:0180H (INT 60H)
        MOV     AX,0                ; Set ES register to the base
                                    ; address of the interrupt vector
        MOV     ES,AX               ; table
        MOV     DI,180H             ; Set DI to offset of INT 60H
                                    ; Offset = 60H * 4
; Entry point of MINIOS kernel is 0000:1000H
```

```
          CLI                       ; Interrupts off while changing
                                    ; table
          CLD                       ; Forward direction
          MOV     AX,1000H          ; AX holds offset
          STOSW                     ; Store offset in low-order word
; String instruction bumps DI to 182H
          MOV     AX,0              ; AX holds segment base
          STOSW                     ; Store base in high-order word
          STI                       ; Interrupts on
; From now on an application can restart the MINIOS kernel by
; executing INT 60H
;***********************************|
;          COMMAND PROCESSOR        |
;***********************************|
COMMAND:
          LEA     SI,MESS_COM       ; Pointer to MINIOS greeting
          CALL    DISPLAY
          CALL    KBR_WAIT          ; Procedure from SOLUTION.LIB
                                    ; to wait for one keystroke
          CMP     AL,'1'            ; System hardware command
          JNE     TEST_2            ; Cascade if not 1
          JMP     COMMAND_1         ; Go to processing routine
TEST_2:
          CMP     AL,'2'            ; Equipment list command
          JNE     TEST_3            ; Cascade
          JMP     COMMAND_2         ; Processing for this command
TEST_3:
          CMP     AL,'3'            ; Memory list command
          JNE     TEST_4            ; Cascade
          JMP     COMMAND_3         ; Processing for this command
TEST_4:
          CMP     AL,'4'            ; Load program command
          JNE     COMMAND           ; Cascade processing ends
          JMP     COMMAND_4         ; Processing for this command
;
;******************************************************************
;                  command execution routines
;******************************************************************
;********************|
;   system hardware  |
;********************|
COMMAND_1:
          CALL    SYS_PARAMS        ; Procedure from SOLUTION.LIB
; Assume first machine type and cascade messages
          LEA     SI,MACH0          ; Personal computer
          CMP     CL,0              ; Test for code
```

```
            JNE      TRY_MACH1      ; If not, test for next machine
            CALL     DISPLAY        ; Display machine type
            JMP      COMMAND        ; Return to command processor
TRY_MACH1:
            LEA      SI,MACH1       ; Model 25/30
            CMP      CL,1           ; Test for code
            JNE      TRY_MACH2      ; If not, test for next machine
            CALL     DISPLAY        ; Display machine type
            JMP      COMMAND        ; Return to command processor
TRY_MACH2:
            LEA      SI,MACH2       ; PC XT
            CMP      CL,2           ; Test for code
            JNE      TRY_MACH3      ; If not, test for next machine
            CALL     DISPLAY        ; Display machine type
            JMP      COMMAND        ; Return to command processor
TRY_MACH3:
            LEA      SI,MACH3       ; Model 50/60
            CMP      CL,3           ; Test for code
            JNE      TRY_MACH4      ; If not, test for next machine
            CALL     DISPLAY        ; Display machine type
            JMP      COMMAND        ; Return to command processor
TRY_MACH4:
            LEA      SI,MACH4       ; PCjr
            CMP      CL,4           ; Test for code
            JNE      TRY_MACH5      ; If not, test for next machine
            CALL     DISPLAY        ; Display machine type
            JMP      COMMAND        ; Return to command processor
TRY_MACH5:
            LEA      SI,MACH5       ; Model 70/80
            CMP      CL,5           ; Test for code
            JNE      TRY_MACH6      ; If not, test for next machine
            CALL     DISPLAY        ; Display machine type
            JMP      COMMAND        ; Return to command processor
TRY_MACH6:
            LEA      SI,MACH6       ; PC AT
            CMP      CL,6           ; Test for code
            JNE      DO_MACH8       ; If not, must be PC Convertible
            CALL     DISPLAY        ; Display machine type
            JMP      COMMAND        ; Return to command processor
DO_MACH8:
            LEA      SI,MACH8       ; Model 25/30
            CALL     DISPLAY        ; Display machine type
            JMP      COMMAND        ; Return to command processor
;*********************|
;  optional equipment |
;*********************|
```

```
COMMAND_2:
        CALL    EQUIPMENT          ; Procedure from SOLUTION.LIB
; Test for number of printer ports and move ASCII to message area
; AH holds binary number of printer ports
        ADD     AH,30H             ; Convert to ASCII
        MOV     BYTE PTR DS:PRNS,AH   ; and store in message area
; AL holds number of serial ports
        ADD     AL,30H             ; To ASCII
        MOV     BYTE PTR DS:S_PORTS,AL; and store in message area
; BH holds number of diskette drives
        ADD     BH,30H             ; To ASCII
        MOV     BYTE PTR DS:DSKTS,BH   ; and store in message area
; BL holds 1 if math coprocessor installed
        ADD     BL,30H             ; To ASCII
        MOV     BYTE PTR DS:COPRO,BL   ; and store in message area
; CH holds 1 if pointing device installed
        ADD     CH,30H             ; To ASCII
        MOV     BYTE PTR DS:MOUSE,CH   ; and store in message area
; Display message
        LEA     SI,EQUIPS          ; Message with equipment data
        CALL    DISPLAY            ; Display equipment message
        JMP     COMMAND            ; Return to command processor
;********************|
;     memory size    |
;********************|
COMMAND_3:
        CALL    EQUIPMENT          ; Procedure from SOLUTION.LIB
; DX holds number of 1K blocks of memory in system. Convert to
; ASCII
        LEA     DI,ASC_BUF         ; Destination space in message
                                   ; area
        CALL    BIN_TO_ASC         ; Procedure from SOLUTION.LIB
; Display message
        LEA     SI,MEM_MS          ; Message with memory-size data
        CALL    DISPLAY
        JMP     COMMAND
;********************|
; load executable file |
;********************|
;
; Operation:
; The program MAKEEF.EXE writes a COM file developed under MS DOS
; starting at logical sector number 5 of the MINIOS system
; diskette
; The present coding reads one diskette sector (512 bytes), loads
; the code into memory, and transfers execution to this program.
```

```
; Note that the load operation assumes that the executable file
; is less than 512 bytes long. The code will require modification
; in order to load longer applications. In this case, the disk
; record of the application file will have to contain a count for
; the number of sectors to be loaded
;
; The MINIOS program execution area is located at 0000:2000H
COMMAND_4:
        LEA     SI,LOAD_MS      ; Load command entry message
        CALL    DISPLAY
;**********************|
;       load          |
;**********************|
; The diskette in drive A contains executable code stored
; starting at DOS logical sector number 5. The BIOS location for
; this sector is:
;       drive = 0
;       head = 0
;       track = 0
;       sector = 6
;
        MOV     AX,0
        MOV     ES,AX           ; Segment address of destination
        MOV     BX,2000H        ; Offset of destination
; The address of the application area is 0000:2000H
        MOV     AH,2            ; BIOS service request
        MOV     AL,1            ; Transfer 1 sector
; Note: The value in AL can be changed to load longer applications
        MOV     DX,0            ; Head 0 and drive 0
        MOV     CH,0            ; track 0
        MOV     CL,6            ; Sector
        INT     13H
; Code assumes no error during transfer
;**********************|
;  transfer execution  |
;**********************|
        MOV     CX,2000H        ; MINIOS applications area
        JMP     CX              ; Transfer control to application
;
;****************************************************************
;                       procedures
;****************************************************************
;
DISPLAY         PROC    NEAR
;                               |********************************|
;                               | procedure listed in MINIBOOT.ASM |
;                               |********************************|
;
```

```
KBR_WAIT        PROC    NEAR
;                               |*********************************|
;                               | procedure listed in KEYBRD.ASM  |
;                               |*********************************|
;
; Code segment temporary storage for system identification codes
SYS_CODE        DB      0
;
SYS_PARAMS      PROC    NEAR
;                               |*********************************|
;                               | procedure listed in AUXSERV.ASM |
;                               |*********************************|
;
;
EQUIPMENT       PROC    NEAR
;                               |*********************************|
;                               | procedure listed in AUXSERV.ASM |
;                               |*********************************|
;
;
BIN_TO_ASC      PROC    NEAR
;                               |*********************************|
;                               | procedure listed in CONVERT.ASM |
;                               |*********************************|
;
CLEAR_5         PROC    NEAR
;                               |*********************************|
;                               | procedure listed in CONVERT.ASM |
;                               |*********************************|
;
;****************************************************************
;                          kernel data
;****************************************************************
MESS_COM        DB      0AH,0DH
        DB      '  MINIOS operating system kernel ',0AH,0DH
        DB      '     MENU OF SYSTEM OPERATIONS',0AH,0DH
        DB      ' 1. Machine type     2. Equipment     ',0AH,0DH
        DB      ' 3. Memory size      4. Load program  ',0AH,0DH
        DB      '   Select operation desired: ',00
;
MACH0   DB      0AH,0AH,0DH,'Personal Computer',0AH,0DH,00
MACH1   DB      0AH,0AH,0DH,'PS/2 Model 25/30',0AH,0DH,00
MACH2   DB      0AH,0AH,0DH,'Personal Computer XT',0AH,0DH,00
MACH3   DB      0AH,0AH,0DH,'PS/2 Model 50/60', 0AH,0DH,00
MACH4   DB      0AH,0AH,0DH,'PCjr',0AH,0DH,00
MACH5   DB      0AH,0AH,0DH,'PS/2 Model 70/80',0AH,0DH,00
```

```
MACH6    DB        0AH,0AH,0DH,'Personal Computer AT',0AH,0DH,00
MACH8    DB        0AH,0AH,0DH,'PC Convertible',0AH,0DH,00
;
EQUIPS   DB        0AH,0AH,0DH
PRNS     DB        20H                        ;Filled by program
         DB        ' printer port(s)',0AH,0DH
S_PORTS  DB        20H                        ;Filled by program
         DB        ' serial port(s)',0AH,0DH
DSKTS    DB        20H                        ;Filled by program
         DB        ' diskette drive(s)',0AH,0DH
COPRO    DB        20H                        ;Filled by program
         DB        ' math coprocessor',0AH,0DH
MOUSE    DB        20H
         DB        ' mouse ports (PS/2 only)',0AH,0AH,0DH,00
;
MEM_MS   DB        0AH,0AH,0DH
ASC_BUF  DB        '     K memory in system',0AH,0AH,0DH,00
;
LOAD_MS  DB        0AH,0AH,0DH,'MINIOS program loader',0AH,0DH
;
CODE     ENDS
         END
```

3.2.4 The TESTEF Executable File

Command number 4 of the MINIOS kernel loads an executable file into the memory space starting at address 2000H and transfers execution to this code. The demonstration program is contained in the file TESTEF.COM. This file is moved to logical sector number 5 (BIOS head 0, track 0, sector 6) of the MINIOS diskette by the MAKEEF program described and listed in Section 3.3.2. The executable program displays a trivial message and waits for a user keystroke before returning control to the MINIOS kernel. The reader can develop another version of the test file by creating an MS DOS program of the COM type. This code can be moved to the MINIOS diskette using the MAKEEF utility.

```
;****************************************************************
;****************************************************************
;                         TESTEF.ASM
;****************************************************************
;****************************************************************
; Test module for an executable file to be loaded by MINIOS
; command number 4
;
; This test program displays a trivial screen message. The code
; then waits for a keystroke to return to the MINIOS kernel
```

```
;**************************** code ****************************
;
CODE      SEGMENT
          ASSUME    CS:CODE
;
          MOV       AX,200H           ; Segment base for data segment
          MOV       DS,AX
          ASSUME    DS:CODE
;
          LEA       SI,MES            ; Set pointer to message text
          CALL      DISPLAY           ; Display message
;
          MOV       AX,0              ; BIOS service to wait for key
          INT       16H
;
          INT       60H               ; Return to kernel using interrupt
;
;*****************************************************************
;                         procedures
;*****************************************************************
DISPLAY           PROC      NEAR
;                           |********************************|
;                           | procedure listed in MINIBOOT.ASM |
;                           |********************************|
;
;**************************** data ****************************
MES       DB        0AH,0AH,0DH,'This message is displayed by the
          DB        ' loaded program...',0AH,0DH
          DB        'Press any key to return to MINIOS',0AH,0DH,00
;
CODE      ENDS
          END
```

3.3 Creating the MINIOS Software

In IBM microcomputers an operating system can reside either on a diskette or on the
fixed disk. The BIOS start-up sequence first checks for a diskette in the first floppy disk
drive. If one is detected, the BIOS attempts to read executable code from side 0, track
0, sector 1 of this medium, transfers the code to memory address 7C00H, and gives it
control. If no diskette is found, the corresponding sector on the hard disk drive is loaded
and executed. For this reason, system code must be recorded in the appropriate sector
of the storage media so that it will be given control by the BIOS bootstrap. The present
discussion is limited to installing system code on diskette media, since the modification
of hard disk sectors can entail the loss of valuable data.

Table 3.1. *IBM Microcomputer Diskette Storage Formats*

MEDIA	NUMBER OF SIDES	TRACKS PER SIDE	SECTORS PER TRACK	STORAGE CAPACITY	MACHINE TYPES
5¼-in SS/DD	1	40	8	160K	PC
	1	40	9	180K	PC
5¼-in DS/DD	2	40	8	320K	PC
	2	40	9	360K	PC/PCXT
5¼-in DS/QD	2	80	9	1.2 Mbytes	PCAT
3½-in DS/DD	2	80	9	720K	PS/2 Model 25/30
3½-in DS/HD	2	80	18	1.4 Mbytes	PS/2

Note that MS DOS numbers the diskette sectors consecutively, starting with sector number 0 and ending with the last one in the media. The MS DOS sector numbering scheme does not take into account the diskette side or track. On the other hand, the IBM BIOS designates diskette sectors by specifying the diskette's side, track, and sector number. In the BIOS scheme the sectors are numbered starting with 1 and ending with the last sector in the track. The term *logical sector* is sometimes used in reference to the MS DOS numbering method and the term *physical sector* to the BIOS method.

The difference between these sector numbering schemes is occasionally a source of programming error. For instance, a program that uses BIOS and MS DOS services in accessing diskette data will have to take into account that MS DOS logical sector number 3 corresponds with BIOS side 0, track 0, sector 4. Furthermore, since the number of sectors per track vary in different media, there can be no single conversion formula from the MS DOS to the BIOS numbering methods. Fortunately, standard sectors contain 512 bytes in both the MS DOS and the BIOS systems. Table 3.1 lists the most common diskette storage formats used in IBM microcomputers.

3.3.1 The MAKEOS Program

The MAKEOS program was developed using MS DOS programming tools. The program creates the MINIOS system diskette from a standard MS DOS data diskette by moving to this media the code contained in the files MINIBOOT.BIN and MINIOS.SYS. The file MINIBOOT.BIN is placed in the diskette's boot record, which corresponds to BIOS physical sector number 1. Physical sector number 2 is not used. Sectors 3, 4, and 5 are loaded with the file MINIOS.SYS. Finally, the MAKEEF program, described and listed in Section 3.3.2, moves a COM type file to physical sector number 6. Figure 3.3 shows a sector map of the MINIOS system diskette.

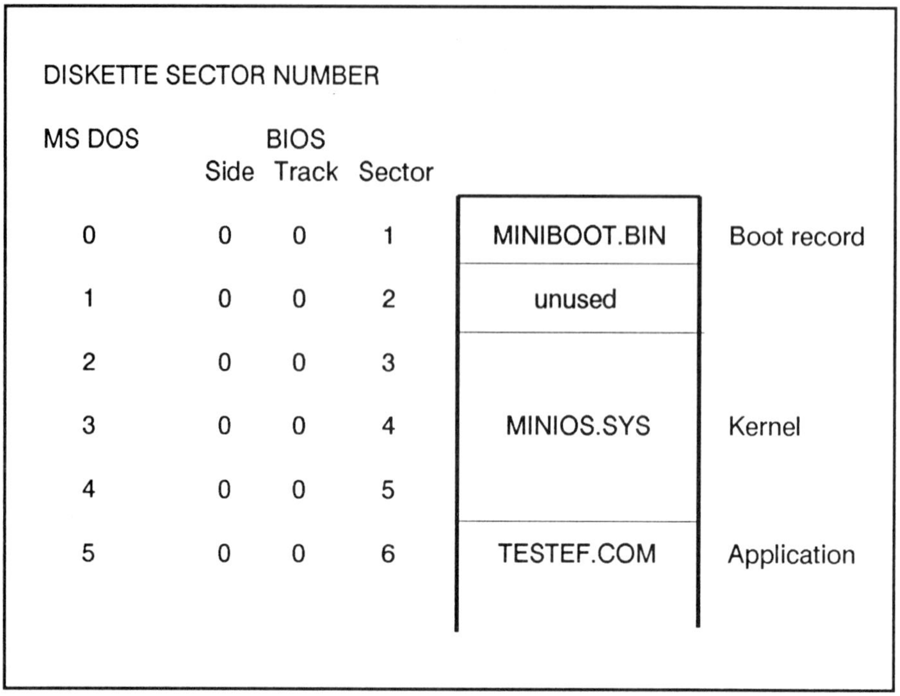

DISKETTE SECTOR NUMBER

MS DOS		BIOS				
	Side	Track	Sector		
0	0	0	1	MINIBOOT.BIN	Boot record
1	0	0	2	unused	
2	0	0	3		
3	0	0	4	MINIOS.SYS	Kernel
4	0	0	5		
5	0	0	6	TESTEF.COM	Application

Figure 3.3. *MINIOS Diskette Sector Map*

```
;*****************************************************************
;*****************************************************************
;                          MAKEOS.ASM
;*****************************************************************
;*****************************************************************
;
; DOS system program to create the MINIOS system diskette
; The code makes the following assumptions:
; 1. There is a data-formatted diskette in drive A
; 2. There is a bootstrap program named MINIBOOT.BIN in the
;    file path
; 3. There is an operating system kernel program named MINIOS.SYS
;    in the file path
;
;*********************** stack ***************************
STACK          SEGMENT        stack
               DB     0400H DUP ('?')       ; Default stack is 1K
STACK_TOP      EQU    THIS BYTE
STACK          ENDS
```

```
;*********************** data ***************************
DATA    SEGMENT
;
;********************|
;  disk transfer area |
;********************|
DTA_BUF DB       128      DUP (00H)
        DB       382      DUP (00H)        ; Pad to 512 bytes
                                           ; for MINIBOOT disk write
        DB       55H                       ; Standard BIOS sector
        DB       0AAH                      ; terminators
        DB       1024     DUP (00H)        ; Extension for 1536-byte
                                           ; records
        DW       0000H
;
;********************|
;  file control blocks |
;********************|
; DOS File control block for the file MINIBOOT.BIN
FCB_BUF1         DB       0
                 DB       'MINIBOOT'       ; Filename
                 DB       'BIN'            ; Extension
                 DB       25 DUP (00H)
                 DW       0000H
; DOS File control block for the file MINIOS.SYS
FCB_BUF2         DB       0
                 DB       'MINIOS   '      ; Filename
                 DB       'SYS'            ; Extension
                 DB       25 DUP (00H)
                 DW       0000H
;
;********************|
;    error messages    |
;********************|
ERR_MS1 DB       'Cannot open file',10,13,'$'
ERR_MS2 DB       'File operation error',10,13,'$'
;
DATA    ENDS
;*********************** code ***************************
;
CODE    SEGMENT
;
        ASSUME  CS:CODE
;
START:
; Establish addressability of the program's data segment
```

```
        MOV     AX,DATA
        MOV     DS,AX
        ASSUME  DS:DATA
; Initialize stack. Note that this instruction is necessary for
; compatibility with non-Microsoft assemblers
        LEA     SP,SS:STACK_TOP ; Stack pointer to top of stack
; Now DS points to start of program's data area
        PUSH    DS
        POP     ES                      ; Reproduce in extra segment
        ASSUME  ES:DATA
;******************************************************************
;                       load the bootstrap file
;******************************************************************
;**********************|
;     set the DTA      |
;**********************|
        MOV     AH,26           ; DOS service request code
        MOV     DX,OFFSET DTA_BUF       ; DTA buffer
        INT     21H             ; DOS service
;**********************|
;   open and load      |
;   MINIBOOT.BIN       |
;**********************|
        MOV     AH,15           ; DOS service request code
        MOV     DX,OFFSET FCB_BUF1      ; File's FCB
        INT     21H                     ; DOS service
; Test exit code for error
        CMP     AL,0FFH         ; Error return code
        JNE     OK_BOOT1        ; No error, continue
        MOV     DX,OFFSET ERR_MS1
        JMP     ERROR
OK_BOOT1:
; File MINIBOOT.BIN is open and FCB is filled by DOS
;**********************|
; read 256 bytes from  |
;  file into DTA_BUF   |
;**********************|
        MOV     AH,20           ; DOS service request code
        MOV     DX,OFFSET FCB_BUF1
        MOV     WORD PTR DS:FCB_BUF1+14,256     ; Record size
        INT     21H             ; DOS service
; Test exit code for error. No error if AL < 4
        CMP     AL,4
        JC      OK_BOOT2
        MOV     DX,OFFSET ERR_MS2
        JMP     ERROR
```

```
; The bootstrap file MINIBOOT.BIN is now in DTA_BUF
; Since MINIBOOT.BIN is less than 256 bytes, only 1 record was
; read
;********************|
;  close MINIBOOT.BIN  |
;********************|
OK_BOOT2:
        MOV     AH,16               ; DOS service request code
        MOV     DX,OFFSET FCB_BUF1
        INT     21H                 ; DOS service
; No error checking after close operation
;********************|
;  write DTA to disk   |
; sector 0, in drive A |
;********************|
; This routine assumes that drive A exists and that it contains
; a formatted diskette. DOS function INT 26H is used to write
; the contents of the DTA_BUF to DOS logical sector 0
; This DOS sector is the boot record
        MOV     AL,0                ; Drive A
        MOV     CX,1                ; 1 sector to write
        MOV     DX,0                ; DOS logical sector 0
        MOV     BX,OFFSET DTA_BUF
        INT     26H
        ADD     SP,2                ; Adjust stack after INT 26H
; No error checking in this operation
;*************************************************************
;               load the operating system kernel file
;*************************************************************
;********************|
;    open MINIOS.SYS   |
;********************|
        MOV     AH,15               ; DOS service request code
        MOV     DX,OFFSET FCB_BUF2
        INT     21H                 ; DOS service
; Test exit code for error
        CMP     AL,0FFH             ; Error return code
        JNE     OK_MINI1            ; No error, continue
        MOV     DX,OFFSET ERR_MS1
        JMP     ERROR
OK_MINI1:
; File MINIOS.SYS is open and FCB is filled by DOS
;********************|
; read 1536 bytes from |
;  file into DTA_BUF   |
;********************|
```

```
        MOV     AH,20               ; DOS service request code
        MOV     DX,OFFSET FCB_BUF2
        MOV     WORD PTR DS:FCB_BUF2+14,1536    ; Record size
        INT     21H                 ; DOS service
; Test exit code for error. No error if AL < 4
        CMP     AL,4
        JC      OK_MINI2
        MOV     DX,OFFSET ERR_MS2
        JMP     ERROR
; The operating system kernel file, MINIOS.SYS, is now in the DTA
; Since MINIOS.SYS is less that 1536 bytes, only one sector was
; read
;*********************|
;    close MINIOS.SYS  |
;*********************|
OK_MINI2:
        MOV     AH,16               ; DOS service request code
        MOV     DX,OFFSET FCB_BUF2
        INT     21H                 ; DOS service
; No error checking after close operation
;*********************|
;   write DTA to disk   |
;*********************|
; This routine assumes that drive A exists and that it contains
; a formatted diskette. DOS function INT 26H is used to write
; the contents of the DTA_BUF
        MOV     AL,0                ; Drive A
        MOV     CX,3                ; 3 sectors to write
        MOV     DX,2                ; DOS logical sector 2
        MOV     BX,OFFSET DTA_BUF
        INT     26H
        ADD     SP,2                ; Adjust stack
; No error checking in this operation
        JMP     DOS_EXIT
;
;****************************************************************
;                    error handler and exit
;****************************************************************
ERROR:
        MOV     AH,9                ; DOS service request code
        INT     21H
;
DOS_EXIT:
        MOV     AH,76               ; DOS service request code
        MOV     AL,0                ; No error code returned
        INT     21H                 ; To DOS
```

```
;
CODE    ENDS
        END     START
```

3.3.2 The MAKEEF Program

The final component of the MINIOS software is called MAKEEF. This program moves a COM type program, created under MS DOS, to side 0, track 0, sector 6 of the MINIOS system diskette (see Figure 3.3). Once located at this position, the file will be executed by the MINIOS load program function (command number 4).

The program execution facility in MINIOS is indeed primitive. It is based on a fixed diskette sector and assumes that the file to be loaded is less than 512 bytes long. A more refined loader would execute programs of variable length and be capable of selecting files with different names, located at various storage addresses. This form of operation usually requires storing program data along with the program code. For example, a simple scheme could be devised whereby the first 10 bytes in the diskette record would contain program information, as listed in Figure 3.4. In this case the loader receives a program name in the command line and checks it against the name stored on sector bytes 0 to 7. When a match is found, the loader obtains the count for the number of sectors in the program from sector bytes 8 and 9 and proceeds to load the required sectors. Finally, the loader transfers execution to the code in memory.

An even more sophisticated scheme devotes one or more sectors, starting at a specific storage address, to hold the location, name, length, and other data regarding the various programs and files contained in the diskette. This control area is sometimes called the *disk* or *diskette directory*. MS DOS uses two directory structures in each storage device: the file allocation table (FAT) and the root directory. MS DOS also stores important data in an area of the boot record extending from offset 03H to offset 1EH. These storage areas, as well as other MS DOS storage conventions and methods, have been well documented in the literature.

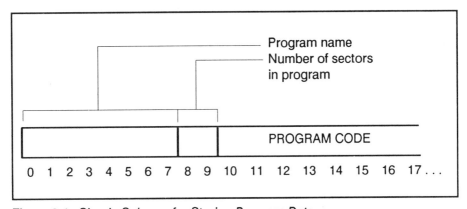

Figure 3.4. *Simple Scheme for Storing Program Data*

```
****************************************************************
;****************************************************************
;                          MAKEEF.ASM
;****************************************************************
;****************************************************************
; DOS system program to move a COM file, created under MS DOS, to
; the MINIOS diskette
; The code assumes that there is a data-formatted diskette in
; drive A
; The program to be moved to MINIOS diskette must be a COM-type
; MS DOS file created with Microsoft MASM assembler, linked with
; a Microsoft linker and converted from .EXE to .COM format using
; the MS DOS utility EXE2BIN
;
;*********************|
;        externals    |
;    from SOLUTION.LIB |
;*********************|
EXTRN    BIO_SHOW_MESS:  FAR
EXTRN    DOS_KBR_INPUT:  FAR
EXTRN    SET_DTA:        FAR
;
; Note: The disk access procedures in the DISKIO.ASM module of
; SOLUTION.LIB are not suited for the disk operations required
; by this program.
;
;************************* stack *************************
STACK          SEGMENT        stack

               DB      0400H DUP ('?')       ; Default stack is 1K
STACK_TOP      EQU     THIS BYTE

STACK          ENDS
;************************* data *************************
DATA    SEGMENT
;
; Disk transfer area
DTA_BUF DB        512       DUP (00H)
        DW        0000H
;
; DOS File control block for the file to be moved
FCB_BUF          DB       0
FCB_NAME         DB       '        '      ; Filename
                 DB       'COM'          ; COM extension
                 DB       25 DUP (00H)
                 DW       0000H
```

```
DOS_IN_BUF       DB      8         ; Maximum number of characters
DOS_COUNT        DB      0         ; Characters typed
DOS_NAME         DB      9 DUP (00H)
                 DW      0000H     ; Separator
;
LOG_SEC          DW      5         ; DOS logical sector number
;
;*********************|
;  display messages   |
;*********************|
ENTRY    DB      'Program to move a COM file created under MS DOS'
         DB      ' to a MINIOS system diskette',0AH,0DH
         DB      'Enter MS DOS filename: ',00H
;
ERR_MS1 DB       'Cannot open file',10,13,'$'
ERR_MS2 DB       'File operation error',10,13,'$'
;
DATA     ENDS
;****************************************************************
;                           code
;****************************************************************
;
CODE     SEGMENT
;
         ASSUME  CS:CODE
;
START:
;*********************|
;     initialize      |
;*********************|
; Establish addressability of the program's data segment
         MOV     AX,DATA
         MOV     DS,AX
         ASSUME  DS:DATA
; Initialize stack. Note that this instruction is necessary for
; compatibility with non-Microsoft assemblers
     LEA     SP,SS:STACK_TOP ; Stack pointer to top of stack
; Now DS points to start of program's data area
         PUSH    DS
         POP     ES                ; Reproduce in extra segment
         ASSUME  ES:DATA
;*********************|
;     set the DTA     |
;*********************|
         MOV     DX,OFFSET DTA_BUF       ; DTA buffer
         CALL    SET_DTA           ; SOLUTION.LIB library procedure
```

```
;***********************|
;   entry messages      |
;***********************|
        LEA     SI,ENTRY           ; Pointer to message text
        CALL    BIO_SHOW_MESS      ; Display procedure in
                                   ; SOLUTION.LIB
;***********************|
;   obtain filename     |
;***********************|
        LEA     DX,DOS_IN_BUF      ; Input buffer
        CALL    DOS_KBR_INPUT      ; Input procedure in SOLUTION.LIB
;***********************|
; move filename to FCB  |
;***********************|
        MOV     CL,DOS_COUNT       ; Bytes in filename
        MOV     CH,0               ; Clear high-order byte of
                                   ; counter
        LEA     SI,DOS_NAME        ; Source pointer
        LEA     DI,FCB_NAME        ; Destination pointer
MOVE_NAME:
        MOV     AL,[SI]            ; Name character from source
        MOV     [DI],AL            ; Into FCB
        INC     SI                 ; Bump pointers
        INC     DI
        LOOP    MOVE_NAME
;***********************|
;   open and load COM   |
;          file         |
;***********************|
        MOV     AH,15              ; DOS service request code
        MOV     DX,OFFSET FCB_BUF
        INT     21H                ; DOS service
; Test exit code for error
        CMP     AL,0FFH            ; Error return code
        JNE     READ_SEC           ; No error, continue
        MOV     DX,OFFSET ERR_MS1
        JMP     ERROR
;***********************|
; read 512 bytes from   |
;  file into DTA_BUF     |
;***********************|
READ_SEC:
        MOV     AH,20              ; DOS service request code
        MOV     DX,OFFSET FCB_BUF
        MOV     WORD PTR DS:FCB_BUF+14,512    ; Set record size
                                   ; to 1 sector
```

```
        INT     21H             ; DOS service
; Test exit code for error. No error if AL < 4
        CMP     AL,4
        JC      OK_FILE2
        MOV     DX,OFFSET ERR_MS2
        JMP     ERROR
;*********************|
;   write DTA to disk |
;*********************|
OK_FILE2:
        PUSH    AX              ; Save exit codes
        CALL    WRITE_26        ; Write procedure using INT 26H
        POP     AX              ; Restore read exit codes
        CMP     AL,1            ; Test for end of file
        JE      CLOSE_FILE      ; Close if end of file
        CMP     AL,3            ; Test for partial record
        JE      CLOSE_FILE      ; Close if partial record read
        JMP     READ_SEC        ; Read next sector
; Note: Although the MAKEEF program can move files that contain
; several records to the MINIOS diskette, the MINIOS load routine,
; as presently coded, assumes that the executable program is just
; one record long. See comments in the COMMAND_4 label of the
; MINIOS.ASM source
;*********************|
;   close disk file   |
;*********************|
CLOSE_FILE:
        MOV     AH,16           ; DOS service request code
        MOV     DX,OFFSET FCB_BUF
        INT     21H             ; DOS service
; No error test on close operation
        JMP     DOS_EXIT        ; End of program
;
;****************************************************************
;                         procedures
;****************************************************************
WRITE_26        PROC    NEAR
; This procedure assumes that drive A exists and that it contains
; a formatted diskette. DOS function INT 26H is used to write
; 512 bytes (one sector) in the DTA buffer to the diskette in
; drive A starting at DOS logical sector number 5
; On entry:
;       LOG_SEC DW  = logical sector number
; On exit:
;       nothing
        MOV     AL,0            ; Drive A
```

```
        MOV     CX,1            ; 1 sector to write
        MOV     DX,LOG_SEC      ; Starts at logical sector 5
        MOV     BX,OFFSET DTA_BUF
        INT     26H
        ADD     SP,2            ; Adjust stack
; No error checking in this operation
        INC     LOG_SEC         ; Bump for next sector
        RET
WRITE_26        ENDP
;
;****************************************************************
;                    error handler and exit
;****************************************************************
ERROR:
        MOV     AH,9            ; DOS service request code
        INT     21H
;
;*********************|
;    exit to DOS      |
;*********************|
DOS_EXIT:
        MOV     AH,76           ; DOS service request code
        MOV     AL,0            ; No error code returned
        INT     21H             ; To DOS
;
CODE    ENDS
        END     START
```

4

Programming the Printer

4.0 Printing Devices

The printer is the device most commonly used to obtain hardcopy of computer data. In the conventional sense, the printer makes a paper record of the stream of alphanumeric characters received from a computer. But recent advances in printing techniques and machinery make possible the reproduction of graphic and photographic images as well as the scaling, rotation, and translation of the traditional alphanumeric characters.

Printing devices have been connected to computers using a multitude of standard and nonstandard interfaces. However, the parallel port is by far the most commonly used means of sending data and control codes to a printer, particularly in the case of the IBM microcomputers. Therefore, in many respects, printer programming is performed through the parallel port. Most commercial programs use the parallel port as the default means for printer access, and many offer no other alternative.

Printing devices can be generally classified as impact and nonimpact types, depending on whether there is a mechanical collision between the printing element and the paper. Dot-matrix and daisy-wheel printers are impact devices. Ink-jet and laser printers are of the nonimpact type. Lower cost seems to be the main advantage of impact printers. A few years ago daisy-wheel printers were considered the standard for high-quality reproduction; today, desktop laser and other types of nonimpact printers surpass daisy-wheel quality at much greater speed and silently.

4.0.1 Useful Printer Applications

Sometimes printer programming in the IBM microcomputers consists simply of monitoring the status of the parallel port and sending to it the desired string of alphanumeric characters. The procedures SEND_PRN and STATUS_PRN in the OUTPUT_ASM module (see Chapter 2) use BIOS services to perform these functions.

MS DOS service number 5, INT 21H, also provides a way of sending a single character to the parallel port. Starting with MS DOS version 2.0, it is also possible to address the printer using the standard device handle number 0004. In any case, the programmer using MS DOS services to access the parallel port will find some difficulties in obtaining the port status. This limitation can hang up the code if the device is not available or if it remains in a busy state. For this reason, parallel port access using MS DOS is not considered in this book.

Often the programmer needs to perform other printer functions in addition to monitoring the status and sending of characters to the parallel port. In the present chapter we have selected some useful programming solutions regarding printer operations. This sample programs software are classified as follows:

1. *Printer filters*. Printer filter routines are generally of two types. *Data filters* intercept individual characters on their way to the parallel and substitute or complement them. *Device filters* intercept the data stream directed at a certain port or device and redirect it to another one. The programs CODEFILT and SERFILT, presented in this chapter, are printer filters.

2. *Printer spoolers*. Spoolers are a special type of filter that intercept printer output and redirect it to a temporary storage area if the device is presently busy. Spoolers increase productivity by operating the printer as a background task. The program SPOOL is a timer-driven, printer spooler.

Table 4.1. *The Centronics Printer Interface (IBM version)*

DB-25 PIN NUMBER	SIGNAL DIRECTION PC	PS/2	VOLTAGE	SIGNAL NAME
1	⇒	⇔	-	STROBE
2	⇒	⇔	+	Data bit number 0
3	⇒	⇔	+	Data bit number 1
4	⇒	⇔	+	Data bit number 2
5	⇒	⇔	+	Data bit number 3
6	⇒	⇔	+	Data bit number 4
7	⇒	⇔	+	Data bit number 5
8	⇒	⇔	+	Data bit number 6
9	⇒	⇔	+	Data bit number 7
10	⇐	⇐	-	Acknowledge (ACK)
11	⇐	⇐	-	Busy
12	⇐	⇐	+	Out of paper (PE)
13	⇐	⇐	+	Select (SLCT)
14	⇒	⇒	-	Auto feed (XT)
15	⇐	⇐	-	Error
16	⇒	⇒	-	Initialize printer (INIT)
17	⇒	⇒	-	Select input (SLCT IN)
18–25				Ground

3. *Laser printer screen dumps.* Laser printers are page-based devices that require a different programming approach than the conventional character-based printers. This is particularly true in respect to the graphics functions. The program PCLDUMP, in Section 4.3.5, is a screen dump utility for a laser printer programmable in Hewlett-Packard Printer Control Language.

4.0.2 The Centronics Standard

The Centronics printer interfaces originated in the practice of a well-known printer manufacturer and were later adopted by the rest of the industry. In IBM microcomputers the Centronics parallel port uses a 25-pin D-shell connector in place of the standard 36-pin form. For this reason connecting a parallel printer to an IBM microcomputer requires a special cable which has a 25-pin D-shell connector at the computer end and a 36-pin Amphenol connector at the other end. Table 4.1 shows the interface lines of the Centronics standard as implemented in IBM microcomputers.

4.0.3 Direct Access to the Parallel Port Hardware

We have mentioned that, for most printer programming purposes, the services provided by the SEND_PRN and the STATUS_PRN routines in the OUTPUT module (see Chapter 2) are sufficient. However, to access the parallel port directly, the programmer must take certain precautions and consider the peculiarities of various IBM hardware in order to ensure the portability of the code. The program SPOOL, presented later in this chapter, contains code to directly access the parallel port.

The base address of the parallel port has varied in the various models of the PC and the PS/2 lines. For instance, in the IBM Personal Computer, the PC XT, and some models of the PS/2 line, the parallel port is located at address 3BCH while in the PCjr, the PC AT, and other models of the PS/2 line it is at 378H. In addition, if more than one port is implemented in a system, the ports can be located at 3BCH, 378H, and 278H. Nevertheless, the BIOS stores the base address of the first parallel port at address 408H, the second parallel port at 40AH, and the third one at 40CH of the BIOS data area. If a port is not implemented, the value stored will be zero. A program can easily retrieve the address of the ports as follows:

```
CODE      SEGMENT
          ASSUME  CS:CODE
              .
; Obtain base address of first parallel port from BIOS data area
          PUSH    DS                  ; Save program's DS
          XOR     AX,AX               ; AX = 0
          MOV     DS,AX               ; Data segment zero for BIOS
          MOV     DX,DS:0408H         ; Base address of LPT1
; The previous line can be edited to access other parallel ports
          POP     DS                  ; Restore program's DS
; The code can now check if DX = 0 to determine whether there is
; a valid LPT1 in the system
```

4.0.4 Coding a TSR

All the programs listed in this chapter, and several others throughout the book, belong to a type of software often called a *terminate-and-stay resident* utility, or TSR. The main difference between a TSR and a conventional program is that the TSR attaches itself to the operating system so that its code can remain resident in memory. This contrasts with MS DOS normal operation, in which a program is assigned a memory space while it is executing and this space is freed by MS DOS when control returns to the system.

The TSR code uses specific MS DOS exit routines to make sure that its image will not be destroyed by the operating system. The traditional exit is via MS DOS interrupt 27H, known as the *terminate-and-stay resident* exit. Service number 49, of INT 21H, sometimes known as the *keep process* exit, can also be used for this purpose. The difference between these methods for returning control to MS DOS, yet preserving the program's code in memory, are related to the allowable size of the TSR code, the way of calculating the memory space to be protected, and the automatic restoration of error handlers by INT 27H. So as to illustrate both methods we have used service number 49, of INT 21H, in the SERFILT and SPOOL programs. The other TSR programs in Chapter 4 use INT 27H.

4.0.5 Accessing the TSR Code

The MS DOS services discussed in Section 4.0.4 serve to protect the TSR code so that it remains in the operating system's memory space, however, accessing the TSR code is an entirely different matter. In a program-relocatable environment, such as MS DOS, applications reside in a variable memory space, which is assigned to each program, by the operating system, at load time. When the program concludes, its memory space is freed for other applications. TSRs constitute the exception to this rule. A TSR's permanent memory residence address is determined during its initialization and remains fixed until the system is restarted. Therefore, if an application program knows the TSR's original address, it will be able to transfer execution to the TSR code at any time.

In the IBM microcomputer environment the most convenient way to store a TRS's residence address is by taking over an interrupt and installing the TSR's address in the corresponding vector. Often a TSR's initialization routine will take over an unused interrupt. In MS DOS the vectors corresponding to INT 60H to 67H are available for user software. These vectors are normally free, but the programmer should note that some systems may use them for other purposes. Other TSRs intercept existing BIOS interrupts. In this case the TSR's code is located at the intercepted vector. Vector manipulations can be simplified by using the corresponding MS DOS services, as shown in the sample programs in this chapter.

4.1 Printer Filters

A printer filter is generally installed at the system level so as to intercept data sent through the parallel port by any application program. In the MS DOS environment the filter is coded as a COM-type file and located in the system's memory space using an

MS DOS *terminate-and-stay resident* service. The filter assumes that the application will access the printer using BIOS service number 17H (as is the case with the procedures SEND_PRN and STATUS_PRN in the OUTPUT module listed in Chapter 2. Output from programs that do not use the BIOS printer service and that access the port directly will bypass the filter.

By intercepting BIOS INT 17H the filter can operate on the data destined to the parallel port. The code can add, discard, or substitute characters and control codes (character filters) or direct the output to another device or port (device filters).

4.1.1 Developing a Character Filter

The following example, named CODEFILT, is a character filter designed to convert certain character strings to uppercase while leaving other strings unchanged. Its usefulness is related to an assembly language coding style which prefers uppercase characters for CPU instructions, labels, names, and other meaningful code and lowercase characters for comments. This coding style, generally adopted in the present book, is designed to improve the readability of the code by emphasizing its meaningful areas. The filter operates on a file composed in a different style so that meaningful code is printed in uppercase characters while the comments remain as originally typed. In operation this is achieved by setting a switch to change to uppercase all characters transmitted to the printer, except those following a semicolon (;) symbol.

```
;****************************************************************
;****************************************************************
;                          CODEFILT.ASM
;****************************************************************
;****************************************************************
;
; Filter to intercept calls to BIOS INT 17H, service number 0,
; print character. The filter will change to uppercase (caps) all
; characters output to the parallel port, except those located
; between a semicolon symbol (;) and the following carriage
; return (0DH). This filter can be used to print assembly
; language source files in the caps/lowercase style
;
; Note:
;     This file was typed using lowercase characters so that
;     it can be used to test the CODEFILT program. All other
;     code listed in this book is typed in the caps/lowercase
;     style
;
; MS DOS commands for creating the run file CODEFILT.COM
;         1. MASM CODEFILT;
;         2. LINK CODEFILT;
;         3. EXE2BIN CODEFILT.EXE CODEFILT.COM;
;         4. ERASE CODEFILT.EXE
```

```
;*************************** code ***************************
;
code    segment
;
        org     0100h               ; COM file origin
        assume  cs:code,ds:code,es:code,ss:code
;
entry:
        jmp     install
;
;****************************************************************
;                       filter routine
;****************************************************************
hex17_int:
; Test for AH = 0 corresponding to the BIOS print character
; service. Ignore other service requests
        cmp     ah,0
        je      filter_char         ; Proceed to filter
;*********************|
;    print character  |
;      via INT 60H    |
;*********************|
print_it:
        int     60h                 ; New vector for INT 17H
        iret
;
; AL = character to be printed
filter_char:
        sti                         ; Interrupts on
;*********************|
;    filter routine   |
;*********************|
; Test for semicolon and turn caps conversion off
        cmp     al,';'              ; Test for start of comment area
        je      caps_off            ; Switch off routine
; Test for carriage return and turn caps conversion on
        cmp     al,0dh              ; Code for end of line
        je      caps_on             ; Switch on routine
; Test for all other control codes and for characters already in
; uppercase (less than 60h)
        cmp     al,60h              ; Less than 60h is control code
                                    ; or uppercase
        jb      print_it            ; Print normally
; Test for caps conversion switch off
        cmp     cs:caps_switch,0        ; Is switch off
        je      print_it            ; Print character as received
```

```
; If execution drops then character must be converted to
; uppercase
        sub     al,20h          ; Convert to uppercase
        jmp     print_it
;**********************|
; caps conversion OFF  |
;**********************|
caps_off:
        mov     cs:caps_switch,0        ; Code for off
        jmp     print_it        ; Print semicolon normally
;**********************|
;  caps conversion ON  |
;**********************|
caps_on:
        mov     cs:caps_switch,1        ; Code for on
        jmp     print_it        ; Print carriage return normally
;
;************************** data ***************************
caps_switch     db      1       ; 0 = print data as received
                                ; 1 = change data to uppercase
                                ; Set to 1 on entry
                dw      0
;
;***********************************************************
;                     installation routine
;***********************************************************
; Operations:
;       1. Obtain vector for INT 17H and store in INT 60H
;       2. Set INT 17H vector to this routine
;       3. Protect memory and exit
;***********************************************************
install:
;*********************|
;     get INT 17H     |
;*********************|
        mov     ah,35h          ; Service request code
        mov     al,17h          ; Code of vector desired
        int     21h
; ES — segment address of installed interrupt handler
; BX — offset address of installed interrupt handler
;*********************|
;   store at INT 60H  |
;*********************|
; Use MS DOS service number 37 to install the original vector
        mov     ah,37           ; Service request code
        mov     al,60h          ; Destination vector
```

```
        push    ds                  ; Save operational DS
        push    es                  ; ES to DS via stack
        pop     ds                  ; to transfer segment base
        mov     dx,bx               ; Offset of address to dx
        int     21h                 ; MS DOS service
        pop     ds                  ; Restore DS
;**********************|
; set new INT 17H in   |
;     vector table     |
;**********************|
; uses DOS service 37 of INT 21H
        mov     ah,25h              ; Service request code
        mov     al,17h              ; Interrupt code
; Data segment = code segment in a .COM file
        mov     dx,offset hex17_int     ; Routine's offset
        int     21h
;**********************|
;  protect memory and  |
;        exit          |
;**********************|
        mov     dx,offset cs:install
        inc     dx                  ; One byte to assure paragraph
        int     27h
;
code    ends
        end     entry
```

4.1.2 Developing a Device Filter

A device filter is a TSR designed to intercept output to a certain hardware device or port and redirect it to another device, port, or file. The more recent versions of MS DOS have built-in redirection facilities which allow some manipulations in this respect. However, the programmer often needs to customize the device filter so as to perform functions not available or documented in the operating system code. The program named SERFILT redirects output to the parallel port, via INT 17H, so that the character stream is output to the serial port instead. The code assumes that the serial port is initialized to the following communications protocol:

> Baud rate 1200
> parity even
> 1 stop bit
> 7 bits per word

Details regarding serial port programming can be found in Chapter 5.

```
;******************************************************************
;******************************************************************
;                         SERFILT.ASM
;******************************************************************
;******************************************************************
;
; Filter for redirecting a character output to the parallel port
; so that it will be transmitted through the serial port
;
; DOS commands for creating the run file
;        1. MASM SERFILT;
;        2. LINK SERFILT;
;        3. EXE2BIN SERFILT.EXE SERFILT.COM
;        4. ERASE HPFILTER.EXE
;
;*************************** code ***************************
CODE    SEGMENT
        ORG     0100H             ; COM file origin
;
        ASSUME  CS:CODE,DS:CODE,ES:CODE,SS:CODE
;
ENTRY:
        JMP     INSTALL
;
;******************************************************************
;                         filter routine
;******************************************************************
HEX17_INT:
        STI
; Test for AH = 0 code of the print character service call
        CMP     AH,0
        JE      SEND_SERIAL       ; Intercept function
;*********************|
; original INT 17H via |
;       INT 60H        |
;*********************|
        INT     60H               ; New vector for INT 17H
        IRET
;*********************|
;  test serial port    |
;*********************|
SEND_SERIAL:
; Wait loop for transmitter holding register empty
        PUSH    AX
        PUSH    DX
        PUSH    AX                ; Save character to transmit
```

```
THRE_WAIT:
        MOV     DX,CS:CARD_BASE
        ADD     DX,5              ; Line status register
        IN      AL,DX            ; Get byte at port
        JMP     SHORT $+2        ; I/O delay
; Test for data received
        TEST    AL,00000001B     ; Data ready
        JNZ     DATA_READY
        TEST    AL,20H           ; THRE bit set ?
        JNZ     OK_2_SEND
        JMP     THRE_WAIT
; Test for XOFF code (decimal 19)
DATA_READY:
        MOV     DX,CS:CARD_BASE
        IN      AL,DX            ; Retrieve character
        CMP     AL,19            ; Test for XOFF
        JNE     THRE_WAIT        ; Ignore character if not XOFF
; Wait for XON
WAIT_4_XON:
        IN      AL,DX            ; Retrieve character
        CMP     AL,17            ; XON character
        JNE     WAIT_4_XON
;*********************|
;    send character   |
;*********************|
OK_2_SEND:
        POP     AX               ; Recover byte to be sent
; Place in transmitter holding register
        MOV     DX,CS:CARD_BASE ; THR register
        OUT     DX,AL            ; Send
        JMP     SHORT $+2        ; I/O delay
; Restore registers used by interrupt service and counter
EXIT_SEND:
        POP     DX
        POP     AX
        MOV     AH,10010000B     ; Not busy and selected
;*********************|
; return from interrupt|
;*********************|
        CLC
        IRET
;
;*************************** data ***************************
CARD_BASE       DW      ?
                DW      0        ; Safety padding
; Calculate code area to be protected on exit
```

```
PROTECT EQU      $-ENTRY
;
;******************************************************************
;                        installation routine
;******************************************************************
;
; Installation operations:
;         1. Obtain vector for INT 17H and move to INT 60H
;         2. Set INT 17H vector to this routine
;         3. Obtain and store base address of RS-232-C card
;         4. Set communications protocol and initialize serial
;            port
;         5. Protect memory and exit
;******************************************************************
;
INSTALL:
;*********************|
;     get INT 17H     |
;*********************|
        MOV      AH,53           ; Service request code
        MOV      AL,17H          ; Code of vector desired
        INT      21H
; ES -> segment address of installed interrupt handler
; BX -> offset address of installed interrupt handler
;*********************|
;   store at INT 60H  |
;*********************|
; Use MS DOS service number 37 to install the original vector
        MOV      AH,37           ; Service request code
        MOV      AL,60H          ; Destination vector
        PUSH     DS              ; Save operational DS
        PUSH     ES              ; ES to DS via stack
        POP      DS              ; to transfer segment base
        MOV      DX,BX           ; Offset of address to DX
        INT      21H             ; MS DOS service
        POP      DS              ; Restore DS
;*********************|
; set new INT 17H in  |
;     vector table    |
;*********************|
; Also uses MS DOS service 37 of INT 21H
        MOV      AH,37           ; Service request code
        MOV      AL,17H          ; Interrupt code
; Data segment = code segment in a .COM file
        MOV      DX,OFFSET HEX17_INT     ; Routine's offset
        INT      21H
```

```
;**********************|
;  set serial protocol |
;**********************|
; Serial communications line is set to:
; Bit mask: 100xxxxx ...... Baud = 1200
;           xxx11xxx ...... Parity = even
;           xxxxx0xx ...... Stop bits = 1
;           xxxxxx10 ...... Word length = 7
;           10011010
          MOV     AL,10011010B      ; Control code
          MOV     AH,0              ; BIOS request number
          MOV     DX,0              ; COM1 in all hardware types
          INT     14H               ; BIOS service request
;**********************|
;   store address of   |
;    RS-232-C card      |
;**********************|
          PUSH    DS                ; Save data segment
          MOV     AX,0
          PUSH    AX
          POP     DS                ; DS -> base of RAM
          MOV     DI,0400H          ; DI -> offset
          MOV     DX, WORD PTR [DI]
          POP     DS                ; Restore data segment
          MOV     CARD_BASE,DX      ; Save as program data
;**********************|
; init modem register  |
;**********************|
; Initialize modem control register for data terminal ready
; (bit 0), and request to send (bit 1). DX still holds the port
; address
          MOV     DL,0FCH           ; MCR address
          MOV     AL,00000011B      ; Bits 0 and 1 set
          OUT     DX,AL
          JMP     SHORT $+2
;**********************|
;    disable serial    |
;    interrupts        |
;**********************|
          MOV     DL,0F9H           ; Interrupt enable register
          MOV     AL,0
          OUT     DX,AL
          JMP     SHORT $+2
;**********************|
; protect TSR and exit |
;**********************|
```

```
; This program uses service number 49, of INT 21H, to terminate
; and stay resident
        MOV     AH,49               ; MS DOS service request number
        MOV     AL,0                ; No error reported system
;********************|
; calculate paragraphs |
;       to protect      |
;********************|
        MOV     DX,((PROTECT+15)/16)+16
                                    ; Formula to have assembler
                                    ; calculate paragraphs to be
                                    ; protected
        INT     21H
;
CODE    ENDS
        END     ENTRY
```

4.1.3 Removing an Installed Filter

Some software filters, as is the case with those listed in the present chapter, are only temporarily useful. Once they have served their purpose, it is often desirable to return the system to its normal state. For example, a user may wish to redirect printer output of a file to the serial port and later restore normal printer operation.

As mentioned previously, many TSR routines operate by intercepting one or more system interrupts and placing their own code at these vectors. If the TSR's installation routine saves the address of the original interrupt, another program can recover this address and restore it. For example, the SERFILT and the CODEFILT programs intercept output to the printer by replacing the INT 17H vector with their own and by moving the address of the original INT 17H to the vector for INT 60H. Both SERFILT and CODEFILT use INT 60H to pass to the original handler the unrelated service calls. Since the original vector for INT 17H is saved at the vector for INT 60H, which is normally available to user software, it is possible to restore the machine's original conditions.

We have seen that, in addition to changing the interrupt vectors, the installation routine of a TSR preserves the program's image in memory by making it part of the operating-system code. Memory protection is achieved by using one of the corresponding MS DOS services — namely, INT 27H or service number 49 if INT 21H — as shown in the programs listed in this chapter. The operation performed by these services reassigns a part of memory, normally available to applications, to the operating-system protected area, thus reducing the memory space available for user software.

On removal of a TSR it would be desirable to free its reserved memory and restore it to the memory pool available to applications. However, although there are MS DOS services to modify the memory allocation of an application, these services are not documented to operate with TSR routines and are not consistently successful in this use. Therefore, except by restarting the system, there is no documented, effective

method in MS DOS for restoring to the application's memory space the area used by a
dead TSR. This effect can be objectionable, depending on the size of the TSR's memory
image, the amount of available memory, and the memory needs of other programs.

The following program, named FILTOFF, reinstalls the INT 17H vector from INT
60H. It can be used to restore normal printer operation with any of the filter programs
listed in this chapter. The removal routine has the drawback that the memory occupied
by the TSR is not reassigned to the user software space. Note that although the
FILTOFF program is coded as a COM-type file, there is no reason why it could not
have been an EXE-type.

```
;****************************************************************
;****************************************************************
;                         FILTOFF.ASM
;****************************************************************
;****************************************************************
;
; Program to restore the original INT 17H, now stored at INT 60H,
;
; MS DOS commands for creating the run file FILTOFF.COM
;       1. MASM FILTOFF;
;       2. LINK FILTOFF;
;       3. EXE2BIN FILTOFF.EXE FILTOFF.COM;
;       4. ERASE FILTOFF.EXE
;
;*************************** code ***************************
;
CODE     SEGMENT
;
         ORG      0100H              ; COM file origin
         ASSUME   CS:CODE,DS:CODE,ES:CODE,SS:CODE
;
;****************************************************************
;                     installation routine
;****************************************************************
; Operations:
;       1. Obtain vector for INT 17H and store at INT 60H
;       2. Normal exit to DOS
;****************************************************************
ENTRY:
;*********************|
;    get vector for   |
;       INT 60H       |
;*********************|
         MOV      AH,53              ; Service request code
         MOV      AL,60H             ; Code of vector desired
         INT      21H
```

```
; ES -> segment address of installed interrupt handler
; BX -> offset address of installed interrupt handler
;*********************|
;      store vector at  |
;          INT 17H      |
;*********************|
; Use MS DOS service number 37 to reinstall the original vector
          MOV     AH,37           ; Service request code
          MOV     AL,17H          ; Destination vector
          PUSH    DS              ; Save operational DS
          PUSH    ES              ; ES to DS via stack
          POP     DS              ; to transfer segment base
          MOV     DX,BX           ; Offset of address to DX
          INT     21H             ; MS DOS service
          POP     DS              ; Restore DS
;******************|
;    exit to DOS      |
;******************|
          MOV     AH,4CH          ; DOS service request code
          MOV     AL,0            ; No error code returned
          INT     21H             ; TO DOS
;
CODE      ENDS
          END     ENTRY
```

4.2 Printer Spoolers

Printer spoolers are a form of multitasking that allows operation of the printer as a background task while other programs continue to execute in the foreground. This use of the word *spool* originates in the mainframe expression: Simultaneous Peripheral Operation On Line. Some printer spoolers include additional memory or hardware devices, while others operate purely as software.

The usefulness of a printer spooler derives from the relative slowness of hardcopy devices. The spooler increases system efficiency by reducing the time that the CPU spends waiting for the printer to become ready for the next transmitted character. In the IBM microcomputers, a typical printer spooler intercepts output to the BIOS parallel port service, at INT 17H. The intercepted characters are stored in memory or disk buffer. When the printer becomes ready to receive, the spooler software recovers the character from memory or disk storage and sends it to the device. In this manner the CPU does not waste time waiting for a slow device.

Ideally, an implementation can use a hardware interrupt to notify the CPU of the printer ready condition. The problem is that the printer interrupt signal does not function correctly in some printer adapters of the IBM PC line. Therefore, a spooler program that aims at operating in any IBM microcomputer model must find another way of detecting a printer ready condition. One option is to poll the printer status register at frequent intervals. But the IBM microcomputer system timer sustains a beat of approximately 18.2 times per second, which is not frequent enough to ensure optimum performance with the faster printing devices. Therefore, an efficient spooling program must get into the complications of speeding up the system timer, and thus ensure that port polling takes place at an adequate frequency.

4.2.1 The SPOOL Program

The program named SPOOL, listed in this section, uses polling to determine a printer ready condition. The system timer is accelerated by a factor of 10 during the initialization routine. Since the BIOS uses the original timer beat for the time-of-day clock and for certain diskette operations, the spooler must transfer execution to the original handler on every tenth beat in order to preserve these system controls. The SPOOL program is also discussed in Chapter 6 (Section 6.2) in relation to interrupt sharing. The details of program operation are shown in the code listing.

```
;****************************************************************
;****************************************************************
;                        SPOOL.ASM
;****************************************************************
;****************************************************************
;
; Clock driven printer spooler with 61K memory buffer
; Changes during installation:
; 1. The BIOS printer interrupt service is relocated from INT 17H
;    to INT 60H and the system clock interrupt from INT 08H to
;    INT 61H
; 2. The system timer is made to run 10 times faster to ensure
;    that the printer status is monitored with the necessary
;    frequency
; 3. New service routines are installed for the printer interrupt
;    and the system timer
; Operation:
; 1. The new interrupt handler at INT 17H filters all BIOS calls
;    to print a character (AH = 0). The character is stored in a
;    buffer, instead of printed
; 2. Other calls to the original INT 17H are passed along to the
;    BIOS handler
; 3. The new interrupt handler at INT 08H gains control with
;    every tick of the system timer. If there is data in the
;    spooler buffer, the code checks if the printer if not busy.
;    If not busy, the character is sent to the printer directly
; 4. If the printer is busy, execution is returned to the current
;    task
; DOS commands for creating the run file SPOOL.COM
```

```
;         1. MASM SPOOL;
;         2. LINK SPOOL;
;         3. EXE2BIN SPOOL.EXE SPOOL.COM
;         4. ERASE SPOOL.EXE
;
;*************************** code **************************
;
CODE    SEGMENT
;
        ORG     0100H              ; COM file origin
        ASSUME  CS:CODE,DS:CODE,ES:CODE,SS:CODE
;
ENTRY:
        JMP     INSTALL
;
;*********************************************************************
;                      new INT 08H handler
;*********************************************************************
; The handler is designed so that a new timer tick cannot take
; place while printing. This is ensured by not sending the 8259
; end-of-interrupt code until the routine's processing is
; complete
;*********************************************************************
;
HEX08_INT:
        STI                        ; Interrupts on
        PUSH    AX                 ; Save registers used by routine
        PUSH    BX
        PUSH    DX
        PUSH    DS
; Make DS = CS
        PUSH    CS
        POP     DS
;********************|
; check buffer for data|
;********************|
        MOV     BX,BUF_OUT         ; Output pointer
        CMP     BX,BUF_IN          ; Input pointer
        JNE     PRINT_CHAR         ; Data in buffer if not equal
;********************|
;   no data in spooler |
;         buffer       |
;********************|
; Decrement counter to determine whether this is the 10th count
; On each 10th count execution is transferred to the original
; handler in order to maintain system integrity
```

```
PRT_EXIT:
        DEC     TIMER_CNT
        JZ      TIME_OF_DAY      ; Exit through time_of_day
;**********************|
;     direct exit      |
;**********************|
        MOV     AL,20H           ; Send end-of-interrupt code
        OUT     20H,AL           ; to 8259 interrupt controller
        POP     DS               ; Restore registers
        POP     DX
        POP     BX
        POP     AX
        IRET                     ; Return from interrupt
;**********************|
;   pass to original   |
;   INT 08H handler    |
;**********************|
TIME_OF_DAY:
        MOV     TIMER_CNT,10     ; Reset counter
        POP     DS
        POP     DX
        POP     BX
        POP     AX
        INT     61H
        IRET
;**********************|
;   data in spooler    |
;       buffer         |
;**********************|
PRINT_CHAR:
; Send character to printer if printer NOT BUSY
        MOV     DX,PRT_BASE      ; Get card address
        INC     DX               ; Point to status port
;**********************|
; check if printer busy|
;**********************|
        IN      AL,DX            ; Get status byte
        TEST    AL,80H           ; Busy ?
        JZ      PRT_EXIT         ; Yes
;**********************|
;   printer not busy   |
;    print character   |
;**********************|
; DX holds printer card base address + 1
        DEC     DX               ; Adjust address to data port
; Get character from buffer and send to printer
```

```
            MOV     AL,CS:[BX]          ; BX holds BUF_OUT pointer
                                        ; AL has character to print
            OUT     DX,AL               ; Write character to printer port
;*********************|
;  pulse STROBE bit   |
;*********************|
            INC     DX                  ; Adjust address to status port
NOT_READY:
            IN      AL,DX               ; Read byte at status port
            TEST    AL,80H              ; Busy ?
            JZ      NOT_READY           ; Continue until not busy
; Pulse printer STROBE bit to transmit character
            INC     DX                  ; Adjust address to control port
            MOV     AL,00001101B        ; STROBE bit 0 on
                                        ; Initialize and select bits also
                                        ; on
            OUT     DX,AL               ; Output to control port
            MOV     AL,00001100B        ; Strobe bit 0 off
            OUT     DX,AL               ; Output to control port
; Test for buffer full
            INC     BX                  ; Bump output pointer
            CMP     BX,OFFSET BUF_END       ; Test for end
            JNE     OK_BUF_END          ; Not at end
;*********************|
;   at end of buffer  |
;*********************|
; Reset buffer pointer
            MOV     BX,OFFSET BUF_START     ; To start of buffer
OK_BUF_END:
            MOV     BUF_OUT,BX          ; Store pointer in variable
; No test for printer error is provided at this time
            JMP     PRT_EXIT
;****************************************************************
;                       new INT 17H handler
;****************************************************************
HEX17_INT:
;
; Test for AH = 0 code of the print character service call
            CMP     AH,0
            JE      STORE_CHAR          ; Intercept function
;*********************|
;   pass to original  |
;       handler       |
;*********************|
            INT     60H                 ; Let pass to original INT 17H
            IRET
```

```
;**********************|
;    store character   |
;  if buffer not full  |
;**********************|
STORE_CHAR:
        STI                    ; Interrupts on
; Save registers used by interrupt service and counter
        PUSH     DS       ; Save data segment
        PUSH     BX
        PUSH     CX
        MOV      CX,0              ; Set error timer
;
        PUSH     CS
        POP      DS                ; Set data segment
STORE_IT:
        MOV      BX,BUF_IN         ; Input buffer pointer
; Test for buffer full
        CMP      BX,OFFSET BUF_END         ; Test for end
        JNE      OK_2_BUMP         ; Not at end. Bump pointer
;**********************|
;    at end of buffer  |
;**********************|
; Reset buffer pointer
        MOV      BX,OFFSET BUF_START       ; To start of buffer
;**********************|
;    store character   |
;**********************|
OK_2_BUMP:
        MOV      [BX],AL           ; Store byte in buffer
        INC      BX                ; Bump buffer pointer
        MOV      BUF_IN,BX         ; New input pointer
        MOV      AH,0              ; Return code used by INT 17H
STORE_EXIT:
        POP      CX
        POP      BX
        POP      DS
        IRET
;**********************|
;    buffer full       |
;**********************|
FULL:
        AAD                        ; Delay
        AAD
        LOOP     STORE_IT
; Printer loop timed out. Reset pointers to start of buffer
; and exit
```

```
        MOV     BX,OFFSET BUF_START
        MOV     BUF_IN,BX       ; Reset input pointer
        MOV     BUF_OUT,BX      ; And output pointer
        MOV     AH,1            ; INT 17H error return code
        JMP     STORE_EXIT
;
;*************************** data ***************************
; Buffer pointers
BUF_IN          DW      BUF_START       ; Input pointer
BUF_OUT         DW      BUF_START       ; Output pointer
;
TIMER_CNT       DB      10              ; Timer counter
PRT_BASE        DW      ?               ; Printer port base address
;*********************|
;  printer buffer area |
;*********************|
BUF_START       LABEL   BYTE
;
        DB      0F000H DUP (00H) ; 61K buffer - can be changed
                                 ; to a maximum of 63K
;
BUF_END         LABEL   BYTE
;
        DW      0000H
;
PROTECT EQU     $-ENTRY
;
;****************************************************************
;                     installation routine
;****************************************************************
; Operations:
;       1. Obtain vector for INT 17H and store in INT 60H
;       2. Obtain vector for INT 08H and store in INT 61H
;       3. Set INT 17H vector to routine in this module
;       4. Speed up system timer by a factor of 10
;       5. Set INT 08H vector to routine in this module
;       6. Find and save base address of printer card
;       7. Protect memory for TSR and exit
;****************************************************************
INSTALL:
;*********************|
;    get INT 17H      |
;*********************|
        MOV     AH,53           ; Service request code
        MOV     AL,17H          ; Code of vector desired
        INT     21H
```

```
; ES -> segment address of installed interrupt handler
; BX -> offset address of installed interrupt handler
;**********************|
;    store at INT 60H   |
;**********************|
; Use MS DOS service number 37 to install the original vector
        MOV     AH,37         ; Service request code
        MOV     AL,60H        ; Destination vector
        PUSH    DS            ; Save operational DS
        PUSH    ES            ; ES to DS via stack
        POP     DS            ; to transfer segment base
        MOV     DX,BX         ; Offset of address to DX
        INT     21H           ; MS DOS service
        POP     DS            ; Restore DS
;
;**********************|
;     get INT 08H       |
;**********************|
        MOV     AH,53         ; Service request code
        MOV     AL,08H        ; Code of vector desired
        INT     21H
; ES -> segment address of installed interrupt handler
; BX -> offset address of installed interrupt handler
;**********************|
;    store at INT 61H   |
;**********************|
; Use MS DOS service number 37 to install the original vector
        MOV     AH,37         ; Service request code
        MOV     AL,61H        ; Destination vector
        PUSH    DS            ; Save operational DS
        PUSH    ES            ; ES to DS via stack
        POP     DS            ; to transfer segment base
        MOV     DX,BX         ; Offset of address to DX
        INT     21H           ; MS DOS service
        POP     DS            ; Restore DS
;
;**********************|
; set new INT 17H in    |
;     vector table      |
;**********************|
; Also uses DOS service 37 of INT 21H
        MOV     AH,37         ; Service request code
        MOV     AL,17H        ; Interrupt code
; Data segment = code segment in a .COM file
        MOV     DX,OFFSET HEX17_INT    ; Routine's offset
        INT     21H
```

```
;**********************|
;    speed up system   |
;      timer by 10     |
;**********************|
; Original divisor = 65,536
; New divisor = 6,555
        CLI                             ; Interrupts off while resetting
        MOV     AL,00110110B            ; 00xx xxxx = channel 0
                                        ; xx11 xxxx = write LSB then MSM
                                        ; xxxx 011x = mode 3
                                        ; xxxx xxx0 = binary system
        OUT     43H,AL
        MOV     BX,6555                 ; New divisor
        MOV     AL,BL
        OUT     40H,AL                  ; Send LSB
        MOV     AL,BH
        OUT     40H,AL                  ; Send MSB
;**********************|
; set new INT 08H in   |
;    vector table      |
;**********************|
; Mask off all interrupts while changing INT 08H vector
        CLI
; Save mask in stack
        IN      AL,21H                  ; Read 8259 mask register
        PUSH    AX                      ; Save in stack
        MOV     AL,0FFH                 ; Mask off IRQ0 to IRQ7
        OUT     21H,AL                  ; Write to 8259 mask register
; Install new interrupt vector
        MOV     AH,25H
        MOV     AL,08H                  ; Interrupt code
        MOV     DX,OFFSET HEX08_INT
        INT     21H
; Restore original interrupt mask
        POP     AX                      ; Recover mask from stack
        OUT     21H,AL                  ; Write to 8259 mask register
        STI                             ; Set 8088 flag
;**********************|
; get and store address|
;   of printer card    |
;**********************|
        PUSH    ES                      ; Save segment
        MOV     AX,0
        MOV     ES,AX                   ; ES -> base of RAM
        MOV     DX,ES:[0408H]           ; DI -> offset
        POP     ES                      ; Restore segment
```

```
        MOV     CS:PRT_BASE,DX  ; Save as program data
;**********************|
; protect TSR and exit |
;**********************|
        MOV     AH,31H          ; Service request code
        MOV     AL,0            ; No error reported on exit
        MOV     DX,((PROTECT+15)/16)+16
        INT     21H
;
CODE    ENDS
        END     ENTRY
```

4.3 Laser Printer Programming

A laser printer uses electrophotographic technology to transfer a dot image created on a sensitive drum or belt onto a sheet of paper. This method is quite similar to that used in many popular types of copy machines. Printers using laser technology have been available since 1975. But they did not gain much popularity in the microcomputer industry until 1984, when Hewlett-Packard introduced the first desktop laser printer, the *LaserJet*. The recent surge in desktop publishing and other graphics applications is attributable in part to the availability of the LaserJet and other moderately priced laser printers.

Shortly after the introduction of the Hewlett-Packard LaserJet printer, Apple Computers announced a desktop laser printer named *Laser Writer*. The Laser Writer printer came with a built-in programming language called *Postscript*, developed by Adobe Corporation, while the LaserJet used a programming language developed by Hewlett-Packard called *Printer Control Language* (PCL). Since then Postscript has been accepted as a major programming language, not only in laser printer programming but in other graphics fields. The Postscript language has been well described, and there are several books on Postscript programming. On the other hand, although PCL printers manufactured by Hewlett-Packard and other companies are extensively used with IBM microcomputers, the PCL language remains relatively undocumented outside the Hewlett-Packard literature.

4.3.1 Hewlett-Packard's Printer Control Language (PCL)

Computer programmers have suffered considerably because of the incompatibility of hardcopy devices. These incompatibilities originate in the use of extended character sets and nonstandard control codes by the various printer manufacturers, to the extreme that programs that output to the printer cannot safely use ASCII characters beyond the range 20H to 7FH or control codes other than the line-feed and carriage return. For instance, controls for horizontal and vertical tabs, page eject, and margin and form settings have often been implemented in a form that is unique for the device.

Hewlett-Packard's PCL is an effort at standardizing printer character sets and control codes so as to ensure program portability. In its original conception, PCL aimed at controlling many types of printers, from the base level, inexpensive devices, to the most intricate laser printers and professional typesetting machines. To this end, five levels of the PCL language have been implemented. PCL Levels IV and V are the page-oriented supersets of the language used in the Hewlett-Packard LaserJet Series II and Series III printers, respectively. PCL Levels I, II, and III are of little use in laser printer applications.

4.3.2 PCL Control Codes

PCL activates printer features through the use of standard control codes and proprietary escape sequences. The PCL printer control codes can be seen in Table 4.2.

Table 4.2. *PCL Control Codes*

| NAME | VALUE | | DESIGNATION | |
	HEX	DECIMAL	HP	ASCII
Backspace	08H	8	B_S	BS
Line feed	0AH	10	L_F	LF
Carriage return	0DH	13	C_R	CR
Form feed	0CH	12	F_F	FF
Escape	1BH	27	E_C	ESC
Horizontal tab	09H	11	H_T	HT
Shift in	0FH	15	S_I	SI
Shift out	0EH	14	S_O	SO

Note in Table 4.2 that the Hewlett-Packard designation consists of a two-letter code, in which the second character is printed as a subscript. This is the conventional format used in PCL. Also notice that the control codes Backspace, Line-feed, Carriage return, Form-feed, and Horizontal tab correspond to printer functions available in any standard laser or nonlaser device. The Shift-out control is used to select characters from a secondary font and Shift-in to reselect the primary font. The Escape code is used to initiate an escape sequence, described in the following section.

4.3.3 PCL Printer Commands

Some controls needed in printer programming require more data that can be encoded in a single control code. Escape sequences are printer commands that begin with the ESC character (1BH) and are followed by other characters. The sequence is interpreted by the printer as a complex command. The PCL language uses escape sequences that consist of two or more characters. For example, in PCL, the command to reset the printer is

$$E_C E$$

while the generic form for the command to position the printer cursor to a certain screen row is

$$E_C \& a\#R$$

Table 4.3 lists some PCL symbols with special meaning in the language and literal codes used in describing PCL commands.

Table 4.3. *PCL Symbols With Special Meaning*

PCL SYMBOL	HEX VALUE OR RANGE	MEANING
E_C	1BH	Start of PCL printer command
#	23H	Represents a value field in the PCL command Characters represented must be in the range "0" to "9", may be signed + or -, and may be fractions.
X	"!" to "/"	ASCII symbol indicating a parameterized escape sequence, for example: & = Job control, cursor positioning, font orientation or pitch, and macro commands (= Symbol set selection, spacing, pitch, and typeface commands) = Soft font creation command * = Font management and graphics commands
y	"`" to "~"	Lowercase character specifying a group control
z_i	"`" to "~"	Lowercase character used in combining escape sequences
Z_n	"@" to "^"	Uppercase character that specifies the value of a zi field

A general printer command can be expressed in PCL using the symbols in Table 4.3. For example, the resolution of a LaserJet Series II or Series III printer can be 75, 100, 150, or 300 dots per inch. In its generic form, the PCL command to set the printer's resolution is

$$E_C*t\#R$$

where the # symbol represents the ASCII characters corresponding to one of the resolutions listed above. The actual command requires transmitting these characters to the printer, usually through the parallel port. On the IBM microcomputers, a convenient method for sending an escape sequence is to set up a data string terminated in a special character. The value 00H can be used as a string terminator since it is not used by PCL for any other purpose. The procedure named SEND_STRING in the PCLDUMP program presented later in this chapter performs the necessary operations. The command string can be set up in a memory variable, as in the following example:

```
RES_150_DOTS     DB        1BH,'*t150R',00H
```

Table 4.4 lists some of the most frequently used PCL commands. The list is far from complete since it does not include symbol set selection, soft-font creation, font management, graphics, macros, and other commands. Complete documentation regarding the PCL language can be obtained from

Hewlett-Packard Company
Boise Division
Documentation Department M.S. 112
P.O. Box 15
Boise, Idaho 83707

Table 4.4. *Frequently Used PCL Commands*

FUNCTION	UNITS/RANGE	PCL COMMAND	SAMPLE ENCODING
Reset		E_CE	DB 1BH,'E',00H
Number of copies	1–99	E_C&l#X	DB 1BH,'&l20X',00H
Eject page		E_C&l0H	DB 1BH,'&l0H',00H
Feed from tray		E_C&l1H	DB 1BH,'&l1H',00H
Manual feed		E_C&l2H	DB 1BH,'&l2H',00H
Envelope feed		E_C&l3H	DB 1BH,'&l3H',00H
Executive form		E_C&l1A	DB 1BH,'&l1A',00H
Letter-size form		E_C&l2A	DB 1BH,'&l2A',00H
Legal-size form		E_C&l3A	DB 1BH,'&l3A',00H
Top margin	No. of lines	E_C&l#E	DB 1BH,'&l12E',00H
Text length	No. of lines	E_C&l#F	DB 1BH,'&l56F',00H
Left margin	Left column	E_C&l#L	DB 1BH,'&l5L',00H
Right margin	Right column	E_C&l#M	DB 1BH,'&l7M',00H
Horizontal motion index	1/20"	E_C&k#H	DB 1BH,'&k6H',00H
Vertical motion index	1/48"	E_C&k#C	DB 1BH,'&k10C',00H
Lines per inch	1, 2, 3, 4, 6, 8, 12, 16, 24, and 48	E_C&l#D	DB 1BH,'&l4D',00H
Set cursor, vertical	Row No.	E_C&a#R	DB 1BH,'&a12R',00H
	Dots	E_C&p#Y	DB 1BH,'&p300Y',00H
	Decipoints	E_C&a#V	DB 1BH,'&a720V',00H
Set cursor, horizontal	Row No.	E_C&a#C	DB 1BH,'&a12C',00H
	Dots	E_C&p#X	DB 1BH,'&p300X',00H
	Decipoints	E_C&a#H	DB 1BH,'&a720H',00H
Set portrait		E_C&l0O	DB 1BH,'&l0O',00H
Set landscape		E_C&l1O	DB 1BH,'&l1O',00H
Set resolution	75, 100, 150, and 300	E_C*t#R	DB 1BH,'*t150R',00H
Start graphics at left margin		E_C*r0A	DB 1BH,'*r0A',00H
at cursor position		E_C*r1A	DB 1BH,'*r1A',00H
Transfer raster image	Bytes per row	E_C*b#W	DB 1BH,'*b80W',00H
End graphics		E_C*rB	DB 1BH,'*rB',00H

4.3.4 The PCL Page

Laser printers are page-oriented devices. The software driver usually begins by setting certain general parameters, sometimes called the *print environment* or *job control commands*, and then proceeds to compose the printed document page by page. In this task PCL uses the concept of a print cursor, which represents the current print position on the page. The concept is a useful one, since programmers can easily relate the print cursor to the flashing screen cursor. Several PCL commands allow positioning the print cursor anywhere on the active page. As in the screen counterpart, the next character transmitted will be printed at the current cursor position.

The PCL coordinate system uses four different units of measurement: columns, rows, dots, and decipoints. The distance between columns is set by a corresponding PCL command. This distance is often called the *horizontal-motion index* (HMI). The distance between rows is set by the PCL command to change the *vertical-motion index* (VMI). Dots in the Hewlett-Packard LaserJet printers are 1/300th of an inch in diameter. Therefore a distance of 300 dots is equal to 1 in. One typographical point is 1/72th of an inch. A decipoint, the smallest unit of cursor movement in PCL, is equivalent to one-tenth point, or 1/720th of an inch. Although the cursor can be moved in decipoint increments, the smallest printable unit in the LaserJet printers is a dot, 1/300th of an inch in diameter. The printable area is the region of a page accessible to the printer. This area is called the *picture frame* in PCL Level V. The maximum printable area changes for different media and devices.

4.3.5 The PCLDUMP Program

The following program is a TSR to substitute the normal function of the Print Screen key with a graphics screen dump to a PCL printer. The program can be used with VGA or MCGA graphics systems in APA modes 17 and 18. These modes use 640 by 480 pixel resolution, which is the best available in the standard IBM graphics hardware of the PS/2 line. The code tests for these graphics modes and makes the necessary adjustments. If neither mode is active, execution is transferred to the original BIOS Print Screen service routine. PCLDUMP uses a printer resolution of 150 dots per inch, but the reader can change this and other parameters by editing the corresponding command strings.

```
;****************************************************************
;****************************************************************
;                          PCLDUMP.ASM
;****************************************************************
;****************************************************************
;
; Program to substitute the normal print screen function with a
; VGA graphic screen dump to a PCL laser printer
; The code is compatible with VGA graphics modes 17 and 18. If
; another video mode is active, the program will beep once and
; transfer execution to the original INT 05H routine, relocated
; to INT 60H
```

```
; PCLDUMP prints two screen images on an 8 1/2 by 11 in page. The
; top image is printed normally. In the bottom image the bit color
; is reversed
;
; DOS commands for creating the run file: PCLDUMP.COM
;       1. MASM PCLDUMP;
;       2. LINK PCLDUMP;
;       3. EXE2BIN PCLDUMP.EXE PCLDUMP.COM
;       4. ERASE PCLDUMP.EXE
;
;***************************** code *************************
;
CODE    SEGMENT
;
        ORG     0100H               ; COM file forced origin
        ASSUME  CS:CODE,DS:CODE,ES:CODE,SS:CODE
;
ENTRY:
        JMP     INSTALL
;
;******************************************************************
;          new INT 05H (print screen) service routine
;******************************************************************
HEX5_INT:
; Interrupts on
        STI
        PUSH    AX                  ; Save operational registers
        PUSH    BX
        PUSH    CX
        PUSH    DX
        PUSH    ES
;*********************|
; test for valid VGA  |
;   graphics modes    |
;*********************|
; Valid modes for this program are VGA modes 17 and 18
; Mode 17 is 640 by 480 pixels in 2 colors
; Mode 18 is 640 by 480 pixels in 16 colors
; A color mask is set so that nonwhite bits in either mode are
; printed as black dots in the top image and as white dots in the
; bottom image
;
        MOV     AX,0                ; Clear AX
        MOV     ES,AX               ; Set ES to access BIOS data area
        MOV     AL,BYTE PTR ES:[0449H]  ; Video mode byte
        CMP     AL,17               ; Valid modes are 17 and 18
```

```
        JB      BAD_VGA_MODE      ; Invalid mode, exit
        CMP     AL,19             ; VGA modes 19 and higher are
                                  ; illegal
        JAE     BAD_VGA_MODE      ; Invalid mode, exit
        MOV     AH,00000111B      ; Color mask for VGA mode 18
        CMP     AL,18             ; VGA mode 18 is default setting
        JE      OK_VGA_MODE       ; Use default color masks
; Must be VGA mode 17. Set masks for 2-color mode
        MOV     AH,00000001B      ; Use map 0 only
        JMP     OK_VGA_MODE
;**********************|
; beep to signal error |
;   in display mode    |
;**********************|
BAD_VGA_MODE:
        MOV     AH,14             ; BIOS service request code
        MOV     AL,7              ; Code for BELL command
        MOV     BX,0              ; Page 0
        INT     10H
;**********************|
; transfer to original |
;       INT 05H        |
;**********************|
        POP     ES
        POP     DX
        POP     CX
        POP     BX
        POP     AX
        INT     60H
        IRET
;**********************|
;    legal VGA mode    |
;**********************|
OK_VGA_MODE:
        MOV     CS:TEST_COLOR,AH         ; Set memory masks
        MOV     CS:NOT_SWITCH,0          ; Reset image switch
                                         ; for first image
;**********************|
;  ES to video buffer  |
;**********************|
        MOV     AX,0A000H         ; VGA graphics mode start address
        MOV     ES,AX             ; in video buffer to ES
;**********************|
;  graphics controller |
;  set to Read Mode 1  |
;**********************|
```

```
        MOV     DX,3CEH              ; Graphic controller address
                                     ; register
        MOV     AL,5                 ; Select Read Type register
        OUT     DX,AL                ; Activate
        INC     DX                   ; Control register is at 3CFH
        MOV     AL,00001000B         ; Set bit 3 for Read Mode 1
        OUT     DX,AL
;*********************|
;   initialize port   |
;*********************|
        MOV     AH,1                 ; BIOS service request number
        MOV     DX,0                 ; Port No. 0
        INT     17H
;*********************|
;   initialize printer |
;*********************|
        LEA     SI,CS:RESET          ; PCL string to reset printer
        CALL    SEND_STRING          ; Send to device
        LEA     SI,CS:START_GRAPH          ; Set graphics mode,
        CALL    SEND_STRING          ; cursor, resolution, and margin
                                     ; for first image
;
;***************************************************************
;                     graphics screen dump
;***************************************************************
; Sequence of operations:
;       1. Set Color Compare and Color Don't Care registers to
;          filters stored during initialization
;       2. Reset row and column counters for VGA graphics modes
;          CX = x coordinate (0 to 79)
;          DX = y coordinate (0 to 479)
;       3. Initialize printer to transfer a row of raster data
;       4. Read pixel byte at CX/DX (using Read Mode 1)
;          Print first image normally
;          NOT byte in AH to second image
;       5. Bump CX to next column
;          If CX = 80 then start a new row
;       7. Bump DX to next row
;          If DX = 480 then check for end of first or second
;          image. Exit if second image
;***************************************************************
;*********************|
;   set Color Compare |
;      register        |
;*********************|
; Set to the background color to be tested, stored in
```

```
; CS:TEST_COLOR
; The default setting is to test for a white background,
; 00000111B. The user may change this default value. All bits
; that do not match the background color are printed
        MOV     DX,3CEH         ; Graphics Controller
        MOV     AL,2            ; Select Color Compare
        OUT     DX,AL
;
        INC     DX              ; Write to Color Compare register
        MOV     AL,CS:TEST_COLOR
        OUT     DX,AL           ; Color loaded
;*********************|
; set Color Don't Care |
;       register        |
;*********************|
; The Color Don't Care register is set to ignore the intensity
; bit so that bright white bits are not printed as black
        MOV     DX,3CEH         ; Graphics Controller
        MOV     AL,7            ; Select Color Don't Care
        OUT     DX,AL
;
        INC     DX              ; Write to Color Don't Care
        MOV     AL,CS:TEST_COLOR ; Ignore bit 3 setting in VGA 18
                                ; and use bit 0 only in VGA 17
        OUT     DX,AL           ; Color mask loaded
;*********************|
;   reset counters    |
;*********************|
DUMP_SCREEN:
        MOV     CX,0            ; Start at first screen column
        MOV     DX,0            ; and first screen row
;*********************|
; initialize printer  |
;      for new row     |
;*********************|
NEW_ROW:
        LEA     SI,CS:START_ROW ; Message string
        CALL    SEND_STRING     ; Send PCL controls to printer
;*********************|
;      print row       |
;*********************|
PRINT_ROW:
        CALL    BYTE_ADD        ; Compute byte address in BX
; Read pixel byte into AL
        MOV     AL,ES:[BX]      ; Read byte in video buffer
                                ; that matches Color Compare
```

```
                                        ; register
;**********************|
;     invert bits on   |
;       second image   |
;**********************|
        CMP     CS:NOT_SWITCH,0 ; Test for switch off
        JE      DONT_NOT        ; First image, do not reverse
        NOT     AL              ; Invert to print nonwhite bits
; Send pixel byte
DONT_NOT:
        CALL    SEND_PIX        ; AL to printer
; Bump column counter
        INC     CX              ; Range = 0 to 79
        CMP     CX,80           ; End of row
        JE      END_OF_ROW
        JMP     PRINT_ROW       ; Continue printing row
;**********************|
;     new pixel row    |
;**********************|
END_OF_ROW:
        INC     DX              ; Range 0 to 479
        CMP     DX,480          ; Last row in this graphic mode
        JE      EXIT_DUMP       ; Color printed
        MOV     CX,0            ; Reset row counter
        JMP     NEW_ROW
;**********************|
;     end of image     |
;**********************|
EXIT_DUMP:
        LEA     SI,CS:END_GRAPH ; Code string to end graphics
        CALL    SEND_STRING
;**********************|
;   test for first or  |
;     second image     |
;**********************|
        CMP     CS:NOT_SWITCH,1         ; 1 is first image
        JE      LAST_IMAGE
;**********************|
;     initialize       |
;     second image     |
;**********************|
        MOV     CS:NOT_SWITCH,1         ; Set NOT switch
        LEA     SI,CS:SECOND_GRAPH      ; Set graphics mode,
        CALL    SEND_STRING     ; cursor, resolution, and margin
                                ; for second image
        JMP     DUMP_SCREEN     ; Dump second image
```

```
;*********************|
;      end of dump      |
;*********************|
LAST_IMAGE:
        LEA     SI,CS:EJECT      ; Code string to eject sheet
        CALL    SEND_STRING
;*********************|
;    restore and exit   |
;*********************|
EXIT_NEW05:
        POP     ES
        POP     DX
        POP     CX
        POP     BX
        POP     AX
        IRET
;
;************************* procedures **********************
SEND_PIX        PROC    NEAR
; Output character to printer using BIOS service number 0
; of INT 17H
        PUSH    AX              ; Save operational registers
        PUSH    CX
        PUSH    DX
        PUSH    ES
;
        MOV     AH,0            ; Service request number
        MOV     DX,0            ; Printer number
        INT     17H             ; BIOS service
        POP     ES
        POP     DX
        POP     CX
        POP     AX
        RET
SEND_PIX        ENDP
;****************************************************************
;
BYTE_ADD        PROC    NEAR
; Address computation from x and y graphic byte coordinates
; On entry:
;               CX = x coordinate of byte (range 0 to 79)
;               DX = y coordinate of byte (range 0 to 479)
; On exit:
;               BX = Byte offset into video buffer
;
        PUSH    AX              ; Save entry registers
```

```
              PUSH      CX
              PUSH      DX
;**********************|
;  calculate address   |
;**********************|
              PUSH      CX                ; Save x coordinate
              MOV       AX,DX             ; y coordinate to AX
              MOV       CX,80             ; Multiplier
              MUL       CX                ; AX = y times 80
              MOV       BX,AX             ; Free AX and hold in BX
              POP       AX                ; x coordinate from stack
              ADD       BX,AX             ; Offset into buffer to BX
;
              POP       DX                ; Restore entry registers
              POP       CX
              POP       AX
              RET
;
BYTE_ADD        ENDP
;****************************************************************
;
SEND_STRING     PROC      NEAR
; Send printer control string terminated in 00H
; On entry:
;         SI -> message
              PUSH      BX                ; Save operational registers
              PUSH      CX
              PUSH      DX
;
SEND_CHAR:
              MOV       AL,CS:[SI]        ; Get character
              CMP       AL,0              ; Test for message terminator ;
              JE        END_PCL           ; End of message
              MOV       DX,0              ; Printer port
              CALL      SEND_ONE          ; Print routine
              INC       SI                ; Bump message pointer
              JMP       SEND_CHAR
END_PCL:
              POP       DX                ; Restore registers
              POP       CX
              POP       BX
              RET
SEND_STRING     ENDP
;****************************************************************
;
SEND_ONE        PROC      NEAR
```

```
; Test printer status and send character when printer ready
; On entry:
;          AL = character to send
;          DX = printer port (valid range is 0 to 2)
;**********************|
;    initialize port   |
;**********************|
INIT_PORT:
        MOV     AH,1            ; Service request number
        INT     17H             ; Transfer to BIOS
        TEST    AH,80H          ; Test printer NOT-BUSY bit
        JNZ     NOT_BUSY
        TEST    AH,1            ; TIME-OUT bit
        JNZ     STATUS_ERROR
        JMP     INIT_PORT       ; Repeat initialization and
                                ; status check
;******************|
;    error exit    |
;******************|
STATUS_ERROR:
        STC                     ; Carry set to signal error
        RET
;*****************|
; send character  |
;*****************|
NOT_BUSY:
        MOV     AH,0            ; Function request code
        INT     17H             ; Transfer to BIOS
        CLC                     ; No error in send operation
        RET
SEND_ONE        ENDP
;
;*********************** data ***************************
;**********************|
;   PCL commands       |
;**********************|
RESET   DB      1BH,45H,00H
EJECT   DB      1BH,26H,6CH,30H,48H,00H
;
;**********************|
; graphics commands    |
;**********************|
START_GRAPH     DB      1BH,'*p600x400Y'  ; Set cursor at x = 600
                                          ; y = 400
                DB      1BH,'*t150R'     ; Set resolution 150 dots
                                          ; per inch
```

```
                DB       1BH,'*r1A',00   ; Set left margin to
                                         ; cursor
SECOND_GRAPH    DB       1BH,'*p600x1650Y'  ; Set cursor at x = 600
                                            ; y = 1650
                DB       1BH,'*t150R'    ; Set resolution 150 dots
                                         ; per inch
                DB       1BH,'*r1A',00   ; Set left margin to
                                         ; cursor
START_ROW       DB       1BH,'*b80W',00  ; Transfer one row
                                         ; of 80 graphic bytes
END_GRAPH       DB       1BH,'*rB',00H   ; End graphics mode
;*********************|
;     color filter    |
;*********************|
TEST_COLOR      DB       00000111B       ; Initialized for VGA 18
;                                ||||_____ Map 0 (BLUE)
;                                |||_____ Map 1 (GREEN)
;                                ||_____ Map 2 (RED)
;                                |_____ Map 3 (INTENSITY)
; Note: The TEST_COLOR mask is also used to set the Color Don't
; Care register
;*********************|
; reverse color switch |
;*********************|
NOT_SWITCH      DB       0       ; Switch to NOT bits read from video
                                 ; memory in second printing
;***************************************************************
;                       installation routine
;***************************************************************
; Installation operations:
;       1. Obtain vector for INT 05H and move to INT 60H
;       2. Set INT 05H vector to this routine
;       3. Protect TSR and exit
;***************************************************************
;*********************|
;     get INT 05H     |
;*********************|
INSTALL:
        MOV     AH,53           ; Service request code
        MOV     AL,05H          ; Code of vector desired
        INT     21H
; ES -> segment address of installed interrupt handler
; BX -> offset address of installed interrupt handler
;*********************|
;    store at INT 60H |
;*********************|
```

```
; Use MS DOS service number 37 to install the original vector
        MOV     AH,37           ; Service request code
        MOV     AL,60H          ; Destination vector
        PUSH    DS              ; Save operational DS
        PUSH    ES              ; ES to DS via stack
        POP     DS              ; to transfer segment base
        MOV     DX,BX           ; Offset of address to DX
        INT     21H             ; MS DOS service
        POP     DS              ; Restore DS
;**********************|
; set new INT 05H in   |
;     vector table     |
;**********************|
; Also uses DOS service 37 of INT 21H
        MOV     AH,37           ; Service request code
        MOV     AL,05H          ; Interrupt code
; Data segment = code segment in a .COM file
        MOV     DX,OFFSET HEX5_INT      ; Routine's offset
        INT     21H
;**********************|
; protect TSR and exit |
;**********************|
        STI
        MOV     DX,OFFSET CS:INSTALL
        INC     DX              ; One more byte
        INT     27H
CODE    ENDS
        END     ENTRY
```

5

Programming Serial Communications

5.0 The Serial Port in the IBM Microcomputers

The serial port on the IBM microcomputers is the system's main communications link to other computers or devices. The terms *serial port*, *RS-232-C port*, and *asynchronous port* are equivalent. They all designate the microcomputer's conventional serial interface. The term RS-232-C corresponds to a standard of the Electronics Industries Association (Recommended Standard 232, Revision C). The RS-232-C standard for serial communications was developed jointly by the Electronic Industries Association (EIA), the Bell Telephone System, and modem and computer manufacturers. The RS-232-C standard has achieved such widespread acceptance that its name is often used as a synonym for the serial port.

Serial communications encode data transmissions in a stream of consecutive electrical pulses. They can be visualized as a series of bits, marching in single file, from the sending device to the receiving device. This image contrasts with that of a parallel transmission, in which the bits march abreast. But not all the bits in the serial file are used to encode data. Some of them serve to synchronize the transmission. This allows the receiving terminal to detect the start of the transmission, identify the bits that encode data, and detect possible errors.

In addition, serial communications require that the sending and the receiving devices agree on the terms and conditions of the transmission operation. For example, both devices must agree on the speed at which the transmission is to take place, the number and function of the control bits, and the number of bits used to encode transmitted data. These terms, which must be accepted by both sender and receiver, are usually called the *communications protocol*.

5.0.1 The RS-232-C Serial Communications Standard

The Electronic Industries Association (EIA) has sponsored the development of several standards for serial communications, for instance, RS-232-C, mentioned above, and also RS-422, RS-423, and RS-449, which extend the transmission distances and speeds possible with the RS-232-C standard. However, the most used and simplest to implement of these standards is the RS-232-C voltage-level convention. According to the RS-232-C convention, a voltage more negative than -3 V is interpreted as a 1 bit and a voltage more positive than +3 V as a 0 bit. The following terms are frequently used in this protocol:

Baud rate. The speed of transmission, measured in bits per second. Serial communications require that the transmitter and the receiver clocks be synchronized to the same baud period. In IBM microcomputers the most frequently used baud rates are 110, 300, 600, 1200, 2400, 4800, 9600, and 19200 Bd.

Start bit. A low-order bit that serves to mark the start of a data transmission.

Character bits. A group of 5, 6, 7, or 8 bits used to encode the data character transmitted. In the RS-232-C protocol, the least significant data bit is always the first one transmitted.

Parity bit. This optional bit is used in detecting transmission errors. If the protocol specifies *even parity*, the transmitter sets or clears the parity bit so as to make the sum of the character's 1 bits and the parity bit an even number. If the protocol specifies *odd parity*, then the parity bit is used to make the sum of 1 bits an odd number. If the protocol is set to *parity none*, this bit is not present. Parity check is enabled if the setting is odd or even. In this case the receiver notifies the transmitter of a parity error by setting an error flag in a special register.

Stop bits. The number of stop bits are determined in the protocol as 1, 1.5, or 2 bits. The stop bit ensures that the receiver will have enough time to make ready for the next character.

5.0.2 Implementations of the Serial Port

The serial port in the IBM microcomputers can either be contained in an optional adapter card or be part of the standard system hardware. On the IBM Personal Computer and PC XT, the serial port is furnished as an optional adapter card called the *Asynchronous Communications Adapter*. A similar card, termed the *Serial/Parallel Adapter*, is used on the IBM PC AT. Since the introduction of the Personal System/2 IBM furnishes the serial port as a standard component.

An IBM microcomputer can be equipped with more than one serial port. This is true for systems that implement the serial port in an adapter card or for those in which the port is part of the motherboard hardware. BIOS uses a 0-based designation to identify the various possible serial ports in a system. The BIOS system refers to the first serial port is port number 0, the second one as port number 1, and so forth. On the other hand, in MS DOS designations for the serial port, the first one is COM1 (communications port number 1), the second one is COM2, and so on. The different bases for the designation of the serial ports have occasionally been the source of programming errors.

5.1 Communications Programming

The problems often encountered in programming the serial port are related to the particular characteristics of the asynchronous methods of communication. In fact, the term *asynchronous* is used in this sense to indicate that there is no synchronization in the data transmission. This means that, if the received character is not removed fast enough from the corresponding holding register, the next character transmitted will overwrite and destroy the old one. The possibility for this type of error depends on the speed of the transmission and the time intervals during which the receiver does not monitor the data register.

5.1.1 Polling Techniques

In communications terminology the word *polling* is used in regard to programming techniques in which the receiving device checks the status of the transmission line with a given frequency. For polling to be effective, this frequency must be sufficiently short to ensure that the transmitting device will not send a new character before the previous one has been removed by the receiver. Therefore, the faster the baud rate, the more frequently the line must be polled in order to prevent character losses.

Practically, data losses in polled communications are almost always traced to the receiving terminal. The situation can be summarized as follows: if the software allows the receiver to frequently monitor the state of the line, serial data transmission can safely take place at high speeds. On the other hand, the risk of data loss increases proportionally to the duration of the time periods during which the receiver ignores the line, usually to perform data manipulations.

For example, a program that stores the received data bit in a memory buffer leaves the line unattended for shorter periods than does a program that must display the character on the video screen. Consider that screen display routines usually have to assume the tasks of managing the end of screen lines and scrolling the display when it is full. In a standard alpha mode, an IBM microcomputer screen consists of 2000 characters and 2000 corresponding attributes. To make space at the bottom of the screen for a new line (scrolling the screen) requires moving 1920 character bytes and 1920 attributes to new screen positions. Consequently, programs that scroll the screen during serial reception must use the slowest baud rates in order to prevent character losses.

In conclusion, at sufficiently slow baud rates, it is often possible to design polled communications routines that work satisfactorily. On the other hand, software that must execute at the higher baud rates or that perform more elaborate processing require other means of synchronization. Another limitation in the use of polling techniques is that the receiver must be an *intelligent* device. Polling is not possible when programming printers or other *dumb* terminals.

5.1.2 Designed Synchronization

The use of handshake techniques enable the receiver to suspend the transmission while it is performing other functions. For example, a serial printer can use handshake signals to force the computer into a wait state while the last character received is mechanically transferred onto the sheet of paper. In this case, typical operation consists in the printer changing the state of a physical communications line to signal a wait period to the sending device.

This form of handshaking, usually called *hardware handshaking*, is based on electronic control signals. A simple protocol can be established using the signals known as *data set ready* (DSR) and *data terminal ready* (DTR). For example, the serial printer will raise the DTR line to inform the computer that it is ready to receive. If the printer wants to suspend transmission, it will lower DTR to a negative voltage. Two other lines, termed *clear-to-send* (CTS) and *request-to-send* (RQS), can also be used for this purpose, or as a subsidiary handshake.

5.1.3 Software Handshake

But often serial devices are connected using such simple wiring that the hardware control lines are not present. For example, the null modem wiring permits connection of two IBM computers through the serial port using only the transmit data line, the receive data line, and a common ground. This three-wire setup does not support a hardware handshake, but several software handshake protocols have been developed to allow serial communications when the standard RS-232-C control signals are not available.

In the XON/XOFF software handshake convention, the character 13H, called XOFF, is used to signal the transmitting device to stop sending characters and the character 17H, called XON, to signal that transmission can resume. This method, based on inserting control codes in the data stream, works well if the control characters will not be used for other purposes. For instance, in the ASCII encoding the values smaller than 20H are used for control codes, since the alphanumeric character codes are all in the range 20H to 7FH.

Therefore, programs that transmit pure ASCII data can implement a software handshake using the XON/XOFF convention. However, communications software must often transmit binary data, such as program code or graphic images, which can contain all possible bit combinations. In this case it is not possible to include control codes in the transmission stream since the receiver has no way of differentiating these codes from other data items. Nevertheless, it is usually possible to develop other serial transmission schemes that allow handshaking without embedding control characters in the data stream.

Consider a program to transmit binary data stored in a disk file. In this case the sending routine can group the data in discrete units — say, of 128 bytes — and use conventional controls to inform the receiver that one of such data packages is ready for transmission. Once the receiver acknowledges the control codes and certifies that it is ready to receive, the 128-byte data package is sent as pure binary data. The receiver has all the time necessary to processes or store the data package because the transmitter will not send the next package until its synchronization codes are acknowledged. The program named SERCOM, presented later in this chapter, uses a similar synchronization method to send and receive MS DOS disk files. The XMODEM convention, developed in 1977, provides a file transfer protocol, with handshaking. The XMODEM protocol is discussed in Section 5.3.2.

5.1.4 Using Communications Interrupts

Another way to synchronize transmitter and receiver during data communications is by using the interrupt facilities of IBM microcomputers. The simplest approach is to have the Universal Asynchronous Receiver and Transmitter (UART) chip generate a hardware interrupt detectable by the CPU. The system can be configured so that this interrupt is generated, by the serial communications hardware, whenever a data item is received. The operation can be visualized as giving the microprocessor a "tap on the shoulder" to let it know that a data byte was acquired. The CPU then interrupts whatever it is doing long enough to remove this byte from the receiver data register and place it in a safe storage location, where it will not be destroyed by the next reception.

Communications programs that use hardware interrupts require elaborate programming; however, these complications are justified if the software has minimum performance requirements. The reader should consider that, without some form of data synchronization, IBM microcomputer communications cannot operate satisfactorily at speeds in excess of 1200 Bd. The reasons for the data losses have been explained starting in Section 5.1. On the other hand, the use of hardware interrupts allows greater freedom of operation to both the receiver and the transmitter, as well as the use of higher baud rates than programs based on polling or handshaking. Incidentally, all serial communications controllers used in the IBM microcomputers support hardware interrupts.

The SERCOM program illustrates both software handshake and interrupt-driven communications techniques. The code contains routines to set up and enable the received data available interrupt and to install an interrupt handler that will process, as a background task, the characters received on the serial communications line. This mode of operation is used while SERCOM is in the *terminal mode*. It allows the SERCOM program to monitor the keyboard and the communications line simultaneously, transmitting all characters typed by the user and displaying those received through the serial line. SERCOM can also be used to transmit binary and ASCII files through the serial port. In this application data package techniques are more convenient than interrupts. Therefore, SERCOM disables the communications interrupt while in the file transfer mode and uses a simple handshaking scheme based on 128-byte data packages.

5.1.5 The Communications Interrupt Service Routine

One of the most important elements of an interrupt-driven communications program is the routine to which execution is transferred when the communications interrupt occurs. For this to happen, the address of the routine must first be placed in the corresponding interrupt vector. A typical service routine performs the following operations:

1. The contents of all registers used by the service routine are pushed on the stack so that they can be preserved for the interrupted code.

2. The service routine executes the required processing.

3. An end-of-interrupt is signaled to the 8259 interrupt controller so that other interrupts can take place.

4. The saved registers are restored from the stack.

5. Execution is returned to the interrupted program.

It is interesting to note that, in some service routines, the programmer may want to access data in the program's data space. However, since there is no way of predicting when execution will be transferred to its code, an interrupt service routine can make no assumptions regarding the state of the CPU registers. For this reason, in order to access local data items, the code must make sure that the data segment contains the correct base. The following instructions can be used to perform this simple operation:

```
; This fragment assumes that the name DATA was used in defining
; the program's data segment
        MOV     DX,DATA         ; Program's name for data segment
        MOV     DS,AX           ; to the DS register
        ASSUME  DS:DATA         ; Assembler directive
```

5.1.6 Circular Buffers

Interrupt-driven programs, whether performing serial communications or other operations, often use a data structure called a *circular buffer*. This arrangement is also called a *first-in-first-out* (FIFO) buffer. This expression accurately describes the order in which the data is received and retrieved in this type of structure. Notice that the concept contrasts with that of a conventional stack, in which the *last* item stored is the first one retrieved, which is why a stack is often described as a *last-in-first-out* (LIFO) structure.

A typical circular buffer is a delimited memory area that can be accessed by two pointers: the *buffer head*, which marks the position of the last item stored in the buffer, and the *buffer tail*, which marks the position of the last item retrieved. When either pointer reaches the end of the buffer, the software must reset it to the buffer start. For this reason, a circular buffer is sometimes called a *wraparound buffer*.

The SERCOM program uses a 20-byte circular buffer named CIRC_BUF. The buffer pointers are the variables named DATA_IN and DATA_OUT. These items are word-size in order to simplify arithmetic operations with the buffer pointers. The interrupt service routine manages the DATA_IN pointer and uses this pointer to store the data received during the communications interrupt. The code of the main program tests the value of the buffer pointers (DATA_IN and DATA_OUT) to determine whether there is new data in the buffer. If there is, the DATA_OUT pointer indicates the offset of the data item to be removed. The following pointer arithmetic is derived from the above concepts and summarizes pointer operations:

1. If DATA_IN = DATA_OUT, no new characters have been received and no display or other manipulation is required.

2. If either buffer pointer, DATA_IN or DATA_OUT, reaches the value of 20, it must be reset to zero. This action makes the pointer wrap around to the start of the circular buffer.

3. If DATA_OUT is not equal to DATA_IN, the new characters in the buffer must be removed.

The size of the buffer is determined by the maximum lag expected between pointers. For the SERCOM program a 20-byte circular buffer proved to be sufficient. Programs that perform more elaborate manipulations may require larger buffers. Figure 5.1 shows a circular buffer and its pointers in the process of receiving and retrieving a message. Although, in theory, it is possible to anticipate the required size for a circular buffer, the calculations could be quite elaborate.

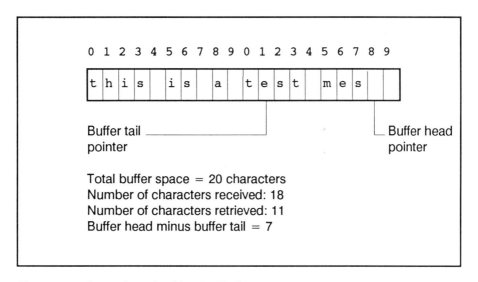

Figure 5.1. *Operation of a Circular Buffer*

5.2 Programming Serial Port Hardware

The serial port is implemented differently in the various models of IBM microcomputers. In general, the designers of the PC line considered serial port hardware as an optional attachment. The exception is the PCjr, which comes equipped with a serial port. In the PS/2 line all models include serial port hardware. In all systems the IBM serial port follows the EIA RS-232-C standard, but there are variations in the connectors.

The basic electronic component of the serial port is an integrated circuit communications controller. The adapters of the PC line, as well as the PCjr and Models 25 and 30 of the PS/2 line, use the 8250 UART or equivalent. The PC AT serial hardware is equipped with the NS-16450 chip; and the Micro Channel models of the PS/2 line, with the NS-16550. However, all these controllers have similar design and are programmed in a very similar manner.

The operation of the serial communications controller can be summarized as follows:

1. The controller converts an 8-bit data value, placed by the processor in the system's output port, into a serial bit stream formatted according to the RS-232-C protocol.

2. During this phase of its operation, the controller inserts the necessary start, stop, and parity bits, according to the protocol parameters presently installed.

3. The controller can also decode an incoming bit stream and place the data byte in the adapter's input port. The CPU can read data at this port.

4. During reception, the controller uses the start, stop, and parity bits to synchronize the transmission, to identify the data bits, and to check for errors.

In the terminology of serial communications, if a device is capable of simultaneously transmitting and receiving data it is said to operate in *full-duplex* mode. If the send and receive functions must take place consecutively, the device is said to operate in *half-duplex* mode. The serial communications controllers used in the IBM microcomputers are all capable of full duplex operation. IBM systems allow the use of more than one serial communications device per machine.

To the programmer, the 8250 UART, the NS-16450, and the NS-16550 appear as 10 internal registers which can be accessed by the CPU through the corresponding ports. In all IBM microcomputers, except the PCjr, the first serial communications controller installed in a system is mapped to ports 3F8H to 3FEH. In this case the controller is said to be configured as communications port number 1, or COM1. The second controller installed, which is frequently a modem device (see Chapter 6), is mapped to ports 2F8H to 2FEH. The second serial port is designated as COM2. In any case, the BIOS initialization routines store the base address of the first serial port (COM1) at memory locations 400H in the BIOS data area. If additional ports are present, their base addresses are stored at memory locations 402H, 404H, and 406H. The SERCOM program obtains the port address from the BIOS storage and copies it into the variable CARD_BASE, where it can be readily accessed.

5.2.1 Preparing for Interrupt-Driven Communications

Programs that use hardware interrupts in communications must go through several preparatory steps in order to configure various electronic components for this type of operation. First, the software must include a service routine that will execute when the interrupt occurs. The design of this routine, as with any other interrupt handler, must take into account that it suspends the execution of the main program and other handlers. For this reason the interrupt handler must be streamlined so as to execute its functions as rapidly as possible. The interrupt handler for the SERCOM program can be found at the label RS232_INT. This routine is located toward the end of the program. This interrupt handler performs the following operations:

1. Saves the interrupted program's register contents on the stack

2. Retrieves the data byte from the receiver data register and stores it in a circular buffer; in case of error the handler replaces the bad character with an inverted question mark

3. Bumps the input pointer (buffer head) and performs the wraparound function if necessary

4. Signals the end-of-interrupt to the interrupt controller

5. Restores the registers of the interrupted program and returns

The actual preparations for interrupt operation are performed by the procedure named COMM_ON of the SERCOM program. This routine executes the following operations:

1. Disables interrupts while changing the interrupt structure so as to prevent clashes

2. Installs the interrupt handler at the corresponding vector. In all IBM microcomputers except the PCjr, the communications interrupt is linked to hardware interrupt line IRQ4, which is vectored through INT 0BH. The PCjr uses IRQ3, vectored through INT 0CH. The routine takes this difference into account.

3. Enables the output 2 signal by setting bit 3 of the modem control register. The DTR and RTS bits are also set.

4. Enables the DATA READY signal for communications interrupts by setting bit 0 of the interrupt enable register.

5. Configures the interrupt mask register within the 8259 interrupt controller by resetting the bits for interrupt lines IRQ3 and IRQ4. This mask is accessed through port 21H.

6. Reenables interrupts.

5.2.2 Disabling Interrupt Communications

The process of disabling communications interrupt consists approximately of the reverse operations used in enabling them (see Section 5.2.1). The COMM_OFF procedure in the SETCOM program disables interrupt-driven communications and enables the normal mode by executing the following steps:

1. Disables interrupts while changing the interrupt structure so as to avoid clashes.

2. Disables the communications interrupt by setting the control bits for the IRQ3 and IRQ4 lines in the interrupt mask register.

3. Restores the original vector for the BIOS handler of the communications interrupt. The address of the original service routine was saved, in the data variables O_INT_OFF and O_INT_SEG, during initialization.

4. Disables the output 2 signal by clearing bit 3 of the modem control register. The DTR and RTS bits of the modem control register are left set so that normal handshake can take place.

5. Reenables interrupts.

Once the COMM_OFF routine executes the system is reset for noninterrupt communications.

5.3 Transmission Error Detection

A valid measure of the quality of a software product is the effectiveness and sophistication of its error handling techniques. Poorly designed programs often hang up or crash on the occurrence of an unforeseen error. Since communications errors are a fact of computing, it is important to include error-checking logic into this type of software. A communications or data transmission program with low reliability is, generally, little more than useless.

5.3.1 Parity Check

Many methods of error detection have been devised in order to improve the reliability of the data received through the communications line. All standard communications protocols contain some form of error control. We have seen in Section 5.0.1 that the RS-232-C standard implements a parity bit with three possible settings. When parity is set to odd or even, this bit is used by the hardware as a rough check for the validity of each transmitted character. If the receiver finds a parity error during transmission, it will immediately set a flag in a special register. This register can be read, at intervals, by the processor to test for error. The parity check is a useful error control method which can be used at the level of each transmitted character. However, the statistical reliability of a parity check is relatively low when used to validate the integrity of a group of characters, a message, or the transmission of an entire file.

5.3.2 The CRC and Checksum Methods

Other methods of error detection are based on performing arithmetic operations on the binary values of the characters contained in groups of a predetermined size. These operations are performed independently by the sender and by the receiver and the resulting values are compared. A mismatch is a sure sign of a transmission error. One powerful technique, called the *cycle redundancy check* (CRC), consists of adding the binary values of all the characters in a block, dividing this sum by a predetermined number, and transmitting the remainder of this division, at the end of the block, as a check value. The same calculations are performed by the receiver, which compares its own CRC remainder with the one received from the sender. If the CRC characters do not match, the block will be retransmitted. A simpler method, sometimes called a *checksum*, is based on adding the binary values of the characters transmitted, often letting the sum overflow, and using a given number of digits of this sum as a check value.

One complication that arises in the design of an error-detection scheme is that the protocol must include specific acknowledgment codes with which the receiver notifies the sender of the accuracy or inaccuracy of the transmission. An error in the transmission of an acknowledgment code can compound the possibility of transmission errors. Consequently, it is possible that an elaborate and sophisticated CRC check will fail because of a transmission error in the acknowledgment code.

A method often used is to have the sender wait for a given time period for the acknowledgment code. If the code is not received, the block is retransmitted. To prevent confusion regarding which block has not been correctly received the blocks are numbered sequentially. If the receiver gets two blocks with the same sequence number, it knows that the block is a retransmission and discards the previous one.

The original version of the XMODEM protocol, mentioned in Section 5.1.3, used a 1-byte arithmetic sum as a check value. Newer versions of XMODEM use a 2-byte CRC check value, which considerably increases transmission accuracy. The XMODEM code 15H, called a *negative acknowledge* or *NAK*, is used by the receiver to signal the sender that data transmission can begin. On the reception of this handshake code, the sender can transmit one 132-byte block (see Figure 5.2). The code 06H, called *acknowledge*, or *ACK*, is issued by the receiver to acknowledge each block received correctly. If the receiver detects errors, it uses the code 15H (NAK) to request from the transmitter to resend the block. The transmission ends with the code 04H, called the *end of transmission*.

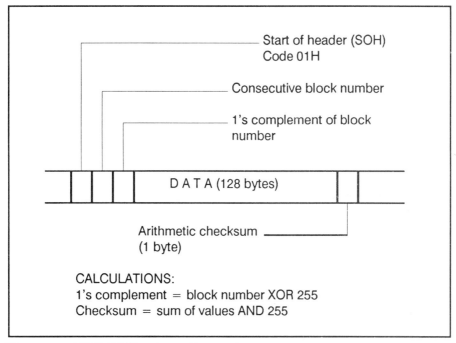

Figure 5.2. *MODEM Checksum Protocol*

The SERCOM program uses unconventional handshake and error-detection methods designed to illustrate the basic principles involved while keeping complications to a minimum. In this program the sender uses the code 01H to signal the transmission of a filename, the code 02H to signal the start of a 128-byte block, and the code 03H to close a file. The receiver uses the letter "R" to acknowledge any of the above operations. The validity of the data is checked with a byte-size checksum that is transmitted at the end of each 128-byte clock. If a checksum error is detected, the receiver sets an error switch, which is read and reported at the end of the transmission, but no resend operation is provided. This method of handshaking and error detection is simpler than any of those described above, but the resulting statistical reliability in the integrity of the transmitted data is also much lower.

5.4 The SERCOM Program

```
;*******************************************************************
;*******************************************************************
;                             SERCOM.ASM
;*******************************************************************
;*******************************************************************
;
; RS-232-C serial communications program
; Program operation:
; SERCOM is interrupt-driven while executing in the terminal mode
; but transmits and receives online while performing disk file
; transfers. The procedure named COMM_ON enables the interrupt-
; driven communications mode and the procedure named COMM_OFF
; disables interrupt communications and sets the online mode
;
; Program functions:
; 1. Serve as a terminal program displaying all characters
;    received through the RS-232-C line and sending all
;    characters typed at the keyboard
; 2. Set the serial communications protocol according to the
;    user's input
; 3. Display the installed serial protocol
; 4. Transmit a disk file through the RS-232-C line
; 5. Receive a disk file through the RS-232-C line
;
;*******************************************************************
;                     procedures in SOLUTION.LIB
;*******************************************************************
EXTRN     DOS_STRING_OUT: FAR
EXTRN     BIO_TTY:        FAR
EXTRN     KBR_FLUSH:      FAR
EXTRN     CLOSE_FILE:     FAR
EXTRN     OPEN_FILE:      FAR
EXTRN     GET_FIRST:      FAR
EXTRN     GET_NEXT:       FAR
EXTRN     KBR_WAIT:       FAR
EXTRN     KBR_STATUS:     FAR
EXTRN     SET_PROTOCOL:   FAR
INCLUDELIB SOLUTION
```

```
;**************************** stack **************************
STACK    SEGMENT stack

                DB      0400H DUP ('?'); Default stack is 1K
STACK_TOP       EQU     THIS BYTE
;
STACK    ENDS
;**************************** data **************************
DATA     SEGMENT
;
; MESSAGES :
MENU_MS DB      '      ** SERCOM Program **',0DH,0AH
        DB      ' <F1> to redisplay this MENU',0DH,0AH
        DB      ' <F2> to set communications protocol',0DH,0AH
        DB      ' <F3> to display protocol installed',0DH,0AH
        DB      ' <F4> to transmit a file',0AH,0DH
        DB      ' <F5> to receive a file',0AH,0DH
        DB      ' <F9> to exit the SERCOM program',0DH,0AH
        DB      ' All other characters typed are transmitted'
        DB      0DH,0AH
        DB      ' Characters received are displayed',0DH,0AH
        DB      0DH,0AH,'$'
;
;*********************|
; serial protocol data |
;*********************|
;
PROT_MS DB      ' * Installed communications protocol *',0DH,0AH
        DB      '       Baud rate: '
BAUD%   DB      '4800',0DH,0AH
        DB      '       Parity: '
PAR%    DB      'even',0DH,0AH
        DB      '       Stop bits: '
STOP%   DB      '1',0DH,0AH
        DB      '       Word length: '
WORD%   DB      '8',0DH,0AH,0AH,'$'
;
BAUD$$  DB      '110 150 300 600 1200240048009600'
PAR$$   DB      'odd noneeven'
;
BAUD_MENU       DB      0DH,0AH,' ** New communications '
        DB      'parameters input **',0DH,0AH
        DB      ' Baud rates:',0DH,0AH
        DB      ' 1 = 110',0DH,0AH
        DB      ' 2 = 150',0DH,0AH
        DB      ' 3 = 300',0DH,0AH
```

```
        DB         ' 4 = 600',0DH,0AH
        DB         ' 5 = 1200',0DH,0AH
        DB         ' 6 = 2400',0DH,0AH
        DB         ' 7 = 4800',0DH,0AH
        DB         ' 8 = 9600 (4800 baud in PCjr)',0DH,0AH
        DB         '          Select: $'
;
PAR_MENU        DB         0DH,0AH,' Parity:',0DH,0AH
        DB         ' 1 = odd',0DH,0AH
        DB         ' 2 = none',0DH,0AH
        DB         ' 3 = even',0DH,0AH
        DB         '          Select: $'
;
STOP_MENU       DB         0DH,0AH,' Stop bits:',0DH,0AH
        DB         ' 1 = 1 stop bit',0DH,0AH
        DB         ' 2 = 2 stop bits',0DH,0AH
        DB         '          Select: $'
;
WORD_MENU       DB         0DH,0AH,' Word length:',0DH,0AH
        DB         ' 1 = 7 bits',0DH,0AH
        DB         ' 2 = 8 bits',0DH,0AH
        DB         '          Select: $'
;
;********************|
;  protocol variables  |
;********************|
BAUD_BYTE       DB         0
PARITY_BYTE     DB         0
STOP_BYTE       DB         0
WORDLEN_BYTE    DB         0
;
;********************|
; program parameters   |
;    and buffers       |
;********************|
CARD_BASE       DW         03F8H   ; Address of RS-232-C card
                                   ; for all hardware types except
                                   ; PCjr (PCjr = 02F8H)
;
; Communications interrupt number:
;                    PCjr ........ IRQ3 ........ 0BH
;            All others ......... IRQ4 ........ 0CH

INT_NUM DB      0CH        ; Offset in BIOS table as follows:
                           ; PC & PS/2- IRQ4 - 0CH * 4 = 30H
                           ; PCjr       IRQ3 - 0BH * 4 = 2CH
```

```
SETUP_BYTE      DB      0BBH     ; Default value
;
; Original interrupt vector address to restore on exit
O_INT_SEG       DW      0000H    ; Segment
O_INT_OFF       DW      0000H    ; Offset
;
; CIRCULAR BUFFER AND POINTERS:
CIRC_BUF        DB      20 DUP (00H)      ;Circular buffer
                DW      0
DATA_IN         DW      0        ; Input pointer
DATA_OUT        DW      0        ; Output pointer
;
;*********************|
;  data area for disk |
;      operations     |
;*********************|
MESS_2   DB        'Filename (or press Enter): $'
;
MESS_3   DB        13,13,10
         DB        'FILE SEND mode ',13,10
         DB        '$'
;
MESS_4   DB        13,13,10
         DB        'FILE RECEIVE mode',13,10
         DB        'Press any key to change mode',13,10,'$'
;
MESS_5   DB        13,10,'FILE RECEIVED - CHECKSUM OK -'
         DB        13,10,'$'
;
MESS_6   DB        13,10,'TERMINATED BY USER',13,13,10,'$'
;
MESS_7   DB        13,10,'RECEIVING FILE: $'
;
MESS_8   DB        13,10,'FILE(S) TRANSMITTED',13,13,10,'$'
;
MESS_9   DB        13,10,'    ***** CHECKSUM ERROR *****'
         DB        13,13,10,'$'
;
MESS_1310       DB      13,13,10,'$'
;
;
;*********************|
;    disk data areas  |
;*********************|
FILE_IN         DB      63       ; Maximum buffered input
IN_COUNT        DB      0        ; Actual input received
```

```
F_NAME          DB      64 DUP (00H)
HANDLE_1        DW      0          ; File handle
;
F_BUFFER        DB      129 DUP (00H)
;
; Scratchpad DTA to be used by DOS in the search for matching
; filenames for global characters
DTA_BUFFER      DB      30 DUP (00H)
NEXT_NAME       DB      13 DUP (00H)
                DB      85 DUP (00H)
;
CHK_ERR         DB      0          ; Checksum error control
;
;********************|
; disk error messages |
;********************|
ERMES_1         DB      'ERROR - Path or file not found ..'
                DB      13,13,10,'$'
ERMES_2         DB      'ERROR - Cannot write sector .....'
                DB      13,13,10,'$'
ERMES_3         DB      'ERROR - Cannot open for read ....'
                DB      13,13,10,'$'
ERMES_4         DB      'ERROR - Cannot open for write ...'
                DB      13,13,10,'$'
;********************|
; general transmission |
;         error        |
;********************|
ERR1_MS         DB      0DH,0AH,'  *** cannot transmit *** '
                DB      13,13,10,'$'
;
DATA    ENDS
;
;*********************** code ***************************
CODE    SEGMENT
        ASSUME  CS:CODE
;
START:
; Establish addressability of the program's data segment
        MOV     AX,DATA
        MOV     DS,AX
        ASSUME  DS:DATA
; Initialize stack. Note that this instruction is necessary for
; compatibility with non-Microsoft assemblers
        LEA     SP,SS:STACK_TOP ; Stack pointer to top of stack
; Set extra segment to data
```

```
            MOV       ES,AX
            ASSUME    ES:DATA
;*********************|
; display program menu |
;*********************|
            MOV       DX,OFFSET MENU_MS        ; Message
            CALL      DOS_STRING_OUT
;*********************|
; get machine type code|
;*********************|
; Examine byte at F000:FFFE
            PUSH      DS                 ; Save operation segment
            MOV       DX,0F000H
            MOV       DS,DX
            MOV       AL,BYTE PTR DS:[0FFFEH] ; Machine type code to AL
;*********************|
; get serial port base |
;      address         |
;*********************|
; Get address of RS-232-C card from BIOS data area
            MOV       DX,0             ; BIOS data area segment
            MOV       DS,DX            ; Data segment to BIOS area
            MOV       CX,DS:0400H      ; Offset of card 1
            POP       DS                       ; Restore program DS
            MOV       CARD_BASE,CX     ; Store in program's DATA
;*********************|
;  determine interrupt |
;       number         |
;*********************|
;       0CH...........IRQ3 .......... PCjr
;       0BH ..........IRQ4 .......... other PC and PS/2 hardware
            CMP       AL,0FDH          ; Code for PCjr
            JNE       SET_ADDRESS
            MOV       INT_NUM,0BH      ; Interrupt number for PCjr
;*********************|
;  get communications  |
;   interrupt vector    |
;*********************|
; Use MS DOS service number 53, INT 21H
SET_ADDRESS:
            MOV       AH,53            ; DOS service request number
            MOV       AL,INT_NUM       ; Interrupt number (0BH or 0CH)
            INT       21H
;*********************|
;  save old interrupt  |
;*********************|
```

```
; ES:BX = segment/offset of original handler
        MOV     O_INT_SEG,ES    ; Save segment
        MOV     O_INT_OFF,BX    ; and offset
;**********************|
;  set communications  |
;  protocol (default)  |
;**********************|
; Default protocol:
; Bit mask: 110xxxxx ...... Baud = 4800
;           xxx11xxx ...... Parity = even
;           xxxxx0xx ...... Stop bits = 1
;           xxxxxx11 ...... Word length = 8
;           10111011
;
        MOV     AL,11011011B    ; Bit mask for default protocol
        MOV     AH,0            ; BIOS service request number
        MOV     DX,0            ; COM1 in all hardware types
        INT     14H             ; BIOS service request
;**********************|
;      set DTA         |
;**********************|
; Set scratchpad DTA inside the program's data area for
; processing filenames with the global characters '?' and '*'
        MOV     AH,26           ; DOS service request number
                                ; to set DTA address
        MOV     DX,OFFSET DTA_BUFFER
        INT     21H
;**********************|
;  initialize serial   |
;    communications    |
;**********************|
        CALL    COMM_ON         ; Interrupt-driven communications
                                ; on
        CALL    KBR_FLUSH       ; Flush keyboard buffer
;
;*****************************************************************
;            command processing and character echo
;*****************************************************************
MONITOR:
        CALL    KBR_STATUS      ; Library procedure for keyboard
                                ; status
        JNC     SER_IMP         ; Nothing in keyboard buffer
        JMP     CHAR_TYPED      ; Character in keyboard buffer
;**********************|
;      delay           |
;**********************|
```

```
; Allow interrupt to occur
SER_IMP:
        STI                          ; Interrupts on
        MOV     CX,50
DELAY:  NOP
        NOP
        LOOP    DELAY
;*********************|
;  new data received? |
;*********************|
        CLI                          ; Interrupts off while reading
                                     ; pointer
        MOV     BX,DATA_OUT          ; Compare pointers
        CMP     BX,DATA_IN
        JNE     NEW_DATA             ; New data items
        STI                          ; Interrupts on
        JMP     MONITOR              ; Repeat cycle
;*********************|
;  new data in buffer |
;*********************|
CHAR_TYPED:
        MOV     AH,0                 ; Code for read keyboard
                                     ; character
        INT     16H                  ; BIOS service
;
; Test for <F1>, <F2>, <F3>  and <F9> keys
        CMP     AX,3B00H             ; <F1>
        JNE     TEST_F2
        JMP     SHOW_MENU            ; <F1> key pressed
TEST_F2:
        CMP     AX,3C00H             ; <F2>
        JNE     TEST_F3
        JMP     SET_NEW_PROT         ; <F2> key pressed
TEST_F3:
        CMP     AX,3D00H             ; <F3>
        JNE     TEST_F4
        JMP     SHOW_PROTOCOL        ; <F3> key pressed
TEST_F4:
        CMP     AX,3E00H             ; <F4>
        JNE     TEST_F5
        JMP     SEND_FILE            ; <F4> key pressed
TEST_F5:
        CMP     AX,3F00H             ; <F5>
        JNE     TEST_F9
        JMP     RECEIVE_FILE         ; <F5> key pressed
TEST_F9:
```

```
        CMP        AX,4300H          ; <F9>
        JE         DOS_EXIT          ; Exit if <F9> key
; If typed character is not a program command then display it
; and transmit it through the serial line
        JMP        SHOW_AND_SEND
;****************|
;     exit       |
;****************|
DOS_EXIT:
; Communications interrupts OFF
        CALL       COMM_OFF
; Exit
        MOV        AH,76             ; DOS service request number
        MOV        AL,0              ; No return code
        INT        21H               ; Exit to DOS
;
;******************************************************************
;                    terminal mode operations
;                    echo data sent and received
;******************************************************************
;*********************|
;  new data in buffer |
;*********************|
NEW_DATA:
        LEA        SI,CIRC_BUF       ; Circular buffer address
        MOV        BX,DATA_OUT       ; Output pointer
        ADD        SI,BX             ; Buffer start + displacement
        MOV        AL,BYTE PTR [SI]
                                     ; Get character
; Update output pointer
        INC        BX                ; Bump
        CMP        BX,20             ; Pointer overflows buffer ?
        JNE        OK_OUT_PTR
        MOV        BX,0              ; Reset to start of buffer
;
OK_OUT_PTR:
        MOV        DATA_OUT,BX       ; Update
; Display byte taken from buffer
        STI
        CALL       TTY
        JMP        MONITOR
;
;*********************|
;     data to send    |
;*********************|
SHOW_AND_SEND:
```

```
; Wait loop for transmitter holding register empty
        MOV     CX,2000         ; Prime wait counter
        PUSH    AX              ; Save character to transmit
THRE_WAIT:
        MOV     DX,CARD_BASE
        ADD     DX,5            ; Line status register
        IN      AL,DX           ; Get byte at port
        JMP     SHORT $+2       ; I/O delay
        TEST    AL,20H          ; THRE bit set ?
        JNZ     OK_2_SEND
        LOOP    THRE_WAIT
; Wait period timed out. Display error message and exit
        POP     AX              ; Restore stack
        MOV     DX,OFFSET ERR1_MS
        CALL    DOS_STRING_OUT  ; Error to screen
        CALL    COMM_ON         ; Interrupt communications on
        JMP     MONITOR
OK_2_SEND:
        POP     AX              ; Retrieve byte
; Place in transmitter holding register to send
        MOV     DX,CARD_BASE    ; THR register
        OUT     DX,AL           ; Send
        JMP     SHORT $+2       ; I/O delay
; Display character
        CALL    TTY
        JMP     MONITOR
;
;****************************************************************
;                       command execution
;****************************************************************
;******************************|
; <F1> command - redisplay MENU |
;******************************|
SHOW_MENU:
        MOV     DX,OFFSET MENU_MS
        CALL    DOS_STRING_OUT  ; Display message routine
        JMP     MONITOR
;
;******************************|
; <F2> command - set new protocol|
;******************************|
SET_NEW_PROT:
; The individual submenus for the selection of BAUD RATE, PARITY,
; STOP BITS, and WORD LENGTH are posted. The value entered is
; moved to the variables and later to the registers required by
; the SET_PROTOCOL procedure in the OUTPUT.ASM module of
```

```
; SOLUTION.LIB
; Selected values are also inserted into the parameters area
; for display.
;
; Interrupts off while resetting protocol
        CALL    COMM_OFF
;**********************|
;   select baud rate   |
;**********************|
BAUD_RATES:
        MOV     DX,OFFSET BAUD_MENU
        CALL    DOS_STRING_OUT
        CALL    KBR_WAIT            ; Get single key input in AL
; Display input at cursor
        CALL    TTY
; Valid range is "1" to "8"
        CMP     AL,'1'             ; Carry set if less than 1
        JC      BAUD_RATES         ; Repeat selection
        CMP     AL,'9'             ; No carry if larger than 8
        JNC     BAUD_RATES
; Input is in valid range.
        SUB     AL,30H             ; ASCII to binary
        MOV     BAUD_BYTE,AL       ; Store baud rate code
; Select 4-byte baud rate message and place in protocol message
; area for display of installed parameters
; Multiply binary code by 4 to compute displacement into table
        SUB     AL,1               ; Adjust
        MOV     CL,4
        MUL     CL        ; AL is now in range 0 to 28 (offset)
        MOV     SI,OFFSET BAUD$$
                                   ; SI -> baud rates message
        MOV     AH,0               ; For addition of AL displacement
        ADD     SI,AX              ; SI -> 4 ASCII characters of
                                   ; baud rate message
; Move baud rate message into protocol display area
        MOV     DI,OFFSET BAUD%
                                   ; Destination message area
        MOV     CX,4               ; 4 bytes to move
        CLD                        ; Forward
        PUSH    DS
        POP     ES
        REP     MOVSB              ; Move them
;
;**********************|
;   select parity      |
;**********************|
```

```
PARITY:
        MOV     DX,OFFSET PAR_MENU
        CALL    DOS_STRING_OUT
        CALL    KBR_WAIT          ; Single-key input in AL
        CALL    TTY               ; Display input at cursor
; Valid input range is "1" to "3"
        CMP     AL,'1'            ; Carry set if less than 1
        JC      PARITY            ; Repeat selection
        CMP     AL,'4'            ; No carry if larger than 3
        JNC     PARITY
; Input is in valid range
        SUB     AL,30H            ; ASCII to binary in range 1 to 3
        MOV     PARITY_BYTE,AL    ; Store selected parity code
; Select 4-byte parity message and place in display area
        SUB     AL,1              ; To range 0 to 2
        MOV     CL,4
        MUL     CL                ; Multiply to obtain offset
        MOV     SI,OFFSET PAR$$
                                  ; SI -> parity messages
        MOV     AH,0              ; For addition of displacement
        ADD     SI,AX             ; SI -> ASCII characters for
                                  ; parity
        MOV     DI,OFFSET PAR%
                                  ; DI -> destination of message
        MOV     CX,4              ; Byte to move
        CLD                       ; Forward
        PUSH    DS
        POP     ES
        REP     MOVSB             ; Move them
;
;*********************|
;   select stop bits  |
;*********************|
STOPBITS:
        MOV     DX,OFFSET STOP_MENU
        CALL    DOS_STRING_OUT
        CALL    KBR_WAIT          ; Get single-key input in AL
        CALL    TTY               ; Display input
; Valid input range is "1" or "2"
        CMP     AL,'1'            ; Carry set if less than 1
        JC      STOPBITS          ; Repeat selection
        CMP     AL,'3'            ; No carry if larger than 2
        JNC     STOPBITS
; Input is in valid range. Move input digit to display area
        MOV     SI,OFFSET STOP%   ; Pointer to display area
        MOV     BYTE PTR [SI],AL
```

```
                                  ; Insert digit
; Convert input digit to binary 1 or 2
        SUB     AL,30H          ; ASCII to binary minus 1
        MOV     STOP_BYTE,AL    ; Store selected stop bits
;
;**********************|
;  select word length  |
;**********************|
WORD_LENGTH:
        MOV     DX,OFFSET WORD_MENU
        CALL    DOS_STRING_OUT
        CALL    KBR_WAIT        ; Single-key input in AL
        CALL    TTY             ; Display input
; Valid input range is "1" or "2"
        CMP     AL,'1'          ; Carry set if less than 1
        JC      WORD_LENGTH     ; Repeat selection
        CMP     AL,'3'          ; No carry if larger than 2
        JNC     WORD_LENGTH
        PUSH    AX              ; Save input
; Input in valid range. Add 6 and move input to display area
        ADD     AL,6            ; 1 = 7 and 2 = 8
        MOV     SI,OFFSET WORD% ; Display area
        MOV     BYTE PTR [SI],AL
        POP     AX              ; Restore input digit
        SUB     AL,30H          ; Convert to binary 1 or 2
        MOV     WORDLEN_BYTE,AL ; Store word-length code
;
;**********************|
;  set up serial line  |
;  with new protocol   |
;**********************|
; Move memory variables into the registers required by
; SET_PROTOCOL
        MOV     AL,BAUD_BYTE
        MOV     BL,PARITY_BYTE
        MOV     BH,STOP_BYTE
        MOV     DL,WORDLEN_BYTE
        CALL    SET_PROTOCOL
; line-feed and carriage return before exit
        MOV     AL,0DH
        CALL    TTY             ; Execute carriage return
        MOV     AL,0AH
        CALL    TTY             ; Execute line-feed
; Communications interrupts on
        CALL    COMM_ON
        JMP     MONITOR
```

```
;*******************************|
; <F3> command - display protocol|
;*******************************|
SHOW_PROTOCOL:
        MOV     DX,OFFSET PROT_MS
        CALL    DOS_STRING_OUT  ; Display message routine
        JMP     MONITOR
;
;*******************************|
;  <F4> command - send file     |
;*******************************|
SEND_FILE:
        CALL    COMM_OFF            ; Communications interrupt off
                                    ; for disk file operations
        MOV     DX,OFFSET MESS_3       ; Send mode message
        CALL    DOS_STRING_OUT
        MOV     DX,OFFSET MESS_2       ; Filename input message
        CALL    DOS_STRING_OUT
;********************|
; get matching file  |
;********************|
        MOV     DX,OFFSET FILE_IN       ; Formatted buffer
        CALL    GET_FIRST               ; Input filename
        JNC     OK_FIRST_NAME           ; First match found
; If carry clear the DTA is ready for the open call
;********************|
;   no matching file |
;   or user aborted  |
;********************|
; Test for empty buffer to determine if user aborted input
        CMP     IN_COUNT,0                  ; No characters except CR
        JE      USER_TERM       ; User terminated input
        MOV     DX,OFFSET ERMES_1
                                ; ERROR - path or file not found
        CALL    DOS_STRING_OUT
        JMP     SEND_EXIT
;********************|
; terminated by user |
;********************|
USER_TERM:
        MOV     DX,OFFSET MESS_6
                                ; TERMINATED BY USER
        CALL    DOS_STRING_OUT
;********************|
;   exit file send   |
;********************|
```

```
SEND_EXIT:
        CALL    COMM_ON              ; Interrupt communications back
                                     ; on
        JMP     MONITOR              ; Exit receive mode
;*********************|
;  filename matched   |
;*********************|
OK_FIRST_NAME:
        MOV     DX,OFFSET NEXT_NAME       ; ASCIIZ filename buffer
        CALL    OPEN_FILE
        JNC     OK_OPEN_FILE
; If carry clear then file was opened. If carry set then the open
; operation failed
NO_OPEN:
        MOV    DX,OFFSET ERMES_3
                                ; ERROR - cannot open file
        CALL   DOS_STRING_OUT
        JMP    RECEIVE_EXIT
OK_OPEN_FILE:
        MOV    HANDLE_1,AX          ; Store file handle
        MOV    DX,OFFSET MESS_1310  ; New line
        CALL   DOS_STRING_OUT
;*********************|
; filename to receiver |
;     (code 01)        |
;*********************|
; The send operation uses the codes 01, 02, and 03 to activate the
; desired receive operations. Each code sent must be acknowledged
; with the code "R" by the receiver
NEXT_ENTRY:
        MOV    AL,01             ; Code to receive filename
        CALL   SEND_ONE
        CALL   ACK_R             ; Wait for receiver to be ready
                                 ; for filename
; Receive mode ready, send the filename and 0FFH terminator
        MOV    SI,OFFSET NEXT_NAME
SEND_NAME:
        MOV    AL,[SI]           ; Filename character
        CALL   SEND_ONE          ; Send character through line
        CMP    AL,0H             ; Test for NULL byte
        JE     NAME_SENT         ; All filename transmitted
        INC    SI                ; Bump pointer
        JMP    SEND_NAME         ; and continue
NAME_SENT:
; Send terminator for filename
        MOV    AL,0FFH           ; Code recognized by the receiver
```

```
                CALL    SEND_ONE
                CALL    ACK_R           ; Wait for acknowledge code
                                        ; before transmitting record
;**********************|
;   read one record    |
;**********************|
READ_RECORD:
; Read one 128-byte disk record using handle and place in buffer
                MOV     AH,63           ; BIOS service request number
                                        ; to read file (handle mode)
                MOV     BX,HANDLE_1     ; File handle from open function
                MOV     CX,128          ; 128 bytes to read (1 record)
                MOV     DX,OFFSET F_BUFFER
                INT     21H
; Determine whether EOF (code = 03) or send sector (code = 02)
; AX = number of bytes read. AX = 0 if EOF
                CMP     AX,0            ; Test AX for EOF
                JE      READ_END        ; AX = 0, EOF encountered
; Disk sector in F_BUFFER is ready to send
                MOV     AL,02           ; Code to receive record
                CALL    SEND_ONE        ; Send through serial line
                CALL    ACK_R           ; Wait for receive ready
                                        ; to start sending record
                CALL    SEND_RECORD     ; Send 128 bytes to receiver
                CALL    ACK_R           ; Wait for receiver to be ready
                                        ; for next record
                JMP     READ_RECORD     ; Read new record and send
;**********************|
;   record was read    |
;**********************|
READ_END:
; Send code to close file
                MOV     AL,03           ; Handshake code to close
                CALL    SEND_ONE        ; Through serial line
                MOV     BX,HANDLE_1     ; Get file handle
                CALL    CLOSE_FILE      ; and close file
;**********************|
;  next matching name  |
;**********************|
; Check for a next filename that satisfies the global MS DOS
; characters, * and ?, in the original input line
                CALL    GET_NEXT
; Carry set if no next file match found
                JC      EXIT_FILE
; Matched filename can be found as an ASCIIZ string in the
; buffer named NEXT_NAME. Use this name to open file and get
```

```
; handle
        MOV       DX,OFFSET NEXT_NAME
        CALL      OPEN_FILE
        JNC       OK_OPEN_NEXT
        JMP       NO_OPEN            ; Open failed error exit
OK_OPEN_NEXT:
        MOV       HANDLE_1,AX        ; Save handle for new operations
        CLC                          ; Return code in carry flag
        JMP       NEXT_ENTRY
;********************|
;    file was sent   |
;    successfully    |
;********************|
EXIT_FILE:
        MOV       DX,OFFSET MESS_8
                                     ; FILE(S) TRANSMITTED
        CALL      DOS_STRING_OUT
        JMP       SEND_FILE          ; Repeat send routine
;
;*****************************|
;   <F5> command - receive file  |
;*****************************|
RECEIVE_FILE:
; Turn off communications interrupt during disk file reception
        CALL      COMM_OFF
;
        MOV       DX,OFFSET MESS_4
        CALL      DOS_STRING_OUT
        MOV       CHK_ERR,0          ; Clear checksum error control
        JMP       NO_R_ENTRY
;********************|
;   monitor line for  |
;    control code     |
;********************|
MONITOR_CODE:
; Monitor the RS-232-C line for a control code and execute
; according to the following:
; No carry, AL has control code:
;       01H = Receive path or filename and open file
;       02H = Receive 128 characters through the RS-232-C line,
;             send "R" to acknowledge and wait for new code
;       03H = Close file, post message and repeat receive
; Carry set if keyboard abort
;
; Send acknowledge code to sender
        MOV       AL,'R'             ; Code
```

```
              CALL    SEND_ONE          ; Through RS-232-C line
       ; Monitor line
       NO_R_ENTRY:
              CALL    GET_232           ; Get character from RS-232-C
              JNC     EXECUTE_CODE      ; Carry set if key pressed
       ; Key pressed, abort operation, post TERMINATED BY USER
       RECEIVE_ABORT:
              MOV     BX,HANDLE_1       ; Get file handle
              CALL    CLOSE_FILE        ; and close file
              MOV     DX,OFFSET MESS_6
                                        ; TERMINATED BY USER
              CALL    DOS_STRING_OUT
       ;*********************|
       ;  receive data exit  |
       ;*********************|
       RECEIVE_EXIT:
              CALL    COMM_ON           ; Interrupt communications back
                                        ; on
              JMP     MONITOR           ; Exit receive mode
       EXECUTE_CODE:
              CMP     AL,01             ; Code to receive filename
              JNE     TST_02            ; Continue testing
              JMP     RECEIVE_FNAME
       TST_02: CMP     AL,02            ; Code to receive a disk sector
              JNE     TST_03            ; Continue testing
              JMP     RECEIVE_128       ; Routine to receive sector
       TST_03: CMP     AL,03            ; Close and continue
              JNE     MONITOR_CODE      ; Illegal code, ignore
       ;
       ;*********************|
       ;   close disk file   |
       ;     (code 03)       |
       ;*********************|
       END_RECEIVE:
       ; Close file, post FILE RECEIVED OK and repeat receive mode
       ; if no checksum error
              MOV     BX,HANDLE_1       ; Get file handle
              CALL    CLOSE_FILE        ; and close file
              CMP     CHK_ERR,1
              JNE     OK_CHKSUM         ; No error
              MOV     DX,OFFSET MESS_9        ; *** CHECKSUM ERROR ***
              CALL    DOS_STRING_OUT
              JMP     RECEIVE_EXIT
       ;
       OK_CHKSUM:
              MOV     DX,OFFSET MESS_5
```

```
        CALL    DOS_STRING_OUT
        JMP     RECEIVE_FILE
;
; Bridge to label
GO_TO_ABORT:
        JMP     RECEIVE_ABORT
;
;**********************|
;    receive sector    |
;       (code 02)      |
;**********************|
; Get 128 characters from communications line and place in DTA
; Checksum is also transmitted
RECEIVE_128:
        MOV     AL,'R'              ; Signal receiver ready
        CALL    SEND_ONE
        MOV     BX,0                ; Clear checksum register
        MOV     DI,OFFSET F_BUFFER
        MOV     CX,128
REP_R_128:
        CALL    GET_232
        JC      GO_TO_ABORT         ; Key pressed, abort
        MOV     [DI],AL             ; Place in receiving buffer
        ADD     BL,AL               ; Add to checksum
        INC     DI                  ; Bump buffer pointer
        LOOP    REP_R_128           ; Repeat until end of sector
; Receive checksum and compare with value in BL
        CALL    GET_232             ; Checksum of sender
        JC      GO_TO_ABORT         ; Key pressed
        CMP     AL,BL               ; Test with sum of received
                                    ; characters
        JE      OK_SUM              ; Checksum OK
        MOV     CHK_ERR,1           ; Set checksum error switch
;**********************|
;   write one sector   |
;**********************|
OK_SUM:
        MOV     AH,64               ; DOS service request number
                                    ; to write file (handle mode)
        MOV     BX,HANDLE_1         ; File handle
        MOV     CX,128              ; Bytes to write
        MOV     DX,OFFSET F_BUFFER
        INT     21H
; Carry flag set if write error occurred
        JNC     OK_WRITE_OP
; Write error
```

```
        MOV      BX,HANDLE_1      ; Get file handle
        CALL     CLOSE_FILE       ; and close file
        MOV      DX,OFFSET ERMES_2
                                  ; ERROR - cannot write sector
        CALL     DOS_STRING_OUT
        JMP      RECEIVE_EXIT     ; Exit receive mode
OK_WRITE_OP:
        JMP      MONITOR_CODE     ; Send 'R' and wait for next
                                  ; control code from sender
;**********************|
;     receive file     |
;      (code 01)       |
;**********************|
; Send mode will transmit up to 64 characters in an ASCIIZ string
; that contains the filename. The code 0FFH will signal that all
; filename has been transmitted
RECEIVE_FNAME:
        MOV      AL,'R'           ; Acknowledge - ready for name
        CALL     SEND_ONE
; Receive filename until 0FFH terminator
        MOV      DI,OFFSET F_NAME
NAME_CHAR:
        CALL     GET_232          ; Receive character through line
        JNC      OK_NAME
        JMP      RECEIVE_ABORT    ; Key pressed, abort operation
OK_NAME:
        CMP      AL,0FFH          ; Test for filename end
        JE       NAME_END         ; End of filename code received
        MOV      [DI],AL          ; Store character
        INC      DI               ; Bump pointer
        JMP      NAME_CHAR        ; Next character
NAME_END:
; Set terminator and save address of end of filename
        MOV      BYTE PTR [DI],00H
        PUSH     DI               ; Save address of terminator
; Create file
        MOV      AH,3CH           ; BIOS service request number
        MOV      CX,0             ; Create with normal attribute
        MOV      DX,OFFSET F_NAME
        INT      21H
; Carry flag is set if create function failed
        JNC      OK_CREATE
; Restore stack, post error message and exit
        POP      DI               ; Adjust stack
        MOV      DX,OFFSET ERMES_4
                                  ; ERROR - cannot open for write
```

```
          CALL      DOS_STRING_OUT   ; Abort with error message
          JMP       RECEIVE_EXIT
OK_CREATE:
          MOV       HANDLE_1,AX      ; Save handle
; Display message RECEIVING FILE: followed by filename
          MOV       DX,OFFSET MESS_7
          CALL      DOS_STRING_OUT
; Substitute 00H terminator in ASCIIZ filename string for the $
; sign to use DOS string display function
          POP       DI               ; Address of NULL byte in stack
          MOV       BYTE PTR [DI],'$'
; Display filename string
          MOV       DX,OFFSET F_NAME
          CALL      DOS_STRING_OUT
; Add line feed and carriage return
          MOV       DX,OFFSET MESS_1310
          CALL      DOS_STRING_OUT
          JMP       MONITOR_CODE
;
;******************************************************************
;                            procedures
;******************************************************************
COMM_ON        PROC      NEAR
; Set communications line for interrupt operation on received
; data
          CLI                        ; Interrupts off
;*********************|
; install new routine |
;    in vector table  |
;*********************|
; Label for this interrupt service routine is: RS232_INT.
; Uses DOS service number 37 of INT 21H.
          MOV       AH,37            ; DOS service request number
          MOV       AL,INT_NUM       ; Machine interrupt number
          MOV       DX,OFFSET CS:RS232_INT
          PUSH      DS               ; Save program data segment
          PUSH      CS
          POP       DS               ; Set DS to segment base of
                                     ; interrupt service routine
          INT       21H
          POP       DS               ; Restore program's DS
;
; Reset buffer pointers to start of buffer
          MOV       DATA_IN,0
          MOV       DATA_OUT,0
; Set DX to base address of RS-232-C card from BIOS
```

```
        MOV     DX,CARD_BASE
;
;**********************|
;    initialize MCR    |
;**********************|
; Initialize modem control register for:
;       DTR (data terminal ready) .... x x x x  x x x 1
;       RTS (request to send) ........ x x x x  x x 1 x
;       OUTPUT 2 ..................... x x x x  1 x x x
;                                      ----------------
;                                      0 0 0 0  1 0 1 1
        MOV     DL,0FCH         ; MCR address
        MOV     AL,00001011B    ; Bits 0, 1 and 3 set
        OUT     DX,AL
        JMP     SHORT $+2
;
; Set bit 7 of the line control register (DLAB) to access
; the interrupt enable register at xF9H.
        MOV     DL,0FBH         ; xFBH = line control register
        IN      AL,DX           ; Read byte at port
        JMP     SHORT $+2       ; I/O delay
        AND     AL,7FH          ; Reset DLAB
        OUT     DX,AL           ; Write to LCR
        JMP     SHORT $+2       ; I/O delay
;
; Enable interrupts for DATA READY only
        MOV     DL,0F9H         ; Interrupt Enable register
        MOV     AL,1            ; DATA READY interrupt
        OUT     DX,AL
        JMP     SHORT $+2
;
; Enable communications interrupts by resetting the bits
; corresponding to the IRQ3 and IRQ4 lines on the interrupt mask
; register (port address = 21H)
        IN      AL,21H          ; Read byte at port
        JMP     SHORT $+2       ; I/O delay
        AND     AL,0E7H         ; Reset bits 3 and 4
        OUT     21H,AL
        JMP     SHORT $+2       ; I/O delay
;
; Reenable interrupts
        STI
        RET
COMM_ON         ENDP
;
COMM_OFF        PROC    NEAR
```

```
; Disable interrupt-driven communications and reset the normal
; transmission mode
        CLI                             ; Interrupts off
; Disable communications interrupts by setting bits for IRQ3 and
; IRQ4 lines on the Interrupt Mask register (port address = 21H)
        IN        AL,21H
        OR        AL,18H                ; Set bits 3 and 4
        OUT       21H,AL
        JMP       SHORT $+2
; Restore original interrupt vector for communications interrupt
        PUSH      DS                    ; Save operational DS
        MOV       AH,37                 ; DOS service request number
        MOV       AL,INT_NUM            ; Machine interrupt number
        MOV       DX,O_INT_OFF          ; Offset to DX
        MOV       AX,O_INT_SEG          ; Segment
        MOV       DS,AX                 ; to DS
        INT       21H
        POP       DS                    ; Restore data segment
;********************|
;    initialize MCR  |
;********************|
; Initialize modem control register for:
;       DTR (data terminal ready) .... x x x x  x x x 1
;       RTS (request to send) ........ x x x x  x x 1 x
;                                      ----------------
;                                      0 0 0 0  0 0 1 1
        MOV       DX,CARD_BASE
        ADD       DX,4                  ; Modem Control register
        MOV       AL,00000011B          ; See codes in table above
        OUT       DX,AL
        JMP       SHORT $+2             ; I/O delay
        STI                             ; Interrupts on
        RET
COMM_OFF        ENDP
;
SEND_RECORD     PROC    NEAR
; Send one disk record (128 bytes) through the RS-232-C line
; and byte-size checksum
        MOV       BL,0                  ; Clear Checksum register
        MOV       SI,OFFSET F_BUFFER
                                        ; Pointer to source buffer
        MOV       CX,128                ; Total bytes to send
                                        ; 1 logical record
REP_S_128:
        MOV       AL,[SI]               ; Get byte to send
        ADD       BL,AL                 ; Add checksum
```

```
              CALL      SEND_ONE          ; Send character though line
              INC       SI                ; Bump pointer
              LOOP      REP_S_128         ; Repeat until end of record
      ;
      ; Send checksum
              MOV       AL,BL
              CALL      SEND_ONE          ; Transmit checksum of sector
              RET
      ;
      SEND_RECORD       ENDP
      ;
      SEND_ONE          PROC      NEAR
      ; Send AL character through the RS 232-C line
              PUSH      AX                ; Save character to send
              MOV       DX,CARD_BASE      ; Serial card base address
              ADD       DX,5              ; Status register
      CHK_THRE:
              IN        AL,DX             ; Status
              JMP       SHORT $ + 2       ; I/O delay
              TEST      AL,20H            ; Transmitter holding register
                                          ; empty?
              JZ        CHK_THRE          ; No
      ; Ready to send
              POP       AX                ; Restore character to send
              MOV       DX,CARD_BASE      ; Transmitter holding register
              OUT       DX,AL             ; Send character
              JMP       SHORT $ + 2       ; I/O delay
              RET
      ;
      SEND_ONE          ENDP
      ;
      GET_232           PROC      NEAR
      ; Receive one character through RS-232-C line
      ; First flush keyboard buffer
              CALL      KBR_FLUSH
              MOV       DX,CARD_BASE      ; Serial card base address
              ADD       DX,5              ; Status register
      CHK_STAT:
              IN        AL,DX             ; Character ready?
              TEST      AL,1              ; Data ready bit on Status
                                          ; register
              JNZ       D_READY           ; Get data
              TEST      AL,1EH            ; Bits 1, 2, 3 and 4 are error
                                          ; bits
              JNZ       DATA_ERROR        ; Go if error bit set
      ; Test for key pressed
```

```
        PUSH    DX                  ; Save card base address
        MOV     AH,1                ; BIOS service request number
        INT     16H                 ; for keyboard status
        POP     DX                  ; Restore card address
        JZ      CHK_STAT            ; No key pressed, continue
; Key was pressed during line monitoring
        STC                         ; Carry flag is return code
        RET
GET_DATA        PROC    NEAR
D_READY:
        MOV     DX,CARD_BASE        ; Receiver register
        IN      AL,DX               ; Read character into AL
        CLC                         ; Normal exit
        RET
DATA_ERROR:
        MOV     AL,0A8H             ; Inverted ? = error received
        CLC                         ; Normal exit
        RET
;
GET_DATA        ENDP
GET_232         ENDP
;
ACK_R   PROC    NEAR
; Wait for receive acknowledge code "R" or abort if a key is
; pressed
        CALL    KBR_FLUSH
GET_STATUS:
        MOV     DX,CARD_BASE        ; Serial card base address
        ADD     DX,5                ; Status register
CHK_4_DATA:
        IN      AL,DX               ; Get status
        TEST    AL,1                ; Data ready bit of status
                                    ; register
        JNZ     DATA_READY          ; Go if set
; Check keyboard for a key pressed
        MOV     AH,1                ; BIOS service request number
        INT     16H                 ; to get keyboard status
        JZ      GET_STATUS          ; No key pressed
; Abort sending
        POP     DX                  ; Adjust stack
        MOV     DX,OFFSET MESS_6
        CALL    DOS_STRING_OUT      ; Display TERMINATED BY USER
        CALL    COMM_ON             ; Interrupt communications back
                                    ; on
        JMP     MONITOR
DATA_READY:
```

```
            CALL     GET_DATA
            CMP      AL,'R'            ; Test for acknowledge code
            JNE      GET_STATUS        ; Repeat if wrong code
            RET                        ; Return if 'R' received
    ;
    ACK_R   ENDP
    ;
    ;
    TTY               PROC    NEAR
    ; Display character or control code at cursor position
    TTY_ONE:
            PUSH     AX                ; Save character
            CALL     BIO_TTY           ; Library service
            POP      AX
    ; Test for carriage return and add line-feed
            CMP      AL,0DH
            JNE      NOT_CR
            MOV      AL,0AH
            JMP      TTY_ONE
    NOT_CR:
            RET
    TTY               ENDP
    ;
    ;******************************************************************
    ;          new communications interrupt service routine
    ;******************************************************************
    RS232_INT:
    ;
            STI                        ; Interrupts on - except for
                                       ; communications
    ;********************|
    ;     save context   |
    ;********************|
    ; Save registers to be used by the service routine in stack
            PUSH     AX
            PUSH     BX
            PUSH     DX
            PUSH     DI
            PUSH     DS
    ; Set DS establish addressability of main program data
            MOV      DX,DATA
            MOV      DS,DX
            ASSUME   DS:DATA
    ;********************|
    ; check for data ready |
    ;********************|
```

```
; Check line status register for reception error and data ready
DATA_CHECK:
        MOV     DX,CARD_BASE    ; Base address of serial port
        MOV     DL,0FDH         ; Line status register
        IN      AL,DX           ; Read port byte
        JMP     SHORT $+2       ; I/O delay
; Check for data ready on line
        TEST    AL,01H          ; Bit 0 is data ready
        JNZ     DATA_INPUT      ; Go if bit set
; Check for error codes
        TEST    AL,1EH          ; Bits 1, 2, 3, or 4 set?
        JNZ     BAD_DATA        ; Go if set
        JMP     DATA_CHECK      ; No data or error codes
;
BAD_DATA:
        MOV     AL,0A8H         ; Inverted ? is error symbol
        JMP     STORE_BYTE      ; Store error code
;**********************|
;    read data byte    |
;**********************|
; Pull data from the receiver data register and store in the
; circular buffer
DATA_INPUT:
        MOV     DL,0F8H         ; Receiver data register address
        IN      AL,DX           ; Get byte
        JMP     SHORT $+2       ; I/O delay
        AND     AL,7FH          ; Mask off high-order bit
;**********************|
; store byte in buffer |
;**********************|
STORE_BYTE:
        LEA     DI,CIRC_BUF     ; Buffer pointer
        MOV     BX,DATA_IN      ; Input pointer
        ADD     DI,BX           ; Point DI to active byte
        MOV     BYTE PTR [DI],AL
                                ; Store in CIRC_BUF
;**********************|
;  bump buffer pointer |
;**********************|
; Reset if pointer overflows buffer
        INC     BX              ; Bump pointer
        CMP     BX,20           ; Past end of buffer ?
        JNE     OK_IN_PTR
; Reset pointer to start of buffer
        MOV     BX,0
OK_IN_PTR:
```

```
        MOV     DATA_IN,BX       ; Store new pointer displacement
;********************|
;   end-of-interrupt |
;********************|
; Signal end-of-interrupt to the Interrupt Command register
        MOV     AL,20H           ; Code
        OUT     20H,AL           ; EOI port address
        JMP     SHORT $+2        ; I/O delay
;********************|
;   restore context  |
;********************|
; Restore registers from stack
        POP     DS
        POP     DI
        POP     DX
        POP     BX
        POP     AX
;********************|
;       return       |
;********************|
        IRET
;
CODE    ENDS
        END     START
```

6

Programming the Modem

6.0 Computer Communications Using Telephone Lines

At the time of the invention of computers the world was already crisscrossed by an impressive network of communication lines. This wiring system was developed and installed by national and international telephone companies. When computer technology identified a need for communicating, it found that the telephone lines provided connecting wires to almost every location on the earth's surface. It was more economical, at that time, to use the existing system than to develop a new one.

However, the use in digital transmissions of a device designed and intended for the exchange of audible signals was not without its drawbacks. A data transmission network, designed for high-speed communications between digital devices, is presently being developed and will someday make unnecessary the use of telephone circuits and lines. For the present, the telephone system hardware is the only available means for data interchange between locations that are not connected through dedicated data transmission lines.

6.0.1 The Modem

The use of telephone circuits requires a modulating-demodulating device, called a *modem*. This is necessary because the telephone system is designed to carry analog signals while most computer equipment operate on digital data. In practice, the modem transforms square waves (digital coding) into oscillating waves (analog coding). In other words, it changes digital representations into audible tones that can be handled by the telephone hardware.

Digital data cannot be directly sent through a telephone wire because of the narrow bandwidth of the telephone system. The sounds produced by a human voice can range between 20 and 20,000 Hz, but the original designers of telephone circuitry determined that a range from 300 to 3000 Hz was a satisfactory compromise between transmission quality and hardware costs. Although the 300 to 3000 Hz range is adequate for voice communications, it is not sufficient for the direct transmission of digital data. This explains the need for a device (modem) to transform digital data into tones that fall within the permissible range, and vice versa.

In addition to modulating and demodulating, the modem can execute commands related to telephone communications; for example, it can be programmed to answer the telephone and remain on the line, to dial a number, or to terminate a connection (hang up).

6.0.2 Internal and External Modems

In the IBM microcomputers modems are furnished as external devices or as adapter cards. Internal modems are usually adapter cards which include serial port hardware. Thus, in a system containing a conventional serial port designated as COM1, the internal modem will usually appear as COM2. External modems are generally connected to an existing serial port, which can be in the range COM1 to COM4.

Most external modems are equipped with visible indicator lights that represent the modem's state of operation. These signals are usually light-emitting diodes (LEDs) labeled with words, initials, or codes; for example, in one device the state of the carrier detect will be visible in a LED labeled CD, and the state of the data terminal ready line in a LED labeled TR. Another advantage of external modems is that their mode of operation can often be configured by setting microswitches and that the volume of the modem speaker can be mechanically controlled by the user. Finally, external modems do not use system expansion resources. Internal modems, on the other hand, provide their own serial port and do not clutter the user's desk.

6.0.3 Modem Communications Standards

In addition to being internal or external, modems and modem communications are classified according to conventions based on the communications speed. The following is a general classification:

1. *300-baud modems*. At 300 Bd/s the voltage signals are converted into audible tones following a convention known as *frequency shift keying* (FSK). In this convention, which is described in the Bell 103 protocol, the originator logical 0 tone has a frequency of 1070 Hz and the logical 1 tone, 1270 Hz. The answerer logical 0 tone has a frequency of 2025 Hz and the logical 1 tone, 2225 Hz.

2. *1200-baud modems*. This baud rate corresponds to the Bell 212A protocol. Modem communications at 1200 Bd are based on phase modulation. This consists of manipulating the carrier signal so that 2 bits can be transmitted simultaneously in each direction. In this manner, the modem can achieve a transmission speed rated at 1200 Bd while using a line frequency of 600 Bd. The method is known as *phase shift keying* (PSK).

3. *2400-baud modems*. 2400-Bd communications are regulated by the CCITT V.22 protocol. This technique, based on creating three amplitudes and 12 phase angles, is known as *phase amplitude modulation* (PAM). These 36 states make possible the

transmission of 6 simultaneous data bits. Consequently, although the line frequency is of 600 Bd, the transmission is rated at 2400 bps (bits per second).

4. *9600- and 19,200-baud modems.* Modems that operate at these high speeds are usually too costly for use in the microcomputer field. The transmission techniques used at these rates combine data compression with amplitude-phase modulation. The present international standard for high-speed modem communications are CCITT V.29 and V.32.

The reader can find additional information regarding serial communications protocols in Chapter 5.

6.1 The Hayes Command Set

The Hayes Microcomputer Products company has specialized in modem design and manufacturing. The products of this firm have achieved such general acceptance that they created a factual standard. In this manner, a modem compatible with the command system created by this manufacturer is often described as being Hayes-compatible. Since most Hayes modem commands begin with the letters AT (attention), the system is also called the AT command set. Table 6.1 lists the most frequently used commands in the Hayes command set.

Two commands in the Hayes command set do not require the AT preface and the carriage return terminator codes. The A command (see Table 6.1) is used to repeat the previous command. The command codes for the repeat command are the characters A/. The escape command is used to instruct an online modem to return to the command mode. It consists of a 1-s initial guard time, followed by the string " + + +", and another 1-s wait. The guard times surrounding the escape code are designed to prevent the modem from accidentally interpreting the data values " + + +" as an escape sequence. Modem register S12 holds the value of the wait periods in 20 ms units. The default value is 50 units, equivalent to 1 s.

6.1.1 Modes of Modem Operation

Programming a modem consists mostly of sending commands and data to the serial port and in reading serial port data. In Hayes-compatible modems the instructions are in the form of the AT or Hayes commands, discussed in Section 6.1. But the programmer should be careful in assuming that all modems are Hayes-compatible. Some popular modems, including the Internal Modem furnished by IBM for the PCjr, do not recognize Hayes commands.

Most modems, Hayes-compatible or not, operate in one of two states, known as the *online* and the *local command* modes. In the local command mode the modem receives and responds to its command language, usually the Hayes set (see Table 6.1). These commands are code as character strings and transmitted through the modem's serial port. For example, the Hayes system modem command

AT DT 727-6319

makes the modem dial the telephone number 727-6319, using touch tones, and remain *listening* on the phone line. Most commands in the Hayes system are terminated by sending the carriage return code 0DH. The sample command strings in Table 6.1 include this terminator, if it is required.

When a modem finishes executing a command, it sends a response message through the serial line. The command AT V (see Table 6.1) can be used to force the modem to output numerical codes or text messages. The default condition is determined by the state of bits 2 and 3 in modem register S12. Table 6.2 lists the most common modem responses.

If a modem establishes a connection with another modem, it automatically goes into the online mode. With the modem online, data output to the serial port is transmitted through the line, not interpreted as a command. A modem in the online mode can be either the originator or the answerer. To establish a connection between two modems, one must play the part of an originating modem and the other one, of an answering modem.

Table 6.1. *Modem Commands in the Hayes System*

COMMAND	SAMPLE COMMAND STRING	ACTION
A/	'A/'	Repeat last command (redial last number)
B<p>	'AT B0',0DH	Enable communications protocol = 0 for CCITT V.22 = 1 for Bell 212A protocol

D<s><n>	"AT DT 727-6319',0DH	Dialing command. — The following subcommmands <s> can be included:
		, = pause (default time 2 seconds)
		T = dial using touch tones
		P = dial using rotary (pulse) tones
		W = wait for dialtone
		; = return to command mode at end
		  of line (voice call dialing)
		<n> = telephone number with optional
		  -,(,) symbols and spaces

E<p>	'AT E0',0DH	Echo characters in command mode p = 0 for no echo p = 1 for echo (default)
H<p>	'AT H0',0DH	Hook control <p> = 0 to hang up (on hook) <p> = 1 to pick up (off hook)
O	'AT O',0DH	Online; return modem to online mode after escape or voice command
S<n> = <p>	'AT S0=3',0DH	Set modem register <n> = register number <p> = value installed in register
S<n>?	'AT S0?',0DH	Report contents of modem register number <n>
V<p>	'AT V1',0DH	Verbal response mode <p> = 0 for numerical result codes <p> = 1 for verbal result codes
<w>+++<w>	+++	Escape sequence — switch from online to command mode. w is 1-s wait.

Table 6.2. *Modem Responses in the Hayes System*

| HAYES RESPONSE | | |
NUMERICAL	VERBAL	DESCRIPTION
0	OK	Command executed with no errors
1	CONNECT	Modem connected
2	RING	Incoming call detected
3	NO CARRIER	Carrier signal was lost or not detected
4	ERROR	Error in command code
5	CONNECT 1200	Communication established at 1200 bps
6	NO DIALTONE	No dialtone detected
7	BUSY	Busy signal detected
8	NO ANSWER	The number dialed did not answer
10	CONNECT 2400	Communication established at 2400 bps

6.1.2 Modem Registers

Hayes system modems contain a set of 28 internal registers, called the *S registers*. These registers are locations in the modem's memory space that store data and parameters used in determining the modem's operation. The S registers are accessible to the programmer through the S= and S? commands (see Table 6.1). The S registers are numbered S0 to S27. Since the Hayes system is an informal standard, the number of S registers and their default contents vary in modems by different manufacturers. For this reason direct programming of the S registers often endangers the portability of the code.

6.2 The DIALER Program

Programs that use the modem to communicate through the telephone lines must act on the characters and codes received and sent by the device. It is the software that must display characters, scroll the screen, transmit keyboard input, send and receive files, and perform any other function required. These characters are transmitted through the serial port using conventional communications routines, as those described and listed in Chapter 5. For example, a modem program to send and receive disk files could be constructed using the same routines that appear in the SERCOM program listed in Chapter 5. The modem itself has no control over the computer hardware, except for the RS-232-C port to which it is connected.

For this reason the program named DIALER, presented in this chapter, illustrates modem programming mostly in regards to the processing and execution of the Hayes command set. Other functions typically performed by modem software, such as serving as a terminal, or transmitting disk files, are not coded any differently than those used in conventional communications through the serial port (see Chapter 5).

```
;*****************************************************************
;*****************************************************************
;                          DIALER.ASM
;*****************************************************************
;*****************************************************************
;
; Modem communications program
;
; Program operation
; 1. The program is a TSR that detects the keystroke
;    Ctrl+Alt+<F1> to gain control of the machine.
; 2. The program operates in alpha modes only
; 3. The contents of the video buffer are saved in the program's
;    memory space and restored on exit
;
;
; Commands for creating the run file DIALER.COM using Microsoft
; Macro Assembler software
;         1. MASM DIALER;
;         2. LINK DIALER;
;         3. EXE2BIN DIALER.EXE DIALER.COM
;         4. ERASE DIALER.EXE
;
;*************************** code ***************************
;
CODE     SEGMENT
;
         ORG    0100H              ; COM file forced origin
         ASSUME CS:CODE,DS:CODE,ES:CODE,SS:CODE
;
ENTRY:
         JMP    INSTALL            ; Jump to installation routine


;*****************************************************************
;                      new INT 09H entry point
;*****************************************************************
NEW09_INT:
         JMP    SHORT HANDLER_09         ; Go to handler routine
;*****************************************************************
;            IBM standard interrupt chaining structure
;                      (16 bytes data area)
;*****************************************************************
; This structure must start at the third byte from the entry
; point of the interrupt handler. The preceding short jump ensures
; this requirement
OLD_VECTOR_09   DD     0       ; Pointer to BIOS handler
```

```
IBM_SIGNATURE    DW       424BH    ; IBM signature for a valid
                                   ; handler
IBM_FLAGS        DB       80H      ; Code to indicate that this is
                                   ; now the first handler in the
                                   ; chain
;**********************|
; jump to unlink code  |
;**********************|
; This jump must be located at the 10th byte from the entry point
        JMP      SHORT UNLINK_THIS_09
;*********************|
;    reserved area    |
;*********************|
                 DB      7 DUP (00H)      ; 7 bytes reserved
;******************************************************************
;                      unlinking routine
;******************************************************************
; The following code is used to discard this handler and restore
; the previous one in the chain. The unlinking routine executes
; if this handler is the one installed at the vector for INT 09H.
; The code is encoded in a FAR procedure so that the RET
; instruction will return execution to the caller
UNLK_09          PROC     FAR
UNLINK_THIS_09:
        CLI                         ; Interrupts off
; The following code is used to obtain the segment:offset address
; at the vector for INT 09H.
        MOV      AX,0               ; Clear registers
        MOV      ES,AX              ; to set ES to segment of table
        MOV      DI,24H             ; Set DI to offset of the vector
                                   ; for INT 09H (09H * 4 = 24H)
;*********************|
; unchain this handler |
;*********************|
; Restore address stored at OLD_VECTOR_09 the vector table
; Abort operation if this value is 0000:0000H
; ES -> to interrupt vector table segment base (0000H)
        MOV      AX,WORD PTR CS:OLD_VECTOR_09
        MOV      BX,WORD PTR CS:OLD_VECTOR_09[2]
; AX = offset and BX = segment address of old vector
; DI -> interrupt vector for INT 09H
        CLD                         ; Direction flag to forward
        STOSW                       ; Store offset
; DI -> to segment address position
        MOV      AX,BX              ; Segment to AX
        STOSW                       ; Store segment
```

```
;***********************|
; FAR return to caller  |
;***********************|
        RET
UNLK_09         ENDP
;*****************************************************************
;                       new interrupt handler
;*****************************************************************
HANDLER_09:
        STI                     ; Interrupts on
; Save registers
        PUSH    DS
        PUSH    ES
        PUSH    SI
        PUSH    DI
        PUSH    AX
        PUSH    BX
        PUSH    CX
        PUSH    DX
; Set DS to CS to simplify coding
        PUSH    CS
        POP     DS
; Test for machine type 1 (PC and XT) or type 2 (AT or PS/2)
        CMP     KB_CHIP,2
        JE      TYPE_2
;***********************|
; processing for type   |
;     1 machines        |
;***********************|
; Get the scan code
        IN      AL,60H
        JMP     SHORT $+2       ; I/O delay
;***********************|
;  test keystroke for   |
;     Ctrl+Alt+<F1>      |
;***********************|
        CALL    TEST_CTAF1      ; Test for Ctrl+Alt+<F1>
                                ; keystroke
; Carry set if not Ctrl+Alt+<F1>
        JNC     RESET_8048      ; Keys pressed were Ctrl+Alt+<F1>
        JMP     NOT_CTAF1       ; Take exit to keyboard interrupt
;***********************|
;  reenable keyboard    |
;  interrupt on 8048    |
;***********************|
RESET_8048:
```

```
            IN      AL,61H              ; Get control byte at port
            MOV     AH,AL               ; and save it in AH
            OR      AL,10000000B        ; Set bit number 7
            OUT     61H,AL              ; Send keyboard acknowledge
            JMP     SHORT $+2           ; I/O delay
            XCHG    AL,AH               ; Recover original control
            OUT     61H,AL              ; Reset keyboard
            JMP     SHORT $+2           ; I/O delay
; Signal end of interrupt
            MOV     AL,20H              ; EOI code
            OUT     20H,AL              ; To 8259 interrupt controller
            JMP     SHORT $+2           ; I/O delay
            JMP     EXECUTE_TSR         ; Execution routine is common to
                                        ; all systems
;*********************|
;   return control to    |
;     original handler   |
;*********************|
NOT_CTAF1:
            POP     DX                  ; Restore registers
            POP     CX
            POP     BX
            POP     AX
            POP     DI
            POP     SI
            POP     ES
            POP     DS
; Exit from new service routine to old service routine
            CLI                         ; Clear interrupt flag
            JMP     DWORD PTR CS:OLD_VECTOR_09
;
;*********************|
; processing for type    |
;     2 machines         |
;*********************|
TYPE_2:
            MOV     AL,0ADH             ; Code to disable keyboard
            CALL    SEND_8042           ; To 8042 controller
;
            CLI                         ; Interrupts off
            MOV     CX,0FFFFH           ; Set up timer counter
WAIT_1:
            IN      AL,64H              ; 8042 status port
            JMP     SHORT $+2           ; I/O delay
            TEST    AL,00000010B        ; Check for input buffer full
            LOOPNZ  WAIT_1              ; Loop until bit set
```

```
                                         ; or timer counter = 0
; Get scan code
        IN     AL,60H            ; Read scan code at 8042 output
                                 ; buffer
        JMP    SHORT $+2         ; I/O delay
        STI
;**********************|
;   test keystroke for |
;    Ctrl+Alt+<F1>     |
;**********************|
        CALL   TEST_CTAF1        ; Test for Ctrl+Alt+<F1>
                                 ; keystroke
; Carry set if not Ctrl+Alt+<F1>
        JNC    RESET_8042        ; Keys pressed were Ctrl+Alt+<F1>
        JMP    NOT_CTAF1         ; Take exit to keyboard interrupt
;**********************|
;  reenable keyboard   |
;  interrupt on 8082   |
;**********************|
RESET_8042:
; Signal end of interrupt and reset controller
        MOV    AL,20H
        OUT    20H,AL            ; Send to interrupt controller
        JMP    SHORT $+2         ; Time delay for PS/2 systems
        MOV    AL,0AEH           ; Code to enable keyboard
        CALL   SEND_8042         ; To 8042 controller
;******************************|
;         TSR execution        |
;******************************|
EXECUTE_TSR:
;**********************|
;   test for graphics  |
;        modes         |
;**********************|
; TSR is not compatible with dot addressable modes
        CALL   BIO_GET_MODE      ; SOLUTION.LIB procedure in the
                                 ; BIOVIDEO module
; AL holds video mode. Legal modes are number 7, monochrome, and
; color alpha modes numbers 0 to 4. All other modes are APA
        CMP    AL,7              ; Monochrome mode is compatible
                                 ; with default settings
        JE     MODE_OK
        CMP    AL,4              ; Test for color alpha mode
        JBE    MODE_OK           ; Less than 4 are legal color
                                 ; modes
; Mode is APA
```

```
            MOV     AL,7            ; Bell code
            CALL    BIO_TTY         ; Beep to signal error
            JMP     EXIT_TSR        ; Abort execution
;*********************|
;   get video buffer  |
;     segment base    |
;*********************|
MODE_OK:
            CALL    ES_TO_VIDEO     ; SOLUTION.LIB procedure in the
                                    ; DAVIDEO module
; ES -> video buffer base address
;*********************|
;   save video image  |
;*********************|
            MOV     CX,2000         ; Words to save
            MOV     SI,0            ; Source pointer to start of
                                    ; buffer
            MOV     DI,OFFSET VIDEO_SAVE
SAVE_IMAGE:
            MOV     AX,ES:[SI]      ; Word from buffer
            MOV     [DI],AX         ; Saved in local memory
            ADD     SI,2            ; Bump pointers
            ADD     DI,2
            LOOP    SAVE_IMAGE
;*********************|
; get and save cursor |
;       position      |
;*********************|
            MOV     BX,0            ; Page 0
            CALL    BIO_GET_CUR     ; SOLUTION.LIB procedure in the
                                    ; BIOVIDEO module
; Present cursor position in DX
            MOV     OLD_CURSOR,DX   ; Store in memory variable
;*********************|
;   clear screen and  |
;  display directory  |
;*********************|
            CALL    CLEAR_SCR       ; Procedure to clear screen
            MOV     DX,0            ; Set cursor to top of screen
            CALL    BIO_SET_CUR     ; SOLUTION.LIB procedure in the
                                    ; BIOVIDEO module
            MOV     SI,OFFSET PHONES_MESS
            CALL    SHOW_MESS
;*********************|
; display program menu |
;*********************|
```

```
        MOV     SI,OFFSET MENU_MESS
        CALL    SHOW_MESS
        CALL    BRIGHT_LINE
;**********************|
;   initialize modem   |
;**********************|
; Default initialization is to no echo. The modem command string
; labeled ENTRY_STR can be edited for other initialization
; commands
        MOV     SI,OFFSET ENTRY_STR     ; Buffer with codes
        CALL    SEND_STRING
;*****************************************************************
;                       command processing
;*****************************************************************
TSR_COMMAND:
        MOV     DH,24
        MOV     DL,0            ; Cursor address to screen bottom
        CALL    BIO_SET_CUR
        MOV     SI,OFFSET F0_PROMPT     ; Message to clear prompt
                                        ; area
        CALL    SHOW_MESS
        MOV     DH,24
        MOV     DL,0            ; Cursor back to start of line
        CALL    BIO_SET_CUR     ; Set cursor
;**********************|
;  monitor typed and   |
;  received characters |
;**********************|
; First check keyboard buffer for new command
KEY_OR_CHAR:
        MOV     AH,1            ; BIOS service to read status
        INT     16H
        JNZ     KEY_READY       ; Go to fetch key routine
; No keystroke in buffer, check for serial reception
        MOV     AH,3            ; Serial line status service
        MOV     DX,COMM_PORT    ; Get BIOS communication port
        INT     14H             ; BIOS serial service interrupt
        AND     AH,00000001B    ; Test bit 0, data ready
        JZ      KEY_OR_CHAR     ; No character
;**********************|
; get serial character |
;**********************|
; Rapidly clear 20 characters in display area
        MOV     DI,3840         ; Offset of screen line 24
        MOV     CX,20           ; 20 characters to clear
        MOV     AL,' '          ; Blank
```

```
CLEAR_20:
        MOV     ES:[DI],AL      ; Place blank in buffer
        INC     DI
        INC     DI              ; Bump pointer, skip attribute
        LOOP    CLEAR_20
SERIAL_1:
        MOV     AH,2            ; Serial line read service
        MOV     DX,COMM_PORT    ; Get BIOS communication port
        INT     14H             ; BIOS serial service interrupt
; Character is returned in AL. Test for line-feed and skip
        CMP     AL,0AH          ; Line-feed code
        JE      KEY_OR_CHAR     ; Skip it
        CALL    BIO_TTY         ; Display others at cursor
        JMP     SERIAL_1
;*********************|
; get command keystroke|
;*********************|
KEY_READY:
        CALL    KBR_WAIT        ; SOLUTION.LIB procedure in the
                                ; KEYBRD module
        CMP     AX,011BH        ; <Esc> key pressed
        JNE     TEST_UP         ; Continue processing if not
                                ; <Esc>
        JMP     TSR_END         ; Exit
TEST_UP:
        CMP     AX,4800H        ; Up arrow?
        JNE     TEST_DOWN       ; Continue if not keystroke
;*********************|
;    up arrow command |
;*********************|
        CMP     BRT_ROW,2       ; Check for limit
        JE      TEST_DOWN       ; Ignore if row at limit
        CALL    NORMAL_LINE     ; Set line to normal attribute
        DEC     BRT_ROW         ; Decrement row if not
        CALL    BRIGHT_LINE     ; Display new line bright
        JMP     TSR_COMMAND     ; Continue monitoring
TEST_DOWN:
        CMP     AX,5000H        ; Down arrow?
        JNE     TEST_RIGHT      ; Continue if not keystroke
;*********************|
;  down arrow command |
;*********************|
        CMP     BRT_ROW,12      ; Check for lower limit
        JE      TEST_RIGHT      ; Ignore command if at limit
        CALL    NORMAL_LINE     ; Set line to normal attribute
        INC     BRT_ROW         ; Increment row
```

```
        CALL     BRIGHT_LINE        ; Set new line as bright
        JMP      TSR_COMMAND
TEST_RIGHT:
        CMP      AX,4D00H           ; Right arrow?
        JNE      TEST_LEFT          ; Continue if not keystroke
;**********************|
; right arrow command  |
;**********************|
        CMP      BRT_COL,39         ; Check for right limit
        JE       TEST_LEFT          ; Ignore command if at limit
        CALL     NORMAL_LINE        ; Set line to normal attribute
        MOV      BRT_COL,39         ; Set to right-hand value
        CALL     BRIGHT_LINE        ; Set new line as bright
        JMP      TSR_COMMAND
TEST_LEFT:
        CMP      AX,4B00H           ; Left arrow?
        JNE      TEST_ENTER         ; Continue if not keystroke
;**********************|
;  left arrow command  |
;**********************|
        CMP      BRT_COL,0          ; Check for right limit
        JE       TEST_ENTER         ; Ignore command if at limit
        CALL     NORMAL_LINE        ; Set line to normal attribute
        MOV      BRT_COL,0          ; Set to left-hand value
        CALL     BRIGHT_LINE        ; Set new line as bright
        JMP      TSR_COMMAND
TEST_ENTER:
        CMP      AL,0DH             ; <Enter> key code
        JNE      TEST_F1            ; Continue if not keystroke
;**********************|
;    dial number in    |
;    selected entry    |
;**********************|
; Calculate offset into buffer using the values stored in BRT_COL
; and BRT_ROW
        MOV      SI,OFFSET PHONES_TEXT    ; Set up buffer pointer
        MOV      AL,BRT_ROW         ; Row to AL. Range is 2 to 12
        SUB      AL,2               ; Reduce value to offset of entry
        MOV      AH,0               ; Clear high-order byte
        MOV      CX,80              ; 80 characters per row
        MUL      CL                 ; AL * CL, product is in AX
        ADD      SI,AX              ; Add offset to pointer
        MOV      AL,BRT_COL         ; Get entry offset value
        MOV      AH,0               ; Clear high-order byte for
                                    ; addition
        ADD      SI,AX              ; Add 0 or 39 for row start
```

```
            ADD     SI,3                 ; Skip consecutive entry number
DIAL_NUMBER:
            CALL    MOVE_PH_NUM          ; Procedure to move digits to
                                         ; dialing buffer
            MOV     SI,OFFSET DIAL_BUF   ; Set pointer
            CALL    SEND_STRING          ; Procedure to send AT and DT
                                         ; command
                                         ; and phone number digits to COM2
            JMP     TSR_COMMAND
TEST_F1:
            CMP     AX,3B00H             ; <F1> key?
            JNE     TEST_F2
;*********************|
;       hang up       |
;*********************|
            MOV     SI,OFFSET HANG_UP    ; Buffer with codes
            CALL    SEND_STRING
            JMP     TSR_COMMAND
TEST_F2:
            CMP     AX,3C00H             ; <F2> key?
            JNE     TEST_F3
;*********************|
; type and dial number |
;*********************|
            MOV     SI,OFFSET F2_PROMPT  ; Message text
            CALL    SHOW_MESS            ; Message displayed at
                                         ; cursor
            MOV     DI,OFFSET INPUT_AREA ; Area for digits
            CALL    KEY_INPUT            ; Enter keyboard
                                         ; characters
            MOV     SI,OFFSET INPUT_AREA
            JMP     DIAL_NUMBER
;
TEST_F3:
            CMP     AX,3D00H             ; <F3> key?
            JNE     TEST_F4
;*********************|
;    modem command    |
;*********************|
            MOV     SI,OFFSET F3_PROMPT  ; Message text
            CALL    SHOW_MESS            ; Message displayed at
                                         ; cursor
            MOV     DI,OFFSET INPUT_AREA ; Area for digits
            CALL    KEY_INPUT            ; Enter keyboard
                                         ; characters
; Add buffer controls to send string
```

```
            MOV     BYTE PTR [DI],0DH        ; String terminator
            INC     DI                       ; Bump buffer pointer
            MOV     BYTE PTR [DI],0H         ; Message terminator
            MOV     SI,OFFSET INPUT_AREA
            CALL    SEND_STRING              ; Procedure to send
            JMP     TSR_COMMAND
TEST_F4:
            CMP     AX,3E00H         ; <F4> key?
            JNE     EXIT_TESTS
;**********************|
;  go to command mode  |
;**********************|
; Send escape command to modem to shift from online to
; command-mode operation. The guard time preceding and following
; the escape command is determined by the setting of modem
; register S12. The code does not have to implement a wait period
            MOV     SI,OFFSET ESCAPE_STR     ; Pointer to command
                                             ; string
            CALL    SEND_STRING      ; Send to RS-232-C port procedure
EXIT_TESTS:
            JMP     TSR_COMMAND
;**********************|
; restore screen image |
;      and exit        |
;**********************|
TSR_END:
            MOV     CX,2000          ; Words to save
            MOV     SI,0             ; Source pointer to start of
                                     ; buffer
            MOV     DI,OFFSET VIDEO_SAVE
RESTORE_IMAGE:
            MOV     AX,[DI]          ; Word from memory area
            MOV     ES:[SI],AX       ; to video buffer
            ADD     SI,2             ; Bump pointers
            ADD     DI,2
            LOOP    RESTORE_IMAGE
;**********************|
;    reset cursor      |
;**********************|
            MOV     DX,OLD_CURSOR
            CALL    BIO_SET_CUR
;**********************|
;      end of TSR      |
;**********************|
EXIT_TSR:
            POP     DX               ; Restore registers
```

```
              POP     CX
              POP     BX
              POP     AX
              POP     DI
              POP     SI
              POP     ES
              POP     DS
              IRET
;
;******************************************************************
;                            procedures
;******************************************************************
MOVE_PH_NUM      PROC     NEAR
; Move a phone digits string into the dialing buffer
; On entry:
;         SI -> start of a string of phone number digits
;
; String can have leading spaces or other invalid characters less
; than 0
              MOV     DI,OFFSET PHONE_NO_BUF
                                          ; Destination buffer
NUM_START:
              MOV     AL,[SI]          ; Character from directory area
              CMP     AL,'0'           ; Skip characters until first
                                       ; digit
              JNB     MOVE_DIGIT       ; Go if not a space
              INC     SI               ; Bump pointer
              JMP     NUM_START        ; Continue searching
; Move all digits in the range 0 to 9. Terminate on space
MOVE_DIGIT:
              MOV     [DI],AL          ; To dialing buffer
              INC     DI               ; Bump destination pointer
SKIP_DIGIT:
              INC     SI               ; Bump source pointer
              MOV     AL,[SI]          ; Get next digit
              CMP     AL,' '           ; Test for terminator
              JE      END_DIGITS       ; End of digits string
              CMP     AL,'0'           ; Test lower limit of range
              JB      SKIP_DIGIT       ; Skip it if less
              CMP     AL,'9'           ; Test upper limit
              JA      SKIP_DIGIT       ; Skip it if larger
              JMP     MOVE_DIGIT       ; Move it to buffer if in range
END_DIGITS:
              MOV     BYTE PTR [DI],0DH     ; Carriage return
              INC     DI               ; Bump buffer pointer
              MOV     BYTE PTR [DI],0  ; NULL-byte terminator
```

```
        RET
MOVE_PH_NUM      ENDP
;*****************************************************************
;
SEND_STRING      PROC    NEAR
; Send command code string to selected serial port
; On entry:
;        SI -> buffer containing codes and numbers to send
;                terminated in a NULL byte
SEND_NUM:
        MOV     AL,[SI]          ; Character from buffer
        CMP     AL,0             ; Test for terminator
        JE      SEND_END         ; Exit routine on terminator
        PUSH    SI               ; Save pointer from BIOS
        MOV     DX,COMM_PORT     ; Get BIOS communications port
        MOV     AH,1             ; BIOS service request code
        INT     14H              ; BIOS service routine
        POP     SI               ; Restore buffer pointer,
        INC     SI               ; bump it
        JMP     SEND_NUM         ; and continue
SEND_END:
        RET
SEND_STRING      ENDP
;*****************************************************************
;
SEND_8042       PROC    NEAR
; Procedure to transmit data or control codes to the 8042
; keyboard controller
; On entry: AL = byte to transmit
        PUSH    CX
        PUSH    AX               ; Save byte to send
        CLI                      ; Interrupts off while accessing
                                 ; controller
        MOV     CX,0FFFFH        ; Set up timer counter
WAIT_4_FULL:
        IN      AL,64H           ; Read status
        TEST    AL,00000010B     ; Test for input buffer full bit
        LOOPNZ  WAIT_4_FULL      ; Wait if not full
;
        POP     AX               ; Recover byte to send
        OUT     64H,AL           ; Send to controller
        STI                      ; Reenable interrupts
        POP     CX
        RET
;
SEND_8042        ENDP
```

```
;********************************************************************
;
TEST_CTAF1       PROC     NEAR
; Test if <F1> key pressed while Ctrl and Alt keys are held
; On entry:
;          AL = last keyboard scan code
; On exit:
;          carry set if not Ctrl+Alt+<F1> keystroke
;
; First test for <F1> key
         CMP      AL,3BH          ; Scan code for <F1>
         JNE      NOT_CAF1        ; Last scan code was not <F1>
; Keystroke was <F1> key. Test for Ctrl key held down
; Ctrl key state is encoded in bit 2 of the BIOS data area byte
; at 0040:0017H
         PUSH     ES              ; Save segment
         XOR      AX,AX           ; Clear AX
         MOV      ES,AX           ; and ES
         MOV      AL,ES:[0417H]   ; Get keyboard control byte
         POP      ES
         TEST     AL,00000100B    ; Bit 2 is Ctrl key pressed
         JNZ      CTRL_PRESSED    ; Go if bit set
         JMP      NOT_CAF1        ; Exit if not
CTRL_PRESSED:
         TEST     AL,00001000B    ; Bit 3 is Alt key pressed
         JNZ      IS_CAF1         ; Go if Alt is also held down
         JMP      NOT_CAF1
IS_CAF1:
         CLC                      ; Return code is carry clear
         RET
NOT_CAF1:
         STC                      ; Carry set if not Ctrl+<F1>
         RET
TEST_CTAF1       ENDP
;********************************************************************
;
SHOW_MESS   PROC     NEAR
; Customized display routine for the DIALER TSR
; On entry:
;          SI -> message terminated in 1AH
         PUSH     AX              ; Save caller's register
         PUSH     BX
SHOW_MS:
         MOV      AL,[SI]         ; Get character
         CMP      AL,1AH          ; Test for terminator
         JE       END_OF_MESS
```

```
        MOV     AH,14           ; BIOS service request number
                                ; for ASCII teletype write
        MOV     BX,0            ; Display page
        INT     10H             ; BIOS service request
        INC     SI              ; Bump pointer
        JMP     SHOW_MS
END_OF_MESS:
        POP     BX              ; Restore caller's register
        POP     AX
        CLC                     ; No error detection
        RET
SHOW_MESS    ENDP
;****************************************************************
;
BRIGHT_LINE     PROC    NEAR
; Display current active phone area in bright characters
        MOV     DH,BRT_ROW      ; To set cursor to active row
        MOV     DL,BRT_COL      ; Column value is 1 or 40
        MOV     CX,39           ; Characters to emphasize
BRT_39:
        PUSH    CX              ; Save counter
        CALL    BIO_SET_CUR     ; Cursor to start of phone area
; Read attribute and character at cursor
        MOV     AH,8            ; BIOS service request number
        MOV     BH,0            ; Display page
        INT     10H
; Ignore attribute returned in AH, set BL to bright
        MOV     BL,BRIGHT_ATT   ; Bright attribute from variable
        CALL    BIO_SHOW_ATR    ; Display the same character with
                                ; a bright attribute
        INC     DL              ; Next column
        POP     CX              ; Restore character counter
        LOOP    BRT_39          ; Continue
        RET
;
BRIGHT_LINE     ENDP
;****************************************************************
;
NORMAL_LINE     PROC    NEAR
; Display current active phone area in bright characters
        MOV     DH,BRT_ROW      ; To set cursor to active row
        MOV     DL,BRT_COL      ; Column value is 1 or 40
        MOV     CX,39           ; Characters to emphasize
NOR_39:
        PUSH    CX              ; Save counter
        CALL    BIO_SET_CUR     ; Cursor to start of phone area
```

```
; Read attribute and character at cursor
        MOV     AH,8            ; BIOS service request number
        MOV     BH,0            ; Display page
        INT     10H
; Ignore attribute returned in AH, set BL to bright
        MOV     BL,NORMAL_ATT   ; Normal attribute from variable
        CALL    BIO_SHOW_ATR    ; Display the same character with
                                ; a bright attribute
        INC     DL              ; Next column
        POP     CX              ; Restore character counter
        LOOP    NOR_39          ; Continue
        RET
;
NORMAL_LINE     ENDP
;
;******************************************************************
;
KEY_INPUT       PROC    NEAR
;
; Keyboard input routine with the following parameters:
; Control codes and exit codes:
;               0DH <Enter> .... Exit with carry clear
;              011BH <Esc> ...... Exit with carry set
; On entry:
;          DI -> storage buffer
; On exit:
;          Text is stored in buffer by DI
;                   DI -> start of character buffer
;                   CX = total characters input
;                   Buffer contains space terminator
;
        MOV     CL,40           ; Maximum characters allowed
;
GET_KEY:
        CALL    KBR_WAIT        ; Get character
;*****************|
; input processing |
;*****************|
        CMP     AL,0DH          ; <Enter> key
        JNE     NOT_0DH
        JMP     KBR_EXIT_0      ; Take exit
NOT_0DH:
        CMP     AX,011BH        ; <Esc> key
        JNE     NOT_ESC
        JMP     KBR_EXIT_1      ; Take exit
NOT_ESC:
```

```
; Test for backspace keystroke
        CMP     AL,08H          ; Backspace key?
        JNE     NOT_08          ; Not backspace
;*********************|
;   backspace key     |
;*********************|
; Test for start of display area
        CMP     CL,40           ; Start value at start of display
        JE      GET_KEY         ; Refuse backspace control
        DEC     DI              ; Adjust pointer
        DEC     CL              ; Adjust character counter
        CALL    BIO_TTY         ; Execute cursor backspace
        MOV     AL,' '          ; Blank to clear screen character
        CALL    BIO_TTY
        MOV     AL,08H          ; Backspace code again
        CALL    BIO_TTY
        JMP     GET_KEY         ; Code not stored in buffer
; Test for buffer full
NOT_08:
        CMP     CL,0            ; CL is the counter
        JNZ     DISPLAY_IT
        MOV     AL,07H          ; Bell code
        CALL    BIO_TTY         ; Beep to signal error
        JMP     GET_KEY         ; Buffer is full
;*****************|
;    display      |
;   character     |
;*****************|
DISPLAY_IT:
        CALL    BIO_TTY
; Store it in buffer
        MOV     [DI],AL
;*****************|
;  bump pointers  |
;*****************|
        INC     DI              ; Bump buffer pointer
        DEC     CL              ; Character counter
        JMP     GET_KEY         ; Continue
;*********************|
;  <Enter> key exit   |
;*********************|
KBR_EXIT_0:
        MOV     AL,' '          ; End of input code
        MOV     [DI],AL         ; Place code in buffer
        CLC                     ; <Enter> key exit, no carry
        RET
```

```
;**********************|
;  <Esc> key pressed   |
;**********************|
KBR_EXIT_1:
        MOV     AL,' '              ; Safety measure to close buffer
        MOV     [DI],AL
        STC
        RET
KEY_INPUT       ENDP
;****************************************************************
;
CLEAR_SCR       PROC    NEAR
; Clear the video display with a block move
; On entry:
;          ES -> video buffer base address (ES_TO_VIDEO)
; On exit:
;        carry clear
        PUSH    AX                  ; Save entry registers
        PUSH    CX
        PUSH    DI
        MOV     DI,0                ; Start at offset 0 in buffer
        MOV     AL,20H              ; Blank byte
        MOV     AH,NORMAL_ATT       ; Normal display attribute
        MOV     CX,2000             ; Repeat 2000 times
        CLD                         ; Forward direction in memory
        REP     STOSW               ; Store 2000 words in buffer
        POP     DI
        POP     CX
        POP     AX                  ; Restore entry registers
        CLC                         ; No error detection
        RET
CLEAR_SCR       ENDP
;
;****************************************************************
;                     SOLUTION.LIB procedures
;****************************************************************
; Note: A TSR program must meet the restrictions of a COM-type
;       file. This restriction makes it necessary to modify the
;       procedures in SOLUTION.LIB to NEAR
;
;****************************************************************
;
BIO_TTY         PROC    NEAR
;                               |********************************|
;                               | procedure listed in BIOVIDEO.ASM |
;                               | module of SOLUTION.LIB           |
```

```
;                       |*********************************|
;*********************************************************************
;
BIO_GET_MODE     PROC        NEAR
;                       |*********************************|
;                       | procedure listed in BIOVIDEO.ASM |
;                       | module of SOLUTION.LIB           |
;                       |*********************************|
;*********************************************************************
;
BIO_SET_CUR      PROC        NEAR
;                       |*********************************|
;                       | procedure listed in BIOVIDEO.ASM |
;                       | module of SOLUTION.LIB           |
;                       |*********************************|
;*********************************************************************
;
BIO_GET_CUR      PROC        NEAR
;                       |*********************************|
;                       | procedure listed in BIOVIDEO.ASM |
;                       | module of SOLUTION.LIB           |
;                       |*********************************|
;*********************************************************************
;
BIO_SHOW_ATR     PROC        NEAR
;                       |*********************************|
;                       | procedure listed in BIOVIDEO.ASM |
;                       | module of SOLUTION.LIB           |
;                       |*********************************|
;*********************************************************************
;
KBR_WAIT    PROC     NEAR
;                       |*********************************|
;                       | procedure listed in KEYBRD.ASM  |
;                       | module of SOLUTION.LIB           |
;                       |*********************************|
;*********************************************************************
;
ES_TO_VIDEO      PROC        NEAR
;                       |*********************************|
;                       | procedure listed in DAVIDEO.ASM  |
;                       | module of SOLUTION.LIB           |
;                       |*********************************|
;*********************************************************************
;                     data (in code segment)
;*********************************************************************
```

```
;**********************|
; buffers and variables|
;**********************|
VIDEO_SAVE        DB      4000 DUP (00H)
                                        ; 4000 bytes storage for alpha
                                        ; mode video image
                  DW      0
OLD_CURSOR        DW      0             ; Cursor position for executing
                                        ; program
;*********************|
; storage for the file |
;     PHONES.ASC       |
;*********************|
PHONES_MESS       DB      '            **** DIRECTORY OF '
                  DB      ' USER TELEPHONES ****',0AH,0DH,0AH,0DH
PHONES_TEXT       DB      958 DUP (20H)
                  DB      00H
                  DB      1AH     ; Guard bytes with EOF
MENU_MESS         DB      78 DUP (0CDH)
                  DB      0AH,0DH
                  DB      'Use arrow keys to select a directory '
                  DB      'number and press <Enter> to dial it',
                  DB      0AH,0DH
                  DB      'Press <F1> to HANG UP',0AH,0DH
                  DB      'Press <F2> to type and dial a new'
                  DB      ' number',0AH,0DH
                  DB      'Press <F3> to enter a modem command'
                  DB      0AH,0DH
                  DB      'Press <F4> for command mode (send escape'
                  DB      ' sequence)',0AH,0DH
                  DB      'Press <Esc> to end execution',1AH
;
F2_PROMPT         DB      'Type phone number and press <Enter>: '
                  DB      1AH
F3_PROMPT         DB      'Enter modem command and press <Enter>: '
                  DB      1AH
F0_PROMPT         DB      '                                        '
                  DB      '                        ',1AH
;
;*********************|
;     controls        |
;*********************|
KB_CHIP           DB      1             ; 1 = Intel 8048 keyboard
                                        ; controller
                                        ; 2 = Intel 8042 keyboard
                                        ; controller
```

```
BRT_ROW          DB      2           ; Screen row to set bright
                                     ; range is 2 to 12
BRT_COL          DB      0           ; Screen column to set bright
                                     ; value is 0 or 40
COMM_PORT        DW      0           ; BIOS code for communications
                                     ; port
                                     ; 0 = COM1
                                     ; 1 = COM2
;**********************|
;  display attributes  |
;**********************|
; Note: The default attributes are compatible with most
;        applications
NORMAL_ATT       DB      07H         ; Normal attribute
BRIGHT_ATT       DB      0FH         ; Bright attribute
;
;**********************|
;   text messages      |
;  and modem commands  |
;**********************|
DIAL_BUF         DB      'ATDT'
PHONE_NO_BUF     DB      30 DUP (00H)
;
HANG_UP          DB      'ATH',0DH,00H
                 DB      00H
;
ENTRY_STR        DB      'ATE0',0DH,00H   ; This command string is
                                          ; sent on program entry
;
ESCAPE_STR       DB      '+++',00H        ; Switch from online to
                                          ; command mode
;
INPUT_AREA       DW      40 DUP (00H)
;
MODEM_COMMAND    DW      40 DUP (00H)
                 DW      0           ; Safety word
PROTECT:
;**********************|
; data to be discarded |
;**********************|
; Note: All code and data below the label named PROTECT are
; discarded from memory after installation
DTA              DB      128 DUP (00H)    ; Disk transfer area
PHONES_NAME      DB      '\PHONES.ASC',00H
                                     ; ASCIIZ string with filename
PH_HANDLE        DW      0           ; File handle for PHONES.ASC
```

```
;*******************************************************************
;                        installation routine
;*******************************************************************
; Installation operations:
;        1. Read a file named PHONES.ASC in the root directory of
;           the active drive into a permanent buffer
;        2. Determine and save hardware type:
;           type 1 = PC, XT, and others using the Intel 8048 chip
;           type 2 = PC AT, PS/2, and others using the Intel 8042
;        3. Obtain vector for INT 09H and store in OLD_VECTOR_09
;        4. Set INT 09H vector to this routine
;        5. Protect TSR and exit
;*******************************************************************
;
INSTALL:
;*********************|
;    read PHONES.ASC  |
;*********************|
; If an ASCII file named PHONES.ASC is found in the root directory
; of the active drive, it is loaded into permanent memory. Note
; that this operation must be done during initialization since
; the TSR cannot use MS DOS services
        MOV     DX,OFFSET CS:DTA   ; Set pointer to program's
                                   ; buffer
        CALL    SET_DTA
        MOV     DX,OFFSET CS:PHONES_NAME ; Pointer to ASCIIZ
                                         ; string
        CALL    OPEN_FILE
        JC      SET_PORT           ; Open operation failed
; If no carry AX contains file handle from open call
        MOV     CS:PH_HANDLE,AX            ; Store handle in
                                          ; variable
;*********************|
; read 958 bytes from |
;   file into buffer  |
;*********************|
; Use MS DOS service number 63, INT 21H, to read 958 bytes into
; a buffer named PHONES_TEXT using the file's handle
        MOV     AH,63              ; Service request code
        MOV     BX,CS:PH_HANDLE ; File handle from open call
        MOV     CX,958             ; Bytes to read
        MOV     DX,OFFSET CS:PHONES_TEXT   ; Destination buffer
        PUSH    CS
        POP     DS                 ; Set DS to storage segment
        INT     21H
; No error processing. File is assumed read into buffer
```

```
;**********************|
;   close PHONES.ASC   |
;**********************|
        MOV     BX,CS:PH_HANDLE ; File handle
        CALL    CLOSE_FILE
;**********************|
;   set communications |
;     port BIOS code   |
;**********************|
; Test the base address for the RS-232-C communications line
; number 2 and change default BIOS port number if not zero
SET_PORT:
        MOV     AX,0            ; Set AX to BIOS data area base
        MOV     ES,AX           ; and move value to ES
        MOV     AX,ES:[402H]    ; Storage address for COM2 port
        CMP     AX,0            ; Value is zero if no second port
        JE      GET_MACHINE
        MOV     AX,1            ; Value for COM2
        MOV     CS:COMM_PORT,AX ; Set value in data area
;**********************|
;   get machine type   |
;**********************|
GET_MACHINE:
        MOV     AX,0FFFFH
        MOV     ES,AX
        MOV     AL,ES:[000EH]   ; Machine ID code
; Test for PCjr code (0FDH) and exit. Processing for the PCjr
; keyboard is not provided in the intercept routine
        CMP     AL,0FDH         ; PCjr
        JNE     NOT_PCJR
; Return to DOS and abort installation
        MOV     AH,76           ; Normal DOS exit code
        MOV     AL,0            ; No error return
        INT     21H
NOT_PCJR:
        CMP     AL,0FCH         ; AT, XT 286, and some PS/2
                                ; systems
        JE      MACHINE_2       ; all use the 8042 controller
; Other systems using the 8042 can be detected by testing bit 4
; of the keyboard data byte at 0040:0096H. If set, the system is
; equipped with 101/102-key keyboard
        XOR     AX,AX           ; Clear AX
        MOV     ES,AX           ; and ES
        MOV     AL,ES:[0496H]   ; Get keyboard data byte
        TEST    AL,00010000B    ; Is bit 4 set?
        JNZ     MACHINE_2       ; Type 2 if bit 4 is set
```

```
            JMP       MACHINE_1          ; It is safe to assume the
                                         ; 8048 keyboard controller
MACHINE_2:
            MOV       CS:KB_CHIP,2       ; Change default machine code
MACHINE_1:
; Use MS DOS service 53 of INT 21H to obtain original vector for
; INT 09H from the vector table
;*********************|
;    get INT 09H      |
;*********************|
            MOV       AH,53              ; Service request code
            MOV       AL,09H             ; Code of vector desired
            INT       21H
; ES -> segment address of installed interrupt handler
; BX -> offset address of installed interrupt handler
;*********************|
; store it in variable|
;*********************|
            MOV       AX,ES              ; Segment to AX
            MOV       DI,OFFSET CS:OLD_VECTOR_09
                                         ; Pointer to storage variable
            MOV       CS:[DI],BX         ; Store offset
            MOV       CS:[DI+2],AX       ; Store segment
;*********************|
; set new INT 09H in  |
;    vector table     |
;*********************|
; Also uses DOS service 37 of INT 21H
            MOV       AH,37              ; Service request code
            MOV       AL,09H             ; Interrupt code
; Data segment = code segment in a .COM file
            MOV       DX,OFFSET CS:NEW09_INT   ; Routine's offset
            INT       21H
;*********************|
; protect TSR and exit|
;*********************|
            STI
            MOV       DX,OFFSET CS:PROTECT
            INC       DX                 ; One more byte
            INT       27H
;
;****************************************************************
;                  procedures used in installation
;****************************************************************
SET_DTA          PROC      NEAR
; Set memory area to be used by DOS as disk transfer area
```

```
;  On entry:
;           DX -> 128-byte buffer to be used as DTA
;
;  On exit:
;           carry clear
;
        MOV     AH,26           ; DOS service request
        INT     21H
        RET
SET_DTA         ENDP
;****************************************************************
;
OPEN_FILE       PROC    NEAR
; Open file using an ASCIIZ string for the filename
; On entry:
;           DX -> buffer containing ASCIIZ string for filename
; On exit:
;           if carry clear file was opened successfully
;           AX = file handle
;           if carry set open operation failed
;           AX = error code
;                1 = invalid function
;                2 = file not found
;                3 = path not found
;                4 = no available handle
;                5 = access denied
;               12 = invalid access code
;
        MOV     AH,61           ; DOS service request number
                                ; to open file (handle mode)
        MOV     AL,2            ; Read-write access
        INT     21H
        RET
OPEN_FILE       ENDP
;****************************************************************
;
CLOSE_FILE      PROC    NEAR
; Close file using file handle
; On entry:
;           BX = file handle
; On exit:
;           carry clear if operation successful - file closed
;           carry set if operation failed - invalid handle or file
;           not open
;
        MOV     AH,62           ; DOS service request
```

```
              INT      21H
              RET
    CLOSE_FILE        ENDP
    ;
    CODE    ENDS
              END      ENTRY
```

6.3 Interrupt Sharing

Some programs and many TSR routines take over interrupts that are used by system software for other purposes. For example, the printer filters and the SPOOL TSR discussed in Chapter 4 intercept the printer interrupt (INT 17H), and the SERCOM program presented in Chapter 5 intercepts the communications interrupt (INT 0BH or INT 0CH). The DIALER program, listed previously in this chapter, intercepts the keyboard interrupt (INT 09H) in order to detect its activation keystrokes. In programs that execute independently, like the program SERCOM in Chapter 5, this form of operation presents no major difficulties. When the program concludes execution it can restore the vectors and other machine hardware to its default state, as performed by the SERCOM code. However, most TSRs operate by intercepting and filtering a system interrupt. Since the TSR does not execute discretely, as does a conventional EXE or COM program, it cannot determine when to remove itself from the system.

For example, the SPOOL TSR (in Chapter 4), intercepts the timer interrupt and speeds up the system clock in order to perform its own functions. But the BIOS code requires an 18.2 counts-per-second timer beat in order to synchronize diskette operations and to update its internal controls. In order to preserve these functions, SPOOL keeps track of the beat of the accelerated clock and returns execution to the BIOS handler at the original rate. SPOOL relocates the original vectors at INT 60H and INT 61H. Superficially, it may seem that it is possible to restore the system to its previous state by exchanging the INT 17H and INT 60H vectors and INT 08H and INT 61H vectors. However, this manipulation would not reset the timer beat to the original 18.2 counts-per-second. In the case of the SPOOL program, in order to completely restore the system to its normal state it would also be necessary to slow down the system timer to its original beat.

6.3.1 Unlinking an Interrupt Handler

Most of the problems associated with TSRs are related to conflicts between the TSR handler and the system software, between the TSR and another TSR, or between the TSR and an application program. Suppose that the SPOOL TSR was furnished as an executable file to a user with no technical knowledge of the program's characteristics. In this case, once SPOOL was installed, the only way that this user could restore the system to normal operation would be to restart it. There would likely be a conflict if this user tried to run other programs that intercepted the same interrupts used by SPOOL or that changed the system clock.

One solution to this problem would be to provide a separate program that will remove a specific TSR and restore the system to its previous state. The FILTOFF program listed in Chapter 4 performs this function. Perhaps a more elegant solution would be to include the removal code as part of the TSR. This routine, which could be visualized as the TSR's self-destruct mechanism, would restore all system parameters and vectors to its normal state and unlink the TSR from the interrupt chain.

Chapter 4 of the *IBM Personal System/2 and Personal Computer BIOS Interface Technical Reference* (see the Bibliography at the end of this book) proposes a protocol for interrupt chaining. It is not too clear in the IBM Manual whether the requirements listed in the protocol apply to software handlers in TSR routines. Furthermore, the sample code provided by IBM does not apply to typical TSR coding. For this reason, in adopting the idea of a TSR that includes its own unlinking routine, we have not followed closely the IBM sample code. However, we have used identical data patterns as those described in the IBM literature so as to create a compatible structure with the same entry point. This structure can be seen at the beginning of the DIALER program.

The program named UNLINK09, listed below, shows the steps necessary for calling a TSR's removal code. UNLINK09 works with any TSR, coded according to the IBM convention and installed at INT 09H. The code can be readily modified to work with other interrupt vectors. The TSR removal code and the calling program are designed so that execution returns to the caller. This makes it possible for another program or TSR to include a routine, within its own code, that unlinks a previous handler in the chain. The mechanism provides a communications path between the system, an application, or a TSR, with an installed interrupt handler that meets the requirements of the IBM protocol mentioned above.

```
;***************************************************************
;***************************************************************
;                         UNLINK09.ASM
;***************************************************************
;***************************************************************
; Program to access the unlinking code contained in the DIALER
; program
;
;************************ stack ****************************
STACK   SEGMENT stack
;
                DB      0400H DUP ('?'); Default stack is 1K
STACK_TOP       EQU     THIS BYTE
;
STACK   ENDS
;************************ data ****************************
DATA    SEGMENT
;*********************|
;  address of handler |
; for CALL instruction |
;*********************|
```

```
PRESENT_09        DD       0
;
EXIT_MS           DB       'INT 09H handler unlinked from chain $'
;
DATA     ENDS
;
;*************************** code ***************************
;
CODE     SEGMENT
         ASSUME  CS:CODE
;
START:
;******************|
;  initialization  |
;******************|
; Establish data and extra segment addressability
         MOV     AX,DATA          ; Address of DATA to AX
         MOV     DS,AX            ; and to DS
         ASSUME  DS:DATA          ; Assume from here on
; Initialize stack. Note that this instruction is necessary for
; compatibility with non-Microsoft assemblers
         LEA     SP,SS:STACK_TOP ; Stack pointer to top of stack
;******************|
;   get address of |
; unlinking routine |
;******************|
         MOV     AX,0             ; Clear register
         MOV     ES,AX            ; Set EX to segment of vector
                                  ; table
         MOV     DI,24H           ; DI -> offset of vector for
                                  ; INT 09H
                                  ; (09H * 4 = 24H)
         MOV     BX,ES:[DI]       ; Offset to BX
         MOV     AX,ES:[DI+2]     ; Segment to AX
; AX -> segment address of installed interrupt handler
; BX -> offset address of installed interrupt handler
; Access to unlinking routine of handler is at its entry point
; plus 9
         ADD     BX,9             ; Set BX to unlink code entry
;********************|
; store it in variable |
;********************|
         MOV     DI,OFFSET PRESENT_09
                                  ; Pointer to storage variable
         MOV     [DI],BX          ; Store offset
         MOV     [DI+2],AX        ; Store segment
```

```
;*********************|
;     go to unlink    |
;     via FAR CALL    |
;*********************|
        CALL    DWORD PTR DS:PRESENT_09
;*********************|
;  display message    |
;  to confirm return  |
;*********************|
        LEA     DX,EXIT_MS      ; Text message in data segment
        MOV     AH,9            ; Service request number for
                                ; MS DOS
        INT     21H
;*********************|
;     exit to DOS     |
;*********************|
DOS_EXIT:
        MOV     AH,4CH          ; DOS service request code
        MOV     AL,0            ; No error code returned
        INT     21H             ; TO DOS
;
CODE    ENDS
        END     START
```

7

Keyboard Programming

7.0 IBM Microcomputer Keyboard Hardware

The IBM microcomputer component that has undergone the most modifications and redesigns is the keyboard. Externally, the changes have consisted in the addition of several new keys, the repositioning of other keys, and the inclusion of light-emitting diodes (LEDs) to indicate the state of the toggle keys. Internally, the keyboard of the PC and XT, the one on the PCjr, and the keyboards of the PC AT and the PS/2 line are completely different.

The keyboard furnished with the original IBM PC and PC XT has 83 keys. The IBM PCjr was released with a 62-key keyboard, popularly dubbed the "Chiclet" keyboard because of the appearance and feel of the keys. It was soon recalled by IBM and replaced with a better model. The IBM PC AT has an 84-key keyboard characterized by a relocated Esc (escape) key and a new system request key, intended for use in multitasking environments. The PS/2 line introduced yet another keyboard with 101 keys on the U.S. version and 102 keys for the models sold outside the United States. The PS/2 keyboards are equipped with two additional function keys and special keypads with duplicate editing and cursor control keys.

Regarding electronic hardware, the PC and XT keyboards use the Intel 8048 keyboard controller while the AT and PS/2 keyboards use the Intel 8042. Although the two chips are different, the 8042 can be programmed to mimic the 8048.

7.0.1 The Keyboard Controller

The main function of the keyboard controller is to relieve the microprocessor from monitoring the state of the key switches. In operation these chips perform as follows:

1. Whenever a key is pressed or released, the 8048 or 8042 stores a code (called a *scan code*) in one of its internal registers. In all IBM systems this register can be read at port 60H. The scan codes are specific for each key but do not correspond with the ASCII value of the key.

2. Once the scan code is stored, the keyboard controller generates an interrupt on the 8259 line IRQ1. If the keyboard interrupt is enabled, the microprocessor transfers execution to the INT 09H handler.

3. The INT 09H handler, located in the system BIOS, reads the scan code at port 60H and converts it into the ASCII or extended ASCII characters. If the keystroke corresponds to a key that requires immediate action, as is the case with the LOCK keys, the Print Screen key or any other hot key, the handler proceeds accordingly. If not, the ASCII code and the original scan code are placed in a BIOS area called the *keyboard buffer*.

7.1 The Keyboard Scan Codes

Some forms of keyboard programming require the identification of keys by their scan codes. We have mentioned in Section 7.0 that every time a key is pressed or released, the keyboard microprocessor places a code, particular to that key, in the register associated with port 60H. The keyboard handler uses these scan codes to determine which key or key combination has been pressed or released and to take action accordingly.

The programming operations necessary for obtaining and interpreting the keyboard scan codes are simple and straightforward. In addition, IBM has maintained the same scan codes for the corresponding keys in the various keyboards. However, the description and listing of the scan codes in the IBM Technical Reference Manuals have created some confusion.

For instance, the *IBM Personal Computer AT Technical Reference Manual* (pages 4-10 to 4-13) lists the make codes for all keys and explains that the break codes are identical to the make codes, but preceded by a value of F0H. Someone reading this table can assume, for example, that the AT < Esc > key generates the make scan code 76H and that the break sequence consists of the break prefix F0H followed by a value of 76H. In reality, the scan codes listed in the table do not correspond with those generated by the AT keyboard during normal operation. For instance, the AT < Esc > key actually produces the make code 01H (not the code 76H listed in the table) and the break code 81H (not the sequence F0H, 76H).

This variation is due to the setting of a bit in the keyboard controller's command register, which forces the AT keyboard into a mode of operation compatible with the PC hardware. The BIOS initialization routines automatically set the AT keyboard in the PC-compatible mode.

The keyboards of the PS/2 line offer three sets of scan codes. Scan code set 1 is compatible with the keyboards of the PC line. Here again, the following statement in the IBM Model 50 and 60 Technical Reference can be easily misinterpreted: "The system defaults to scan set 2, but can be switched to set 1 or set 3." It is not hard to construe, from these words, that scan set 2 is normally active; in reality, during normal execution the PS/2 BIOS initialization code automatically selects scan set 1.

Table 7.1 shows that the make and break scan codes for some common control keys are identical in several models of IBM microcomputers.

Table 7.1. *Keyboard Make–Break Scan Codes*

KEY	PC & XT	AT	PCjr	PS/2
< Esc >	01H–81H	01H–81H	01H–81H	01H–81H
< F1 >	3BH–BBH	3BH–BBH	3BH–BBH	3BH–BBH
< F2 >	3CH–BCH	3CH–BCH	3CH–BCH	3CH–BCH
< F3 >	3DH–BDH	3DH–BDH	3DH–BDH	3DH–BDH
< F4 >	3EH–BEH	3EH–BEH	3EH–BEH	3EH–BEH
< F5 >	3FH–BFH	3FH–BFH	3FH–BFH	3FH–BFH
< F6 >	40H–C0H	40H–C0H	40H–C0H	40H–C0H
< F7 >	41H–C1H	41H–C1H	41H–C1H	41H–C1H
< F8 >	42H–C2H	42H–C2H	42H–C2H	42H–C2H
< F9 >	43H–C3H	43H–C3H	43H–C3H	43H–C3H
< F10 >	44H–C4H	44H–C4H	44H–C4H	44H–C4H
< Scroll Lock >	46H–C6H	46H–C6H	46H–C6H	46H–C6H
< Backspace >	0EH–8EH	0EH–8EH	0EH–8EH	0EH–8EH
< Ins >	52H–D2H	52H–D2H	52H–D2H	52H–D2H
< Del >	53H–D3H	53H–D3H	53H–D3H	53H–D3H
< Num Lock >	45H–C5H	45H–C5H	45H–C5H	45H–C5H
< Tab >	0FH–8FH	0FH–8FH	0FH–8FH	0FH–8FH
< Enter >	1CH–9CH	1CH–9CH	1CH–9CH	1CH–9CH
< Caps Lock >	3AH–BAH	3AH–BAH	3AH–BAH	3AH–BAH
< Left Shift >	2AH–AAH	2AH–AAH	2AH–AAH	2AH–AAH
< Right Shift >	36H–B6H	36H–B6H	36H–B6H	36H–B6H
< Left Ctrl >	1DH–9DH	1DH–9DH	1DH–9DH	1DH–9DH
< Up Arrow >	48H–C8H	48H–C8H	48H–C8H	48H–C8H
< Left Arrow >	4BH–CBH	4BH–CBH	4BH–CBH	4BH–CBH
< Right Arrow >	4DH–CDH	4DH–CDH	4DH–CDH	4DH–CDH
< Down Arrow >	50H–D0H	50H–D0H	50H–D0H	50H–D0H

7.2 The Keyboard Interrupt (INT 09H)

The IBM keyboard controllers are normally programmed to generate an interrupt every time a make or break scan code is placed in port 60H. The BIOS keyboard handler, located at the vector for INT 09H, gains control during this interrupt. The action performed by the handler depends on the key or key combination that originated the interrupt.

1. If the scan code in port 60H corresponds to a character key, the handler places the corresponding ASCII code, together with the scan code, in the keyboard buffer.

2. If the scan code corresponds to the make or break action of the Shift, Ctrl, Alt, Ins, Num Lock, Cap Lock, Scroll Lock, or SysRq key, the handler updates the state of the corresponding bit(s) in a memory area known as the *keyboard status byte.*

3. If the scan code corresponds to the Del key, and if the Ctrl-Alt keys are held down simultaneously, the handler transfers execution to the BIOS warm boot routine.

4. If the scan code for the Pause key, or an equivalent sequence, is detected, the handler enters a wait loop until the next valid keystroke is received.

5. If the scan code corresponds to the Print Screen key or key combination, the handler executes interrupt 05H.

6. If the scan code corresponds to the Ctrl Break sequence, the handler executes interrupt 1BH.

7.2.1 Classification of Keys and Keystrokes

According to their function, the keys can be classified into the following groups:

1. The character keys are commonly used in the creation of text: the letters of the alphabet, the keys for the Arabic numerals, and the symbol keys. These keys are often called the *ASCII set.*

2. The SOFTWARE CONTROL keys are noncharacter keys used by system and applications programs for executing user controls and commands. This group includes the function keys, labeled F1 to F12, the Ins (Insert), Del (Delete), Home, End, PgUp (Page-Up), PgDn (Page-Down), Tab (Tabulate), Backspace, Esc (Escape), and the arrow keys.

3. The HOT keys and keystroke combinations are those that generate an immediate action at the system or application level. The Pause, Print Screen, Ctrl-Alt-Del, and SysRq actions correspond with system level functions. The Ctrl-Break sequence is available as a programmable HOT keystroke combination.

4. The ALTERNATE STATE keys are those that temporarily activate an alternative interpretation of another key. They are the Shift, Ctrl, and Alt keys.

5. The TOGGLE keys are those that permanently activate one of two states, which are recorded at the system level. Caps Lock, Num Lock, and Scroll Lock are toggle keys.

When the keyboard handler detects a scan code corresponding to an ASCII or a SOFTWARE CONTROL key (groups 1 and 2 above) it looks up the code corresponding to the key and stores it in a dedicated area of RAM.

The HOT keys (group 3) determine an immediate action either in the form of a routine internal to the keyboard handler or associated with a software interrupt. Some HOT keys consist of several keystrokes; for instance, the Ctrl-Alt-Del sequence activates the warm boot action and the Ctrl-Break sequence transfers control to interrupt 1BH.

Some ALTERNATE STATE keys (group 4) determine a different interpretation of a keystroke by the handler; for instance, if a character key is pressed while the Shift key is held down, the keystroke is recorded in uppercase. Other ALTERNATE STATE keys are merely recorded by the handler and the interpretation is left to the application.

This action also applies to the TOGGLE keys (group 5). On the PC AT and the PS/2 keyboards each TOGGLE key is furnished with an indicator light, sometimes called a *keyboard LED*. In these keyboards, the indicator light is also controlled by the handler at INT 09H.

The Print Screen Function. All IBM microcomputers provide a hot key or keystroke combination that activates a screen dump to the parallel printer port. The BIOS handler for this function is located at the vector for INT 05H.

The System Request Function. The system request key, labeled Sys Req, is found in the top, right hand corner of the AT keyboard. This key was conceived for use in multitasking environments, but the developers of OS/2 adopted the Ctrl-Esc and the Alt-Esc keystrokes instead. In the PS/2 keyboards the system request function, labeled SysRq, requires the Alt-Print Screen keystroke combination. No system request function is implemented in the original PC, the XT, or the PCjr, since the processor used in these computers does not support multitasking.

The AT and the PS/2 systems, on detecting the system request key or keystroke combinations, will load the AH registers with the value 85H and execute INT 15H. If the action was caused by a make code, the AL register holds 00H. If the action was caused by a break code, AL holds 01H. Since BIOS does not provide a function for service number 85H, of INT 15H, the keystroke will normally appear to have no action. But an application could take over this service for its own purposes.

The Pause Function. All IBM microcomputers go into a wait loop whenever the Pause key or keystroke combination is detected by the interrupt 09H handler. This allows the user to instantly detain an application or system function, such as a screen listing or printer operation. The paused program will resume when an ASCII key is pressed. In the PS/2 keyboards this is a dedicated key labeled Pause. In the PC, XT, and AT keyboards the pause function activates with the Ctrl-Num Lock sequence. In the PCjr the pause function requires the Fn-Q keystroke.

The Keyboard Break Function. The BIOS keyboard handler in all IBM microcomputers recognizes certain key combinations as a keyboard break. This function is provided so that a system program or an application can regain control of runaway code, interrupt undesired execution, or exit an endless loop. This is possible because the function is triggered by a hardware interrupt physically linked to the key or keystroke combination designated as the keyboard break. If the keyboard interrupt is enabled, this action will always invoke interrupt 1BH.

There is a typographical error in page 5-19 of the *IBM Technical Reference Manual for the Personal Computer AT*, which states that the Ctrl-Break keystrokes generate an interrupt 1AH. Interrupt 1AH correspond to the system timer services; the text should have said 1BH.

When the break handler concludes, it should proceed in the same manner as any hardware interrupt routine. This means that the code should send the End of Interrupt command to the interrupt controller, reenable interrupts, and exit via the IRET instruction, for example:

```
        MOV     AL,20H              ; Issue EOI command
        OUT     20H,AL              ; to interrupt controller
        STI                         ; Interrupts ON
        IRET                        ; Return for interrupt
```

The Ctrl-C Handler.   MS DOS provides its own break handler which is activated with
the keystrokes Ctrl-C. The DOS routine terminates any currently active process and
returns control to the parent process. This constitutes an actual abort operation, but it
does not close any open files nor restore vectors or drivers. The most important
difference between the DOS Ctrl-C handler and the keyboard break is that the DOS
handler is not interrupt-driven. When DOS is in control, it checks the keyboard buffer
for the special keystrokes, but the execution of an application cannot be interrupted by
pressing Ctrl-C.

7.2.2 The SHOWSCAN Program

Programmers often need to obtain the scan code for a certain keystroke so that it can
be intercepted and processed by the software. Because of the imprecisions of some
published scan code tables it is convenient to have at hand a small utility that displays
the actual codes generated by the hardware. The following program performs this
function in the simplest way possible:

```
;****************************************************************
;****************************************************************
;                       SHOWSCAN.ASM
;****************************************************************
;****************************************************************
;
; Program for displaying the hexadecimal value of the make and
; break keyboard scan codes
;
; Program operation:
; The program intercepts the BIOS keyboard handler at INT 09H and
; installs the intercept code located at the label HEX09_INT
;
; The intercept routine performs the following operations:
; 1. Reads the raw scan code at port 60H
; 2. Converts its binary value into two hexadecimal digits
; 3. Displays this value
;
; The <Esc> key will end execution and return to DOS. The
; original vector is restored on exit
;
;****************************************************************
;                   procedure in SOLUTION.LIB
;****************************************************************
;
```

```
        EXTRN   BIO_SHOW_MESS:  FAR
        ;
        INCLUDELIB SOLUTION
        ;
        ;*********************** stack ***************************
        STACK   SEGMENT stack
                        DB      0400H DUP ('?'); Default stack is 1K
        STACK_TOP       EQU     THIS BYTE
        ;
        STACK   ENDS
        ;*********************** data ****************************
        DATA    SEGMENT
        ;
        OLD_VECTOR_09   DD      0   ; Storage for the original INT 09H
                                    ; vector
        ENTRY_MSG       DB      'Scan code display utility - values in'
                        DB      ' hexadecimal - Press <Esc> to exit'
                        DB      0AH,0DH,0AH,0DH,00H
        ;
        SCAN_MSG        DB      '  H',0AH,0DH,00H
        DATA    ENDS
        ;*********************** code ****************************
        CODE    SEGMENT
                ASSUME  CS:CODE
        START:
        ;********************|
        ;    initialization  |
        ;********************|
        ; Establish data and extra segment addressability
                MOV     AX,DATA         ; Address of DATA to AX
                MOV     DS,AX           ; and to DS
                ASSUME  DS:DATA         ; Assume from here on
        ; Initialize stack. Note that this instruction is necessary for
        ; compatibility with non-Microsoft assemblers
                LEA     SP,SS:STACK_TOP ; Stack pointer to top of stack
                MOV     ES,AX           ; Reproduce DS in ES
                ASSUME  ES:DATA
        ;********************|
        ;    display entry   |
        ;      message        |
        ;********************|
                LEA     SI,ENTRY_MSG    ; Pointer to message
                CALL    BIO_SHOW_MESS   ; Display message
        ;********************|
        ;  get INT 09H vector |
        ;********************|
```

```
        ; Interrupts off while changing the vector table
                CLI
        ; Uses DOS service 35H of INT 21H to obtain original vector for
        ; INT 09H from the vector table
                MOV     AH,35H      ; Service request code
                MOV     AL,09H      ; Code of vector desired
                INT     21H
        ; ES -> Segment address of BIOS handler
        ; BX -> Offset address of BIOS handler
                MOV     SI,OFFSET OLD_VECTOR_09
        ; Offset of forward pointer in 16-byte structured table
                MOV     [SI],BX         ; Save offset of original handler
                MOV     [SI+2],ES       ; and segment
        ;*********************|
        ; install new handler |
        ;     for INT 09H     |
        ;*********************|
        ; Uses DOS service 25H if INT 21H to set address of new service
        ; routine in the vector table
                MOV     AH,25H      ; Service request code
                MOV     AL,09H      ; Interrupt code
        ; Set DS to CS for DOS service
                PUSH    DS                  ; Save program's DS
                PUSH    CS
                POP     DS
                MOV     DX,OFFSET CS:HEX09_INT   ; Offset of service rtn
                INT     21H
                POP     DS                  ; Restore DS register
        ; Reenable interrupts
                STI
        ;*********************|
        ;   wait for interrupt |
        ;*********************|
        ; Do nothing while waiting for keyboard interrupt
        DO_NOTHING:
                NOP
                JMP     DO_NOTHING
        ;************************************************************
        ;                     INT 09H intercept routine
        ;************************************************************
        HEX09_INT:
        ;*********************|
        ;     get scan code   |
        ;*********************|
                IN      AL,60H          ; Read scan code at port 60H
                CALL    BIN8_2_HEXBX    ; Convert to ASCII hexadecimal
```

```
        ; AL = binary scan code
        ; BX = ASCII value of AL
        ;*********************|
        ;  display scan code  |
        ;*********************|
                LEA     DI,SCAN_MSG
                MOV     [DI],BH         ; Store first ASCII digit
                INC     DI              ; Bump pointer
                MOV     [DI],BL         ; Store second ASCII digit
                LEA     SI,SCAN_MSG
                CALL    BIO_SHOW_MESS   ; Display routine in SOLUTION.LIB
        ;*********************|
        ;   send acknowledge  |
        ;*********************|
        ; The keyboard acknowledge signal consists in first setting
        ; and then clearing bit 7 of the byte at port 61H
                PUSH    AX              ; Save scan code
                IN      AL,61H          ; Read control port
                MOV     AH,AL           ; Save value of port 61H in AH
                OR      AL,10000000B    ; Set keyboard acknowledge bit
                OUT     61H,AL          ; Send to control port
                XCHG    AH,AL           ; Restore original control
                AND     AL,01111111B    ; Turn OFF bit 7
                OUT     61H,AL          ; Send to control port
        ;*********************|
        ;  discard keystroke  |
        ;*********************|
        ; Discard the keystroke by exiting interrupt
                CLI                     ; Turn OFF interrupts
                MOV     AL,20H          ; Send EOI code
                OUT     20H,AL          ; to interrupt controller
                STI                     ; Interrupts ON
        ;*********************|
        ;  test for <Esc> key |
        ;*********************|
        ; Test for <Esc> key break code to exit
                POP     AX              ; Restore scan code
                CMP     AL,01H          ; <Esc> key make code
                JE      EXIT_RTN
                IRET                    ; Return to DO_NOTHING loop
        ;*********************|
        ;  restore old INT 09H |
        ;*********************|
        EXIT_RTN:
        ; Restore original keyboard interrupt vector
                MOV     SI,OFFSET OLD_VECTOR_09
```

```
; Set DS:DX to original segment and offset of keyboard interrupt
; vector
        MOV     DX,[SI]             ; DX -> offset
        MOV     AX,[SI+2]           ; Segment to AX
        MOV     DS,AX               ; and to DS
        MOV     AH,25H              ; DOS service request
        MOV     AL,09H              ; Keyboard interrupt vector
        INT     21H
;********************|
;    exit to DOS     |
;********************|
        MOV     AH,4CH              ; DOS service request code
        MOV     AL,0                ; No error code returned
        INT     21H                 ; TO DOS
;****************************************************************
;                           procedures
;****************************************************************
BIN8_2_HEXBX    PROC    NEAR
; Convert an 8-bit binary number into two ASCII hexadecimal
; digits
; On entry:
;       AL holds binary value (preserved)
; On exit:
;       BH = first hexadecimal digit
;       BL = second hexadecimal digit
;
        PUSH    AX
        PUSH    CX
;
        PUSH    AX                  ; Save input binary
        MOV     CL,4                ; Set counter for shifting nibble
        SHR     AL,CL               ; Isolate high-order nibble
        CALL    BIN_2_ASCHEX
        MOV     BH,AL               ; Save ASCII in BH
        POP     AX                  ; Restore input
        AND     AL,0FH              ; Clear high-order nibble
        CALL    BIN_2_ASCHEX
        MOV     BL,AL               ; Save ASCII in BL
        POP     CX                  ; Restore input
        POP     AX
        RET
BIN8_2_HEXBX    ENDP
;****************************************************************
BIN_2_ASCHEX    PROC    NEAR
; Convert a binary into an ASCII hexadecimal digit
; Input and output in AL
```

```
          CMP      AL,9              ; Test for digit or letter
          JA       LETTER            ; Go if greater than 9
          ADD      AL,30H            ; Convert digit to ASCII
          RET
LETTER:
          ADD      AL,37H            ; Convert letter to ASCII
          RET
BIN_2_ASCHEX      ENDP
;**************************************************************
CODE      ENDS
          END      START
```

7.3 Keyboard Data in BIOS

Keyboard data is stored in three BIOS areas:

1. The byte at absolute address 0040:0017H, known as the first keyboard status byte

2. The byte at absolute address 0040:0018H, known as the second keyboard status byte

3. The buffer pointers and keyboard data buffer starting at absolute address 0040:001AH

IBM has maintained the same address for these areas from the original PC to the PS/2 line.

7.3.1 The First Keyboard Status Byte

Figure 7.1 lists the bit structure of the first keyboard status byte located at address 0040:0017H.

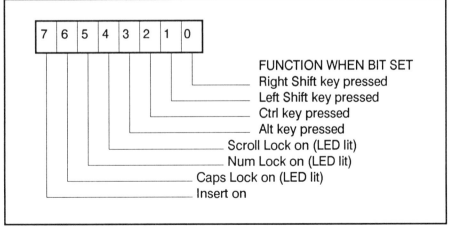

Figure 7.1. *First Keyboard Status Byte at 0000:0417H*

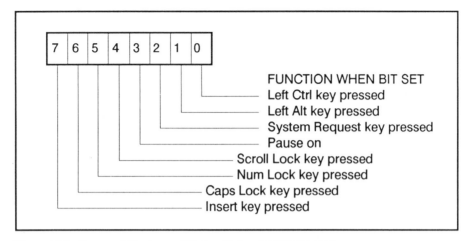

Figure 7.2. *Second Keyboard Status Byte at 0000:0418H*

7.3.2 The Second Keyboard Status Byte

Figure 7.2 lists the bit structure of the second keyboard status byte located at address
0040:0018H. Note that bits 4, 5, 6, and 7 on both status bytes refer to the Scroll Lock,
Num Lock, Caps Lock, and Ins keys, respectively. In the first status byte the bits indicate
the active state. In the second status byte they indicate whether these keys were pressed
simultaneously with the last keystroke. Bits 0 and 1 of the second status byte are
meaningful for PS/2 systems only, since previous keyboards do not have Left Alt and
Left Ctrl keys. Bit number 2 of this byte is also used, in the PCjr, to indicate the state
of the keyboard click function.

An application can change the alternate state or toggle keys by modifying the
corresponding bit in the keyboard status bytes. This operation can be used for presetting
the lock key status. In the AT and PS/2 keyboards the state of the toggle keys is
represented by an illuminated indicator (LED). Changing the corresponding bit to 1 or
0 will turn the light on or off.

7.3.3 The Keyboard Buffer and Buffer Pointers

The keyboard buffer is used by the interrupt 09H handler to store the ASCII values for
keystrokes. Applications and system programs can retrieve these values using the BIOS
keyboard services of INT 16H or by reading the buffer directly. The handler at INT 09H
converts the original scan codes into the corresponding ASCII, extended ASCII, and
control codes of the IBM character set, prior to storing the keystrokes in the buffer.

The keyboard buffer uses two buffer pointers. The output pointer, called
BUFFER_HEAD, is located at address 0040:001AH. The input pointer, called
BUFFER_TAIL, is located at address 0040:001CH. The storage area of the buffer starts
at address 0040:001EH and extends for 16 words. Two storage bytes are used for each
keystroke, one for the ASCII value and another one for the scan code. Since the last
word in the buffer is not used for character storage, the total capacity is 15 characters.

If the keyboard buffer is empty, then the BUFFER_HEAD pointer and the BUFFER_TAIL pointer are equal. This can be used to flush any old characters from the buffer. The following code fragment shows a way of flushing the keyboard buffer.

```
CLI                          ; Interrupts OFF while changing
                             ; pointers
MOV    AX,0040H              ; BIOS data area segment
MOV    ES,AX                 ; indirectly to ES
MOV    AL,ES:[001AH]         ; Get BUFFER_HEAD
MOV    ES:[001CH],AL         ; Set BUFFER_TAIL to this value
STI                          ; Interrupts back on
```

An alternative way of flushing the keyboard buffer is a loop that tests for characters in the buffer and discards them. The procedure named KBR_FLUSH in the KEYBRD module of SOLUTION.LIB performs this operation (see Chapter 2).

One or more characters can be entered directly into the buffer so as to appear to an application as having been typed from the keyboard. In this case the buffer pointers will also require adjustment, since they must signal both ends of the new string. One possible use of this technique is to force DOS to execute a program or command on exit from another program.

7.4 System and Keyboard Performance

The use of more advanced microprocessors, superior data storage devices, and better display hardware are well-known ways to make a software run faster. This type of performance improvement needs no explanation; it is easy to see why a more advanced machine will make programs more productive. On the other hand, the claims of simple utilities and routines to great performance improvements have the ring of a phony sales plot. It is hard to believe that a substantial gain can come cheaply.

Undoubtedly, some types and degrees of software ineffectiveness require hardware solutions. For example, some programs that are slow in performing numerical calculations can be improved only by installing a mathematical coprocessor chip. Nevertheless, not all software performance problems are caused by inefficient hardware. System software handlers for keyboard operation have often been designed to operate at relatively slow speeds, apparently to accommodate the more sluggish typist. The substitution of a slow keyboard handler by a faster one often produces an impressive improvement in software performance.

7.4.1 Measuring Performance

It is difficult to measure the performance of some types of computer programs by technical evaluations of their speed or by standard benchmark tests. This is particularly true regarding editors and word processors. When we state that a certain word processor is faster than another one, we usually mean that one of the programs can be used more effectively. The statement does not necessarily mean that equivalent routines in one program execute so many milliseconds faster than those in the other one, but rather that we perceive one program as being suppler.

Certain elements of program operation particularly enhance this feeling of responsiveness. For instance, in editors and word processors the speed and ease with which the user can move through the text file is probably the most important factor. This is so because a substantial portion of the editing time is spent repositioning the cursor along the file. While writing the present paragraph, the author has scrolled back several times to reread the preceding ones. As the text grows, this movement along the file becomes more laborious. The easier and faster a program performs these manipulations, the more limber it will seem.

It should be noted that this recipe for program agility requires two equally important ingredients: ease and speed. The user should be able to move the cursor along a document rapidly and by the simplest possible commands. Elaborate keystroke combinations are distracting and difficult to remember. Four keys are sufficient to encode all possible maneuvers, since the cursor can move only up, down, left, and right. Most programmers have found that the arrow keys are well suited for this purpose.

7.4.2 Typematic Action

The use of the arrow keys to execute all cursor movements presents some problems. Suppose that the cursor is positioned at the start of a screen line containing 70 characters and that you wish to edit a word located toward the end. In this case, to move the cursor from the start to the end of the line you may have to press the right-arrow key 60 times or more. By the same token, to move from the first line in a page to the last line would requires one keystroke for every line.

Fortunately for the typist, computer hardware can assist in repeating keystrokes. When a key is held down by the user, the keyboard can be made to continue to send codes to the system at a certain rate. IBM calls this operation a *typematic action*. The number of keystrokes repeated per second is called the *typematic rate*. In order to prevent the involuntary repetition of single keystrokes, the keyboard does not begin the typematic burst until after an initial time lapse. This wait period is called the *delay*. The typematic action is represented graphically in Figure 7.3.

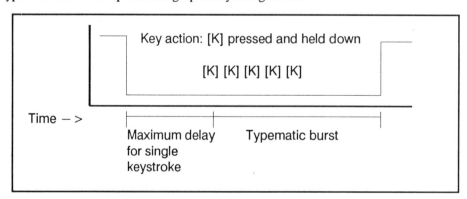

Figure 7.3. *Typematic Action*

7.4.3 Typematic Action in PC Keyboards

All IBM keyboards have typematic action, but the function is not always implemented in the same manner. The IBM PC and PC XT keyboards have a delay period of approximately 500 ms (0.5 s) and a typematic rate of approximately 10 keystrokes per second. In these keyboards, the delay and rate are fixed and cannot be reprogrammed. Applications running on PC and PC XT hardware will always receive typematic keystrokes at this rate, unless some other form of keystroke repetition is implemented.

Most experienced users of text editors and word processors find that the typematic parameters of the PC and PC XT keyboards are too slow. An initial delay of 0.5 s and a burst rate of 10 characters per second require a minimum of 7 s to move the cursor from the start to the end of a 65-character line. To an impatient typist 7 s can seem a long wait. The first IBM microcomputer which allowed reprogramming the typematic rate was the PCjr, but, unrealistically, the reprogramming could consist only in increasing the delay or slowing the burst rate. Since the typematic parameters of the PCjr are similar to those of the PC and PC XT, it is difficult to imagine a user that could profit from this option.

7.4.4 Typematic Action in AT and PS/2 Keyboards

The PC AT was the first IBM machine to allow the user to diminish the delay and increase the burst rate by reprogramming the keyboard hardware. The AT delay could be set at 250, 500, 750, and 1000 ms and the burst rate varied between a maximum of 30 and a minimum of 2 characters per second. The default values, which are the same as the fixed parameters of the PC and PC XT, consist of a 0.5 s delay and a 10 character-per-second burst rate.

The keyboards of the computers of the PS/2 line are also reprogrammable within the same range as the PC AT. In this sense, the AT and the PS/2 keyboards appear identical. The quick-reference diskette provided with computers of the PS/2 line allow the user to select a normal or a fast keyboard speed. But the fast speed is considerably slower than the maximum rate permitted by the hardware.

In systems that allow changing the typematic rate this operation can be performed by either using a BIOS service or accessing the controller registers directly. The AT BIOS dated 11/15/85 and after, the BIOS in the PC XT 286, and the one in PS/2 machines, contain service number 3, of INT 16H, which allows setting the delay and the typematic rate within the scope mentioned above. Machines equipped with AT-type keyboard hardware, which interface with the system via ports 60H and 64H, can always be reprogrammed directly. This is true even if the BIOS does not support service number 3 to set typematic parameters.

7.5 The SETKBD Program

The following program will set the typematic rate and the keystroke delay in a computer equipped with an AT or PS/2 keyboard. The SETKBD program will also preset the Scroll Lock, Caps Lock, and Num Lock keys.

```
;***************************************************************
;***************************************************************
;                        SETKBD.ASM
;***************************************************************
;***************************************************************
;
; Program to preset the typematic delay and burst rate. Also
; to toggle the Num Lock, Caps Lock, and Scroll Lock keys ON
; or OFF
; The code is compatible with computers using AT and PS/2
; keyboards equipped with the 8042 keyboard controller. Since the
; code accesses the controller directly, it will operate in
; machines that do not have BIOS service number 3, of INT 16H
;
; Program operation:
; User values are passed in the DOS command tail as follows:
;
;                              Command tail offset:
;                |————————> +2
;                | |————————> +4
;                | | |————————> +6
;                | | | |————————> +8
;                | | | | |————> +10
;       SETKBD x,x,x,x,x
;                | | | | |————> 1 = Scroll Lock ON
;                | | | |           0 = Scroll Lock OFF
;                | | | |————> 1 = Caps Lock ON
;                | | |             0 = Caps Lock OFF
;                | | |————> 1 = Num Lock ON
;                | |               0 = Num Lock OFF
;                | |
;                | |————————> Keyboard delay
;                |                 0 = 250 ms   1 = 500 ms
;                |                 2 = 750 ms   3 = 1000 ms
;                |
;                |————————> Burst rate (characters per second)
;     0 = 30.0    1 = 26.7    2 = 24.0    3 = 21.8    4 = 20.0
;     5 = 18.5    6 = 17.1    7 = 16.0    8 = 15.9    9 = 13.3
;     A = 12.0    B = 10.9    C = 10.0    D =  9.2    E = 8.6
;     F = 8.0     G = 7.5     H = 6.7     I =  6.0    J = 5.5
;     K = 5.0     L = 4.6     M = 4.3     N =  4.0    O = 3.7
;     P = 3.3     Q = 3.0     R = 2.7     S =  2.5    T = 2.3
;     U = 2.1     V = 2.0
;
; For example, to set a 20.0-cps burst rate, a 500-ms delay
; and to turn OFF all TOGGLE keys the command line will read:
```

```
;                     SETKBD 4,1,0,0,0
;
; If no command tail is typed, the program will set the default
; delay and burst rate. In this case, the TOGGLE keys will not
; be changed
;
;*************************** stack ***************************
STACK   SEGMENT stack
;
                DB      0400H DUP ('?'); Default stack is 1K
STACK_TOP       EQU     THIS BYTE
;
STACK   ENDS
;*************************** code ***************************
;
CODE    SEGMENT
        ASSUME  CS:CODE
;
;
START:
;*********************|
;   read command tail |
;*********************|
; Note: On entry to an executable file the DS segment is set to
;       the MS DOS data area. For this reason the program's
;       command tail, located at DS:0080H, can be read by setting
;       an offset register
        MOV     AL,DS:[0080H]   ; Length of command tail
; Test for no command tail
        CMP     AL,0
        JNE     OK_TAIL          ; There is a command tail
; Reset default values for the delay and the typematic rate
        MOV     AL,2CH           ; 00101100 bit pattern
                                 ;    01100 = 10-cps rate
                                 ;    01    = 500-ms delay
        CALL    SET_DELAY_RATE
        JMP     DOS_EXIT
OK_TAIL:
;********************|
;   set toggle keys  |
;********************|
; Keyboard control byte at 0040:0017H
; Bits: 7 6 5 4 3 2 1 0
;       x 1 x x x x x x = Caps Lock ON
;       x x 1 x x x x x = Num Lock ON
;       x x x 1 x x x x = Scroll lock ON
```

```
        MOV     AL,0                ; Clear setup byte
;**********************|
;      Num Lock key    |
;**********************|
        MOV     AH,DS:[0086H]       ; Num Lock code offset in
                                    ; command tail
        SUB     AH,30H              ; Convert to binary 1 or 0
        MOV     CL,5                ; Bit code for Num Lock
        SHL     AH,CL               ; To corresponding bit position
        OR      AL,AH               ; Into setup byte
;**********************|
;      Caps Lock key   |
;**********************|
        MOV     AH,DS:[0088H]       ; Caps Lock code offset
        SUB     AH,30H              ; Convert to binary 1 or 0
        MOV     CL,6                ; Bit code for Caps Lock
        SHL     AH,CL               ; To corresponding bit position
        OR      AL,AH               ; Into setup byte
;**********************|
;      Scroll Lock key |
;**********************|
        MOV     AH,DS:[008AH]       ; Scroll Lock offset
        SUB     AH,30H              ; Convert to binary 1 or 0
        MOV     CL,4                ; Bit code for Scroll Lock
        SHL     AH,CL               ; To corresponding bit position
        OR      AL,AH               ; Into setup byte
; OR setup byte into BIOS keyboard data area
        MOV     DX,0040H            ; Segment base for BIOS data area
        MOV     ES,DX               ; To ES
        MOV     ES:[0017H],AL       ; Directly into keyboard flag
;**********************|
;    get burst rate    |
;**********************|
; Read command tail parameters
        MOV     BL,DS:[0082H]       ; Typematic rate
; Convert ASCII parameter in BL into binary code required by
; the SET_DELAY_RATE procedure
; Operations:
;       1. If input is in the range '0' to '9' then subtract
;          30H to convert to the binary range 0 to 9
;       2. If input is in the range 'A' to 'X' then subtract
;          37H to convert to the binary range AH to 1FH
;
        CMP     BL,'9'              ; Test first range
        JG      RANGE_2
; Execute step 1 conversion
```

```
          SUB       BL,30H
          JMP       GET_DELAY
RANGE_2:
          SUB       BL,37H              ; Convert from second range
;*********************|
;      get delay      |
;*********************|
GET_DELAY:
          MOV       AL,DS:[0084H]    ; Delay
          SUB       AL,30H           ; Convert to binary
; AL holds binary encoding for the keyboard delay, in the
; 000000xx bit positions. Shift right 5 bit positions to obtain
; the required 0xx00000 bit pattern for the delay bits. See bit
; map in the SET_DELAY_RATE procedure
          MOV       CL,5             ; Counter for 5-bit shift
          SAL       AL,CL            ; Shift AL
; BL = 000xxxxx bit pattern for typematic rate
; AL = 0xx00000 bit pattern for delay
; Combine AL and BL
          OR        AL,BL            ; Set bit pattern 0ddrrrrr
;*********************|
;  set delay and burst |
;       rate          |
;*********************|
          CALL      SET_DELAY_RATE
;*********************|
;     exit to DOS     |
;*********************|
DOS_EXIT:
          MOV       AH,76            ; DOS service request code
          MOV       AL,0             ; No error code returned
          INT       21H              ; TO DOS
;
;*****************************************************************
;                         procedures
;*****************************************************************
SET_DELAY_RATE  PROC      NEAR
; Set delay and typematic rate using direct port access
; On entry:
;         AL = encoded bit pattern for delay and typematic
;              rate according to the following bit map:
;
; BITS: 7  6  5  4  3  2  1  0
;       0  |  |  |  |  |  |  |
;          |  |  |__|__|__|__|_____ CSP burst rate
;          |  |                      00000 = 30.0    00001 = 26.7
```

```
;              |  |                        00010 = 24.0    00011 = 21.8
;              |  |                        00100 = 20.0    00101 = 18.5
;              |  |                        00110 = 17.1    00111 = 16.0
;              |  |                        01000 = 15.0    01001 = 13.3
;              |  |                        01010 = 12.0    01011 = 10.9
;              |  |                        01100 = 10.0    01101 = 9.2
;              |  |                        01110 = 8.0     01111 = 8.0
;              |  |                        10000 = 7.5     10001 = 6.7
;              |  |                        10010 = 6.0     10011 = 5.5
;              |  |                        10100 = 5.0     10101 = 4.6
;              |  |                        10110 = 4.3     10111 = 4.0
;              |  |                        11000 = 3.7     11001 = 3.3
;              |  |                        11010 = 3.0     11011 = 2.7
;              |  |                        11100 = 2.5     11101 = 2.3
;              |  |                        11110 = 2.1     11111 = 2.0
;              |  |
;              |__|_____ Delay
;                                          00 = 250 ms   01 = 500 ms
;                                          10 = 750 ms   11 = 1000 ms
;
; The default value is 00101100B (2CH), for a 500-ms delay and a
; 10.0-cps burst rate.
;
        PUSH    AX                  ; Save entry value
; Disable keyboard interface using command code ADH
        MOV     AL,0ADH
        CALL    COM_8042            ; Send command to port 64H
; Send command code F3H to set delay and typematic rate
        MOV     AL,0F3H
        CALL    WRITE_8042          ; Write to system command to
                                    ; port 60H
; Restore input bit pattern for delay and typematic rate
        POP     AX
        CALL    WRITE_8042
; Reenable keyboard using command code AEH
        MOV     AL,0AEH
        CALL    COM_8042
; Send command to clear output buffer and restart scanning
        MOV     AL,0F4H
        CALL    WRITE_8042
        RET
SET_DELAY_RATE  ENDP
;****************************************************************
;
COM_8042        PROC    NEAR
; Issue command to 8042 keyboard controller port 64H
```

```
; On entry:
;              AL = command code
         PUSH    AX              ; Save command code
         CLI                     ; Interrupts off
         MOV     CX,0FFFFH       ; Set counter
TEST_4_FULL:
         IN      AL,64H          ; Read STATUS port
         TEST    AL,00000010B    ; Input buffer full?
         LOOPNZ  TEST_4_FULL     ; Loop if CX not zero and if
                                 ; zero flag = 0
; Input buffer is empty, send command
         POP     AX              ; Restore entry value (in AL)
         OUT     64H,AL          ; Send command
         STI                     ; Reenable interrupts
         RET
COM_8042         ENDP
;****************************************************************
;
WRITE_8042       PROC    NEAR
; Write a byte of data to 8042 keyboard controller port 60H
; On entry:
;              AL = data byte to write
; Set ES to BIOS data area
         MOV     CX,40H          ; Offset 0400H segment base
         MOV     ES,CX
;
         MOV     BH,AL           ; Save entry AL in BH
         MOV     BL,03           ; Counter for repeat effort
REPEAT_3:
         CLI                     ; Interrupts off
; Make sure that bits 4 and 5 of the keyboard flag byte at
; 0040:0097H are cleared. The function of these bits is:
;        bit 4 = Acknowledgment received
;        bit 5 = Resend receive flag
;
         MOV     AL,01001111B    ; Mask to clear bits 4 and 5
         AND     ES:[0097H],AL
TEST_FULL:
         IN      AL,64H          ; Read STATUS port
         TEST    AL,00000010B    ; Input buffer full?
         LOOPNZ  TEST_FULL       ; Loop if CX not zero and if
                                 ; zero flag = 0
         MOV     AL,BH           ; Recover entry value to write
         OUT     60H,AL          ; Write byte to port 60H
         STI                     ; Reenable interrupts
; Wait for keyboard flag bit 4 (Acknowledge) ON
```

```
          MOV       CX,6656           ; Cycles to wait
WAIT_4_FLAGS:
          TEST      BYTE PTR ES:[0097H],00010000B
; Exit if bit 4 is set
          JNZ       EXIT_WRITE
          LOOP      WAIT_4_FLAGS
; 6656 cycles elapsed and bits not set. Repeat 3 times
          DEC       BL                ; BL primed to 3
          JNZ       REPEAT_3
; Operation failed after 3 tries. Set keyboard TRANSMIT ERROR
; flag and exit
          OR        BYTE PTR ES:[0097H],10000000B   ; Bit 7 set
EXIT_WRITE:
          RET
WRITE_8042     ENDP
;*****************************************************************
;
CODE      ENDS
          END       START
```

7.6 Supercharging the PC Keyboard

The keyboard hardware of the PC, the XT, and compatible systems does not support reprogramming of the typematic parameters. These microcomputers are designed with an initial delay period of 0.5 s and a burst rate of 10 characters per second and no provisions are made for changing these values. However, it is possible for a program, or a TSR utility, to take over the keystroke repetition function. When correctly executed, the resulting keyboard action appears to a user as if the typematic delay and burst rate had been effectively changed.

7.6.1 Designing a Keystroke Repetition Handler

By assuming keystroke repetition directly, the programmer is able to implement this function in a more sophisticated manner. The software will be able to not only reduce the delay and increment the burst rate beyond the limits imposed by the AT and PS/2 keyboard hardware but also make possible refinements that are not available in the hardware version. For example, the keystroke repetition handler can be made to select the keys to be repeated, or to use several simultaneous repeat rates for different keys.

A simple design for a software keystroke repetition handler, for use with editors and word processor programs, is as follows:

1. The handler sets the simulated typematic parameters according to the user's input. The upper limit is fixed at 100 ms of initial delay and a burst rate of 50 characters per second, since keyboard operation becomes very difficult at higher rates.

2. The user defines the keystrokes to be repeated. Usually the four arrow keys will be included. Many editors and word processor programs will also benefit if the < Del > key is repeated.

3. The handler can be made to recognize special key combinations that will multiply the normal rate of keystroke repetition. For instance, if the left shift key is held down, the typematic burst can be made to execute at double the normal rate. This "turbo" keystroke is useful in performing fast translations within the document.

Other features can be added at will, but the programmer should be careful not to exceed the limits imposed by physical system performance.

7.6.2 Coding the Handler

Implementing keystroke repetition in software requires two basic elements: a way of receiving the raw scan codes generated by the keyboard and a timing mechanism for the delay and the burst rate. Both elements can be achieved through well-known programming techniques.

In order to monitor keyboard action, the customized handler must intercept the scan codes before they reach BIOS interrupt 09H. Standard programming consists in saving the address of the original handler in a memory variable, then placing the address of the new handler at the corresponding vector. Once interrupt 09H has been intercepted, the program can examine the raw keyboard scan codes; if it corresponds to one of the keys to be operated by the handler, execution is directed to the program's keystroke delay logic; if not, execution is transferred to the original BIOS interrupt.

The second element in the keystroke handler is a timing mechanism to measure the delay and to synchronize the burst rate. All IBM microcomputer models are equipped with a system timer which, in the default setting, generates a pulse rate of 18.2 beats per second. Every beat of this timer generates a hardware interrupt vectored through interrupt 08H. The keystroke handler can intercept this interrupt and use the system's clock beat as a timing device.

One difficulty is that the default pulse rate of 18.2 beats per second limits the burst rate to this frequency. In the PC and PC XT, in which the normal burst rate is 10 characters per second (cps), 18 cps is a substantial increase that will satisfy most users. In any case, the system timer can be reprogrammed to a higher rate. For instance, doubling the timer frequency generates a beat of 36.4 times per second, which allows a burst rate of 36.4 cps. The program named FAST48, listed later in this chapter, uses the normal burst rate as the default but allows the user to speed up the system clock to twice, four times, or six times the default rate.

Care should be taken, when reprogramming the timer, to preserve the original beat in the BIOS handler. This must be done in order to maintain the accuracy of the system clock and related controls. If the timer rate is doubled to 36.4 beats per second, the original 18.2 beats per second rate can be maintained by sending every other beat to the BIOS handler. The FAST48 program implements this manipulation for all allowed burst rates.

7.7 The FAST48 Program

The FAST48 program, listed below, is a TSR utility that reprograms the system timer and intercepts the keyboard and the timer interrupts so as to implement keystroke repetition in software. FAST48 operates in relation to the four arrow keys and the <Del> key. The left-shift key acts as a "turbo" keystroke by doubling the burst rate. Although the sample program is in the form of a TSR, the basic coding can be used in other types of executable code. FAST48 allows the user to vary the delay and the burst rate, within certain limits, by entering values in the command tail.

```
;*****************************************************************
;*****************************************************************
;                          FAST48.ASM
;*****************************************************************
;*****************************************************************
;
; Keyboard enhancer for IBM microcomputers that use the 8048
; keyboard controller (IBM PC, XT, PCjr, and compatible)
;
; The code assumes the following hardware:
; 1. Keyboard equipped with 8048 controller and keyboard
;    interrupt vectored at INT 09H
; 2. 8253 or 8254 timer chips and timer interrupt vectored at
;    INT 08H
;
; Program operation:
; The program installation routine reads the DOS command tail to
; install a delay (in clock cycles) and to speedup the system
; timer. The first single-character parameter in the command tail
; is the delay factor and the second one the clock speedup.
; For example, the command:
;                    FASTPC 8,4
; introduces a delay of 8 time cycles and speeds up the system
; timer by a factor of 4. Valid values for the delay are the
; following:
;                                      Delay
;                    Digit        (in clock cycles)
;                      2                  2
;                      3                  3
;                      4                  4 (default)
;                      5                  5
;                      6                  6
;                      7                  7
;                      8                  8
;                      9                  9
;                      A                 10
```

```
;                         B              11
;                         C              12
;                         D              13
;                         E              14
;                         F              15
;                         G              16
;                         H              17
;
; Valid values for the clock speedup factors are the following:
;                    Digit          Speedup action:
;                      1            maintain clock speed (default)
;                      2            clock speed times 2
;                      4            clock speed times 4
;                      6            clock speed times 6
;
; Sample MS DOS command line:
;                    FAST48 A,4
; This command will install a delay of 10 clock cycles and speed
; up the system timer by a factor of 4
;
; Actions performed by the INT 09H intercept:
; (Receives control every time a key is pressed)
;    1. If scan code is a make for a keypad arrow key or for the
;       <Del> key, the code is stored in the variable KEY_CODE
;       and the interrupt is discarded
;    2. If not, FFH is stored in variable KEY_CODE and execution
;       is restored to the original handler
;
; Actions performed by the INT 08H intercept
; (receives control with every tick of the system timer)
;    1. If the variable KEY_CODE holds a scan code for a keypad
;       arrow key or for the <Del> key, the key code is placed
;       in the BIOS keyboard buffer
;    2. If the <left><shift> key is pressed, the code is stored
;       twice in order to increase the speed. If the <Ctrl> key
;       is pressed, the code is shipped 4 times
;    3. If the variable KEY_CODE holds the value FFH, the
;       intercept routine does nothing
;    4. Execution is returned to the original INT 08H handler
;       maintaining the original clock rate of 18.2 ticks per
;       second
;
; DOS commands for creating the run file:
;    1. MASM FAST48;
;    2. LINK FAST48;
;    3. EXE2BIN FAST48.EXE FAST48.COM
```

```
;            4. ERASE FAST48.EXE
;
;
;*****************************************************************
;                  equates for BIOS keyboard data
;*****************************************************************
BUFFER_HEAD     EQU     001AH     ; Pointer to head of buffer
BUFFER_TAIL     EQU     001CH     ; Pointer to tail
;
KB_BUFFER       EQU     001EH     ; Offset of buffer start
KB_BUFFER_END   EQU     003EH     ; Offset of buffer end
;
KB_CONTROL      EQU     0017H     ; First keyboard status byte
;
;*************************** code ***************************
CODE    SEGMENT
;
        ORG     0100H             ; COM file forced origin
        ASSUME  CS:CODE,DS:CODE,ES:CODE,SS:CODE
;
ENTRY:
        JMP     INSTALL
;*****************************************************************
;                    new INT 09H entry point
;*****************************************************************
NEW_HEX08:
        JMP     SHORT HANDLER_08          ; Go to handler routine
;
;*****************************************************************
;          IBM standard interrupt chaining structure
;                    (16 bytes data area)
;*****************************************************************
; This structure must start at the third byte from the entry point
; of the interrupt handler. The preceding short jump ensures this
; requirement
OLD_VECTOR_08   DD      0         ; Pointer to BIOS handler
IBM_SIGNATURE   DW      424BH     ; IBM signature for a valid
                                  ; handler
IBM_FLAGS       DB      80H       ; Code to indicate that this is
                                  ; now the first handler in the
                                  ; chain
;*********************|
; jump to unlink code |
;*********************|
; This jump must be located at the 10th byte from the entry point
        JMP     SHORT UNLINK_THIS_08
```

```
;**********************|
;    reserved area     |
;**********************|
                DB       7 DUP (00H)      ; 7 bytes reserved
;****************************************************************
;                     unlinking routine
;****************************************************************
; The following code is used to discard this handler and restore
; the previous one in the chain. The unlinking routine executes
; if this handler is the one installed at the vector for INT 08H
; The code is entered in a FAR procedure so that the RET
; instruction will return execution to the caller
; The unlink routine is customized for this handler. It restores
; the original vector for INT 08H (system timer) and INT 09H
; (keyboard) and, if necessary, resets the system timer to its
; original beat
UNLK_08         PROC     FAR
UNLINK_THIS_08:
        CLI                     ; Interrupts off
; The following code is used to obtain the segment:offset address
; at the vector for INT 08H.
;**********************|
; unchain this INT 08H |
;**********************|
        MOV      AX,0           ; Clear registers
        MOV      ES,AX          ; to set ES to segment of table
        MOV      DI,20H         ; Set DI to offset of the vector
                                ; for INT 08H (08H * 4 = 20H)
; Restore address stored at OLD_VECTOR_08 to the vector table
; Abort operation if this value is 0000:0000H
; ES -> to interrupt vector table segment base (0000H)
        MOV      AX,WORD PTR CS:OLD_VECTOR_08
        MOV      BX,WORD PTR CS:OLD_VECTOR_08[2]
; AX = offset and BX = segment address of old vector
; DI -> interrupt vector for INT 08H
        CLD                     ; Direction flag to forward
        STOSW                   ; Store offset
; DI -> to segment address position
        MOV      AX,BX          ; Segment to AX
        STOSW                   ; Store segment
; Repeat processing to unchain INT 09H
;**********************|
; unchain this INT 09H |
;**********************|
        MOV      DI,24H         ; Set DI to offset of the vector
                                ; for INT 09H (09H * 4 = 24H)
```

```
; Restore address stored at OLD_VECTOR_09 to the vector table
; Abort operation if this value is 0000:0000H
; ES -> to interrupt vector table segment base (0000H)
        MOV      AX,WORD PTR CS:OLD_VECTOR_09
        MOV      BX,WORD PTR CS:OLD_VECTOR_09[2]
; AX = offset and BX = segment address of old vector
; DI -> interrupt vector for INT 09H
        CLD                         ; Direction flag to forward
        STOSW                       ; Store offset
; DI -> to segment address position
        MOV      AX,BX              ; Segment to AX
        STOSW                       ; Store segment
;*********************|
; restore system clock |
;   to 18.2 beats per  |
;       second         |
;*********************|
; To reset the system clock it is not necessary to know its
; present rate
        MOV      AL,00110110B       ; 00xx xxxx = channel 0
                                    ; xx11 xxxx = write LSB then MSM
                                    ; xxxx 011x = mode 3
                                    ; xxxx xxx0 = binary system
        OUT      43H,AL
        JMP      SHORT $ + 2        ; I/O delay
        MOV      AX,65535           ; Original divisor
        OUT      40H,AL             ; Send LSB
        JMP      SHORT $ + 2        ; I/O delay
        MOV      AL,AH
        OUT      40H,AL             ; Send MSB
        JMP      SHORT $ + 2        ; I/O delay
;*********************|
; FAR return to caller |
;*********************|
        RET
UNLK_08          ENDP
;
;****************************************************************
;               new system timer interrupt handler
;                          INT 08H
;****************************************************************
HANDLER_08:
; Save registers
        PUSH     AX
        PUSH     BX
        PUSH     SI
```

```
        PUSH    ES
        MOV     AL,CS:KEY_CODE
;********************|
;   test for AT break  |
;********************|
; Ignore if stored scan code is AT break code announcer
        CMP     AL,0F0H          ; AT break code announcer
        JE      NO_ACTION
        CMP     AL,0FFH                    ; Last keypad scan code
                                           ; was FFH?
        JNE     KP_MAKE                    ; No
;********************|
; reset delay counter   |
;       and exit        |
;********************|
NO_ACTION:
        MOV     AL,CS:DELAY
        MOV     CS:DELAY_COUNT,AL
        JMP     EXIT_TIMER                 ; Yes, exit
;********************|
;   execute delay       |
;********************|
KP_MAKE:
; Test for initial delay exhausted or for first iteration
        MOV     AL,CS:DELAY_COUNT
        CMP     AL,0                       ; Delay exhausted
        JE      EXECUTE_KEY
; Decrement delay counter
        DEC     CS:DELAY_COUNT
; Test for first iteration exception
        CMP     AL,CS:DELAY                ; AL = delay count on
                                           ; entry
        JE      EXECUTE_KEY                ; Execute first iteration
        JMP     NORMAL_KEY
;********************|
;   execute keystroke   |
;********************|
EXECUTE_KEY:
; Set ES to BIOS data segment base at 40H
        MOV     AX,0040H
        MOV     ES,AX
;********************|
;   turbo controls      |
;********************|
; Set repetition factor by testing for <left><shift> and
; <Ctrl> keys pressed
```

```
          MOV      AL,ES:KB_CONTROL          ; First keyboard status
                                             ; byte
          MOV      CS:REPEAT,2               ; Assume 2 repetitions
          TEST     AL,00000010B              ; <left><shift> key
                                             ; pressed
          JNZ      REPEAT_KEY
          MOV      CS:REPEAT,4               ; Assume 4 repetitions
          TEST     AL,00000100B              ; <Ctrl> key pressed
          JNZ      REPEAT_KEY
          MOV      CS:REPEAT,1               ; Send code once
          JMP      REPEAT_KEY
REPEAT_KEY:
; Load scan code for keypad key into AH and clear AL
          MOV      AH,CS:KEY_CODE
          MOV      AL,0
;*********************|
; store key in keyboard|
;       buffer        |
;*********************|
          MOV      BX,ES:BUFFER_TAIL         ; [0040:001CH]
          MOV      SI,BX                     ; Save pointer in SI
; Bump buffer pointer to next available storage
          INC      BX
          INC      BX
          CMP      BX,KB_BUFFER_END          ; End of buffer?
          JNE      NOT_AT_END
; If at end of buffer reset pointer to start of buffer
          MOV      BX,KB_BUFFER              ; Reset to buffer start
; Test for buffer wraparound
NOT_AT_END:
          CMP      BX,ES:BUFFER_HEAD         ; Buffer-full condition
          JE       EXIT_TIMER                ; Do not store
          MOV      ES:[SI],AX                ; Store code in buffer
; Bump buffer tail
          MOV      ES:BUFFER_TAIL,BX
;*********************|
; execute repetitions |
;     if turbo on     |
;*********************|
          DEC      CS:REPEAT
          JZ       EXIT_TIMER                ; Go if last repetition
          JMP      REPEAT_KEY
;*********************|
;         exits       |
;*********************|
; If the count is a multiple of the speedup factor, execution is
```

```
        ; transferred to the original handler. This ensures that the BIOS
        ; INT 08H routine receives control 18.2 times per second.
        EXIT_TIMER:
                DEC     CS:TIMER_COUNT
                JZ      EXIT_TO_08
        ;*********************|
        ;    end of interrupt |
        ;*********************|
        ; Bypass BIOS INT 09H (time-of-day) service
                CLI
                MOV     AL,20H          ; End-of-interrupt code
                OUT     20H,AL          ; to interrupt controller
        ; Restore entry registers
                POP     ES
                POP     SI
                POP     BX
                POP     AX
                IRET
        ;*********************|
        ; exit via BIOS service|
        ;*********************|
        EXIT_TO_08:
        ; Restore timer count from RATE variable
                MOV     AL,CS:RATE
                MOV     CS:TIMER_COUNT,AL
        NORMAL_KEY:
        ; Restore entry registers
                POP     ES
                POP     SI
                POP     BX
                POP     AX
                STC                             ; Continue processing
                JMP     DWORD PTR CS:OLD_VECTOR_08
        ;
        ;****************************************************************
        ;                   INT 09H intercept routine
        ;                      keyboard interrupt
        ;****************************************************************
        ;
        NEW_HEX09:
        ;*********************|
        ;    get scan code    |
        ;*********************|
                PUSH    AX              ; Save accumulator
                PUSHF                   ; and flags
                IN      AL,60H          ; Read scan code at port 60H
```

```
;***********************|
;    test for keypad    |
; arrows and <Del> key  |
;***********************|
;         Key pad keys:                          Scan codes:
;                                                 make/break
;       7        8        9       47H/C7H    48H/C8H    49H/C9H
;       Home     ^        PgUp
;
;       4        5        6       4BH/CBH    4CH/CCH    4DH/CDH
;       <-                ->
;
;       1        2        3       4FH/CFH    50H/D0H    51H/D1H
;       End      |        PgDn
;
;                        <Del>                              53H/D3H
        CMP     AL,4BH                  ; Left arrow?
        JE      STORE_SCAN_CODE
        CMP     AL,48H                  ; Up arrow?
        JE      STORE_SCAN_CODE
        CMP     AL,4DH                  ; Right arrow?
        JE      STORE_SCAN_CODE
        CMP     AL,50H                  ; Down arrow?
        JE      STORE_SCAN_CODE
        CMP     AL,53H                  ; <Del> key?
        JNE     EXIT_VIA_09             ; Go if not <Del> key
;*********************|
;     test for        |
;  <Ctrl>+<Alt>+<Del> |
;*********************|
; The RESET sequence must be tested by the handler since the
; <Del> keystroke is part of this sequence
        PUSH    AX                      ; Save accumulator
        PUSH    ES                      ; and ES
        MOV     AX,0040H                ; Segment for BIOS data area
        MOV     ES,AX                   ; To ES
        MOV     AL,ES:KB_CONTROL        ; Keyboard flag
        TEST    AL,00001100B            ; ALT_CTRL keys pressed
        POP     ES                      ; Restore registers
        POP     AX
        JZ      STORE_SCAN_CODE ; Recognize <Del> key if CTRL+ALT
                                ; not pressed
;*********************|
;   exit via original |
;    INT 09H handler  |
;*********************|
```

```
EXIT_VIA_09:
; Store FFH in KEY_CODE variable and return control to the
; original INT 09H handler in BIOS
        MOV     AL,0FFH         ; For intercept routine
        MOV     CS:KEY_CODE,AL  ; stored in variable
        POPF                    ; Restore flags
        POP     AX              ; and accumulator
; No data in buffers. Transfer execution to original vector
; The code can safely assume a valid vector at INT 09H
        JMP     DWORD PTR CS:OLD_VECTOR_09
;
;********************|
;   store scan code  |
;********************|
STORE_SCAN_CODE:
        MOV     CS:KEY_CODE,AL
;********************|
;   send acknowledge |
;      to 8048 chip  |
;********************|
        IN      AL,61H          ; Read control port
        MOV     AH,AL           ; Save value in port 61H
        OR      AL,80H          ; Set keyboard acknowledge bit
        OUT     61H,AL          ; Send to control port
        XCHG    AH,AL           ; Restore original control
        OUT     61H,AL          ; Send to controller
;********************|
;   discard keystroke |
;********************|
; Discard this keystroke by exiting interrupt
        CLI                     ; Turn off interrupts
        MOV     AL,20H          ; Send EOI code
        OUT     20H,AL          ; to interrupt controller
        POP     AX              ; Discard flags
        POP     AX              ; Restore AX
        IRET
;
;*****************************************************************
;                   code segment data
;*****************************************************************
OLD_VECTOR_09   DD      0       ; Pointer to original 09H
                                ; interrupt
;
KEY_CODE        DB      0FFH    ; Last keypad keystroke received
                                ; or FFH
REPEAT          DB      1       ; Switch for left-shift key
```

```
                                 ; and Left-Ctrl key iteration
                                 ; Holds 1, 2, or 4 accordingly
TIMER_COUNT        DB       1    ; Counter for timer pulses
;
DELAY_COUNT        DB       4    ; Counter for first-key delay
;
; Typematic parameters. Can be modified in the command tail
DELAY              DB       4    ; Default delay period is of 4 clock
                                 ; beats
RATE               DB       1    ; Speedup factor for the typematic
                                 ; rate as a function of the original
                                 ; system clock rate of 18.2 beats
                                 ; per second
                                 ; The default value of 1 does not
                                 ; change the speed of the system
                                 ; clock
;
;**************************************************************
;                       installation routine
;**************************************************************
; Installation operations:
;          1. Read the MS DOS command tail to get the entry values
;             typed by the user for the delay and clock rate. Test
;             for values in valid range and set control variables
;          2. Obtain vector for INT 09H and store in OLD_VECTOR_09
;          3. Set INT 09H vector to this routine
;          4. Speed up system timer according to memory variable
;             or leave default rate
;          5. Obtain vector for INT 08H and store in OLD_VECTOR_08
;          6. Set INT 08H vector to this routine
;          5. Protect TSR and exit
;**************************************************************
INSTALL:
;********************|
;   read command tail  |
;********************|
; Test for input parameters in the program's command tail at
; offset 0080H of the PSP
          MOV      DI,80H          ; Use DI as pointer into PSP
          MOV      AL,DS:[DI]      ; Get command tail character
          CMP      AL,0            ; count. 0 = no command tail
          JE       NO_TAIL         ; Execute with default values
;********************|
;   set up keystroke  |
;      delay          |
;********************|
```

```
; Read command tail value entered by the user
        ADD     DI,2            ; Skip space
        MOV     AL,DS:[DI]      ; Delay factor (2 to H)
        SUB     AL,30H          ; Convert to binary
; Valid range for delay is 2 to 17
        CMP     AL,2            ; Test lower limit of range
        JB      NO_TAIL         ; Invalid value, use default
        MOV     CS:DELAY,AL     ; Store in program variables
        MOV     CS:DELAY_COUNT,AL
;*********************|
;   read command tail |
;*********************|
        ADD     DI,2            ; Skip comma
        MOV     AL,DS:[DI]      ; System clock speedup factor
        SUB     AL,30H          ; To binary range
;*********************|
;  set new clock rate |
;*********************|
; Valid values for clock speedup factor are 2, 4, and 6
        CMP     AL,2            ; Test valid values in cascade
        JE      SET_NEW_RATE
        CMP     AL,4
        JE      SET_NEW_RATE
        CMP     AL,6
        JNE     NO_TAIL
SET_NEW_RATE:
        MOV     CS:RATE,AL      ; Store in program variables
        MOV     CS:TIMER_COUNT,AL
;*********************|
;  get INT 09H vector |
;*********************|
NO_TAIL:
; Interrupts off while changing the vector table
        CLI
; Uses DOS service 35H of INT 21H to obtain original vector for
; INT 09H from the vector table
        MOV     AH,35H          ; Service request code
        MOV     AL,09H          ; Code of vector desired
        INT     21H
; ES -> Segment address of installed interrupt handler
; BX -> Offset address of installed interrupt handler
;*********************|
;  save old vector in |
;    memory variable  |
;*********************|
        MOV     SI,OFFSET CS:OLD_VECTOR_09
```

```
        ; Offset of forward pointer in 16-byte structured table
                MOV     CS:[SI],BX   ; Save offset of original handler
                MOV     CS:[SI+2],ES    ; and segment
        ;**********************|
        ; install new INT 09H  |
        ;**********************|
        ; Uses DOS service 25H if INT 21H to set address of new service
        ; routine in the vector table
                MOV     AH,25H        ; Service request code
                MOV     AL,09H        ; Interrupt code
        ; Set DS to CS for DOS service
                PUSH    CS
                POP     DS
                MOV     DX,OFFSET CS:NEW_HEX09   ; Offset of service
                                                 ; routine
                INT     21H
        ;**********************|
        ;   speed up system    |
        ;        timer         |
        ;**********************|
        ; Speed up timer channel 0 by the value in the RATE variable
        ; If RATE = 4, then:
        ; Original divisor = 65,535
        ; New divisor 65,535/4 = 16,383
                MOV     CL,CS:RATE       ; Get value from variable
                CMP     CL,1             ; Test for default value
                JE      CLOCK_OK         ; Leave default clock rate
                MOV     AL,00110110B     ; 00xx xxxx = channel 0
                                         ; xx11 xxxx = write LSB then MSB
                                         ; xxxx 011x = mode 3
                                         ; xxxx xxx0 = binary system
                OUT     43H,AL
                JMP     SHORT $ + 2      ; I/O delay
                MOV     AX,65535         ; Original divisor
                MOV     CL,CS:RATE
                MOV     CH,0             ; Clear high-order byte of
                MOV     DX,0             ; divisor and dividend
                DIV     CX               ; AX = new divisor
                OUT     40H,AL           ; Send LSB
                JMP     SHORT $ + 2      ; I/O delay
                MOV     AL,AH
                OUT     40H,AL           ; Send MSB
                JMP     SHORT $ + 2      ; I/O delay
        ;**********************|
        ; get INT 08H vector   |
        ;**********************|
```

```
CLOCK_OK:
; Uses DOS service 35H of INT 21H to obtain original vector for
; INT 08H from the vector table
        MOV     AH,35H              ; Service request code
        MOV     AL,08H              ; Code of vector desired
        INT     21H
; ES -> Segment address of installed interrupt handler
; BX -> Offset address of installed interrupt handler
;**********************|
;   save old vector in |
;     memory variable  |
;**********************|
        MOV     SI,OFFSET CS:OLD_VECTOR_08
; Offset of forward pointer in 16-byte structured table
        MOV     CS:[SI],BX          ; Save offset of original handler
        MOV     CS:[SI+2],ES        ; and segment
;**********************|
; install new INT 08H  |
;**********************|
; Use DOS service 25H of INT 21H
        MOV     AH,25H
        MOV     AL,08H              ; Interrupt code
; DS already set to ES
        MOV     DX,OFFSET CS:NEW_HEX08
        INT     21H
        STI                         ; Reenable interrupts
;**********************|
;     terminate and    |
;     stay resident    |
;**********************|
; Exit to DOS protecting the service routine above the label
; INSTALL
        MOV     DX,OFFSET CS:INSTALL
        INC     DX                  ; One more byte
        INT     27H
;
CODE    ENDS
        END     ENTRY
```

8

Programming the 80x87
Math Coprocessor

8.0 Low-level Mathematics

To the typical IBM microcomputer programmer one of the most arcane and difficult fields is that of low-level mathematics. Those working in high-level languages have available an assortment of mathematical operators and functions, varying in richness and precision according to the language. The arithmetic, logarithmic, and trigonometric services offered by high-level languages are usually sufficient for the task at hand. It is not a common occasion that in which a high-level language programmer must develop a mathematical routine to correct a limitation of the language.

Programmers working in assembly language are not as fortunate, in the sense that the language is not equipped with a collection of comparable mathematical services. The apparently simple task of multiplying or dividing two decimal numbers, which a high-level language programmer resolves with a single program statement, results in a major task for a low-level language. The reason is that the microprocessors used in the present generation of IBM microcomputers are capable only of very primitive mathematical operations. For example, the processors of the Intel 8086/8088 family, up to the 286 chip, are limited to integer arithmetic using byte- or word-size operands.

These limitations stem from the instruction set of the Intel 80x86 family, up to the 80286, which allow only addition, subtraction, multiplication, and division of unsigned integer numbers. The operands cannot exceed word size; consequently, the result will not exceed a doubleword. Because the 80386 registers have greater capacity than those of its predecessors, this chip can perform arithmetic operations on doubleword operands and generate quadword results. All this means that programs coded for the Intel 80x86 family must perform many common mathematical operations in software or through a mathematical coprocessor chip.

8.1 The 80x87 Math Coprocessors

The builders of the 8086 chip were quite aware of the mathematical limitations of their product. Almost simultaneously with the 8086, Intel developed a coprocessor chip to provide these badly needed mathematical functions. This coprocessor, designated as the 8087 *Numerical Data Processor*, was furnished as an option. The 8086 could be used by itself, with its limited arithmetic, or an 8087 could be added to the system to extend its mathematical capabilities into high-speed, floating-point operations, logarithms, and trigonometry. Most 80x86 computers contained an empty socket destined for the optional coprocessor.

Note that the 8087 mathematical coprocessor was the first hardware implementation of the ANSI/IEEE standard for binary floating-point arithmetic, first proposed in 1979. This chip brought to the microcomputer field the numerical processing power that was available only with larger computer systems. The 8087 chip is also known as the *Numeric Data Processor* (NDP), *Numeric Data Coprocessor*, and *Numeric Processor Extension* (NPX). In this book we will use the generic designation 80x87, as well as the acronym NDP, to indicate any Intel mathematical coprocessor of this family, namely, the 8087, 80287, and 80387.

To 8086 programmers the 8087 is a mixed blessing. The chip does provide considerable mathematical capabilities, if present in the system, but the fact that it is an optional attachment complicates matters considerably, because programs intended for the general public cannot assume that all IBM microcomputers are equipped with the 80x87 coprocessor. In reality only a small percentage of the installed base includes the coprocessor chip. On the other hand, to assume the nonexistence of a coprocessor would be to waste processing power in those machines equipped with it.

The 80x87 can load and store values encoded in seven different data types, but all internal processing is done in a numeric format designated as the *extended precision real*. Most application software store coprocessor data in the *double precision format*, which provides high precision with considerable safety margin for internal rounding off operations and overflow errors. The double precision format can hold decimal numbers of up to 18 digits without rounding. A map of the 80x87 data types can be seen in Figure 8.1.

8.1.1 80x87 Data Conversions

The 80x87 chip is a binary machine. It operates on encoded binary numbers in a floating-point format designed to simplify calculations and minimize storage. There are no conversion facilities in the chip, although some instructions can be used to assist in this operation. The transformation of the user's input, usually in ASCII decimals, to the binary format accepted by the chip is left mostly to the application. By the same token, the software must also provide conversion routines from the internal binary format, in which the results are stored in the chip's registers, into a humanly readable form.

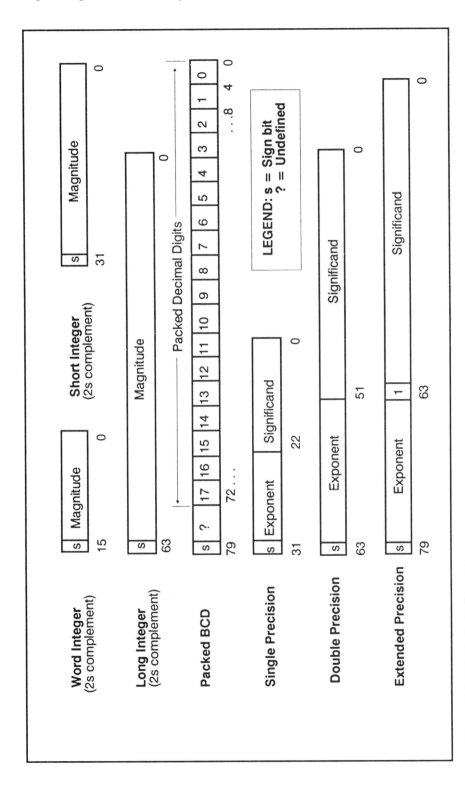

Figure 8.1. *80x87 Data Formats*

8.1.2 The IOX87 Program

For this reason, in addition to knowledge regarding the 80x87 processor and skills in using floating-point instructions, the programmer must have at hand the necessary conversion routines for loading values into the NDP and for translating numerical data in the coprocessor registers.

   User input/output is in the form of ASCII decimal numbers, in general-purpose programs, or in scientific notation, in technical programs. For this reason, in a conversion step unrelated to the 80x87, the code must be able to transform numbers in conventional decimal form into scientific notation. The procedure named ASCII_TO_FPD, in the IOX87 program presented later in this chapter, performs this conversion. This preliminary step is also convenient because it standardizes input into the conversion routine that loads a value into an 80x87 register. This input routine is named INPUT_8087 in the IOX87 program. Finally there must be a routine to transform a number in the 80x87 stack, stored in the extended precision format, into a form that can be output to the user. This conversion is performed by the routine named OUTPUT-8087.

```
;*****************************************************************
;*****************************************************************
;                          IOX87.ASM
;*****************************************************************
;*****************************************************************
;
;
; Description
; Input and output conversion routines for the 80x87 math
; coprocessor
;
; Procedures in the module:
; 1. ASCII_TO_FPD - Conversion of an ASCII decimal number into
;                    a floating-point decimal string
;
; 2. INPUT_8087 - Load of a floating-point decimal string
;                    into the 80x87 stack top register
;
; 3. OUTPUT_8087 - Store of the 80x87 stack top register into
;                    a floating-point decimal string
;*****************************************************************
;
;*********************|
;        notes        |
;*********************|
; 1. To generate emulated code remove the comment symbol from the
;     following line and make sure E87MACS.INC is in the DOS path
; INCLUDE E87MACS.INC
```

```
; 2. This module can be assembled and the object file added to the
;    library named SOLUTION.LIB developed in Chapter 2
;
;******************************************************************
;                            publics
;******************************************************************
;
PUBLIC  ASCII_TO_FPD
PUBLIC  INPUT_8087
PUBLIC  OUTPUT_8087
;
;******************************************************************
;                         temporary data
;******************************************************************
ROUT_DATA       SEGMENT
; Temporary storage buffers for conversion routines
TEMP_REAL       DT      ?
                DB      0
WORK_BUF        DB      18 DUP (?)
                DB      0
; 8087 caller's environment storage area
STATE_8087      DB      94 DUP (?)
;
; Binary and BCD variables and constants
PACKED_EXP      DT      ?       ; 18-digit BCD exponent
PACKED_SIG      DT      ?       ; 18-digit BCD significand
BINARY_EXP      DW      ?       ; Storage for binary exponent
SIGN_OF_EXP     DB      ?       ; 1 = negative
                                ; 0 = positive
TEN_TO_17       DT      00100000000000000000
TEN             DW      10
NAN_CODE        DD      0FFFFFFFFH      ; Not a number encoding
INF_NEGATIVE    DD      0FF800000H      ; Negative infinity
INF_POSITIVE    DD      07F800000H      ; Positive infinity
;
USERS_CW        DW      ?       ; Storage for caller's control
                                ; word
DOWN_CW         DW      17FFH   ; Temporary control word to
                                ; force
                                ; rounding down
;
; Text for clearing the caller's buffer
FPD_MES         DB      '    .                   E      '
; Status word storage and error messages
ERROR_AL1       DB      ' NONORMAL                      '
ERROR_AL2       DB      ' INFINITY                      '
```

```
ERROR_AL3        DB       ' NOT-A-NUMBER              '
ERROR_AL4        DB       ' EMPTY                     '
NUMBER_0         DB       ' 0.00000000000000000 E+0   '
STATUS_WORD      DW       ?
;
; Intermediate buffer for 5 exponent ASCII digits
EXP_BUFFER       DB       '      ',00H
;
; Storage for entry pointers
ENTRY_SI         DW       0          ; Start of caller's input string
ENTRY_DI         DW       0          ; Start of caller's output
                                     ; buffer
                 DB       0
;
ROUT_DATA        ENDS
;
;*************************** code ***************************
CODE     SEGMENT
         ASSUME  CS:CODE
;
;*****************************************************************
;                  numerical conversion procedures
;*****************************************************************
;
;*****************************|
;   ASCII to floating-point   |
;         conversion          |
;*****************************|
ASCII_TO_FPD     PROC     FAR
; Conversion of an ASCII decimal number into floating-point
; decimal string
; On entry:
;       DS:SI ->  an ASCII decimal string, terminated in a NULL
;                 byte, which holds the caller's ASCII decimal
;                 input
;              Note: The caller's buffer may contain the $ sign
;                    and commas as formatting symbols. The string
;                    terminator (00H) may be preceded by a CR
;                    (0DH) or LF (0AH) control code. If the
;                    characters E or e are in the string, the
;                    procedure assumes that the string is already
;                    in floating-point notation
;
;       DS:DI ->  a 27-byte unformatted memory area which will
;                 be filled with the floating-point decimal
;                 output
```

```
; On exit:
;         DS:DI -> the caller's buffer with the input number
;                  reformatted in floating-point decimal format
;                  as follows:
;
;                  sm.mmmmmmmmmmmmmmmmmm ESeeee
;
; where
; s = sign of number (blank = +)
; m = 18 significand digits
; . = decimal point following the first significand digit
; E = letter E signals the start of the exponent field
; S = + or - sign of exponent
; e = up to 4 exponent digits
;                  All registers are preserved
;
;*********************|
;    save caller's    |
;       segments      |
;*********************|
          PUSH    DS
          PUSH    ES
; Set ES -> caller's data
          PUSH    DS
          POP     ES
; Set DS to -> routine's data
          MOV     AX,ROUT_DATA     ; AX to local data
          MOV     DS,AX            ; then to DS
          ASSUME  DS:ROUT_DATA
;*********************|
; save input pointers |
;*********************|
          MOV     ENTRY_SI,SI      ; Values passed by caller
          MOV     ENTRY_DI,DI
;*********************|
; save input registers|
;*********************|
          PUSH    AX               ; Push registers used by routine
          PUSH    CX
          PUSH    DX
          PUSH    SI
          PUSH    DI
;*********************|
;    test for E or e  |
;       character     |
;*********************|
```

```
; The caller's string may already be in floating-point format
TEST_4_FPF:
        CMP     BYTE PTR ES:[SI],'E'
        JE      STRING_ISFP             ; String in floating-
                                        ; point format
        CMP     BYTE PTR ES:[SI],'e'
        JE      STRING_ISFP
        CMP     BYTE PTR ES:[SI],' '    ; Less than 20H is
                                        ; end
                                        ; of string
        JB      NOT_FPF                 ; Not floating point
        INC     SI
        JMP     TEST_4_FPF
;**********************|
; move data to output  |
;       buffer         |
;**********************|
STRING_ISFP:
        MOV     SI,ENTRY_SI     ; Restore input string pointer
; Clear 27 bytes in output buffer
        PUSH    DI              ; Save output pointer
        MOV     CX,27           ; Set up digits counter
PREP_27:
        MOV     BYTE PTR ES:[DI],' '    ; Place blank in buffer
        INC     DI
        LOOP    PREP_27
        POP     DI              ; Restore output buffer pointer
; Move up to 27 digits from input to output buffers. No checks
; are made for an invalid input string
        MOV     CX,27           ; Digits counter
MOVE_INPUT:
        MOV     AL,ES:[SI]      ; Get character
        CMP     AL,' '          ; Less than 20H ends input string
        JB      END_ISTRING     ; End move if terminator
        MOV     ES:[DI],AL      ; Move character to output buffer
        INC     SI              ; Bump pointers
        INC     DI
        LOOP    MOVE_INPUT
END_ISTRING:
        JMP     A2FP_EXIT
;**********************|
; clear output area    |
;**********************|
NOT_FPF:
        MOV     SI,ENTRY_SI     ; Restore input buffer pointer
        PUSH    DI              ; Save output pointer
```

```
            LEA     SI,NUMBER_0       ; Zero is default value
            MOV     CX,27             ; Byte to clear
CLEAR_27:
            MOV     AL,[SI]           ; Get message character
            MOV     ES:[DI],AL        ; Place in buffer area
            INC     DI                ; Bump pointers
            INC     SI
            LOOP    CLEAR_27          ; Continue
; Caller's buffer is now formatted. Restore pointer
            MOV     SI,ENTRY_SI       ; Start of caller's buffer
            POP     DI                ; Output buffer start
;*********************|
;      get sign       |
;*********************|
; Find first significant character in the caller's string
; Skip leading blanks, $ and # signs, and other invalid symbols
GET_NB:
            MOV     AL,ES:[SI]        ; Get character
            CMP     AL,'+'            ; Test for + sign
            JAE     FIRST_NB          ; Go if equal or larger
            INC     SI
            JMP     GET_NB
; first nonblank is a symbol or number larger than the + sign
FIRST_NB:
            CMP     AL,'+'            ; Test for +
            JE      SIGN_IS_PLUS
            CMP     AL,'-'            ; Test for -
            JE      SIGN_IS_MINUS
; First nonblank character is not a sign. Assume a digit and
; force a positive significand
            JMP     IMPLICIT_POS
;*********************|
;     negative sign   |
;*********************|
SIGN_IS_MINUS:
            MOV     BYTE PTR ES:[DI],'-'    ; Set minus sign in
                                            ; caller's buffer
; Positive numbers are formatted with a leading blank
SIGN_IS_PLUS:
            INC     SI                ; Bump source pointer
IMPLICIT_POS:
            INC     DI                ; Bump destination pointers
;*********************|
;   skip leading zeros |
;*********************|
SKIP_ZERO:
```

```
; Leading zeros are not significant. Skip them
        CMP     BYTE PTR ES:[SI],'0'    ; Test for 0
        JNE     NOT_LEAD0
        INC     SI                      ; Bump to next digit
        JMP     SKIP_ZERO
;**********************|
;  find decimal point  |
;**********************|
;  Clear counter for digits preceding the decimal point
NOT_LEAD0:
        MOV     DX,0                    ; DX is integer digit counter
        PUSH    SI                      ; Save pointer to caller's
                                        ; leading digit
; Caller's string must end in a NULL byte (00H) but it can have
; other embedded control characters, for example, 0DH
; Test for an integer zero input
        CMP     BYTE PTR ES:[SI],' '    ; Smaller than 20H is
                                        ; end of input buffer
        JAE     GET_POINT               ; Continue if not end
        JMP     NUM_ISZERO              ; Number is zero
GET_POINT:
        MOV     AL,ES:[SI]              ; Get caller's characters
        CMP     AL,'.'                  ; Test for decimal point
        JE      POINT_FOUND
        CMP     AL,','                  ; Test for formatting comma
                                        ; in the caller's string
        JE      SKIP_COMMA              ; Ignore comma
        CMP     AL,0                    ; String terminator
        JNE     LOOK_4_PT               ; Continue searching
        JMP     NO_POINT                ; No decimal point in string
LOOK_4_PT:
        INC     DX                      ; Count one integer digit
;**********************|
;      skip comma      |
;**********************|
SKIP_COMMA:
        INC     SI                      ; Bump integer digits counter
        JMP     GET_POINT
;**********************|
; string is a decimal  |
;      fraction        |
;**********************|
; If DX = 0 then the caller's string < 1 and the EXPONENT IS
;           NEGATIVE or the number is zero
; If DX = 1 then the caller's string is already normalized
;           and the EXPONENT = +0
```

```
; If DX > 1 then the caller's string is a number =< 10 and
;          the EXPONENT IS POSITIVE
;
POINT_FOUND:
        CMP     DX,1                ; Test for normalized input
        JNE     TEST_4_DX0
;*********************|
; string is =< 10     |
;*********************|
; Number is between 1 and 10. Set exponent sign and value
        MOV     SI,ENTRY_DI         ; SI -> start of output buffer
        ADD     SI,22               ;      -> first character after E
; DS:SI -> position for exponent sign in output buffer
        MOV     BYTE PTR ES:[SI],'+'    ; Sign must be +
        INC     SI
        MOV     BYTE PTR ES:[SI],'0'    ; Set zero exponent
; Move exponent digits from conversion buffer into output buffer
        JMP     EXP_MOVED
TEST_4_DX0:
        CMP     DX,0                ; Test for negative exponent
        JE      DX_ISZERO           ; Go to DX = 0 processing
; If not zero, treat number as integer. Adjust exponent
        INC     DX
        JMP     NO_POINT
;*********************|
;    string is < 1,   |
; exponent is negative,|
;    or number = 0    |
;*********************|
; Possible cases:
;   nonzero ->   000.002345
;   nonzero ->      .2345
;     zero ->     0.00
;     zero ->      .0
; Count decimal digits to normalized position, that is, following
; the first nonzero digit
; DX is used as counter
; SI -> decimal point
DX_ISZERO:
        INC     SI                  ; Skip decimal point
        INC     DX                  ; Count one digit
NORM_SIGNF:
        CMP     BYTE PTR ES:[SI],'0'    ; Test for zero
        JE      ZERO_DIGIT
        JB      NUM_ISZERO
; If not equal or less, it must be larger
```

```
        JMP     OK_SIGNF        ; Normalized position found
ZERO_DIGIT:
        INC     SI              ; Bump pointer
        INC     DX              ; and digits counter
        JMP     NORM_SIGNF
;*********************|
;    string = 0       |
;*********************|
NUM_ISZERO:
; Zero is the default floating-point value in the buffer
; but exponent may have been changed
        MOV     SI,ENTRY_DI     ; SI -> start of output buffer
        ADD     SI,22           ;     -> first character after E
; DS:SI -> position for exponent sign in output buffer
        MOV     BYTE PTR ES:[SI],'+'   ; Sign must be +
        INC     SI
        MOV     BYTE PTR ES:[SI],'0'   ; Set zero exponent
        POP     SI
        JMP     A2FP_EXIT       ; Exit conversion
OK_SIGNF:
; Test for an invalid digit indicating a zero input
        POP     AX              ; Discard old pointer in stack
        PUSH    SI              ; Save pointer to first nonzero
                                ; digit
        MOV     SI,ENTRY_DI     ; SI -> start of output buffer
        ADD     SI,22           ;     -> first character after E
; DS:SI -> position for exponent sign in output buffer
        MOV     BYTE PTR ES:[SI],'-'   ; Sign must be -
        JMP     CONV_EXPONENT
;*********************|
; string is an integer |
;*********************|
NO_POINT:
; Exponent of integer is positive
        MOV     SI,ENTRY_DI     ; SI -> start of output buffer
        ADD     SI,22           ;     -> first character after E
; DS:SI -> position for exponent sign in output buffer
        MOV     BYTE PTR ES:[SI],'+'   ; Sign must be +
        INC     SI
; String has no decimal point. DX = exponent plus 2
        DEC     DX
        DEC     DX
CONV_EXPONENT:
        LEA     DI,EXP_BUFFER   ; Buffer for conversion
        CALL    BIN_TO_ASC      ; Binary in DX to a 5-digit
                                ; ASCII in EXP_BUFFER
```

```
            MOV     SI,ENTRY_DI      ; SI -> start of output buffer
            ADD     SI,23            ;    -> first character after
                                     ; exponent sign
;**********************|
;   move digits to     |
;   output buffer      |
;**********************|
; Caller's string pointer in stack
; DI -> first nonzero ASCII digit in conversion buffer
TO_OUTPUT_BUF:
            MOV     AL,[DI]          ; Get character
            CMP     AL,0             ; Test for end of buffer
            JE      EXP_MOVED        ; Exponent digits have been moved
            MOV     ES:[SI],AL       ; Place digit in output buffer
            INC     SI               ; Bump pointers
            INC     DI
            JMP     TO_OUTPUT_BUF
EXP_MOVED:
            POP     SI               ; Pointer to first nonzero digit
                                     ; in the caller's input
;**********************|
; move up to 18 digits |
;**********************|
            MOV     DI,ENTRY_DI      ; Start of output buffer
            INC     DI               ; Skip sign of significand
; Move one digit preceding the decimal point. Caller's string
; will have at least one digit at this point
            MOV     AL,ES:[SI]       ; Get digit
; Test for invalid values
            CMP     AL,'0'           ; Lower limit
            JAE     VALID_1          ; Go if OK
            JMP     NUM_ISZERO       ; Force zero if invalid digit
VALID_1:
            CMP     AL,'9'           ; Upper limit of digit
            JBE     VALID_2          ; Go if OK
            JMP     NUM_ISZERO       ; Force zero if invalid digit
VALID_2:
            MOV     ES:[DI],AL       ; Move to buffer
            INC     DI               ; Bump buffer pointers
            INC     SI
            INC     DI               ; Skip decimal point in buffer
            MOV     CX,17            ; Load digits counter
UPTO_17:
            MOV     AL,ES:[SI]       ; Get digit
            CMP     AL,'.'           ; Test for period symbol
                                     ; in caller's string
```

```
            JE          SKIP_SYMBOL         ; Skip it
            CMP         AL,','              ; and for commas
            JE          SKIP_SYMBOL
            CMP         AL,' '              ; Test for terminator symbol
            JB          A2FP_EXIT           ; Go if less than 20H
; Test for invalid values
            CMP         AL,'0'              ; Lower limit
            JAE         VALID_3             ; Go if OK
            JMP         NUM_ISZERO          ; Force zero if invalid digit
VALID_3:
            CMP         AL,'9'              ; Upper limit of digit
            JBE         VALID_4             ; Go if OK
            JMP         NUM_ISZERO          ; Force zero if invalid digit
VALID_4:
            MOV         ES:[DI],AL          ; Move digit into buffer
            INC         DI                  ; Bump pointers
            INC         SI
            LOOP        UPTO_17
            JMP         A2FP_EXIT
;**********************|
;    skip period       |
;**********************|
; Skip period without decrementing character counter
SKIP_SYMBOL:
            INC         SI
            JMP         UPTO_17
;**********************|
;    exit routine      |
;**********************|
A2FP_EXIT:
            POP         DI                  ; Restore caller's data registers
            POP         SI
            POP         DX
            POP         BX
            POP         AX
            POP         ES                  ; and segment registers
            POP         DS
            RET
ASCII_TO_FPD    ENDP
;
;
;*****************************|
;    floating-point number to |
;       80x87 stack top        |
;*****************************|
INPUT_8087      PROC    FAR
```

```
; On entry:
;     DS:DX points to the caller's buffer which holds an ASCII
;     decimal number formatted in floating-point decimal notation:
;
;                     sm.mmmmmmmmmmmmmmmmmm ESeeee
; where
; s = sign of number (blank = +)
; m = up to 18 significant digits. Extra digits are ignored
; . = decimal point following the first significand digit
;     if no decimal point in string, it is assumed
; E = explicit letter E (or e) to signal start of exponent
; S = + or - sign of exponent. If no sign, positive is assumed
; e = up to four exponent digits. The numerical value of the
;     exponent cannot exceed +/- 4932
; One or more spaces can be used to separate the last digit of
; the significand and the start of the exponent
;
; Examples of input:
;                     1.781252345E-1
;                     -3.14163397  E+0
;                     1.2233445566778899 e1387
;
; On exit:
;     a. If carry flag clear
;        Input number is loaded into 8087 stack top register
;        Previous values in the stack are pushed down one
;        register
;        AL = 0 (no error)
;     b. If carry flag set
;        AL holds error code
;        AL = 1 for no E or e symbol in the caller's string
;             NAN encoding is loaded into ST(0)
;        AL = 2 for exponent exceeds valid range
;             Overflow - positive infinity is loaded into ST(0)
;             Underflow - negative infinity is loaded into ST(0)
;        AL = 3 for invalid character in caller's string
;             NAN encoding is loaded into ST(0)
;
;        AX is destroyed. All other registers are preserved.
;        The caller's 8087 environment is also preserved, except
;        the stack top register
;
;**********************|
;     save caller's    |
;   segment registers  |
;**********************|
```

```
              PUSH      DS
              PUSH      ES
      ; Set ES -> caller's data
              PUSH      DS
              POP       ES
      ; Set DS to -> routine's data
              MOV       AX,ROUT_DATA        ; AX to local data
              MOV       DS,AX               ; Then to DS
              ASSUME    DS:ROUT_DATA
      ;*********************|
      ;  save caller's 80x87 |
      ;    environment and   |
      ;       registers      |
      ;*********************|
              FSAVE     STATE_8087
              FWAIT
              PUSH      CX                  ; Save registers used by routine
              PUSH      DX
              PUSH      SI
              PUSH      DI
      ;*********************|
      ; clear BCD significand|
      ;        buffer        |
      ;*********************|
              LEA       DI,PACKED_SIG
              MOV       CX,10               ; Bytes in buffer
      CLEAR_10:
              MOV       BYTE PTR [DI],0     ; Clear with zero
              INC       DI                  ; Bump pointer
              LOOP      CLEAR_10
      ;*********************|
      ; clear working buffer |
      ;*********************|
              LEA       DI,WORK_BUF
              MOV       CX,18
      CLEAR_18:
              MOV       BYTE PTR [DI],0     ; Clear byte
              INC       DI
              LOOP      CLEAR_18
      ;*********************|
      ;   move digits into   |
      ;   working buffers    |
      ;*********************|
      ; DS:DX -> caller's buffer with ASCII decimal number in
      ; floating-point decimal notation
              MOV       SI,DX               ; Copy source to SI
```

```
              LEA     DI,WORK_BUF        ; Destination
              MOV     CX,18              ; Maximum digits to move
      MOVE_18:
              MOV     AL,ES:[SI]         ; Get character from user buffer
              INC     SI                 ; Bump source pointer
              CMP     AL,'.'             ; Do not move decimal point
              JE      MOVE_18
              CMP     AL,'+'             ; or + and - signs
              JE      MOVE_18
              CMP     AL,'-'
              JE      MOVE_18
              CMP     AL,' '             ; Skip spaces
              JE      MOVE_18
      ;********************|
      ; test for terminator |
      ;********************|
      ; Test for E or e field terminators
              CMP     AL,'E'             ; Start of exponent
              JE      END_MOVE_18        ; End move if E
              CMP     AL,'e'             ; Lowercase e also allowed
              JE      END_MOVE_18        ; End move if e
      ; Test for invalid digit, larger than ASCII 9 or smaller than
      ; ASCII 0
              CMP     AL,'9'             ; High limit
              JA      BAD_ASCII          ; Exit if larger than 9
              CMP     AL,'0'             ; Low limit
              JB      BAD_ASCII
      ; Value is in legal range
      OK_ASCII:
              MOV     [DI],AL            ; Place ASCII in buffer
              INC     DI
              LOOP    MOVE_18
              JMP     END_MOVE_18
      ;********************|
      ;  illegal character  |
      ;      in string      |
      ;********************|
      BAD_ASCII:
              MOV     AL,3               ; Error code for illegal
                                         ; character in caller's string
              JMP     INPUT_ERROR
      ;********************|
      ;      read sign      |
      ;********************|
      END_MOVE_18:
      ; BCD significand is to be formatted as follows:
```

```
;                    s0|dd|dd|dd|dd|dd|dd|dd|dd|dd
; where
; s = sign of significand. 1000 if number is negative
;                          0000 if number is positive
; d = 18 significand digits in packed BCD format
; 0 = required zero
;
;**********************|
;    set up buffer     |
;        pointers      |
;**********************|
          MOV      SI,DX            ; Caller's input buffer
          LEA      DI,PACKED_SIG    ; Output buffer
          ADD      DI,9             ; Point to sign byte
          MOV      AL,ES:[SI]       ; Get sign of number
          CMP      AL,'-'           ; Test for negative
          JNE      POS_NUMBER       ; Go if not negative
          MOV      BYTE PTR [DI],80H      ; Set sign byte
POS_NUMBER:
          DEC      DI               ; Point to byte number 8
;**********************|
;    convert ASCII to  |
;       packed BCD     |
;**********************|
          LEA      SI,WORK_BUF      ; Significand's digits
CONVERT_8:
          MOV      AH,[SI]          ; Get ASCII digit
          CMP      AH,0             ; All characters read ?
          JE       FIND_E           ; Exit if zero
                                    ; Nothing to store at this point
          INC      SI               ; Bump pointer to next digit
          SUB      AH,30H           ; Convert to binary
          MOV      CL,4             ; Set up shift counter
          SHL      AH,CL            ; Shift bits to high-order
                                    ; nibble of AL
; High-order BCD digit now in AH
          MOV      AL,[SI]          ; Get ASCII digit
          CMP      AL,0             ; All characters read ?
          JNE      OK_DIGIT         ; Continue if not
; There is a valid digit in AH which must be stored
          MOV      [DI],AH          ; Store it
          JMP      FIND_E           ; and exit routine
OK_DIGIT:
          SUB      AL,30H           ; Convert to binary
          OR       AL,AH            ; Pack BCD digits in AL
          MOV      [DI],AL          ; Place in significand's buffer
```

```
            INC     SI                  ; Point to next character
            DEC     DI                  ; Bump pointers
            JMP     CONVERT_8
;*********************|
;    find start of    |
;      exponent       |
;*********************|
FIND_E:
            MOV     SI,DX               ; Caller's input buffer
            MOV     CX,22               ; Maximum character count
                                        ; preceding the E symbol
SEARCH_4_E:
            MOV     AL,ES:[SI]          ; Get character
            CMP     AL,'E'
            JE      VALID_EXP           ; Valid symbol
            CMP     AL,'e'
            JE      VALID_EXP           ; Also valid
            INC     SI                  ; Bump buffer pointer
            LOOP    SEARCH_4_E
; No E or e in caller's input string
            MOV     AL,1                ; Error code number 1
;*********************|
;      input error    |
;*********************|
INPUT_ERROR:
            FRSTOR  STATE_8087          ; Restore environment
            FWAIT
            FLD     NAN_CODE            ; Load NOT-A-NUMBER code
ERROR_RETURN:
            STC                         ; Error
            JMP     RESTORE_EXIT
;*********************|
;   convert exponent  |
;*********************|
VALID_EXP:
            INC     SI                  ; Point to exponent sign or
                                        ; to first exponent digit
;*********************|
;   sign of exponent  |
;*********************|
            MOV     SIGN_OF_EXP,0       ; Assume positive
            MOV     AL,ES:[SI]          ; Get sign of exponent
            CMP     AL,'-'              ; Test for negative
            JNE     POS_EXPON           ; Go if not negative
            MOV     SIGN_OF_EXP,1       ; Code for negative exponent
            INC     SI
```

```
                JMP     READ_EXP
        POS_EXPON:
                CMP     AL,'+'              ; Test for explicit positive
                JNE     READ_EXP           ; Pointer is OK
                INC     SI                 ; Skip + sign
        ;**********************|
        ;  convert digits to   |
        ;      binary          |
        ;**********************|
        READ_EXP:
                CALL    ASC_2_BIN          ; Convert to binary (in DX)
                MOV     BINARY_EXP,DX
        ;**********************|
        ;   test for exponent  |
        ;     out of range     |
        ;**********************|
        ; Absolute value of exponent cannot exceed the limit of the 8087
        ; double-precision format
                CMP     DX,4933            ; Test for limit
                JB      EXPONENT_OK        ; Go if smaller than 4933
        ;**********************|
        ;       encode         |
        ;    + or - infinity   |
        ;**********************|
        ; Restore caller's environment
                FRSTOR  STATE_8087         ; Restore environment
                FWAIT
                MOV     AL,2               ; Exit code for this error
        ; Exponent is out of range. Determine if underflow or overflow
                CMP     SIGN_OF_EXP,1      ; Test for negative
                JE      UNDERFLOW          ; Encode negative infinity
        ; Overflow. Encode positive infinity
                FLD     INF_POSITIVE       ; Load code for positive infinity
                JMP     ERROR_RETURN
        UNDERFLOW:
                FLD     INF_NEGATIVE       ; Load code for negative infinity
                JMP     ERROR_RETURN
                MOV     AL,2               ; Error code number 2
                JMP     INPUT_ERROR
        ;**********************|
        ; load BCD significand |
        ;**********************|
        EXPONENT_OK:
                FBLD    TEN_TO_17          ; 10^17   | EMPTY  |
                FBLD    PACKED_SIG         ; sig     | 10^17  | EMPTY  |
                FDIV    ST,ST(1)           ; sig/10^17| 10^17 | EMPTY  |
```

```
        FXCH    ST(1)           ;   10^17  |   SIG  |  EMPTY |
        FSTP    ST(0)           ;   SIG    |  EMPTY |
;*********************|
;  select conversion  |
;        mode         |
;*********************|
; Option 1: If exponent = 0 then significand remains unchanged
; Option 2: If exponent is negative (SIGN_OF_EXP = 1) then divide
;           significand by 10^exponent
; Option 3: If exponent is positive (SIGN_OF_EXP = 0) then
;           multiply significand by 10^exponent
; DX holds binary exponent
        CMP     DX,0            ; Test option 1
        JNE     TEST_EXP_POS    ; Test for positive if not zero
        JMP     EXPONENT_ZERO
TEST_EXP_POS:
        CMP     SIGN_OF_EXP,0   ; Exponent positive ?
        JNE     EXPONENT_NEG
        JMP     EXPONENT_POS    ; Exponent must be positive
;*********************|
; exponent is negative |
;*********************|
EXPONENT_NEG:
;                               |  SIG   |  EMPTY  |
        FILD    BINARY_EXP      ;  exp   |   SIG   |  EMPTY  |
        CALL    TEN_2_X         ; 10^exp |   SIG   |  EMPTY  |
        FDIVP   ST(1),ST        ; number |  EMPTY  |
        JMP     EXIT_INPUT_87
;*********************|
; exponent is positive |
;*********************|
EXPONENT_POS:
;                               |  SIG   |  EMPTY  |
        FILD    BINARY_EXP      ;  exp   |   SIG   |  EMPTY  |
        CALL    TEN_2_X         ; 10^exp |   SIG   |  EMPTY  |
        FMULP   ST(1),ST        ; number |  EMPTY  |
        JMP     EXIT_INPUT_87
;*********************|
;  exponent is zero   |
;*********************|
EXPONENT_ZERO:
        JMP     EXIT_INPUT_87
;*********************|
;   restore 8087      |
;   environment       |
;*********************|
```

```
EXIT_INPUT_87:
        FSTP      TEMP_REAL        ; Save numbers in memory
        FRSTOR    STATE_8087       ; Restore original 8087
                                   ; environment
        FWAIT
        FLD       TEMP_REAL        ; Load number into 8087 stack
        CLC                        ; No error
        MOV       AL,0             ; Error code zero
;*********************|
;   exit routine      |
;*********************|
RESTORE_EXIT:
        POP       DI               ; Restore caller's registers
        POP       SI
        POP       DX
        POP       CX
        POP       ES
        POP       DS
        RET
INPUT_8087        ENDP
;
;
;******************************|
; 80x87 stack top register into |
;        ASCII decimal          |
;******************************|
OUTPUT_8087       PROC    FAR
; Operation:
;          Converts the value in the top register of the 8087
; stack into an ASCII decimal number in scientific notation
;
; On entry:
;          DS:DX points to an unformatted caller's buffer area
;          with minimum space for 25 bytes of storage
;
; On exit:
;          a. Carry flag clear
;          The caller's buffer will contain the ASCII decimal
;          representation of the number at the 8087 stack top
;          register, formatted in scientific notation, as follows:
;
;                      sm.mmmmmmmmmmmmmmmmmm ESeeee
; where
; s = sign of number (blank = +)
; m = 18 significand digits
; . = decimal point following the first significand digit
```

```
; E = explicit letter E to signal start of exponent
; S = + or - sign of exponent
; e = up to four exponent digits
;
; Examples of output:
;                     1.78125234500000000 E-12
;                    -3.14163397000000000 E+0
;                     1.22334455667788998 E+1388
;
;        b. Carry flag set (invalid value in top of stack)
;           Error code in AL
;              AL = 1 for nonnormal real numbers
;                   Buffer message = NONNORMAL
;              AL = 2 for infinity
;                   Buffer message = INFINITY
;              AL = 3 for not a number
;                   Buffer message = NOT-A-NUMBER
;              AL = 4 for empty register
;                   Buffer message = EMPTY
;
;        Zero is reported as  0.00000000000000000 E+0
;
;        AX is destroyed. All other registers and the caller's
;        environment are preserved
;
;********************|
;    save caller's  |
;  segment registers |
;********************|
        PUSH    DS
        PUSH    ES
; Set ES -> caller's data
        PUSH    DS
        POP     ES
; Set DS to -> routine's data
        MOV     AX,ROUT_DATA          ; AX to local data
        MOV     DS,AX                 ; Then to DS
        ASSUME  DS:ROUT_DATA
;********************|
;   examine ST(0)    |
;********************|
; Get condition codes for stack top register and store for later
; reference
        FXAM                      ; Examine condition codes
        FWAIT
        FSTSW   STATUS_WORD       ; Store status word in memory
```

```
        FWAIT
;*********************|
;  save caller's 80x87 |
;   environment and    |
;       registers      |
;*********************|
        FSTP    TEMP_REAL           ; Save stack top in memory
        FLD     TEMP_REAL           ; Restore stack top value
        FSAVE   STATE_8087
        FWAIT
        FLD     TEMP_REAL           ; Restore stack top value
        PUSH    CX                  ; Save registers used by routine
        PUSH    DX
        PUSH    SI
        PUSH    DI
;*********************|
;   test for invalid   |
;        values        |
;*********************|
        MOV     AX,STATUS_WORD          ; Status word to AX
; Clear all noncondition code bits
        AND     AH,01000111B            ; Mask to clear bits
; Condition code settings:
;   AH bits: 7  6  5  4  3  2  1  0
;            3           2  1  0
;            |_____|__|__|_____ Condition codes settings:
;                                    0001 - 0011 = NAN
;                                    0101 - 0111 = INFINITY
;               0000 - 0010 - 1100 - 1110 = NONNORMAL
;               1001 - 1011 - 1101 - 1111 = EMPTY
;                                    1000 - 1010 = ZERO
;                                    0100 - 0110 = NORMAL
; Test for normal
        CMP     AH,00000100B
        JE      NORMAL
        CMP     AH,00000110B
        JE      NORMAL
        JMP     TEST_4_NAN
;*********************|
;         normal       |
;*********************|
NORMAL:
        JMP     GET_EXPONENT
TEST_4_NAN:
        CMP     AH,00000001B
        JE      IS_NAN
```

```
            CMP     AH,00000011B
            JE      IS_NAN
            JMP     TEST_4_INF
;**********************|
;     not-a-number     |
;**********************|
IS_NAN:
            LEA     SI,ERROR_AL3
            CALL    FILL_CALLERS
            MOV     AL,3                ; Error code for NAN
;**********************|
;     output ERROR     |
;**********************|
ERROR_EXIT:
            FRSTOR  STATE_8087          ; Restore original 8087
                                        ; environment
            FWAIT
; Restore registers
            POP     DI
            POP     SI
            POP     DX
            POP     CX
            POP     ES
            POP     DS
            STC                         ; Set carry flag
            RET
;**********************|
;  test for infinity   |
;**********************|
TEST_4_INF:
            CMP     AH,00000101B
            JE      IS_INFINITY
            CMP     AH,00000111B
            JE      IS_INFINITY
            JMP     TEST_4_NON
;**********************|
;      infinity        |
;**********************|
IS_INFINITY:
            LEA     SI,ERROR_AL2
            CALL    FILL_CALLERS
            MOV     AL,2                ; Error code for INFINITY
            JMP     ERROR_EXIT
;**********************|
;  test for nonnormal  |
;**********************|
```

```
        TEST_4_NON:
                CMP     AH,00000000B
                JE      NONNORMAL
                CMP     AH,00000010B
                JE      NONNORMAL
                CMP     AH,01000100B
                JE      NONNORMAL
                CMP     AH,01000110B
                JE      NONNORMAL
                JMP     TEST_4_ZERO
        ;*********************|
        ;       nonnormal     |
        ;*********************|
        NONNORMAL:
                LEA     SI,ERROR_AL1
                CALL    FILL_CALLERS
                MOV     AL,1                ; Error code for NONNORMAL
                JMP     ERROR_EXIT
        TEST_4_ZERO:
                CMP     AH,01000000B
                JE      IS_ZERO
                CMP     AH,01000010B
                JE      IS_ZERO
        ;*********************|
        ;       empty         |
        ;*********************|
                LEA     SI,ERROR_AL4
                CALL    FILL_CALLERS
                MOV     AL,4                ; Error code for EMPTY
                JMP     ERROR_EXIT
        ;*********************|
        ;       zero          |
        ;*********************|
        IS_ZERO:
                LEA     SI,NUMBER_0
                CALL    FILL_CALLERS
                MOV     AL,0                ; No error
                FRSTOR  STATE_8087          ; Restore original 8087
                                            ; environment
                FWAIT
        ;*********************|
        ;   restore registers |
        ;*********************|
                POP     DI
                POP     SI
                POP     DX
```

```
        POP     CX
        POP     ES
        POP     DS
        CLC                     ; No error
        RET
;***********************|
;  calculate exponent   |
;***********************|
GET_EXPONENT:
        FSTCW   USERS_CW        ; Save caller's control word
        FWAIT
        FLDCW   DOWN_CW         ; Force rounding down
;                               |  ST(0)  |  ST(1)  |  ST(2)  |
        FLD     ST(0)           ;    #    |    #    |  EMPTY  |
        FABS                    ;   |#|   |    #    |  EMPTY  |
        FLD1                    ;    1    |   |#|   |    #    |
        FXCH    ST(1)           ;   |#|   |    1    |    #    |
        FYL2X                   ; Log2-X  |    #    |
        FLDL2T                  ; Log2-10 | Log2-X  |    #    |
        FXCH    ST(1)           ; Log2-X  | Log2-10 |    #    |
        FDIV    ST,ST(1)        ;  exp    | Log2-10 |    #    |
        FXCH    ST(1)           ; Log2-10 |  exp    |    #    |
        FSTP    ST(0)           ;  exp    |    #    |  EMPTY  |
        FRNDINT                 ;  EXP    |    #    |  EMPTY  |
        FLD     ST(0)           ;  EXP    |   EXP   |    #    |
;
        FBSTP   PACKED_EXP      ;  EXP    |    #    |  EMPTY  |
        FISTP   BINARY_EXP      ;   #     |  EMPTY  |
;
        FLDCW   USERS_CW        ; Restore original control word
;***********************|
;      calculate        |
;      significand       |
;***********************|
;                               |  ST(0)  |  ST(1)  |  ST(2)  |
;                               |    #    |  EMPTY  |  EMPTY  |
        FLD     ST(0)
        FLD     ST(0)           ;    #    |    #    |    #    |
; Round and store significand, just in case number is an integer
MANTISSA:
        FRNDINT
        FBSTP   PACKED_SIG      ;    #    |    #    |  EMPTY  |
;                               |    #    |    #    |  EMPTY  |
; Test for BCD digits number 18 not zero
        FWAIT
        LEA     SI,PACKED_SIG
```

```
        ADD     SI,8                ; To most significand BCD byte
        MOV     AL,[SI]
        CMP     AL,0FFH             ; Integer is too large to test
        JE      TOO_LARGE
        AND     AL,11110000B        ; Mask to clear bits 0 to 3
        JNZ     END_MANTISSA
        FILD    TEN
        FMULP   ST(1),ST
        FLD     ST(0)
        JMP     MANTISSA
TOO_LARGE:
        FILD    TEN
        FDIVP   ST(1),ST
        FLD     ST(0)
        JMP     MANTISSA
END_MANTISSA:
        FSTP    ST(0)
;*********************|
;    restore 80x87    |
;    environment      |
;*********************|
        FRSTOR  STATE_8087          ; Restore original 8087
environment
        FWAIT
;*********************|
;   format caller's   |
;       buffer        |
;*********************|
        LEA     SI,FPD_MES          ; Blank message
        CALL    FILL_CALLERS
;*********************|
;  construct decimal  |
;       number        |
;*********************|
; The decimal number is built from the data stored in the buffers
; PACKED_SIG and PACKED_EXP. The number is formatted in
; floating-point decimal notation in the user's buffer
        LEA     SI,PACKED_SIG       ; Significand source
        ADD     SI,9                ; To sign byte of BCD
        MOV     DI,DX               ; User's buffer area
        MOV     AL,[SI]             ; Get sign byte from BCD
        CMP     AL,0                ; Zero is positive
        JE      POS_SIGNIF          ; Significand is positive
        MOV     BYTE PTR ES:[DI],'-'    ; Set negative sign
POS_SIGNIF:
        INC     DI                  ; Bump decimal buffer pointer
```

```
                DEC     SI                      ; and BCD significand pointer
; Move digit preceding the significand's decimal point
                MOV     AL,[SI]                 ; Get packed BCD digits into AL
                CALL    NIBBS_2_DEC             ; Decimal digits in AH and AL
                MOV     ES:[DI],AH              ; Set first decimal digit
                INC     DI                      ; Skip decimal point
                INC     DI
                MOV     ES:[DI],AL              ; Set second digit
                INC     DI                      ; Bump pointer
; Move next seven BCD digit pairs as a block
                DEC     SI                      ; Point to next BCD pair
                MOV     CX,8                    ; Digits to move
MOVE_8_DIGITS:
                MOV     AL,[SI]                 ; Get packed BCD digits into AL
                CALL    NIBBS_2_DEC             ; Decimal digits in AH and AL
                MOV     ES:[DI],AH              ; Set first digit
                INC     DI                      ; Bump decimal digits pointer
                MOV     ES:[DI],AL              ; Place second digit
                INC     DI                      ; Bump pointer
                DEC     SI                      ; Source pointer to next BCD pair
                LOOP    MOVE_8_DIGITS
                ADD     DI,2                    ; Bump to exponent sign position
;*********************|
;   sign of exponent  |
;*********************|
                LEA     SI,PACKED_EXP           ; Exponent BCD storage
                ADD     SI,9                    ; To sign byte of BCD
                MOV     BYTE PTR ES:[DI],'+'  ; Assume positive exponent
                MOV     AL,[SI]                 ; Get sign byte from BCD
                CMP     AL,0                    ; Zero is positive
                JE      POS_EXPONENT            ; Significand is positive
                MOV     BYTE PTR ES:[DI],'-'    ; Set negative sign
POS_EXPONENT:
                INC     DI                      ; Bump decimal buffer pointer
;*********************|
; four exponent digits |
;*********************|
                LEA     SI,PACKED_EXP           ; Reset pointer
                INC     SI                      ; to first BCD digit pair of
                                                ; exponent
; Move 4 exponent digits, skipping leading zeros
; BL = 0 if first nonzero digit not yet found
                MOV     BL,0                    ; Switch for first nonzero
                MOV     CX,2                    ; Counter for 2 packed BCDs
MOVE_2_DIGITS:
                MOV     AL,[SI]                 ; Get packed BCD digits into AL
```

```
        CALL    NIBBS_2_DEC         ; Decimal digits in AH and AL
        CMP     BL,0                ; Execute leading zero test ?
        JNE     NO_LEAD_TEST1       ; Switch OFF, skip test
; Test for leading zero
        CMP     AH,'0'              ; Zero ASCII digit ?
        JE      SKIP_LEAD0_1        ; Skip leading zero
; Valid no zero digit, reset lead zero test switch
        MOV     BL,0FFH             ; BL not zero
NO_LEAD_TEST1:
        MOV     ES:[DI],AH          ; Set first decimal digit
        INC     DI                  ; Bump buffer pointer
SKIP_LEAD0_1:
; Second test for leading zeros
        CMP     BL,0                ; Execute test ?
        JNE     NO_LEAD_TEST2       ; Switch OFF, skip test
        CMP     AL,'0'              ; Zero ASCII digit ?
        JE      SKIP_LEAD0_2
NO_LEAD_TEST2:
        MOV     ES:[DI],AL          ; Set second digit
; Valid no zero digit, reset lead zero test switch
        MOV     BL,0FFH             ; BL not zero
        INC     DI                  ; Bump buffer pointer
SKIP_LEAD0_2:
        DEC     SI                  ; To next BCD digit pair
        LOOP    MOVE_2_DIGITS
;*********************|
;    test for all zeros |
;*********************|
; If exponent is all zeros the leading zero switch will be set
        CMP     BL,0                ; Is exponent all zeros?
        JNE     EXIT_OUTPUT         ; No, exit
; Set a zero digit in the exponent
        MOV     BYTE PTR ES:[DI],'0'
;*********************|
;   restore and exit   |
;*********************|
EXIT_OUTPUT:
        POP     DI
        POP     SI
        POP     DX
        POP     CX
        POP     ES                  ; Restore caller's registers
        POP     DS
        CLC                         ; No error exit
        RET
OUTPUT_8087    ENDP
```

```
;****************************************************************
;                          procedures
;****************************************************************
;*****************************|
;    raise 10 to a power      |
;*****************************|
TEN_2_X              PROC    NEAR
;                                     |  ST(0)  |  ST(1)  |  ST(2)  |
        FLDL2T                        ; Log2-10 |    #    |  EMPTY  |
        FMULP    ST(1),ST             ;E=#*L2-10|  EMPTY  |
;
; Set control word rounding control to - infinity
        FSTCW    USERS_CW             ; Store caller's control word
        FLDCW    DOWN_CW              ; Temporary control word for
                                      ; rounding down
;
        FLD1                          ;    1    |    E    |  EMPTY  |
        FCHS                          ;   -1    |    E    |  EMPTY  |
        FLD      ST(1)                ;    E    |   -1    |    E    |
        FRNDINT                       ;  INT(E) |   -1    |    E    |
        FLDCW    USERS_CW             ; Restore caller's control word
        FXCH     ST(2)                ;    E    |   -1    | INT(E)  |
        FSUB     ST,ST(2)             ; F = E-1 |   -1    |    I    |
        FSCALE                        ;   F/2   |   -1    |    I    |
        F2XM1                         ;F/2^2-1  |   -1    |    I    |
        FSUBRP   ST(1),ST             ;2 ^F/2   |    I    |  EMPTY  |
        FMUL     ST,ST(0)             ; 2 ^F    |    I    |  EMPTY  |
        FSCALE                        ; 2 ^(1+F)|    I    |  EMPTY  |
        FXCH     ST(1)                ;    I    | 2 ^(1+F)|  EMPTY  |
        FSTP     ST(0)                ; 2 ^(1+F)|  EMPTY  |
        RET                           ; 10 ^X   |
TEN_2_X              ENDP
;****************************************************************
;
;*****************************|
;  convert ASCII to binary    |
;*****************************|
ASC_2_BIN            PROC    NEAR
; On entry:
;               SI -> start ASCII buffer
; On exit:
;               DX = binary number (range 0 to 65,535)
;
        MOV      DX,0                 ; Clear binary output
ASC0:   MOV      AL,ES:[SI]           ; Get ASCII digit
        INC      SI                   ; Bump pointer to next digit
```

```
            SUB     AL,30H          ; ASCII to decimal
            JL      EXASC           ; Exit if invalid ASCII
            CMP     AL,9            ; Test for highest value
            JG      EXASC           ; Exit if larger than 9
            CBW                     ; Extend to AX
            PUSH    AX              ; Save digit in stack
            MOV     AX,DX           ; Move into output register
            MOV     CX,10           ; Decimal multiplier
            MUL     CX              ; Perform AX = AX * 10
            MOV     DX,AX           ; Move product to output register
            POP     AX              ; Restore decimal digit
            ADD     DX,AX           ; Add in digit
            JMP     ASC0            ; Continue
EXASC:  RET
ASC_2_BIN       ENDP
;****************************************************************
;
;*****************************|
;       binary to ASCII        |
;*****************************|
BIN_TO_ASC      PROC    NEAR
; Convert a 16-bit binary in the DX register to an ASCII decimal
; number
; On entry:
;               DX = binary source
;               DS:DI -> 5-byte output buffer
;
; Clear the buffer with blanks
            PUSH    DI              ; Save buffer start
            MOV     CX,5            ; Five digits to clear
            MOV     AL,' '          ; Blank character
CLEAR_5:
            MOV     [DI],AL         ; Clear digit
            INC     DI              ; Bump pointer
            LOOP    CLEAR_5         ; Repeat for 5 digits
            DEC     DI              ; Adjust buffer pointer to last
                                    ; digit
;
            MOV     CX,0            ; Clear counter
BINA0:  PUSH    CX              ; Save count
            MOV     AX,DX           ; Add in numerator
            MOV     DX,0            ; Clear top half
            MOV     CX,10           ; Enter decimal divisor
            DIV     CX              ; Perform division AX/CX
            XCHG    AX,DX           ; Get quotient
            ADD     AL,30H          ; Make digit ASCII
```

```
                MOV     [DI],AL           ; Store digit in buffer
                DEC     DI                ; Bump destination pointer
                POP     CX                ; Restore counter
                INC     CX                ; Count the digit
                CMP     DX,0              ; Test for end of binary
                JNZ     BINA0             ; Continue if not end
;
                POP     DI                ; Restore pointer to start of
                                          ; buffer
; Skip leading blanks in buffer
BUF_BLANK:
                MOV     AL,[DI]           ; Get buffer digit
                CMP     AL,' '            ; Test for ASCII blank
                JNE     NOT_BLANK         ; Exit if not leading blank
                INC     DI
                JMP     BUF_BLANK
; ES:DI -> first nonzero digit in buffer
NOT_BLANK:
                RET
BIN_TO_ASC      ENDP
;*****************************************************************
;
;*****************************|
;     AL to ASCII digits      |
;*****************************|
NIBBS_2_DEC     PROC    NEAR
; Convert binary value in low- and high-order nibble of AL into
; 2 ASCII decimal digits in AH and AL
; On entry:
;       AL holds 2 packed BCD digits in the range 0 to 9
;
; On exit:
;       AH = high-order ASCII digit (from AL bits xxxx ????)
;       AL = low-order ASCII digit (from AL bits ???? xxxx)
;
                PUSH    CX                ; Preserve entry register
                MOV     AH,AL             ; Copy AL in AH
                MOV     CL,4
                SHR     AH,CL             ; Isolate high-order nibble
                ADD     AH,30H            ; Convert to ASCII
;
                AND     AL,0FH            ; Isolate low-order nibble
                ADD     AL,30H            ; Convert to ASCII
                POP     CX
                RET
NIBBS_2_DEC     ENDP
```

```
;*************************************************************************
;
;*****************************|
;  message to caller's buffer |
;*****************************|
FILL_CALLERS      PROC     NEAR
; Fill caller's buffer by DS:DX with 27-byte message by ES:SI
            MOV      DI,DX           ; Set up destination pointer
            MOV      CX,27           ; Characters to clear
CLEAR_26:
            MOV      AL,[SI]         ; Character from source
            MOV      ES:[DI],AL      ; Into buffer area
            INC      DI              ; Bump pointers
            INC      SI
            LOOP     CLEAR_26
            RET
FILL_CALLERS      ENDP
;*************************************************************************
;
CODE     ENDS
         END
```

8.2 80x87 Trigonometry

Trigonometric and logarithmic functions are not directly available using 80x87 code. In regard to trigonometric functions, only a partial tangent can be obtained, and it is limited to an angle in the range 0 to $\pi/4$ radian. Sine and cosine functions must be calculated from this partial tangent and user input must first be scaled to the above range. The following procedures convert degrees to radian, and compute the sine, cosine, and tangent functions. Two support procedures named GET_SINE and GET_COS are also listed. All procedures assume that a valid input is already loaded into the 8087 stack top register. The conversion routines to load data into the 80x87 registers appear in Section 8.1.2.

8.2.1 80x87 Trigonometric Procedures

```
;****************************|
;      degrees to radian     |
;****************************|
DEG_2_RADS        PROC     NEAR
; Assumes a doubleword constant in memory defined as follows:
; ONE_80          DD       180.0
; Convert degrees (in ST) to radian
```

```
;                              ;    ST(0)   |    ST(1)   |    ST(2)
;                              ;      d     |   empty    |   empty
          FLD      ONE_80  ;    180    |     d      |
          FLDPI            ;    pi     |    180     |     d     |
          FDIV     ST,ST(1);  pi/180   |    180     |     d     |
          FSTP     ST(1)   ;  pi/180   |     d      |
          FMUL     ST,ST(1);    r      |     d      |
          FSTP     ST(1)   ;    r      |   empty    |
; Angle in ST is now in radian measure
          RET
DEG_2_RADS        ENDP
;******************************************************************
;
;****************************|
;         tangent            |
;****************************|
TANGENT PROC     NEAR
; Compute tangent of an angle in the range 0 to pi/2 radian
; On entry:
;         ST = a valid angle in radian
;         STATUS_WORD = A word-size memory variable defined as
;                       follows:
;                       STATUS_WORD    DW      0
; On exit:
;         ST = tangent of angle
; Formulas for finding tangent of r
;   a) if 0 > r < pi/4 ... tangent = tangent r
;   b) if pi/4 > r < pi/2  tan = cotan (pi/4-remainder of r-pi/4)
; Find case a or b
; using pi/4 as a modulus for a partial remainder operation
;                              ;    ST(0)   |    ST(1)   |    ST(2)
;                              ;      r     |   empty    |   empty
          FCLEX
          FLDPI            ;    pi     |     r      |
          FDIV     FOUR    ;   pi/4    |     r      |
          FXCH             ;    r      |    pi/4    |
          FPREM            ;   REM     |    pi/4    |
          FSTSW    STATUS_WORD
          FWAIT
; Condition code C1 is bit 9 of the status word
; If C1 = 1 then use formula b, else use formula a
; Load high-order byte of status word
          MOV      AH,BYTE PTR STATUS_WORD+1
          TEST     AH,00000010B    ; Condition code C1
          JNZ      TAN_FORM_B      ; Bit set indicates b
; Use formula a for tangent
```

```
        FSTP    ST(1)   ;    REM       |  empty   |
        FPTAN           ;   y(opp)      |  x(adj)  |
        FXCH            ;    x          |   y      |
        FDIV    ST,ST(1);   TAN r       | ? |
        FSTP    ST(1)   ;   tan r       |  empty   |
        RET
;
TAN_FORM_B:
;                       |   REM         |  pi/4    |
        FXCH            ;   pi/4        |  REM     |
        FSUB    ST,ST(1); pi/4 - REM    |  REM     |
        FSTP    ST(1)   ; pi/4 - REM    |  empty   |
; Use formula b for tangent
        FSTP    ST(1)   ;    REM        |  empty   |
        FPTAN           ;   y(opp)      |  x(adj)  |
        FDIV    ST,ST(1); cotan r       | ? |
        FSTP    ST(1)   ; cotan r       |  empty   |
        RET
;
TANGENT ENDP
;****************************************************************
;
;****************************|
;          sine             |
;****************************|
SINE    PROC    NEAR
; Compute sine of an angle in the range 0 to pi/2 radian
; On entry:
;       ST = a valid angle in radian
;       STATUS_WORD = A word-size memory variable defined as
;                     follows:
;                     STATUS_WORD    DW       0
; On exit:
;       ST = sine of angle
; Formula for finding radius of r
;  a) if 0 > r < pi/4 ... sine = sine r
;  b) if pi/4 > r < pi/2  sine = cos (pi/4-remainder of r-pi/4)
;
; Find case a or b
; using pi/4 as a modulus for a partial remainder operation
;                       ;    ST(0)    |    ST(1)    |    ST(2)
                        ;      r      |   empty     |   empty
        FCLEX
        FLDPI           ;     pi      |     r       |
        FDIV    FOUR    ;    pi/4     |     r       |
        FXCH            ;      r      |    pi/4     |
```

```
          FPREM              ;   REM      |   pi/4   |
          FSTSW     STATUS_WORD
          FWAIT
; Condition code C1 is bit 9 of the status word
; If C1 = 1 then use formula b, else use formula a
; Load high-order byte of status word
          MOV       AH,BYTE PTR STATUS_WORD+1
          TEST      AH,00000010B     ; Condition code C1
          JNZ       SINE_FOR_B       ; Bit set indicates b
; Use formula a for sine
          FSTP      ST(1)   ;   REM      |  empty   |
          CALL      GET_SINE
          RET
;
SINE_FOR_B:
;                           |   REM      |   pi/4   |
          FXCH             ;   pi/4     |   REM    |
          FSUB      ST,ST(1); pi/4 - REM |   REM    |
          FSTP      ST(1)   ; pi/4 - REM |  empty   |
          CALL      GET_COS
          RET
SINE      ENDP
;****************************************************************
;
;***************************|
;          cosine           |
;***************************|
COSINE    PROC      NEAR
; Compute cosine of an angle in the range 0 to pi/2 radian
; which is 0 to 90 degrees
; On entry:
;       ST = a valid angle in radian
;       STATUS_WORD = A word-size memory variable defined as
;                     follows:
;                     STATUS_WORD   DW      0
; On exit:
;       ST = sine of angle
; Formula for finding radius of r
;  a) if 0 > r < pi/4 ... cos = cos r
;  b) if pi/4 > r < pi/2  cos = sine (pi/4 - remainder of r-pi/4)
;
; Find case a or b
; using pi/4 as a modulus for a partial remainder operation
;                         ;   ST(0)    |   ST(1)    |   ST(2)
;                         ;    r       |   empty    |   empty
          FCLEX
```

```
        FLDPI            ;    pi      |    r      |
        FDIV     FOUR    ;    pi/4    |    r      |
        FXCH            ;    r       |   pi/4    |
        FPREM           ;    REM     |   pi/4    |
        FSTSW    STATUS_WORD
        FWAIT
; Condition code C1 is bit 9 of the status word
; If C1 = 1 then use formula b, else use formula a
; Load high-order byte of status word
        MOV      AH,BYTE PTR STATUS_WORD+1
        TEST     AH,00000010B     ; Condition code C1
        JNZ      COS_FORM_B       ; Bit set indicates b
; Use formula a for sine
        FSTP     ST(1)   ;    REM     |  empty    |
        CALL     GET_COS
        RET
;
COS_FORM_B:
;                        |   REM     |   pi/4    |
        FXCH            ;   pi/4    |   REM     |
        FSUB     ST,ST(1); pi/4 - REM |  REM     |
        FSTP     ST(1)   ; pi/4 - REM |  empty    |
        CALL     GET_SINE
        RET
;
COSINE   ENDP
;******************************************************************
;
GET_SINE         PROC    NEAR
; On entry:
;       ST = angle in radian in the range 0 to pi/4
; On exit:
;       ST = sine of angle
; Find sine using formula Sin @ = y / SQR (x^2 + y^2)
        FPTAN           ;    x(adj)   |   y(opp)   |
        FMUL     ST,ST(0);    x^2     |    y       |
        FXCH            ;    y       |    x^2     |
        FLD      ST(0)   ;    y       |    y       |   x^2   |
        FXCH     ST(3)
        FSTP     ST(0)   ;    y       |    x^2     |   y     |
        FMUL     ST,ST(0);    y^2     |    x^2     |   y     |
        FADD     ST,ST(1); y^2+x^2   |    x^2     |   y     |
        FSQRT           ; SQ(y^2+x^2) |   x^2     |   y     |
        FXCH            ;    x^2     | SQ(y^2+x^2)|   y     |
        FSTP     ST(0)   ; SQ(y^2+x^2) |    y      |
        FXCH            ;    y       | SQ(y^2+x^2)|
```

```
              FDIV    ST,ST(1);  sine r      | ? |
              FSTP    ST(1)   ;  sine r      |   empty   |
              RET
;
GET_SINE         ENDP
;*********************************************************************
;
GET_COS PROC     NEAR
; On entry:
;         ST = angle in radian in the range 0 to pi/4
; On exit:
;         ST = cosine of angle
; Find cosine using formula Cos = x / SQR (x^2 + y^2)
              FPTAN              ;   x(adj)     | y(opp)   |
              FLD     ST(0)   ;      x        |    x     |   y    |
              FXCH    ST(3)
              FSTP    ST(0)   ;      x        |    y     |   x    |
              FMUL    ST,ST(0);    x^2        |    y     |   x    |
              FXCH               ;   y        |   x^2    |   x    |
              FMUL    ST,ST(0);    y^2        |   x^2    |   x    |
              FADD    ST,ST(1);  y^2+x^2      |   x^2    |   x    |
              FSQRT              ; SQ(y^2+x^2) |   x^2    |   x    |
              FXCH               ;    x^2     | SQ(y^2+x^2)|  x    |
              FSTP    ST(0)   ; SQ(y^2+x^2) |    x     |
              FXCH               ;    x       | SQ(y^2+x^2)|
              FDIV    ST,ST(1);  cosine r    | SQ(y^2+x^2 |
              FSTP    ST(1)   ;  cosine r    |  empty    |
              RET
;
GET_COS ENDP
```

8.3 Software Emulation of the 80x87

The solution to the dilemma created by the optional nature of the 80x87 coprocessor is a program that imitates the operations of the chip. This software, sometimes called an *8087 emulator*, can be used in systems not equipped with the hardware component. If correctly designed and coded, the emulator will substitute the 8087 so that programs that use 8087 instructions can be modified to run in machines not equipped with the chip.

Most high-level languages for IBM microcomputers are capable of generating programs that will run in systems with or without the 8087. The term *virtual* is sometimes used in relation to the emulated environment and the term *real* in relation to systems equipped with the 8087 hardware component. In this manner, most implementations of high-level language for IBM microcomputers are furnished with a minimum of two math libraries. The real math library is used in the compilation of programs intended for systems equipped with the 80x87 component. The virtual or emulated library is used in compiling programs for systems that do not contain the mathematical coprocessor. In addition, some high-level programming languages contain a library which uses the 8087 chip, if one is installed, or emulates it in software if not.

The 80x87 emulator software is often classified as full or partial emulators. Most emulators used with high-level languages are partial emulators, which implement only the mathematical functions and operations required by the language. In addition, the mathematical services in many high-level language libraries are coded as procedures, often labeled with whimsical, undocumented names. Those that do use code compatible with the 8087 instruction often require start-up routines that are furnished by the language compiler.

In conclusion, most emulator libraries provided with IBM microcomputer high-level language systems are not easy to use from assembly language. Furthermore, while most assembler programs are capable of generating 80x87 instructions, which will run in systems equipped with this hardware, 80x87 software emulators are not included with popular assemblers and development packages. To our knowledge, the only assembly language development system presently available that can be purchased with a full 8087 emulator and support software is the one by Intel; its Numerics Support Library, which includes the emulator and other programs, must be purchased separately. Other systems, such as Microsoft's MASM, contain functions and operations that seem intended for use with emulator software, but the emulator itself is not furnished as a standard, or even as an optional component.

Emulator programs and mathematical packages that can be used from assembly language are available from various commercial sources other than Intel Corporation. In purchasing these packages the buyer is well advised to carefully investigate the quality of the product as well as the distribution rights granted by the vendor. Ideally, software that incorporates an emulator or other commercial math libraries should not be subject to additional distribution fees or copyright statements in favor or the developer of the emulator or library. For a commercial venture it would be better to purchase an expensive system with few or no restrictions rather than an inexpensive one that requires the payment of fees or other concessions.

In time, the problems created by the optional nature of the 80x87 coprocessor will cease to plague program developers. The Intel 486 processor includes the floating-point unit and can execute the 80x87 instructions without additional hardware. There is no coprocessor in 486 machines, because the numerical operations previously performed by the 80x87 chips are now part of the main processor's instruction set. When machines equipped with the 486 chip replace all 8086, 8088, 80286, and 80386 systems, the coprocessor issue will disappear and so will the need for software emulators.

8.3.1 Details of Emulator Operation

Developing an emulator program for the 8087 coprocessor is a major project. A full emulator usually takes up 16K to 20K of code. The 8087, which is the simplest member of this math coprocessor family, contains a set of 69 operation codes to perform arithmetic, data transfer, comparison, transcendental, constant, and processor control instructions. The chip can operate on seven data types, according to various processing and rounding modes, and generates elaborate error codes and exceptions. Designing and coding a software version of this device is a difficult undertaking and requires mathematical knowledge in addition to programming skills.

The ideal emulator is unrecognizable from the hardware component, except by its slower speed of execution. It performs all 80x87 instructions, using all valid operands and addressing modes. The emulator recognizes the chip's rounding, infinity, and precision controls, uses the same internal data structures, and generates identical error exceptions. In short, the perfect emulator is a software version of the 80x87 chip. Although this ideal is impossible to achieve, the various Intel emulators for the 80x87 family come remarkably close. This should not be surprising considering that Intel is the company that developed the hardware processors.

Note that the emulator software cannot operate on the same opcodes used by the 80x87. The processor-coprocessor architecture designed by Intel is based on hard wiring the 80x87 to the CPU's TEST line. The 80x86 WAIT instruction tests this line and enters into a wait state if the line is not active. Consequently, if a WAIT opcode is executed in a system not equipped with the NDP, the machine hangs up, because the CPU can wait forever for a TEST line that will never become active. Since every NDP instruction is automatically preceded with a WAIT opcode, any effort at emulating the 80x87 while running 80x87 code is predestined to fail.

This introduces the first difficulty in emulating the 80x87 chip, which is that the 80x87 instructions must be replaced or patched with the opcodes recognized by the emulator. The ideal solution would be to have the same opcodes execute in systems with or without and 80x87 component, but, as we have seen, this is technically impossible in IBM microcomputers. With this restriction in mind, emulation can be achieved in the following ways:

1. The assembler program can be made to generate emulator opcodes on detection 80x87 instructions. For example, Microsoft MASM contains the /E switch, which generates emulator opcodes on 80x87 mnemonics. As mentioned previously, this option is of little use to the assembly language programmer since Microsoft has not made available a usable emulator program.

2. The assembler program can be made to recognize special mnemonics, different than those of the 80x87, to represent the emulator opcodes. This option allows developing programs that contain both real and emulated code.

3. The modifications in the opcodes can be introduced after assembly. For instance, in the Intel ASM 86 environment the 80x87 opcodes are changed into emulator opcodes at link time. This means that object files for use with the hardware component or with the emulator are identical.

4. An executable file containing 80x87 opcodes can be patched so that these are replaced with emulator opcodes, and vice versa. This method offers the advantage that the conversion can be made without access to the source or the object files of the program. For example, a commercial program coded for executing in an 80x87 system can be modified to run in an emulated system.

8.3.2 An 80x87 Emulator Include File for MASM

Programmers working with the Intel ASM86 system and the corresponding 80x87 Numeric Support Libraries require few additional software tools for creating real and emulated 80x87 programs. The Intel package includes the emulator, as well as conversion, elementary functions, complex number, and error-handler libraries. However, programmers working in other development systems, including Microsoft's MASM, do not have access to this support software. The following include file can be used to generate emulator code, compatible with the Intel emulators, from Microsoft's MASM version 5.1 and later.

```
;******************************************************************
;******************************************************************
;                            E87MACS.INC
;******************************************************************
;******************************************************************
;
; Macro file to convert 80x87 opcodes into emulator opcodes
; The resulting object file is compatible with the Intel and
; other compatible emulators
;
; Programs assembled with this include file must use the MASM
; version 5.1 or later and the assembler options /Z/W0
;
;*******************************████|
;    80x87 code conversion into   |
;    Intel system emulated code    |
;*******************************████|
; Operation:
; All 80x87 instructions in the no-wait form are in the range:
;              9BH D8H ........
;         to   9BH DFH ........
; except for the segment override instructions described below
;
; Intel system emulator instructions require changing the byte
; 9BH for CDH, for example:
; Instruction        80x87 opcode          Emulator opcode
; FLDZ ............... 9B D9 EE ............. CD D9 EE
; FINIT .............. 9B DB E3 ............. CD DB E3
;
; 8087 instructions with the segment override prefix must be
; modified for the emulator by changing the segment override
; byte to an emulator interrupt (INT), as follows:
;        80x87          Segment        INT        Emulator
;        opcode         override                  Opcode
;        9B 26 ......... ES ............. D4 ....... CD D4
```

```
;        9B 2E ........ CS ............. D5 ....... CD D5
;        9B 36 ........ SS ............. D6 ....... CD D6
;        9B 3E ........ DS ............. D7 ....... CD D7
; This operation is performed with the aid of the @SEGOR macro
; (see end of the module)
;*******************************|
;    editing this macro file    |
;*******************************|
; The macros in the file E87MACS.INC use Intel 80x87 mnemonics to
; generate emulator opcodes. This is possible because MASM
; version 5.1 gives precedence to a macro expansion over an
; instruction opcode
; The names of the macros in this file can be edited so as to
; create a different mnemonic for emulator opcodes. For example,
; by appending the @ symbol to the FLD1 macro it becomes @FLD1.
; This change will allow coding as follows:
;        @FLD1              ; Emulated instruction to load 1
;        FLD1               ; 80x87 instruction to load 1
; Having different mnemonic for the real and the emulated
; instructions, and using a macro file to generate the emulator
; opcodes, makes possible the use of real and emulated code in
; the same program
;
;*******************************|
;        example of macro       |
;*******************************|
; FLD    MACRO    DEST
;
;        IFE    4-TYPE DEST    ;; If operand is a 4-byte real
;        DB     0CDH           ;; Single precision
;        ESC    8,DEST
;        ENDIF
;        ENDM
;
; 1. DEST is a dummy macro parameter that serves as a
;    placeholder for the operand actually used in the instruction
;
; 2. The TYPE operator serves to evaluate the number of bytes
;    in the operand of the instruction, for example:
;            if DEST is an ST(i) register ...... TYPE = 0
;            if DEST is a byte ................ TYPE = 1
;            if DEST is a word ................ TYPE = 2
;            if DEST is single precision or integer.  TYPE = 4
;            if DEST is double precision or integer .  TYPE = 8
;            if DEST is extended precision ..... TYPE = 10
;            if DEST is a packed decimal ....... TYPE = 10
```

```
; 3. The subtraction in the example (4-TYPE DEST) serves to
;    test for a specific operand size. In this case, 4-TYPE
;    DEST equals zero if the destination is single-precision
;    or short integer operand
;
; 4. The IFE (IF Empty) tests the value of the expression
;    4-TYPE DEST and executes the block of conditional
;    instructions if the result is zero
;
; Use of ESC in the macro expansion
; The ESC instruction provides a way for generating 8086 opcodes
; as follows:
;       ESC       xxxyyyB,DEST   =  11011xxx ??yyy???
;
; where ??yyy??? is
;                       MOD REG r/m
;                       ?? yyy ???
;
; The changeable 6-bit field provides the following combinations:
;       11011000B to 11011111B generate opcodes from D8H to DFH
;            ^^^            ^^^
;       ??000???B to ??111???B generate 8 different encodings that
;         ^^^            ^^^
;       are unrelated to the REG function of this field
;
; For example:
;             ESC          1AH,SHORT_INT
; evaluates to:
;       1AH =          011        010         fields
;       ESC =     11011xxx    ??xxx???
;MOD   r/m =                  00   110  for direct memory operand
;                    _____
;   Opcode =     11011011    00010110 = DBH 16H
;
; Values in macro expansions
;         TYPE ST(i) = 0 therefore,
;         TYPE DEST = 0 if DEST is an ST(i) register
;
; The assembler assigns a value to the 80x87 stack registers
; according to the register number (i), for example:
;             DB       0DH,C0H+ST(2)
; evaluates to        0DH,C0H+2 or 0DH,0C2H
;
; The conditional directive IFDEF (if defined) can be used
; in a macro to test if an operand exists, for instance:
;         IFDEF     DEST
```

```
; will expand the macro if DEST exists in the operand
; See the @FXCH macro. The opposite is achieved with:
;         IFB       <DEST>
; In this case the macro will be expanded if <DEST> is a NULL
; string, see the @FADD macro
;
;*******************************|
;              notes            |
;*******************************|
; 1. Requires Microsoft MASM version 5.1 or later
;
; 2. No-wait mnemonics for processor control instructions
;    generate identical emulator code as the wait form. These
;    macros are provided to facilitate the conversion of 80x87
;    code
;
; 3. Floating-point instructions with segment override, for
;    example, FSTSW  ES:MEM_WORD, are handled separately, since
;    the use of the ESC form would add an extra byte to the
;    opcode
;
;*****************************************************************
;                      8087 emulator macros
;*****************************************************************
;******************|
;      loads       |
;******************|
FLD    MACRO   DEST
;
;; Call segment override test macro @SEGOR
        @SEGOR  DEST
;; SBYTE = 0 if no segment override in operand. Else, SBYTE holds
;; emulated segment override byte D4H, D5H, D6H, or D7H
;
        IFE     TYPE DEST         ; If operand is a constant (STi)
                                  ; there can be no segment
                                  ; override
        DB      0CDH
        DB      0D9H,0C0H+DEST
        ENDIF
;
        IFE     4-TYPE DEST       ; If operand is a 4-byte real
        DB      0CDH
;; Test for segment override
        IF      SBYTE             ; Test for SBYTE not zero
;; Generate segment override opcode
```

```
        DB      SBYTE
        DW      06D9H               ; Hand-code 2 bytes of opcode
                                    ; Corresponding to ESC xx
        DW      N_OFF               ; Add offset of destination
;; Generate non-segment override using ESC
        ELSE
        ESC     8,DEST
        ENDIF
        ENDIF
;
        IFE     8-TYPE DEST         ; If operand is an 8-byte real
        DB      0CDH
;; Test for segment override
        IF      SBYTE               ; Test for SBYTE not zero
;; Generate segment override opcode
        DB      SBYTE
        DW      06DDH               ; Hand-code 2 bytes of opcode
                                    ; Corresponding to ESC xx
        DW      N_OFF               ; Add offset of destination
;; Generate nonsegment override using ESC
        ELSE
        ESC     40,DEST
        ENDIF
        ENDIF
;
        IFE     10-TYPE DEST        ; If operand is extended precision
        DB      0CDH
;; Test for segment override
        IF      SBYTE               ; Test for SBYTE not zero
;; Generate segment override opcode
        DB      SBYTE
        DW      2EDBH               ; Hand-code 2 bytes of opcode
                                    ; Corresponding to ESC xx
        DW      N_OFF               ; Add offset of destination
;; Generate nonsegment override using ESC
        ELSE
        ESC     1DH,DEST
        ENDIF
        ENDIF
        ENDM
;****************************************************************
;
FILD    MACRO   DEST
;; Call segment override test macro @SEGOR
        @SEGOR  DEST
;; SBYTE = 0 if no segment override in operand. Else, SBYTE holds
```

```
;; emulated segment override byte D4H, D5H, D6H, or D7H
;
        IFE     2-TYPE DEST     ; If operand is a word integer
        DB      0CDH
;; Test for segment override
        IF      SBYTE           ; Test for SBYTE not zero
;; Generate segment override opcode
        DB      SBYTE
        DW      06DFH           ; Hand-code 2 bytes of opcode
                                ; Corresponding to ESC xx
        DW      N_OFF           ; Add offset of destination
;; Generate nonsegment override using ESC
        ELSE
        ESC     38H,DEST
        ENDIF
        ENDIF
;
        IFE     4-TYPE DEST     ; If operand is a short integer
        DB      0CDH
;; Test for segment override
        IF      SBYTE           ; Test for SBYTE not zero
;; Generate segment override opcode
        DB      SBYTE
        DW      06DBH           ; Hand-code 2 bytes of opcode
                                ; Corresponding to ESC xx
        DW      N_OFF           ; Add offset of destination
;; Generate nonsegment override using ESC
        ELSE
        ESC     18H,DEST
        ENDIF
        ENDIF
;
        IFE     8-TYPE DEST     ; If operand is a long integer
        DB      0CDH
;; Test for segment override
        IF      SBYTE           ; Test for SBYTE not zero
;; Generate segment override opcode
        DB      SBYTE
        DW      2EDFH           ; Hand-code 2 bytes of opcode
                                ; Corresponding to ESC xx
        DW      N_OFF           ; Add offset of destination
;; Generate nonsegment override using ESC
        ELSE
        ESC     3DH,DEST
        ENDIF
        ENDIF
```

```
        ENDM
;****************************************************************
;
FBLD    MACRO   DEST
;; Call segment override test macro @SEGOR
        @SEGOR  DEST
;; SBYTE = 0 if no segment override in operand. Else, SBYTE holds
;; emulated segment override byte D4H, D5H, D6H, or D7H
;
        DB      0CDH
;; Test for segment override
        IF      SBYTE           ; Test for SBYTE not zero
;; Generate segment override opcode
        DB      SBYTE
        DW      26DFH           ; Hand-code 2 bytes of opcode
                                ; Corresponding to ESC xx
        DW      N_OFF           ; Add offset of destination
;; Generate nonsegment override using ESC
        ELSE
        ESC     3CH,DEST
        ENDIF
        ENDM
;****************************************************************
;
;******************|
;     stores       |
;******************|
FST     MACRO   DEST
;; Call segment override test macro @SEGOR
        @SEGOR  DEST
;; SBYTE = 0 if no segment override in operand. Else, SBYTE holds
;; emulated segment override byte D4H, D5H, D6H, or D7H
;
        IFE     TYPE DEST       ; If operand is a constant (STi)
        DB      0CDH
        DB      0DDH,0D0H+DEST
        ENDIF
;
        IFE     4-TYPE DEST     ; If operand is a 4-byte real
        DB      0CDH
;; Test for segment override
        IF      SBYTE           ; Test for SBYTE not zero
;; Generate segment override opcode
        DB      SBYTE
        DW      16D9H           ; Hand-code 2 bytes of opcode
                                ; Corresponding to ESC xx
```

```
            DW      N_OFF            ; Add offset of destination
;; Generate nonsegment override using ESC
            ELSE
            ESC     10,DEST
            ENDIF
            ENDIF
;
            IFE     8-TYPE DEST      ; If operand is an 8-byte real
            DB      0CDH
;; Test for segment override
            IF      SBYTE            ; Test for SBYTE not zero
;; Generate segment override opcode
            DB      SBYTE
            DW      16DDH            ; Hand-code 2 bytes of opcode
                                     ; Corresponding to ESC xx
            DW      N_OFF            ; Add offset of destination
;; Generate nonsegment override using ESC
            ELSE
            ESC     2AH,DEST
            ENDIF
            ENDIF
            ENDM
;****************************************************************
;
FSTP    MACRO   DEST
;; Call segment override test macro @SEGOR
            @SEGOR  DEST
;; SBYTE = 0 if no segment override in operand. Else, SBYTE holds
;; emulated segment override byte D4H, D5H, D6H, or D7H
;
            IFE     TYPE DEST        ; If operand is a constant (STi)
            DB      0CDH
            DB      0DDH,0D8H+DEST
            ENDIF
;
            IFE     4-TYPE DEST      ; If operand is a 4-byte real
            DB      0CDH
;; Test for segment override
            IF      SBYTE            ; Test for SBYTE not zero
;; Generate segment override opcode
            DB      SBYTE
            DW      1ED9H            ; Hand-code 2 bytes of opcode
                                     ; Corresponding to ESC xx
            DW      N_OFF            ; Add offset of destination
;; Generate nonsegment override using ESC
            ELSE
```

```
          ESC     0BH,DEST
          ENDIF
          ENDIF
;
          IFE     8-TYPE DEST     ; If operand is an 8-byte real
          DB      0CDH
;; Test for segment override
          IF      SBYTE           ; Test for SBYTE not zero
;; Generate segment override opcode
          DB      SBYTE
          DW      1EDDH           ; Hand-code 2 bytes of opcode
                                  ; Corresponding to ESC xx
          DW      N_OFF           ; Add offset of destination
;; Generate nonsegment override using ESC
          ELSE
          ESC     2BH,DEST
          ENDIF
          ENDIF
;
          IFE     10-TYPE DEST    ; If operand is extended precision
          DB      0CDH
;; Test for segment override
          IF      SBYTE           ; Test for SBYTE not zero
;; Generate segment override opcode
          DB      SBYTE
          DW      3EDBH           ; Hand-code 2 bytes of opcode
                                  ; Corresponding to ESC xx
          DW      N_OFF           ; Add offset of destination
;; Generate nonsegment override using ESC
          ELSE
          ESC     1FH,DEST
          ENDIF
          ENDIF
          ENDM
;*****************************************************************
;
FIST    MACRO   DEST
;; Call segment override test macro @SEGOR
          @SEGOR  DEST
;; SBYTE = 0 if no segment override in operand. Else, SBYTE holds
;; emulated segment override byte D4H, D5H, D6H, or D7H
;
          IFE     2-TYPE DEST     ; If operand is a word integer
          DB      0CDH
;; Test for segment override
          IF      SBYTE           ; Test for SBYTE not zero
```

```
        ;; Generate segment override opcode
                DB      SBYTE
                DW      16DFH           ; Hand-code 2 bytes of opcode
                                        ; Corresponding to ESC xx
                DW      N_OFF           ; Add offset of destination
        ;; Generate nonsegment override using ESC
                ELSE
                ESC     3AH,DEST
                ENDIF
                ENDIF
        ;
                IFE     4-TYPE DEST     ; If operand is a short integer
                DB      0CDH
        ;; Test for segment override
                IF      SBYTE           ; Test for SBYTE not zero
        ;; Generate segment override opcode
                DB      SBYTE
                DW      16DBH           ; Hand-code 2 bytes of opcode
                                        ; Corresponding to ESC xx
                DW      N_OFF           ; Add offset of destination
        ;; Generate nonsegment override using ESC
                ELSE
                ESC     1AH,DEST
                ENDIF
                ENDIF
                ENDM
        ;****************************************************************
        ;
        FISTP   MACRO   DEST
        ;; Call segment override test macro @SEGOR
                @SEGOR  DEST
        ;; SBYTE = 0 if no segment override in operand. Else, SBYTE holds
        ;; emulated segment override byte D4H, D5H, D6H, or D7H
        ;
                IFE     2-TYPE DEST     ; If operand is a word integer
                DB      0CDH
        ;; Test for segment override
                IF      SBYTE           ; Test for SBYTE not zero
        ;; Generate segment override opcode
                DB      SBYTE
                DW      1EDFH           ; Hand-code 2 bytes of opcode
                                        ; Corresponding to ESC xx
                DW      N_OFF           ; Add offset of destination
        ;; Generate nonsegment override using ESC
                ELSE
                ESC     3BH,DEST
```

```
          ENDIF
          ENDIF
;
          IFE     4-TYPE DEST     ; If operand is a short integer
          DB      0CDH
;; Test for segment override
          IF      SBYTE           ; Test for SBYTE not zero
;; Generate segment override opcode
          DB      SBYTE
          DW      1EDBH           ; Hand-code 2 bytes of opcode
                                  ; Corresponding to ESC xx
          DW      N_OFF           ; Add offset of destination
;; Generate nonsegment override using ESC
          ELSE
          ESC     1BH,DEST
          ENDIF
          ENDIF
;
          IFE     8-TYPE DEST     ; If operand is a long integer
          DB      0CDH
;; Test for segment override
          IF      SBYTE           ; Test for SBYTE not zero
;; Generate segment override opcode
          DB      SBYTE
          DW      3EDFH           ; Hand-code 2 bytes of opcode
                                  ; Corresponding to ESC xx
          DW      N_OFF           ; Add offset of destination
;; Generate nonsegment override using ESC
          ELSE
          ESC     3FH,DEST
          ENDIF
          ENDIF
          ENDM
;****************************************************************
;
FBSTP  MACRO    DEST
;; Call segment override test macro @SEGOR
          @SEGOR  DEST
;; SBYTE = 0 if no segment override in operand. Else, SBYTE holds
;; emulated segment override byte D4H, D5H, D6H, or D7H
;
          DB      0CDH
;; Test for segment override
          IF      SBYTE           ; Test for SBYTE not zero
;; Generate segment override opcode
          DB      SBYTE
```

```
          DW      36DFH              ; Hand-code 2 bytes of opcode
                                     ; Corresponding to ESC xx
          DW      N_OFF              ; Add offset of destination
;; Generate nonsegment override using ESC
          ELSE
          ESC     3EH,DEST
          ENDIF
          ENDM
;****************************************************************
;******************|
;    exchange      |
;******************|
;
FXCH   MACRO    DEST
          IFDEF   DEST               ; If operand is ST(i)
          DB      0CDH
          DB      0D9H,0C8H+DEST
;
          ELSE                       ; If FXCH has no operands
          DB      0CDH
          DB      0D9H,0C9H
          ENDIF
          ENDM
;****************************************************************
;******************|
;    addition      |
;******************|
;
FADD   MACRO    DEST,SOURCE
;
;; Test for FADD (no operands)
          IFB     <DEST>
          DB      0CDH,0DEH,0C1H
          EXITM
          ENDIF
;
;; Call segment override test macro @SEGOR
          @SEGOR  DEST
;; SBYTE = 0 if no segment override in operand. Else, SBYTE holds
;; emulated segment override byte D4H, D5H, D6H, or D7H
;
          IFE     TYPE DEST          ; If FADD  ST(i),ST
                                     ; or FADD  ST,ST(i)
          IF      DEST EQ 0          ; Test for ST as destination
          DB      0CDH
          DB      0D8H,0C0H+SOURCE
```

```
            EXITM
            ENDIF
;
            IF      SOURCE EQ 0     ; Test for ST as source operand
            DB      0CDH
            DB      0DCH,0C0H+DEST
            ENDIF
            ENDIF
;
            IFE     4-TYPE DEST     ; If operand is a 4-byte real
            DB      0CDH
;; Test for segment override
            IF      SBYTE           ; Test for SBYTE not zero
;; Generate segment override opcode
            DB      SBYTE
            DW      06D8H           ; Hand-code 2 bytes of opcode
                                    ; Corresponding to ESC xx
            DW      N_OFF           ; Add offset of destination
;; Generate nonsegment override using ESC
            ELSE
            ESC     00H,DEST
            ENDIF
            ENDIF
;
            IFE     8-TYPE DEST     ; If operand is an 8-byte real
            DB      0CDH
;; Test for segment override
            IF      SBYTE           ; Test for SBYTE not zero
;; Generate segment override opcode
            DB      SBYTE
            DW      06DCH           ; Hand-code 2 bytes of opcode
                                    ; Corresponding to ESC xx
            DW      N_OFF           ; Add offset of destination
;; Generate nonsegment override using ESC
            ELSE
            ESC     20H,DEST
            ENDIF
            ENDIF
            ENDM
;****************************************************************
;
FADDP   MACRO   DEST,SOURCE
;; FADDP has one format only
            DB      0CDH
            DB      0DEH,0C0H+DEST
            ENDM
```

```
;*******************************************************************
;
FIADD   MACRO   DEST
;; Call segment override test macro @SEGOR
        @SEGOR  DEST
;; SBYTE = 0 if no segment override in operand. Else, SBYTE holds
;; emulated segment override byte D4H, D5H, D6H, or D7H
;
        IFE     2-TYPE DEST     ; If operand is a word integer
        DB      0CDH
;; Test for segment override
        IF      SBYTE           ; Test for SBYTE not zero
;; Generate segment override opcode
        DB      SBYTE
        DW      06DEH                   ; Hand-code 2 bytes of opcode
                                        ; Corresponding to ESC xx
        DW      N_OFF                   ; Add offset of destination
;; Generate nonsegment override using ESC
        ELSE
        ESC     30H,DEST
        ENDIF
        ENDIF
;
        IFE     4-TYPE DEST     ; If operand is a short integer
        DB      0CDH
;; Test for segment override
        IF      SBYTE           ; Test for SBYTE not zero
;; Generate segment override opcode
        DB      SBYTE
        DW      06DAH                   ; Hand-code 2 bytes of opcode
                                        ; Corresponding to ESC xx
        DW      N_OFF                   ; Add offset of destination
;; Generate nonsegment override using ESC
        ELSE
        ESC     10H,DEST
        ENDIF
        ENDIF
        ENDM
;*******************************************************************
;
;******************|
;   subtraction    |
;******************|
FSUB    MACRO   DEST,SOURCE
;
;; Test for FSUB (no operands)
```

```
          IFB      <DEST>
          DB       0CDH,0DEH,0E9H
          EXITM
          ENDIF
;
;; Call segment override test macro @SEGOR
          @SEGOR   DEST
;; SBYTE = 0 if no segment override in operand. Else, SBYTE holds
;; emulated segment override byte D4H, D5H, D6H, or D7H
;
          IFE      TYPE DEST      ; If FSUB  ST(i),ST
                                  ; or FSUB  ST,ST(i)
          IF       DEST EQ 0      ; Test for ST as destination
          DB       0CDH
          DB       0D8H,0E0H+SOURCE
          EXITM
          ENDIF
;
          IF       SOURCE EQ 0    ; Test for ST as source operand
          DB       0CDH
          DB       0DCH,0E8H+DEST
          ENDIF
          ENDIF
;
          IFE      4-TYPE DEST    ; If operand is a 4-byte real
          DB       0CDH
;; Test for segment override
          IF       SBYTE          ; Test for SBYTE not zero
;; Generate segment override opcode
          DB       SBYTE
          DW       26D8H          ; Hand-code 2 bytes of opcode
                                  ; Corresponding to ESC xx
          DW       N_OFF          ; Add offset of destination
;; Generate nonsegment override using ESC
          ELSE
          ESC      04H,DEST
          ENDIF
          ENDIF
;
          IFE      8-TYPE DEST    ; If operand is an 8-byte real
          DB       0CDH
;; Test for segment override
          IF       SBYTE          ; Test for SBYTE not zero
;; Generate segment override opcode
          DB       SBYTE
          DW       26DCH          ; Hand-code 2 bytes of opcode
```

```
                                    ; Corresponding to ESC xx
        DW       N_OFF              ; Add offset of destination
;; Generate nonsegment override using ESC
        ELSE
        ESC      24H,DEST
        ENDIF
        ENDIF
        ENDM
;******************************************************************
;
FSUBP   MACRO    DEST,SOURCE
;; FSUBP has one format only
        DB       0CDH
        DB       0DEH,0E8H+DEST
        ENDM
;******************************************************************
FISUB   MACRO    DEST
;; Call segment override test macro @SEGOR
        @SEGOR   DEST
;; SBYTE = 0 if no segment override in operand. Else, SBYTE holds
;; emulated segment override byte D4H, D5H, D6H, or D7H
;
        IFE      2-TYPE DEST       ; If operand is a word integer
        DB       0CDH
;; Test for segment override
        IF       SBYTE             ; Test for SBYTE not zero
;; Generate segment override opcode
        DB       SBYTE
        DW       26DEH             ; Hand-code 2 bytes of opcode
                                   ; Corresponding to ESC xx
        DW       N_OFF             ; Add offset of destination
;; Generate nonsegment override using ESC
        ELSE
        ESC      34H,DEST
        ENDIF
        ENDIF
;
        IFE      4-TYPE DEST       ; If operand is a short integer
        DB       0CDH
;; Test for segment override
        IF       SBYTE             ; Test for SBYTE not zero
;; Generate segment override opcode
        DB       SBYTE
        DW       26DAH             ; Hand-code 2 bytes of opcode
                                   ; Corresponding to ESC xx
        DW       N_OFF             ; Add offset of destination
```

```
;; Generate nonsegment override using ESC
        ELSE
        ESC     14H,DEST
        ENDIF
        ENDIF
        ENDM
;*****************************************************************
;
FSUBR   MACRO   DEST,SOURCE
;
;; Test for FSUBR (no operands)
        IFB     <DEST>
        DB      0CDH,0DEH,0E1H
        EXITM
        ENDIF
;
;; Call segment override test macro @SEGOR
        @SEGOR  DEST
;; SBYTE = 0 if no segment override in operand. Else, SBYTE holds
;; emulated segment override byte D4H, D5H, D6H, or D7H
;
        IFE     TYPE DEST       ; If FSUBR ST(i),ST
                                ; or FSUBR ST,ST(i)
        IF      DEST EQ 0       ; Test for ST as destination
        DB      0CDH
        DB      0D8H,0E8H+SOURCE
        EXITM
        ENDIF
;
        IF      SOURCE EQ 0     ; Test for ST as source operand
        DB      0CDH
        DB      0DCH,0E0H+DEST
        ENDIF
        ENDIF
;
        IFE     4-TYPE DEST     ; If operand is a 4-byte real
        DB      0CDH
;; Test for segment override
        IF      SBYTE           ; Test for SBYTE not zero
;; Generate segment override opcode
        DB      SBYTE
        DW      2ED8H           ; Hand-code 2 bytes of opcode
                                ; Corresponding to ESC xx
        DW      N_OFF           ; Add offset of destination
;; Generate nonsegment override using ESC
        ELSE
```

```
            ESC     05H,DEST
            ENDIF
            ENDIF
;
            IFE     8-TYPE DEST     ; If operand is an 8-byte real
            DB      0CDH
;; Test for segment override
            IF      SBYTE           ; Test for SBYTE not zero
;; Generate segment override opcode
            DB      SBYTE
            DW      2EDCH           ; Hand-code 2 bytes of opcode
                                    ; Corresponding to ESC xx
            DW      N_OFF           ; Add offset of destination
;; Generate nonsegment override using ESC
            ELSE
            ESC     25H,DEST
            ENDIF
            ENDIF
            ENDM
;****************************************************************
;
FSUBRP MACRO    DEST,SOURCE
;; FSUBRP has one format only
            DB      0CDH
            DB      0DEH,0E0H+DEST
            ENDM
;****************************************************************
;
FISUBR MACRO    DEST
;; Call segment override test macro @SEGOR
            @SEGOR  DEST
;; SBYTE = 0 if no segment override in operand. Else, SBYTE holds
;; emulated segment override byte D4H, D5H, D6H, or D7H
;
            IFE     2-TYPE DEST     ; If operand is a word integer
            DB      0CDH
;; Test for segment override
            IF      SBYTE           ; Test for SBYTE not zero
;; Generate segment override opcode
            DB      SBYTE
            DW      2EDEH           ; Hand-code 2 bytes of opcode
                                    ; Corresponding to ESC xx
            DW      N_OFF           ; Add offset of destination
;; Generate nonsegment override using ESC
            ELSE
            ESC     35H,DEST
```

```
            ENDIF
            ENDIF
;
            IFE     4-TYPE DEST        ; If operand is a short integer
            DB      0CDH
;; Test for segment override
            IF      SBYTE             ; Test for SBYTE not zero
;; Generate segment override opcode
            DB      SBYTE
            DW      2EDAH             ; Hand-code 2 bytes of opcode
                                      ; Corresponding to ESC xx
            DW      N_OFF             ; Add offset of destination
;; Generate nonsegment override using ESC
            ELSE
            ESC     15H,DEST
            ENDIF
            ENDIF
            ENDM
;*******************************************************************
;*****************|
;   multiplication |
;*****************|
FMUL    MACRO   DEST,SOURCE
;; Call segment override test macro @SEGOR
            @SEGOR  DEST
;; SBYTE = 0 if no segment override in operand. Else, SBYTE holds
;; emulated segment override byte D4H, D5H, D6H, or D7H
;
            IFE     TYPE DEST         ; If FMUL  ST(i),ST
                                      ; or FMUL  ST,ST(i)
            IF      DEST EQ 0         ; Test for ST as destination
            DB      0CDH
            DB      0D8H,0C8H+SOURCE
            EXITM
            ENDIF
;
            IF      SOURCE EQ 0       ; Test for ST as source operand
            DB      0CDH
            DB      0DCH,0C8H+DEST
            ENDIF
            ENDIF
;
            IFE     4-TYPE DEST       ; If operand is a 4-byte real
            DB      0CDH
;; Test for segment override
            IF      SBYTE             ; Test for SBYTE not zero
```

```
;; Generate segment override opcode
        DB      SBYTE
        DW      0ED8H               ; Hand-code 2 bytes of opcode
                                    ; Corresponding to ESC xx
        DW      N_OFF               ; Add offset of destination
;; Generate nonsegment override using ESC
        ELSE
        ESC     01H,DEST
        ENDIF
        ENDIF
;
        IFE     8-TYPE DEST         ; If operand is an 8-byte real
        DB      0CDH
;; Test for segment override
        IF      SBYTE               ; Test for SBYTE not zero
;; Generate segment override opcode
        DB      SBYTE
        DW      0EDCH               ; Hand-code 2 bytes of opcode
                                    ; Corresponding to ESC xx
        DW      N_OFF               ; Add offset of destination
;; Generate nonsegment override using ESC
        ELSE
        ESC     21H,DEST
        ENDIF
        ENDIF
        ENDM
;****************************************************************
;
FMULP   MACRO   DEST,SOURCE
;; FMULP has one format only
        DB      0CDH
        DB      0DEH,0C8H+DEST
        ENDM
;****************************************************************
;
FIMUL   MACRO   DEST
;; Call segment override test macro @SEGOR
        @SEGOR  DEST
;; SBYTE = 0 if no segment override in operand. Else, SBYTE holds
;; emulated segment override byte D4H, D5H, D6H, or D7H
;
        IFE     2-TYPE DEST         ; If operand is a word integer
        DB      0CDH
;; Test for segment override
        IF      SBYTE               ; Test for SBYTE not zero
;; Generate segment override opcode
```

```
            DB       SBYTE
            DW       0EDEH                 ; Hand-code 2 bytes of opcode
                                           ; Corresponding to ESC xx
            DW       N_OFF                 ; Add offset of destination
    ;; Generate nonsegment override using ESC
            ELSE
            ESC      31H,DEST
            ENDIF
            ENDIF
    ;

            IFE      4-TYPE DEST           ; If operand is a short integer
            DB       0CDH
    ;; Test for segment override
            IF       SBYTE                 ; Test for SBYTE not zero
    ;; Generate segment override opcode
            DB       SBYTE
            DW       0EDAH                 ; Hand-code 2 bytes of opcode
                                           ; Corresponding to ESC xx
            DW       N_OFF                 ; Add offset of destination
    ;; Generate nonsegment override using ESC
            ELSE
            ESC      11H,DEST
            ENDIF
            ENDIF
            ENDM
    ;****************************************************************
    ;
    ;******************|
    ;     division     |
    ;******************|
    FDIV    MACRO    DEST,SOURCE
    ;
    ;; Test for FDIV (no operands)
            IFB      <DEST>
            DB       0CDH,0DEH,0F9H
            EXITM
            ENDIF
    ;
    ;; Call segment override test macro @SEGOR
            @SEGOR   DEST
    ;; SBYTE = 0 if no segment override in operand. Else, SBYTE holds
    ;; emulated segment override byte D4H, D5H, D6H, or D7H
    ;
            IFE      TYPE DEST             ; If FDIV  ST(i),ST
                                           ; or FDIV  ST,ST(i)
            IF       DEST EQ 0             ; Test for ST as destination
```

```
            DB      0CDH
            DB      0D8H,0F0H+SOURCE
            EXITM
            ENDIF
    ;
            IF      SOURCE EQ 0     ; Test for ST as source operand
            DB      0CDH
            DB      0DCH,0F8H+DEST
            ENDIF
            ENDIF
    ;
            IFE     4-TYPE DEST     ; If operand is a 4-byte real
            DB      0CDH
    ;; Test for segment override
            IF      SBYTE           ; Test for SBYTE not zero
    ;; Generate segment override opcode
            DB      SBYTE
            DW      36D8H           ; Hand-code 2 bytes of opcode
                                    ; Corresponding to ESC xx
            DW      N_OFF           ; Add offset of destination
    ;; Generate nonsegment override using ESC
            ELSE
            ESC     06H,DEST
            ENDIF
            ENDIF
    ;
            IFE     8-TYPE DEST     ; If operand is an 8-byte real
            DB      0CDH
    ;; Test for segment override
            IF      SBYTE           ; Test for SBYTE not zero
    ;; Generate segment override opcode
            DB      SBYTE
            DW      36DCH           ; Hand-code 2 bytes of opcode
                                    ; Corresponding to ESC xx
            DW      N_OFF           ; Add offset of destination
    ;; Generate nonsegment override using ESC
            ELSE
            ESC     26H,DEST
            ENDIF
            ENDIF
            ENDM
    ;****************************************************************
    ;
    FDIVP   MACRO   DEST,SOURCE
    ;; FDIVP has one format only
            DB      0CDH
```

```
        DB      0DEH,0F8H+DEST
        ENDM
;****************************************************************
FIDIV   MACRO   DEST
;; Call segment override test macro @SEGOR
        @SEGOR  DEST
;; SBYTE = 0 if no segment override in operand. Else, SBYTE holds
;; emulated segment override byte D4H, D5H, D6H, or D7H
;
        IFE     2-TYPE DEST     ; If operand is a word integer
        DB      0CDH
;; Test for segment override
        IF      SBYTE           ; Test for SBYTE not zero
;; Generate segment override opcode
        DB      SBYTE
        DW      36DEH           ; Hand-code 2 bytes of opcode
                                ; Corresponding to ESC xx
        DW      N_OFF           ; Add offset of destination
;; Generate nonsegment override using ESC
        ELSE
        ESC     36H,DEST
        ENDIF
        ENDIF
;
        IFE     4-TYPE DEST     ; If operand is a short integer
        DB      0CDH
;; Test for segment override
        IF      SBYTE           ; Test for SBYTE not zero
;; Generate segment override opcode
        DB      SBYTE
        DW      36DAH           ; Hand-code 2 bytes of opcode
                                ; Corresponding to ESC xx
        DW      N_OFF           ; Add offset of destination
;; Generate nonsegment override using ESC
        ELSE
        ESC     16H,DEST
        ENDIF
        ENDIF
        ENDM
;****************************************************************
;
FDIVR   MACRO   DEST,SOURCE
;
;; Test for FDIVR (no operands)
        IFB     <DEST>
        DB      0CDH,0DEH,0F1H
```

```
        EXITM
        ENDIF
;
;; Call segment override test macro @SEGOR
        @SEGOR  DEST
;; SBYTE = 0 if no segment override in operand. Else, SBYTE holds
;; emulated segment override byte D4H, D5H, D6H, or D7H
;
        IFE     TYPE DEST       ; If FDIVR  ST(i),ST
                                ; or FDIVR  ST,ST(i)
        IF      DEST EQ 0       ; Test for ST as destination
        DB      0CDH
        DB      0D8H,0FBH+SOURCE
        EXITM
        ENDIF
;
        IF      SOURCE EQ 0     ; Test for ST as source operand
        DB      0CDH
        DB      0DCH,0F0H+DEST
        ENDIF
        ENDIF
;
        IFE     4-TYPE DEST     ; If operand is a 4-byte real
        DB      0CDH
;; Test for segment override
        IF      SBYTE           ; Test for SBYTE not zero
;; Generate segment override opcode
        DB      SBYTE
        DW      3ED8H           ; Hand-code 2 bytes of opcode
                                ; Corresponding to ESC xx
        DW      N_OFF           ; Add offset of destination
;; Generate nonsegment override using ESC
        ELSE
        ESC     07H,DEST
        ENDIF
        ENDIF
;
        IFE     8-TYPE DEST     ; If operand is an 8-byte real
        DB      0CDH
;; Test for segment override
        IF      SBYTE           ; Test for SBYTE not zero
;; Generate segment override opcode
        DB      SBYTE
        DW      3EDCH           ; Hand-code 2 bytes of opcode
                                ; Corresponding to ESC xx
        DW      N_OFF           ; Add offset of destination
```

```
        ;; Generate nonsegment override using ESC
                ELSE
                ESC      27H,DEST
                ENDIF
                ENDIF
                ENDM
        ;*****************************************************************
        ;
        FDIVRP MACRO    DEST,SOURCE
        ;; FSUBRP has one format only
                DB       0CDH
                DB       0DEH,0F0H+DEST
                ENDM
        ;*****************************************************************
        ;
        FIDIVR MACRO    DEST
        ;; Call segment override test macro @SEGOR
                @SEGOR   DEST
        ;; SBYTE = 0 if no segment override in operand. Else, SBYTE holds
        ;; emulated segment override byte D4H, D5H, D6H, or D7H
        ;
                IFE      2-TYPE DEST       ; If operand is a word integer
                DB       0CDH
        ;; Test for segment override
                IF       SBYTE             ; Test for SBYTE not zero
        ;; Generate segment override opcode
                DB       SBYTE
                DW       3EDEH             ; Hand-code 2 bytes of opcode
                                           ; Corresponding to ESC xx
                DW       N_OFF             ; Add offset of destination
        ;; Generate nonsegment override using ESC
                ELSE
                ESC      37H,DEST
                ENDIF
                ENDIF
        ;
                IFE      4-TYPE DEST       ; If operand is a short integer
                DB       0CDH
        ;; Test for segment override
                IF       SBYTE             ; Test for SBYTE not zero
        ;; Generate segment override opcode
                DB       SBYTE
                DW       3EDAH             ; Hand-code 2 bytes of opcode
                                           ; Corresponding to ESC xx
                DW       N_OFF             ; Add offset of destination
        ;; Generate nonsegment override using ESC
```

```
            ELSE
            ESC     17H,DEST
            ENDIF
            ENDIF
            ENDM
;
;****************************************************************
;******************|
; other arithmetic |
;     operations   |
;******************|
FSQRT   MACRO
            DB      0CDH
            DB      0D9H,0FAH
            ENDM
;****************************************************************
;
FSCALE MACRO
            DB      0CDH
            DB      0D9H,0FDH
            ENDM
;****************************************************************
;
FPREM   MACRO
            DB      0CDH
            DB      0D9H,0F8H
            ENDM
;****************************************************************
;
FRNDINT         MACRO
            DB      0CDH
            DB      0D9H,0FCH
            ENDM
;****************************************************************
;
FXTRACT         MACRO
            DB      0CDH
            DB      0D9H,0F4H
            ENDM
;****************************************************************
;
FABS    MACRO
            DB      0CDH
            DB      0D9H,0E1H
            ENDM
;****************************************************************
```

```
FCHS    MACRO
        DB      0CDH
        DB      0D9H,0E0H
        ENDM
;****************************************************************
;
;******************|
;   comparison     |
;******************|
FCOM    MACRO   DEST
;
;; Test for FCOM (no operands)
        IFB     <DEST>
        DB      0CDH,0D8H,0D1H
        EXITM
        ENDIF
;
;; Call segment override test macro @SEGOR
        @SEGOR  DEST
;; SBYTE = 0 if no segment override in operand. Else, SBYTE holds
;; emulated segment override byte D4H, D5H, D6H, or D7H
;
        IFE     TYPE DEST       ; If FCOM ST(i)
        DB      0CDH
        DB      0D8H,0D8H+DEST
        ENDIF
;
        IFE     4-TYPE DEST     ; If operand is a 4-byte real
        DB      0CDH
;; Test for segment override
        IF      SBYTE           ; Test for SBYTE not zero
;; Generate segment override opcode
        DB      SBYTE
        DW      16D8H           ; Hand-code 2 bytes of opcode
                                ; Corresponding to ESC xx
        DW      N_OFF           ; Add offset of destination
;; Generate nonsegment override using ESC
        ELSE
        ESC     02H,DEST
        ENDIF
        ENDIF
;
        IFE     8-TYPE DEST     ; If operand is an 8-byte real
        DB      0CDH
;; Test for segment override
        IF      SBYTE           ; Test for SBYTE not zero
```

```
        ;; Generate segment override opcode
                DB      SBYTE
                DW      16DCH           ; Hand-code 2 bytes of opcode
                                        ; Corresponding to ESC xx
                DW      N_OFF           ; Add offset of destination
        ;; Generate nonsegment override using ESC
                ELSE
                ESC     22H,DEST
                ENDIF
                ENDIF
                ENDM
;*******************************************************************
FCOMP   MACRO   DEST
;
;; Test for FCOMP (no operands)
                IFB     <DEST>
                DB      0CDH,0D8H,0D9H
                EXITM
                ENDIF
;
;; Call segment override test macro @SEGOR
                @SEGOR  DEST
;; SBYTE = 0 if no segment override in operand. Else, SBYTE holds
;; emulated segment override byte D4H, D5H, D6H, or D7H
;
                IFE     TYPE DEST       ; If FCOMP ST(i)
                DB      0CDH
                DB      0D8H,0D8H+DEST
                ENDIF
;
                IFE     4-TYPE DEST     ; If operand is a 4-byte real
                DB      0CDH
        ;; Test for segment override
                IF      SBYTE           ; Test for SBYTE not zero
        ;; Generate segment override opcode
                DB      SBYTE
                DW      1ED8H           ; Hand-code 2 bytes of opcode
                                        ; Corresponding to ESC xx
                DW      N_OFF           ; Add offset of destination
        ;; Generate nonsegment override using ESC
                ELSE
                ESC     03H,DEST
                ENDIF
                ENDIF
;
                IFE     8-TYPE DEST     ; If operand is an 8-byte real
```

```
        DB        0CDH
;; Test for segment override
        IF        SBYTE              ; Test for SBYTE not zero
;; Generate segment override opcode
        DB        SBYTE
        DW        1EDCH              ; Hand-code 2 bytes of opcode
                                     ; Corresponding to ESC xx
        DW        N_OFF              ; Add offset of destination
;; Generate nonsegment override using ESC
        ELSE
        ESC       23H,DEST
        ENDIF
        ENDIF
        ENDM
;****************************************************************
;
FCOMPP MACRO
;; FCOMPP has one format only
        DB        0CDH
        DB        0DEH,0D9H
        ENDM
;****************************************************************
;
FICOM  MACRO     DEST
;; Call segment override test macro @SEGOR
        @SEGOR    DEST
;; SBYTE = 0 if no segment override in operand. Else, SBYTE holds
;; emulated segment override byte D4H, D5H, D6H, or D7H
;
        IFE       2-TYPE DEST        ; If operand is a word integer
        DB        0CDH
;; Test for segment override
        IF        SBYTE              ; Test for SBYTE not zero
;; Generate segment override opcode
        DB        SBYTE
        DW        16DEH              ; Hand-code 2 bytes of opcode
                                     ; Corresponding to ESC xx
        DW        N_OFF              ; Add offset of destination
;; Generate nonsegment override using ESC
        ELSE
        ESC       32H,DEST
        ENDIF
        ENDIF
;
        IFE       4-TYPE DEST        ; If operand is a short integer
        DB        0CDH
```

```
;; Test for segment override
        IF      SBYTE           ; Test for SBYTE not zero
;; Generate segment override opcode
        DB      SBYTE
        DW      16DAH           ; Hand-code 2 bytes of opcode
                                ; Corresponding to ESC xx
        DW      N_OFF           ; Add offset of destination
;; Generate nonsegment override using ESC
        ELSE
        ESC     12H,DEST
        ENDIF
        ENDIF
        ENDM
;
;******************************************************************
;
FICOMP MACRO   DEST
;; Call segment override test macro @SEGOR
        @SEGOR  DEST
;; SBYTE = 0 if no segment override in operand. Else, SBYTE holds
;; emulated segment override byte D4H, D5H, D6H, or D7H
;
        IFE     2-TYPE DEST     ; If operand is a word integer
        DB      0CDH
;; Test for segment override
        IF      SBYTE           ; Test for SBYTE not zero
;; Generate segment override opcode
        DB      SBYTE
        DW      1EDEH           ; Hand-code 2 bytes of opcode
                                ; Corresponding to ESC xx
        DW      N_OFF           ; Add offset of destination
;; Generate nonsegment override using ESC
        ELSE
        ESC     33H,DEST
        ENDIF
        ENDIF
;
        IFE     4-TYPE DEST     ; If operand is a short integer
        DB      0CDH
;; Test for segment override
        IF      SBYTE           ; Test for SBYTE not zero
;; Generate segment override opcode
        DB      SBYTE
        DW      1EDAH           ; Hand-code 2 bytes of opcode
                                ; Corresponding to ESC xx
        DW      N_OFF           ; Add offset of destination
```

```
;; Generate nonsegment override using ESC
        ELSE
        ESC     13H,DEST
        ENDIF
        ENDIF
        ENDM
;
;*****************************************************************
;
FTST    MACRO
        DB      0CDH
        DB      0D9H,0E4H
        ENDM
;*****************************************************************
;
FXAM    MACRO
        DB      0CDH
        DB      0D9H,0E5H
        ENDM
;*****************************************************************
;******************|
;  transcendental  |
;******************|
FPTAN   MACRO
        DB      0CDH
        DB      0D9H,0F2H
        ENDM
;*****************************************************************
;
FPATAN  MACRO
        DB      0CDH
        DB      0D9H,0F3H
        ENDM
;*****************************************************************
;
F2XM1   MACRO
        DB      0CDH
        DB      0D9H,0F0H
        ENDM
;*****************************************************************
;
FYL2X   MACRO
        DB      0CDH
        DB      0D9H,0F1H
        ENDM
;*****************************************************************
```

```
FYL2XP1         MACRO
        DB      0CDH
        DB      0D9H,0F9H
        ENDM
;****************************************************************
;******************|
;       constants  |
;******************|
FLDZ    MACRO
        DB      0CDH
        DB      0D9H,0EEH
        ENDM
;****************************************************************
;
FLD1    MACRO
        DB      0CDH
        DB      0D9H,0E8H
        ENDM
;****************************************************************
;
FLDPI   MACRO
        DB      0CDH
        DB      0D9H,0EBH
        ENDM
;****************************************************************
;
FLDL2T MACRO
        DB      0CDH
        DB      0D9H,0E9H
        ENDM
;****************************************************************
;
FLDL2E MACRO
        DB      0CDH
        DB      0D9H,0EAH
        ENDM
;****************************************************************
;
FLDLG2 MACRO
        DB      0CDH
        DB      0D9H,0ECH
        ENDM
;****************************************************************
;
FLDLN2 MACRO
        DB      0CDH
```

```
        DB      0D9H,0EDH
        ENDM
;***************************************************************
;******************|
; processor control |
;******************|
FINIT   MACRO
        DB      0CDH
        DB      0DBH,0E3H
        ENDM
;***************************************************************
;
FDISI   MACRO
        DB      0CDH
        DB      0DBH,0E1H
        ENDM
;***************************************************************
;
FENI    MACRO
        DB      0CDH
        DB      0DBH,0E0H
        ENDM
;***************************************************************
;
FLDCW   MACRO   DEST
;; Call segment override test macro @SEGOR
        @SEGOR  DEST
;; SBYTE = 0 if no segment override in operand. Else, SBYTE holds
;; emulated segment override byte D4H, D5H, D6H, or D7H
;
        DB      0CDH
;; Test for segment override
        IF      SBYTE           ; Test for SBYTE not zero
;; Generate segment override opcode
        DB      SBYTE
        DW      2ED9H                   ; Hand-code 2 bytes of opcode
                                        ; Corresponding to ESC xx
        DW      N_OFF                   ; Add offset of destination
;; Generate nonsegment override using ESC
        ELSE
        ESC     0DH,DEST
        ENDIF
        ENDM
;***************************************************************
;
FSTCW   MACRO   DEST
```

```
;; Call segment override test macro @SEGOR
        @SEGOR  DEST
;; SBYTE = 0 if no segment override in operand. Else, SBYTE holds
;; emulated segment override byte D4H, D5H, D6H, or D7H
;
        DB      0CDH
;; Test for segment override
        IF      SBYTE               ; Test for SBYTE not zero
;; Generate segment override opcode
        DB      SBYTE
        DW      3ED9H               ; Hand-code 2 bytes of opcode
                                    ; Corresponding to ESC xx
        DW      N_OFF               ; Add offset of destination
;; Generate nonsegment override using ESC
        ELSE
        ESC     0FH,DEST
        ENDIF
        ENDM
;****************************************************************
;
FSTSW   MACRO   DEST
;; Call segment override test macro @SEGOR
        @SEGOR  DEST
;; SBYTE = 0 if no segment override in operand. Else, SBYTE holds
;; emulated segment override byte D4H, D5H, D6H, or D7H
;
        DB      0CDH
;; Test for segment override
        IF      SBYTE               ; Test for SBYTE not zero
;; Generate segment override opcode
        DB      SBYTE
        DW      3EDDH               ; Hand-code 2 bytes of opcode
                                    ; Corresponding to ESC xx
        DW      N_OFF               ; Add offset of destination
;; Generate nonsegment override using ESC
        ELSE
        ESC     2FH,DEST
        ENDIF
        ENDM
;****************************************************************
;
FCLEX   MACRO
        DB      0CDH
        DB      0DBH,0E2H
        ENDM
;****************************************************************
```

```
FSTENV MACRO    DEST
;
;; Call segment override test macro @SEGOR
        @SEGOR  DEST
;; SBYTE = 0 if no segment override in operand. Else, SBYTE holds
;; emulated segment override byte D4H, D5H, D6H, or D7H
;
        DB      0CDH
;; Test for segment override
        IF      SBYTE           ; Test for SBYTE not zero
;; Generate segment override opcode
        DB      SBYTE
        DW      36D9H           ; Hand-code 2 bytes of opcode
                                ; Corresponding to ESC xx
        DW      N_OFF           ; Add offset of destination
;; Generate nonsegment override using ESC
        ELSE
        ESC     0EH,DEST
        ENDIF
        ENDM
;***************************************************************
;
FLDENV MACRO    DEST
;; Call segment override test macro @SEGOR
        @SEGOR  DEST
;; SBYTE = 0 if no segment override in operand. Else, SBYTE holds
;; emulated segment override byte D4H, D5H, D6H, or D7H
;
        DB      0CDH
;; Test for segment override
        IF      SBYTE           ; Test for SBYTE not zero
;; Generate segment override opcode
        DB      SBYTE
        DW      26D9H           ; Hand-code 2 bytes of opcode
                                ; Corresponding to ESC xx
        DW      N_OFF           ; Add offset of destination
;; Generate nonsegment override using ESC
        ELSE
        ESC     0CH,DEST
        ENDIF
        ENDM
;***************************************************************
;
FSAVE  MACRO    DEST
;; Call segment override test macro @SEGOR
        @SEGOR  DEST
```

```
;; SBYTE = 0 if no segment override in operand. Else, SBYTE holds
;; emulated segment override byte D4H, D5H, D6H, or D7H
;
        DB      0CDH
;; Test for segment override
        IF      SBYTE           ; Test for SBYTE not zero
;; Generate segment override opcode
        DB      SBYTE
        DW      36DDH                   ; Hand-code 2 bytes of opcode
                                        ; Corresponding to ESC xx
        DW      N_OFF                   ; Add offset of destination
;; Generate nonsegment override using ESC
        ELSE
        ESC     2EH,DEST
        ENDIF
        ENDM
;*****************************************************************
;
FRSTOR MACRO   DEST
;; Call segment override test macro @SEGOR
        @SEGOR  DEST
;; SBYTE = 0 if no segment override in operand. Else, SBYTE holds
;; emulated segment override byte D4H, D5H, D6H, or D7H
;
        DB      0CDH
;; Test for segment override
        IF      SBYTE           ; Test for SBYTE not zero
;; Generate segment override opcode
        DB      SBYTE
        DW      26DDH                   ; Hand-code 2 bytes of opcode
                                        ; Corresponding to ESC xx
        DW      N_OFF                   ; Add offset of destination
;; Generate nonsegment override using ESC
        ELSE
        ESC     2CH,DEST
        ENDIF
        ENDM
;*****************************************************************
;
FINCSTP         MACRO
        DB      0CDH
        DB      0D9H,0F7H
        ENDM
;*****************************************************************
;
FDECSTP         MACRO
```

```
        DB      0CDH
        DB      0D9H,0F6H
        ENDM
;****************************************************************
;
FFREE   MACRO   DEST
        DB      0CDH
        DB      0DDH,0C0H+DEST
        ENDM
;****************************************************************
;
FNOP    MACRO
        DB      0CDH
        DB      0D9H,0D0H
        ENDM
;****************************************************************
;
FWAIT   MACRO
        DB      90H
        ENDM
;****************************************************************
;
;******************|
; processor control |
;   no-wait form    |
;******************|
FNINIT MACRO
        DB      0CDH
        DB      0DBH,0E3H
        ENDM
;****************************************************************
;
FNDISI MACRO
        DB      0CDH
        DB      0DBH,0E1H
        ENDM
;****************************************************************
;
FNENI   MACRO
        DB      0CDH
        DB      0DBH,0E0H
        ENDM
;****************************************************************
;
FNSTCW MACRO    DEST
;; Call segment override test macro @SEGOR
```

```
                @SEGOR  DEST
;; SBYTE = 0 if no segment override in operand. Else, SBYTE holds
;; emulated segment override byte D4H, D5H, D6H, or D7H
;
        DB      0CDH
;; Test for segment override
        IF      SBYTE           ; Test for SBYTE not zero
;; Generate segment override opcode
        DB      SBYTE
        DW      3ED9H                   ; Hand-code 2 bytes of opcode
                                        ; Corresponding to ESC xx
        DW      N_OFF                   ; Add offset of destination
;; Generate nonsegment override using ESC
        ELSE
        ESC     0FH,DEST
        ENDIF
        ENDM
;*****************************************************************
;
FNSTSW MACRO   DEST
;; Call segment override test macro @SEGOR
        @SEGOR  DEST
;; SBYTE = 0 if no segment override in operand. Else, SBYTE holds
;; emulated segment override byte D4H, D5H, D6H, or D7H
;
        DB      0CDH
;; Test for segment override
        IF      SBYTE           ; Test for SBYTE not zero
;; Generate segment override opcode
        DB      SBYTE
        DW      3EDDH                   ; Hand-code 2 bytes of opcode
                                        ; Corresponding to ESC xx
        DW      N_OFF                   ; Add offset of destination
;; Generate nonsegment override using ESC
        ELSE
        ESC     2FH,DEST
        ENDIF
        ENDM
;*****************************************************************
;
FNCLEX MACRO
        DB      0CDH
        DB      0DBH,0E2H
        ENDM
;*****************************************************************
FNSTENV         MACRO   DEST
```

```
;; Call segment override test macro @SEGOR
        @SEGOR  DEST
;; SBYTE = 0 if no segment override in operand. Else, SBYTE holds
;; emulated segment override byte D4H, D5H, D6H, or D7H
;
        DB      0CDH
;; Test for segment override
        IF      SBYTE           ; Test for SBYTE not zero
;; Generate segment override opcode
        DB      SBYTE
        DW      36D9H           ; Hand-code 2 bytes of opcode
                                ; Corresponding to ESC xx
        DW      N_OFF           ; Add offset of destination
;; Generate nonsegment override using ESC
        ELSE
        ESC     0EH,DEST
        ENDIF
        ENDM
;****************************************************************
;
FNSAVE MACRO    DEST
;; Call segment override test macro @SEGOR
        @SEGOR  DEST
;; SBYTE = 0 if no segment override in operand. Else, SBYTE holds
;; emulated segment override byte D4H, D5H, D6H, or D7H
;
        DB      0CDH
;; Test for segment override
        IF      SBYTE           ; Test for SBYTE not zero
;; Generate segment override opcode
        DB      SBYTE
        DW      36DDH           ; Hand-code 2 bytes of opcode
                                ; Corresponding to ESC xx
        DW      N_OFF           ; Add offset of destination
;; Generate nonsegment override using ESC
        ELSE
        ESC     2EH,DEST
        ENDIF
        ENDM
;****************************************************************
;********************************|
;     segment override macro     |
;********************************|
@SEGOR  MACRO   DEST
; This macro is called by other floating-point macros that access
; memory operands. @SEGOR checks if there is a segment override
```

```
; string in the instruction's destination operand and assigns the
; corresponding opcode value to the variable SBYTE
;
        SBYTE = 00H;; Default value indicates no
;; segment override in operand
;
ESSEG    INSTR    <DEST>,<ES:>;; Test for ES: string
         IF       ESSEG
         SBYTE = 0D4H
         N_OFF = OFFSET DEST      ;; Calculate simple offset of
                                  ;; operand
         ENDIF
;
CSSEG    INSTR    <DEST>,<CS:>;; Test for CS: string
         IF       CSSEG
         SBYTE = 0D5H
         N_OFF = OFFSET DEST      ;; Calculate simple offset of
                                  ;; operand
         ENDIF
;
SSSEG    INSTR    <DEST>,<SS:>;; Test for SS: string
         IF       SSSEG
         SBYTE = 0D6H
         N_OFF = OFFSET DEST      ;; Calculate simple offset of
                                  ;; operand
         ENDIF
;
DSSEG    INSTR    <DEST>,<DS:>;; Test for DS: string
         IF       DSSEG
         SBYTE = 0D7H
         N_OFF = OFFSET DEST      ;; Calculate simple offset of
                                  ;; operand
         ENDIF
         ENDM
;
; END OF MODULE
```

9

VGA Graphics Programming

9.0 Graphics Facilities in IBM Microcomputers

The original IBM microcomputer, released in 1981, was furnished with two optional video systems. One was a monochrome, alphanumeric display, and the other was a color, graphics system. The monochrome version was named the Monochrome Display Adapter (MDA) and the color system, the Color Graphics Adapter (CGA). The MDA system contained 4K of on-board video memory and the CGA was furnished with 16K. The main difference between these systems was that the CGA allowed graphics programming by controlling the individual screen dots while the MDA did not. However, both devices contained an alphanumeric character set with special symbols that could be used in drawing boxes and in shading rectangular screen areas.

Since 1981 IBM has marketed several other graphics systems, including the Enhanced Graphics Adapter (EGA) and its descendant, the Video Graphics Array (VGA). The EGA was first offered in 1985 as an optional color graphics upgrade. The VGA was introduced with the PS/2 line in 1987. Other IBM microcomputer graphics systems are the Video Gate Array used in the PCjr, and the Multicolor Graphics Array (MCGA) that is furnished with the low-end computers of the PS/2 line. IBM also offers two high-resolution graphics systems. The one intended for the PC line is designated as Professional Graphics System (PGS) and the 8514/A for the PS/2 computers.

This abundance of video standards and options, many with totally different characteristics, would likely create programming difficulties. Nevertheless, if the software limits its output to alphanumeric characters and executes in text modes, it is possible to ensure a high degree of portability, because IBM, thus far, has maintained many of the original display alpha modes, with identical numbers of screen rows and columns, as well as the same character set. Therefore, a well-designed application written for the original MDA card will probably run without a glitch in a CGA, PCjr, EGA, MCGA, VGA, and any other IBM or IBM-compatible video hardware.

Table 9.1. *IBM Video Modes*

MODE	TYPE	DEFINITION	MONO OR COLOR	BUFFER ADDRESS	BUFFER SIZE	CHARACTER BOX SIZE	MDA	CGA	EGA	PCjr	VGA	MCGA
							PC LINE				PS/2 LINE	
0	Text	40 x 25	B & W	B8000H	2K	8 x 8		X	X	X	X	X
1	Text	40 x 25	Color	B8000H	2K	8 x 8		X	X	X	X	X
2	Text	80 x 25	B & W	B8000H	2K	8 x 8		X	X	X	X	X
3	Text	80 x 25	Color	B8000H	4K	8 x 8		X	X	X	X	X
4	APA	320 x 200	Color	B8000H	8K	8 x 8		X	X	X	X	X
5	APA	320 x 200	B & W	B8000H	8K	8 x 8		X	X	X	X	X
6	APA	640 x 200	B & W	B8000H	16K	8 x 8		X	X	X	X	X
7	Text	80 x 25	B & W	B0000H	4K	9 x 14	X		X		X	
8	APA	160 x 200	Color	B8000H	16K	8 x 8				X		
9	APA	320 x 200	Color	B8000H	32K	8 x 8				X		
10	APA	640 x 200	Color	B8000H	32K	8 x 8				X		
13	APA	320 x 200	Color	A0000H	8K	8 x 8			X		X	
14	APA	640 x 200	Color	A0000H	16K	8 x 8			X		X	
15	APA	640 x 350	B & W	A0000H	28K	8 x 14			X		X	
16	APA	640 x 350	Color	A0000H	28K	8 x 14			X		X	
17	APA	640 x 480	Color	A0000H	38K	8 x 16					X	X
18	APA	640 x 480	Color	A0000H	38K	8 x 16					X	
19	APA	640 x 480	Color	A0000H	38K	8 x 8					X	X

Abbreviations: MDA = Monochrome Display Adapter   CGA = Color Graphics Adapter   MCGA = PS/2 Multicolor Graphics Array
EGA = Enhanced Graphics Adapter   VGA = PS/2 Video Graphics Array

However, note that this portability is limited to the alphanumeric modes of these standards. Each new graphics system introduced by IBM, or by other companies, has brought increased definition or expanded color or graphics options and, consequently, have had to implement new display modes. For example, the highest definition in the CGA system is obtained in mode 6, with 640 by 200 pixels; in the EGA the highest definition is in mode 16, with 640 by 350 pixels, while in the VGA standard mode 18 provides 640 by 480 pixels. To the graphics programmer each of these modes represents a completely different and incompatible machine, which is programmed differently. Table 9.1 lists the characteristics of the video modes in the most popular graphics hardware of the PC and the PS/2 lines.

9.0.1 The VGA Standard

In 1987 IBM introduced two new video standards named the MCGA, and the VGA. These graphics systems are furnished as standard components in the computers of the PS/2 line. Originally, the lower-end Models 25 and 30 were equipped with MCGA graphics and the remaining systems, Models 50, 60, and 80 were equipped with VGA. Later on IBM extended the VGA standard to Model 30-286. In August 1990 IBM announced a line of inexpensive, home computers designated as the PS/1 line. The models of the PS/1 line are also equipped with VGA graphics, which probably signals the demise of the MCGA standard.

Another major change brought about by the MCGA and VGA standards is a conversion from digital to analog display driver technology. Analog monitors can produce a much larger array of colors than their digital counterparts. This explains why the monitors of the PC line are incompatible with the MCGA and VGA, and vice versa.

VGA graphics systems are furnished with 256K of video memory divided into four 64K video maps, sometimes called *bit planes*. VGA supports all the display modes in MDA, CGA, and EGA. In addition, VGA implements a new graphics mode with 640-by-480-pixel resolution in 16 colors. This mode, designated with the number 18, is exclusive of the VGA standard. The effective resolution of the text modes is 720 by 400 pixels. Three different text fonts can be selected to display text in the alphanumeric modes. The VGA circuitry uses a digital-to-analog converter (DAC) to drive the monitor hardware.

9.0.2 Portability of Graphics Software

Although most IBM graphics systems have enjoyed days of popularity and preponderance, from a technological viewpoint, many of these standards are of only historical interest. However, developers of commercial software products must take into account not only state-of-the-art equipment but also the existence of an installed base of machines that use the older technology. This practical consideration forces complications in program design and coding, so that the software will be compatible with as many systems as possible.

To the graphics programmer the EGA and the VGA appear somewhat similar. Both standards contain the same programmable registers mapped to the same addresses, use similar bit mapping of the color planes, and the same BIOS services. One important difference between the EGA and the VGA standards is related to the maximum resolution possible in the system. In EGA this resolution is 640 by 350 pixels (modes 15 and 16) while the VGA is capable of 640 by 480 pixels (VGA modes 17, 18, and 19). These 640 by 480 modes are not available in EGA. Another difference is that most VGA programmable registers support read and write operations while in EGA, many of these registers cannot be read.

The MCGA system, on the other hand, can be considered a watered-down version of VGA. The only VGA graphics mode not available in the MCGA is mode 18 (see Table 9.1). On the other hand, this mode is the most powerful and popular one in the VGA standard. Fortunately for the graphics programmer, the MCGA standard was short-lived and never very popular.

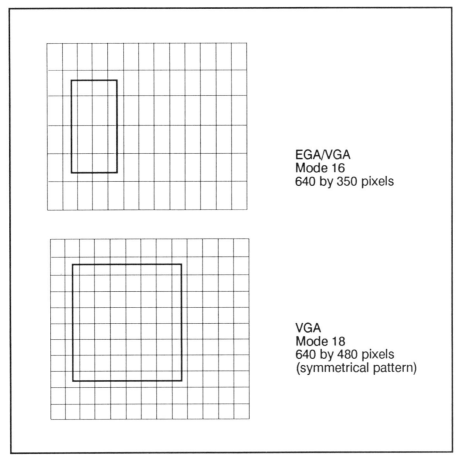

EGA/VGA
Mode 16
640 by 350 pixels

VGA
Mode 18
640 by 480 pixels
(symmetrical pattern)

Figure 9.1. *Resolution Symmetry in IBM Graphics Systems*

9.0.3 Resolution Symmetry

In spite of its historical importance, the EGA standard is no longer active. Few, if any, EGA systems are manufactured or marketed at the present time. In addition, the differences between EGA and VGA are not at all minor. One of the most important is related to resolution symmetry.

Video display resolution can be expressed in terms of the total number of separately addressable elements per unit area. This graphics density is often measured in pixels per inch. For example, a VGA system in graphics mode 18 has a horizontal and vertical resolution of 80 pixels per inch. This density is determined by 640 horizontal pixels per each 8-in row and 480 vertical pixels per each 6-in column. The EGA system, on the other hand, offers 640 horizontal pixels per each 8-in row, with a horizontal density of 80 pixels per inch, but only 350 vertical pixels per each 6-in column, which results in a vertical density of approximately 58 pixels per inch.

Equal vertical and horizontal resolutions, as in VGA mode 18, result in a pixel structure that forms a symmetrical grid. While, if vertical and horizontal resolutions are different, as in EGA mode 15, the pixel grid is asymmetrical. It is easy to see that a symmetrical pixel grid facilitate graphics plotting, while an asymmetrical grid deforms geometrical screen forms and makes a square appear as a rectangle and a circle as an ellipse. Figure 9.1 shows symmetrical and asymmetrical pixel grids.

9.0.4 VGA Video Memory Structure

The EGA standard introduced a new way of organizing video memory. In the MDA, CGA, and PCjr, the program code sets or clears screen pixels directly by writing ones or zeros to the corresponding address in video RAM. In these systems there is no interference from the display hardware. On the other hand, in some EGA and VGA graphics modes, a read or write operation to an address in video memory requires moving 4 data bytes to four individual bit planes in the buffer. Which of these four bit planes is accessed by the CPU depends on the setting of the corresponding latch registers.

In VGA mode 18 (see Table 9.1) the 256K of video RAM are divided into four 64K blocks. It is these blocks that form video maps 0 to 3, which are also referred to as *bit planes*. The 16 possible combinations of these four bit planes give rise to 16 colors. Figure 9.2 lists the memory structure of VGA video mode 18.

In the example of Figure 9.2 the second screen pixel is set according to the state of bit 6 in each video map. Since pixels in the blue and green maps are clear, these elements do not form part of the final color. In this case, the pixel color, bright red, results from the red and the intensity bit maps. The intensity map serves to add a bright hue to any color displayed. Figure 9.3 lists the possible color combinations that can be generated using the I, R, G, and B bit maps.

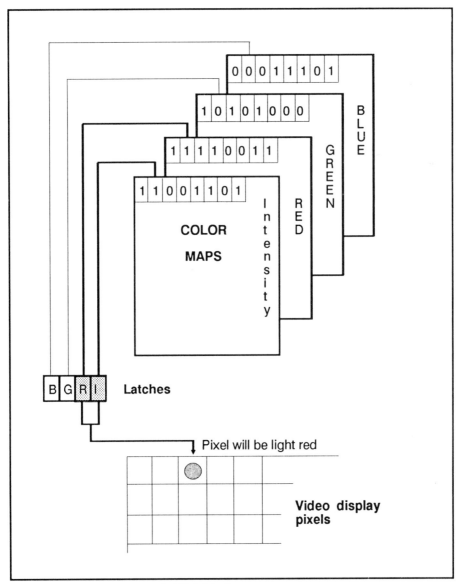

Figure 9.2. *Video Memory in VGA Mode 18*

9.1 VGA Programming

The memory layout depicted in Figure 9.2 appears relatively straightforward. Each of four bit maps serves to control the color elements in each pixel. In practice, however, the linear memory space reserved for video functions in the IBM microcomputers is not sufficient to store all the data required for some EGA and VGA modes. Note that, in the MS DOS environment, the memory area available for video functions extends from

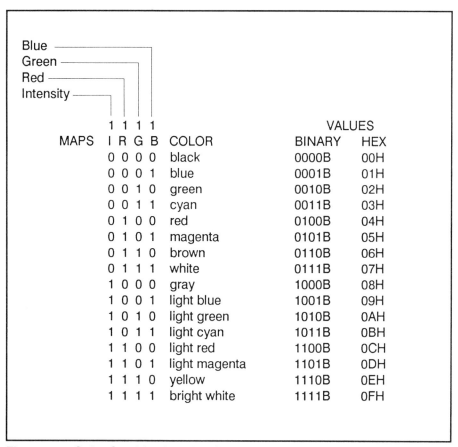

MAPS	I	R	G	B	COLOR	VALUES BINARY	HEX
	0	0	0	0	black	0000B	00H
	0	0	0	1	blue	0001B	01H
	0	0	1	0	green	0010B	02H
	0	0	1	1	cyan	0011B	03H
	0	1	0	0	red	0100B	04H
	0	1	0	1	magenta	0101B	05H
	0	1	1	0	brown	0110B	06H
	0	1	1	1	white	0111B	07H
	1	0	0	0	gray	1000B	08H
	1	0	0	1	light blue	1001B	09H
	1	0	1	0	light green	1010B	0AH
	1	0	1	1	light cyan	1011B	0BH
	1	1	0	0	light red	1100B	0CH
	1	1	0	1	light magenta	1101B	0DH
	1	1	1	0	yellow	1110B	0EH
	1	1	1	1	bright white	1111B	0FH

Figure 9.3. *Color Combinations in VGA Mode 18*

A0000H to BFFFFH, 131,071 bytes (128K). This space is insufficient for the 153,600 bytes of storage required for VGA graphics mode 18, and even less sufficient for the 256,000 bytes for VGA graphics mode 19. As a result of this conflict, the designers of the EGA and VGA systems had to invent nonlinear schemes in order to compress video data into the allotted space.

This scheme consists of a folded video memory implemented through latch registers. The somewhat confusing result is that the various color maps are located at the same physical address. Each memory map is imaged consecutively through a latching mechanism. Fortunately, most complications of this manipulation are handled automatically by the hardware, while the programmer continues to see video memory as a physical space and controls the color of each pixel by loading the video controller register with the desired IRGB encoding (see Figure 9.3).

An important difference between the EGA and VGA high-resolution graphics modes and their alphanumeric modes is the start address of video memory. Alphanumeric applications find the start of the video buffer at physical address B0000H in monochrome systems and at address B8000H in color systems. This last address is also used in some low resolution graphics modes. However, in the high-resolution modes, starting with mode 13, the EGA, MCGA, and the VGA have the video buffer located at physical address A0000H, as listed in Table 9.1. Graphics programs that access the video buffer directly use A000H as a segment base.

9.1.1 Selecting a Read Mode

We have mentioned that, in spite of its apparent complications, programming a folded video memory space is handled almost automatically by the hardware. For example, the EGA and the VGA provide two different read modes. Read Mode 0, which is the default, loads the CPU with the contents of one of the bit maps designated with the letter I, R, G, or B. Which map is read into the CPU depends on the current setting of another VGA register, fittingly named the *Read Map Select* register. Bits 0 and 1 of the Read Map Select register determine which map is *latched* onto the CPU. In order to read the contents of all four maps, the code would have to execute four read operations at the same address. In this case, each read cycle is preceded by instructions that appropriately set the read map select register.

While Read Mode 0 is useful in obtaining the contents of one or more video maps, Read Mode 1 is more convenient when the programmer wishes to test for the presence of pixels that are set to a specific color or pattern. In Read Mode 1 the contents of all four maps is compared with a predetermined bit mask. This mask must have been stored beforehand in a VGA register named the *Color Compare* register. For example, if the code wishes to test for the presence of bright blue pixels, the corresponding bit pattern (which is 1001B in IRGB encoding) is stored in the Color Compare register. Thereafter, a buffer read operation appears to execute four successive logical ANDs with this mask. If a bit in any of the four maps matches the bit mask in the Color Compare register, it will be set in the CPU; otherwise it will be clear.

The program named PCLDUMP, listed in Chapter 4, uses VGA Read Mode 1 to test for nonwhite pixels. The code shows the setting of a EGA or VGA write mode and the loading and operation of the Color Compare and Color Don't Care registers of the Graphics Controller.

9.1.2 The VGA Write Modes

In order to make these devices more useful and flexible, the designers of the EGA and its descendant, the VGA, implemented several ways in which to write data to the video display. These are known as the *write modes*. The EGA allows three and the VGA allows four different write modes. The programmer selects the write mode by setting the graphics mode select register of the graphics controller. The code to perform this operation is shown in the SET_WRITE_MODE procedure that is part of the GAL-LERY program, listed later in this chapter. The fundamental functions of the various write modes are as follows:

Write mode 0 is the default mode. Many programmers consider this mode the most useful and flexible one. In write mode 0 the CPU, map mask register of the sequencer, and the bit mask register of the graphics controller are used to set a screen pixel to any desired color. Other video controller registers are also used for specific effects. For example, the graphics controller's logical operation select and data rotate register has two fields which are significant during write mode 0 operations. The data rotate field (bits 0 to 3) determines how many positions to rotate the CPU data to the right before performing the write operation. The logical operation select field (bits 3 and 4) determines how the data stored in video memory is logically combined with the CPU data. The options are to write the CPU data unmodified or to AND, OR, or XOR it with the latched data. The XOR data mode is discussed in later sections of this chapter in relation to animation techniques.

In *write mode 1* the contents of the latch registers, previously loaded by a read operation, are copied directly onto the color maps. This write mode, which can be used in moving one area of video memory into another, is probably the simplest and the easiest to understand. Write mode 1 becomes particularly useful when the program wants to take advantage of the unused portions of video RAM. The location and amount of this unused memory varies in different systems and modes. For example, we have seen that in VGA graphics mode 18 each video map contains 64K RAM. The total number of pixels is of 640 per row by a total of 480 rows. This means that, in this VGA mode, only 38,400 bytes are actually used while the remaining 27,135 bytes are available to the programmer for storing images or data.

Write mode 2 is a simplified version of write mode 0. Like mode 0, it allows setting an individual pixel to any desired color. In write mode 2 the data rotate function of the logical operation select and data rotate register and the set-reset function are not available. Write mode 2 offers the advantage of a higher execution speed than write mode 0, which is something to consider if the graphics routine can do without these functions. Another difference between these write modes is that, in write mode 2 routines, the pixel color is defined by the contents of the CPU and not by the setting of the sequencer's map mask register or the enable set-reset and set-reset registers. This simplifies the code and is one of the factors that determines the higher execution speed of this mode. The procedure named WRITE_PIX in the program GALLERY presented later in this chapter, is a fast output routine that uses VGA write mode 2.

Write mode 3 is proprietary of the VGA systems. There is no equivalent mode in EGA. The logical operation select and data rotate register operates in the same manner as in write mode 0. The CPU data is ANDed with the bit mask register. The resulting bit pattern performs the same function as the bit mask register in write modes 0 and 2. The set-reset register also performs the same function as in write mode 0. However, the enable set-reset register is not used. Therefore, the pixel color can be determined by programming either the set-reset register or the map mask register. The map mask register can also be programmed to selectively enable or disable the individual maps.

Various read and write modes can be used in the same program without conflict. For instance, the program named GALLERY, listed later, uses write modes 0 and 2 alternatively. The procedure named SET_WRITE_MODE performs the mode changes. These changes in read and write modes do not affect the displayed image. However, a change in video mode will normally clear the screen and reset all programmable registers.

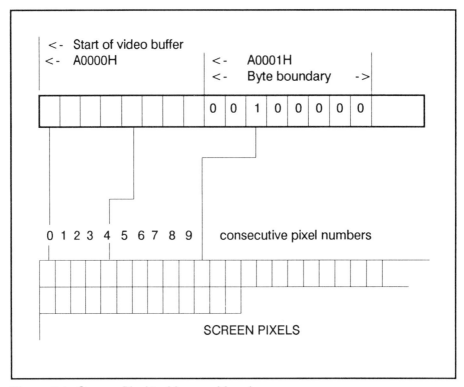

Figure 9.4. *Screen Pixel-to-Memory Mapping*

9.1.3 Address Mapping

An important characteristic of the pixel mapping scheme used in the EGA and VGA standards is that the state of each pixel is determined, in certain graphics modes, by the setting of several memory bits. For example, in VGA mode 18 we have seen that each screen pixel depends on the state of 4 IRGB bits mapped to the pixel's address. This means that each screen pixel is mapped to 4 memory bits, located at the same physical address. But the read and write instructions performed by the 80x86 CPU take place at a byte level. The chip's instruction set does not allow reading an individual memory bit. Therefore, in order to access the individual pixels, a graphics program has to perform some sort of bit masking operation. Figure 9.4 illustrates pixel-to-memory mapping in the EGA and VGA standards.

   In reference to Figure 9.4, to read or write screen pixel number 10, the program must first calculate the bit address in video memory that is mapped to this pixel. The actual arithmetic varies in the different display modes, according to the number of pixels per row and the total number of screen rows. However, in all cases, the mapping operation requires calculating two components: the byte-level address that contains the corresponding memory bit and the mask required to access the bit. In the example of Figure 9.4, the address of the byte that is mapped to the 10th screen pixels is A0001H, and the mask required to isolate this individual pixel is 00100000B.

9.1.4 Byte-Level Operations

Not all graphics routines require the fine degree of screen control achieved through bit mapping. Many graphics applications manipulate relatively large screen areas, usually in rectangular form, which are often displayed in a single color. One advantage of using routines that read or write pixels at the byte level is that they achieve substantially better performance than do those that read or write the pixels individually.

Byte-level graphics routines operate on the byte boundaries listed in Figure 9.4. Frequently these routines bypass mask calculations by using a bit pattern that will set all bits. This is the case in the routine named COARSE_FILL that is part of the GALLERY program. However, there is no reason why this mask has to set all the pixels encoded in a video memory byte. It is possible to use alternative bit patterns in byte-level graphics routines in order to create color shades, hatches, bars, other symmetrical patterns, or even random effects. For example, the COARSE_FILL routine loads the bit pattern 11111111B into the AH register in order to set all pixels controlled by a video memory byte. This mask creates a solid color in the displayed area. If the mask were changed to 00001111B, a series of vertical lines would be displayed instead.

In this type of routine, while the horizontal boundary is at the byte level, there is no required unit of vertical definition. The COARSE_FILL routine of the GALLERY program divides the 480 rows of the video display (assuming VGA mode 18) into 60 stripes of 8 pixel rows. In the routine's terminology these horizontal stripes are named ranks. The chosen value of 8 pixel rows per rank is proportional to the 8 horizontal pixels controlled by each video memory byte. However, this number of pixel rows is arbitrary and there is no reason why it cannot be varied.

The pixel address calculations in byte-level graphics routines are quite simple. The routine named COARSE_ADD of the GALLERY program shows the multiplications necessary to obtain a byte offset into the video buffer from the values passed by the program.

9.1.5 Bit-Level Operations

When a EGA or VGA graphics program must read or write an individual screen pixel it must first obtain the address of the byte to which this pixel is mapped, and then calculate the mask that will isolate this pixel from the other 7 pixels mapped to this same byte. A typical routine for VGA mode 18 receives from the caller the x coordinate (range 0 to 639) and the y coordinate (range 0 to 479) of the pixel to be accessed. The conversion routine calculates the byte offset into the video buffer and the bit mask that isolates the individual pixel. In write modes 0 and 2, this bit mask must be placed in the bit mask registers of the graphics controller.

One way of determining this bit mask is by shifting to the right the unit bit pattern 10000000B. The shift count usually comes as a remainder from the of the byte offset calculations. Another method is to use this remainder as an index into a look-up table that contains the eight possible masks. The procedure named PIXEL_ADD in the GALLERY program illustrates the right hand shift method for performing pixel mask calculations.

9.2 Graphics Primitive Routines

The VGA graphics programmer requires a set of fundamental routines on which it is possible to construct a graphics program, a graphics library, a graphics programming language, or a graphics extension to a language. The graphics manipulations that are performed by the fundamental routines are indeed simple: to read the attributes of a pixel located at certain screen coordinates and to write a pixel at a certain screen coordinate using a given attribute. Services 12 and 13 of BIOS interrupt 10H provide pixel write and read functions, but these BIOS services are generally too slow and too restricted for practical use.

The program named PCLDUMP (see Chapter 4) contains a routine named BYTE_ADD that calculates the offset in the video buffer of successive groups of 8 screen pixels. The program sets the Color Compare and Color Don't Care registers of the graphics controller so that all nonwhite pixels are reported as black. The video buffer is read 1 byte at a time. Each byte, which encodes the state of 8 screen pixels, is then dumped to the PCL printing device.

The GALLERY program, listed in this chapter, contains several graphics routines for performing write operations. The procedure named COARSE_FILL first calls the auxiliary procedure COARSE_ADD to calculate the byte-level address into the video buffer. Then COARSE_FILL passes this data, together with the desired pixel color and an all-1s mask, to a procedure named WRITE_PIX, which actually sets the corresponding screen byte.

Another procedure named VARI_PATTERN is used by the GALLERY program for displaying an encoded bit pattern of variable size. The procedure receives two pointers from the calling routine. One pointer is to an array that contains the dimensions and parameters for the bit pattern to be displayed. The last item retrieved from this pointer is a bit map of the graphic object to be displayed. The second pointer contains the address of a matrix of color attributes to be used in displaying each pixel in the object. In VGA mode 18 only 4 bits are required to encode each pixel color. However, to simplify processing, the VARI_PATTERN procedure uses 1 byte to encode the color of each pixel. In this manner, while the bit map for the cross-hair symbol displayed in the GALLERY program contains 240 pixels, the color matrix for this object contains 240 bytes. The same proportion applies for the *duck object*.

The dimensions and display parameters contained under the first pointer passed to the VARI_PATTERN procedure are the x and y screen coordinates at which the object is to be displayed, the number of rows in the object's bit pattern, and the number of bytes per row. VARI_PATTERN calls the routine PIXEL_ADD to obtain the video buffer offset and bit map for accessing the screen pixel, then passes this data to the general-purpose pixel write routine named WRITE_PIX.

The reader should note that the graphics routines used by the GALLERY program are those required for its functions. These routines are by no means sufficient for a general graphics library. The bibliography lists three titles that contain fundamental graphics information and routines for the EGA and VGA standards.

9.3 Text in VGA Graphics

Most graphics programs require some form of text display. In the EGA and VGA standards there are several ways of generating text characters. Some of these forms are readily usable in a program, while others require extensive coding.

BIOS service number 9, INT 10H, can be used to display a character at the current cursor position. Note that this is the only BIOS character display service that can be used in a graphics mode. Service number 2, INT 10H, to set the cursor position can be used, in conjunction with the character display function, to set a display position. The procedure named GRAPHIC_TEXT in the GALLERY program displays a text string using services 2 and 9 of BIOS INT 10H. In VGA systems, BIOS service number 17, INT 10H, can be used to load one of three available fonts. The loaded font will be the one used by service number 9, but only in alphanumeric modes.

Many graphics and alphanumeric programs create large display lettering by using the graphics characters in the IBM extended ASCII character set. These solid blocks are generated by the extended ASCII codes EBH, ECH, EDH, EEH, and EFH. It is usually easier to design large letters and symbols using quadrille paper. The resulting codes appear as data for a string display routine. The GALLERY program uses this technique to create oversize letters to form the word *Gallery*. The encoding can be seen under the variable GAL_MS in the program's data segment. Other symbols can also be created by manipulating these characters. The GALLERY program draws the figure of a mouse using the extended ASCII symbols. Figure 9.5 presents the IBM Character Set.

The programmer should be aware that the number of text characters per screen row and the total number of screen rows on the video display differ between the graphics and alphanumeric modes. For instance, in VGA mode 18, alphanumeric display, using the default font, is based on 30 horizontal rows of 80 characters each.

9.3.1 Creating Screen Fonts

When the existing screen fonts are not adequate and the creation of characters using the extended ASCII blocks and symbols does not offer satisfactory results, the programmer can resort to a customized bit-mapped font. The encoding of bit mapped fonts, while not technically difficult, can be a time-consuming task. The bit-mapped characters are designed in a similar manner as the duck and cross-hair symbols in the GALLERY program. The same display routine, named VARI_PATTERN, can be used to position the characters on the screen at a pixel level.

9.4 Computer Animation

Computer animation is the imitation of lifelike features using computer technology. We often think of animation as the creation of an illusion of movement, but, strictly speaking, the concept of animation extends to any lifelike feature, such as speech or emotion. In this sense a cartoon figure can be animated by turning the characters's face red to convey the impression of anger, or by simulating talk. Nevertheless, it is undeniable that the

Hex	0	1	2	3	4	5	6	7
0		►		0	@	P	`	p
1	☺	◄	!	1	A	Q	a	q
2	☻	↕	"	2	B	R	b	r
3	♥	‼	#	3	C	S	c	s
4	♦	¶	$	4	D	T	d	t
5	♣	§	%	5	E	U	e	u
6	♠	▬	&	6	F	V	f	v
7	•	↨	'	7	G	W	g	w
8	◘	↑	(	8	H	X	h	x
9	○	↓	)	9	I	Y	i	y
A	◎	→	*	:	J	Z	j	z
B	♂	←	+	;	K	[	k	{
C	♀	∟	,	<	L	\	l	¦
D	♪	↔	-	=	M	]	m	}
E	♫	▲	.	>	N	^	n	~
F	☼	▼	/	?	O	_	o	∆

Figure 9.5. *IBM Character Set*

Hex	8	9	A	B	C	D	E	F
Ø	Ç	É	á	░	└	╨	α	≡
1	ü	æ	í	▒	┴	╤	β	±
2	é	Æ	ó	▓	┬	╥	Γ	≥
3	â	ô	ú	│	├	╙	π	≤
4	ä	ö	ñ	┤	─	╘	Σ	⌠
5	à	ò	Ñ	╡	┼	╒	σ	⌡
6	å	û	ª	╢	╞	╓	μ	÷
7	ç	ù	º	╖	╟	╫	τ	≈
8	ê	ÿ	¿	╕	╚	╪	Φ	○
9	ë	Ö	⌐	╣	╔	┘	Θ	•
A	è	Ü	¬	║	╩	┌	Ω	·
B	ï	¢	½	╗	╦	█	δ	√
C	î	£	¼	╝	╠	▄	∞	ⁿ
D	ì	¥	¡	╜	═	▌	φ	²
E	Ä	₧	«	╛	╬	▐	∈	■
F	Å	ƒ	»	┐	┴	▀	∩	

Figure 9.5. *IBM Character Set (continued)*

imitation of movement is the most effective means by which to create the illusion of life or of lively action.

Computer animation falls into one of two general categories: frame-by-frame and real-time animation. The most important use of frame-by-frame animation techniques is in graphics systems designed to *assist* in the creation of animated images, which are presented using a different medium. For instance, computer graphics systems sometimes aid in the creation of the consecutive images required for the production of cartoon films. These computer images are photographed individually and later projected at sufficient speed to create the illusion of movement.

This type of animation does not impose a critical performance rate on the computer system, which could take as long as necessary in creating each image. Real-time animation, on the other hand, produces results that are visible on the computer terminal as they are generated. Electronic arcade games are a form of real-time animation. In this case, computer performance is an important factor since it determines the speed of the animation and the quality of the generated imagery.

9.4.1 Visual Retention

It is known that our visual organs retain, for a short time, the images of objects that no longer exist in the real world. This phenomenon, called *retention*, is related to the chemistry and the structure of the cells and neurons in the retina. Visual retention is the reason why we can create the illusion of movement by flashing consecutive still images before our eyes. If the flashing rate exceeds a minimum critical speed, often estimated at 15 frames per second, visual retention causes the viewer to mentally merge the images together and perceive the individual flashes as one continuous, flickerless, change.

Computer animation often consists on frame-by-frame projections of successive images. If the rate at which the images are flashed is close to the critical rate of 15 per second, then the animation appears smooth and pleasant. On the other hand, if the software cannot approximate this critical rate, the animation appears coarse and bumpy, and the user perceives a disturbing flicker. It is this rate of retention which imposes performance requirements on real-time animated systems. If a computer animation program is to create a smooth and pleasant effect, all the manipulations and changes from image to image must be performed in less than 1/15 of a second (1/15 s). Raster scan video systems with bit-mapped buffers, such as those in the IBM microcomputers, are not well suited for computer animation.

9.4.2 Interference

A raster scan display system operates by projecting an electron beam on each horizontal row of screen pixels. The scanning proceeds, row by row, from the top left screen corner to the bottom right. To avoid visible interference the electron beam is turned off during the period in which the gun is re-aimed back to the start of the next pixel row (horizontal retrace). It is also turned off while it is re-aimed from the last pixel on the bottom right corner of the screen to the first pixel at the top left corner (vertical retrace). Because of the distance and directions involved, the vertical retrace period takes much longer than the horizontal retrace.

In the original versions of the CGA card, the programmer had to time the program's access to the video buffer with the vertical retrace cycle of the CRT controller. Failure to perform this timing operation would result in a visible interference, often called *snow*. The newer graphics systems, including the EGA and VGA, are designed to avoid this form of interference, but only when using conventional display methods. Not so in animated programs, which must flash consecutive screen images at a rapid rate. In this case, if the access to video hardware is not timed with the vertical retrace cycle, there will be visible interference, although different from the CGA snow.

This timing requirement introduces an additional burden on animated graphics software. For example, the screen refresh periods in EGA and VGA graphics modes takes place at an approximate rate of 70 times per second. An animated program that must flash images on the screen at a minimum rate of 15 per second (see Section 9.4.1) must take into account that each display operation must be timed with a vertical retrace cycle that takes place at a rate of 70 times per second. If the routine is to maintain a critical display rate, this synchronization delay must be added to the processing time. The procedure named TIME_VRC in the GALLERY program detects the start of the CRT vertical retrace cycle so that video access operations can be synchronized.

9.4.3 XOR Operations in Animation Routines

The illusion of movement in a screen object is often produced by geometrically transforming the object. The simple geometrical transformations consist of translation, rotation, and scaling. Complex animation is performed by combining two or more of these transformations; for instance, a screen object can be made to move across the screen while it is made progressively larger. The combined transformations create the illusion that a three-dimensional object is diagonally approximating the viewer.

In any case, the transformation is performed by replacing the previous image of the object with a new image. In simple lateral translation, an object can be made to appear to move across the screen, from right to left, by progressively redrawing it at consecutively smaller x coordinates. The duck in the GALLERY program is translated in this manner. Note that the graphics software must not only draw a series of consecutive images, but also erase the previous images from the screen. Otherwise, the animated object will leave a pixel track. Also note that erasing the screen object is at least as time consuming as drawing it, since each pixel in the object must be changed to its previous state.

The cycle of erasing and redrawing the screen object can be performed in several ways. The most direct method is to save that portion of the screen image that is to be occupied by the object before it is displayed. The object can then be erased by redisplaying the saved image. This method adds an additional burden to the graphics routine, which must also read and store every screen pixel that will be occupied by the object, but in many situations it is the only satisfactory solution.

Another method of erasing the screen image that sometimes offers satisfactory results is based on the logical XOR operation. The effect of the exclusive OR is that a bit in the result is set if both operands contain opposite values. Consequently, XORing the same value twice restores the original contents, as in the following example:

$$
\begin{array}{rl}
 & 10000001B \\
\text{XOR} & 10110011B \\
= & 00110010B \\
\text{XOR} & 10110011B \\
= & 10000001B
\end{array}
$$

The XOR method can be used in EGA and VGA systems because the data rotate register of the Graphics Controller can be programmed to write data normally, or to AND, OR, or XOR, the CPU data with the one in the latches. The procedures DATA_XOR and DATA_NORMAL in the GALLERY program perform these operations. Note that BIOS service number 9 of INT 10H, used in displaying text on the graphics screen, always sets the data rotate register to the normal mode.

In graphics programming, and particularly in animation routines, the XOR mode provides a convenient way of drawing and erasing an object on the screen. The advantages of the XOR method are simpler and faster execution and the certainty that the original screen image will always be restored. This is particularly useful when more than one moving object can coincide on the same screen position. Such is the case in the GALLERY program, in which the duck and the cross-hair symbol can be overlaid. The disadvantage of the XOR method is that the object's color depends on the color of the background over which it is displayed. If a graphics object is moved over different backgrounds, its colors will change. The reader can observe that the cross-hair symbol of the GALLERY program appears in different colors when overlaid over the duck than when over the gray background. In this case the effect is not objectionable, and may be even interesting, but in other applications it could make the XOR technique unsuitable.

9.4.4 Generating the Timed Pulse

We have seen that a popular form of computer animation consists of successively displaying and erasing a screen image at a certain rate. Sometimes this technique is referred to as *timed-pulse animation*. Ideally, the redraw rate in timed-pulse animation should be not less than 24 images per second. In any case, a rate of less than 15 images per second will produce a bumpy and flickery effect that proves tiring and unpleasant. The programmer has several methods of producing the timed pulse at which the animated image is updated. Which method is selected often depends on the characteristics of the application.

The most direct method of updating the screen image of an animated object is in a simple software loop. This loop can include the necessary processing operations as well as one or more polling routines. The main disadvantage of the loop method is that the animation pulse is not really timed. If there are polling operations inside the loop, then the duration of the pulse can vary from iteration to iteration. That, in turn, translates into a nonuniform movement of the animated object.

IBM microcomputers are equipped with an automatic timer which can be intercepted by an application. The default rate of the system timer is approximately of 18.2 beats per second. Apparently this pulse is sufficient to create a smooth animation, but when the synchronization operations mentioned in Section 9.4.2 are taken into account, the pulse rate approximates the borderline. However, it is possible to accelerate the system timer to practically any desired pulse rate. The program named SPOOL (presented in Chapter 4) reprograms and intercepts the system timer. Animation routines can obtain a timed pulse by intercepting the system timer interrupt at INT 08H, at either the original rate or an accelerated rate.

9.4.5 The Vertical Retrace Interrupt

For many graphics applications the most satisfactory method for obtaining a timed pulse is by programming the EGA or VGA CRT controller to generate an interrupt at the start of the vertical retrace cycle. The EGA and VGA screen refresh rate, which is 70 cycles per second, is more than sufficient to produce totally smooth animation. In fact, the most important objection to this method is that it leaves very little time in which to perform any image or data processing between timed pulses.

The greatest advantage of using the vertical retrace interrupt as a timed-pulse generator is that screen interference is automatically avoided. In this case the interrupt intercept routine receives control at the beginning of the vertical retrace cycle of the CRT controller. How much processing can be done in 1/70 s depends on the particular system hardware, mainly the type and speed of the CPU and the wait states in memory access.

For programs that animate small objects, the use of the vertical retrace interrupt is an attractive option. The larger the animated object, or the more complicated the processing, the harder it is to perform it during the vertical retrace cycle. A partial solution would be to skip every other vertical retrace interrupt. This would double the time between object updates, but the screen changes must take place while vertical retrace is in progress. In addition, this operation requires a time overhead in keeping track of the interrupt pulses.

Another solution, occasionally possible, is to move the animated object as close as possible to the bottom of the screen. The advantage of this technique is that the processing time includes, not only the duration of the vertical retrace cycle but also the time in which the unanimated part of the screen is refreshed. Note that the animated duck in the GALLERY program is displayed toward the bottom of the screen. An earlier version of this program, in which the duck traveled at the center of the screen, would operate satisfactorily only in machines equipped with the 80386 CPU.

The GALLERY program contains code to enable the vertical retrace interrupt on a VGA system and to intercept its vector at INT 0AH. The retrace interrupt handler in the GALLERY program is located at the label HEX0A_INT. This handler first certifies that a vertical retrace is, in fact, in progress. This operation is necessary because other devices, such as the mouse and the hard disk, use this same vector. The code then reactivates the vertical retrace, erases and redisplays the duck at the new coordinates, and restores normal operation of the interrupt system.

9.5 Interactive Animation

Another type of animated object is one that is moved at will by the user. A mouse-controlled cursor, for example, is an interactively animated screen object. Interactively animated objects share many characteristics and requirements with timed-pulse animated objects described in Sections 9.4.3 to 9.4.5. One important difference is that interactive objects are not moved at discrete intervals, but whenever the user desires.

The GALLERY program employs a cross-hair symbol that is interactively animated by the action of the mouse device. The game simulates a shooting gallery. The user points the gun by translating the crosshair symbol across the screen and fires by pressing the left-hand mouse button. The code animates the duck symbol at a pulse rate of 70 cycles per second, which is the vertical retrace rate. The movement of the cross-hair symbol is interactive with the movement of the mouse device.

9.5.1 Programming the Mouse

The PS/2 extension to the IBM BIOS implements a pointing device interface linked to service number 194 of INT 15H. Although the functions in this service seem sufficient for low-level operation of a mouse device, there are several inconveniences. Probably the most important difficulty is the scarcity of documentation regarding this services. The information related to the pointing device interface in the *IBM BIOS Interface Technical Reference Manual* (see Bibliography) is not sufficient for programming the device. Another possible problem is related to the compatibility of these services with different mouse hardware. In addition, various non-IBM versions of the BIOS do not support service number 194 of INT 15H. Finally, the service is not recognized in the DOS mode of OS/2.

A disadvantage of all alternative solutions is that they require the use of a TSR mouse driver. This means that a program that uses the mouse device has these alternatives: (1) satisfactory execution will be conditioned to the user previously loading the mouse driver, (2) the software will have to provide an installation routine that loads the driver, or (3) the program will have to include a low-level driver for the mouse device.

If the BIOS mouse services of INT 15H were operational and compatible with standard mouse hardware, a program could use these services from within its code, in the same way that it accesses the printer or the communications port.

9.5.2 Microsoft Mouse Services (INT 33H)

Microsoft Corporation, which pioneered the mouse device in IBM microcomputers, developed a mouse programming interface that has achieved general acceptance. These services, which are associated with INT 33H, provide 36 mouse programming and control functions that are more than sufficient for any conventional purpose. The most important disadvantage of this interface, as discussed in Section 9.5.1, is that its use requires the previous loading of the device driver software. Most mouse hardware for IBM microcomputers is furnished with a driver program compatible with the Microsoft interface. The mouse services grouped under INT 33H are well documented in the book

Microsoft Mouse Programmer's Reference, published by Microsoft Press (see Bibliography).

The Microsoft mouse interface is designed to provide sufficient and easy control of the mouse device from high- and low-level languages. Alphanumeric programs benefit the most from the Microsoft mouse software. The services of INT 33H include functions to display and manage a mouse-controlled cursor, to set the mouse sensitivity and rate, and to initialize and install interrupt handlers that take control when the mouse is moved or when the mouse buttons are operated. Many graphics programs for EGA and VGA systems are unable to take advantage of some of these services, because the Microsoft driver reprograms the video hardware in ways that can conflict with an application.

For this reason, graphics programs must often assume the display and management of the mouse-operated cursor and limit its use of the interface to the fundamental services. For applications of this type the most important services in the Microsoft interface are the following:

1. Service number 0, INT 33H, is used to reset the mouse device and to obtain its status. An application usually calls this service to certify that the mouse driver is resident and to initialize the device parameters. The program named GALLERY performs this check during initialization.

2. Service number 12, INT 33H, initializes a service routine that receives control from the interface when the mouse is moved or when the buttons are pressed or released. The GALLERY program contains a service routine named MOUSE_BUT, which executes when the left or right mouse button is pressed by the user.

3. Service number 11, INT 33H, is used to read the motion counters maintained by the mouse driver. The driver stores the motion parameters in 1/200-in units called *mickeys*. The changes in the motion counters, that have taken place since the last time the function was called, are returned in machine registers. These values are signed integers in 2's complement form. Negative values indicate horizontal movement to the left or upward vertical movement. The GALLERY program inspects the motion counters in a loop that calls service number 11, INT 33H. This routine appears at the label MOUSE_MOVE. If the counters are not zero (zero indicates no change), the procedures MOVE_CURSOR, UPDATE_X, and UPDATE_Y, take care of repositioning the cross-hair cursor.

9.6 The GALLERY Program

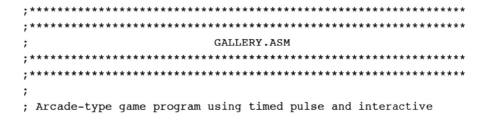

```
;****************************************************************
;****************************************************************
;                         GALLERY.ASM
;****************************************************************
;****************************************************************
;
; Arcade-type game program using timed pulse and interactive
```

```
; animation
;
; The code has the following system requirements:
; 1. VGA graphics system
; 2. MS DOS 3.0 or later
; 3. IBM PS/2, Microsoft, or compatible mouse, and installed
;    driver
;
;
;******************************************************************
;                    procedures in SOLUTION.LIB
;******************************************************************
EXTRN    KBR_FLUSH:       FAR
EXTRN    KBR_STATUS:      FAR
EXTRN    KBR_WAIT:        FAR
EXTRN    DOS_STRING_OUT:  FAR
EXTRN    SOUND:           FAR
EXTRN    RANDOM_NUM:      FAR
EXTRN    BIN_TO_ASC:      FAR
EXTRN    BIO_SET_MODE:    FAR
EXTRN    BIO_SET_CUR:     FAR
;
INCLUDELIB SOLUTION
;
;************************* equates *************************
;
; Limits of cursor movement
; The following values limit the movement of the crosshair symbol
; to the gray rectangular area
CUR_LIM_RIGHT    EQU     620
CUR_LIM_LEFT     EQU     5
CUR_LIM_UP       EQU     362
CUR_LIM_DOWN     EQU     454
;
; The following values determine the on-target error allowance
; Increasing these values makes scoring easier and vice versa
; Units are screen pixels
ON_X             EQU     10
ON_Y             EQU     08
;
; The following value determines the speed at which the duck
; travels across the screen. Increasing this value will make the
; duck travel faster
DUCK_SPEED       EQU     6
;
;************************** stack **************************
```

```
STACK     SEGMENT stack
;
                DB       0400H DUP ('?'); Default stack is 1K
STACK_TOP       EQU      THIS BYTE
;
STACK     ENDS
;**************************** data ****************************
;
DATA      SEGMENT
;*********************|
;  parameter storage  |
;*********************|
NUM_BUFFER      DB       5 DUP(20H)        ; 5-digit buffer used by
                DW       0        ; conversion routines
;
;*********************|
;      text blocks     |
;*********************|
; Graphics block message for the words Shooting GALLERY
GALL_MS DB       2                 ; Start row
        DB       2                 ; Start column
        DB       10000011B         ; Color attribute
;
        DB       'S h o o t i n g',0FFH,0FFH
;
        DB       7 DUP(0DCH),0FFH
;
; Graphics encoding of the word Gallery using the IBM character
; set
        DB       20H,0DBH,0DCH,3 DUP(20H),0DBH,0FFH
;
        DB       20H,0DBH,0DBH,6 DUP(20H),0DBH,0DFH,0DBH,20H,20H
        DB       0DFH,0DBH,3 DUP(20H),0DFH,0DBH,3 DUP(20H),0DFH
        DB       0DBH,0DFH,0DBH,20H,0DFH,0DBH,0DFH,0DBH,0DCH,20H
        DB       0DFH,0DBH,20H,0DBH,0DFH,0FFH
;
        DB       20H,0DBH,0DBH,6 DUP(20H),0DBH,20H,0DBH,3 DUP(20H)
        DB       0DBH,4 DUP(20H),0DBH,4 DUP(20H),0DBH,4 DUP(20H)
        DB       0DBH,20H,20H,0DBH,20H,20H,0DBH,20H,0DBH,0FFH
;
        DB       20H,0DBH,0DBH,20H,0DBH,0DFH,0DBH,20H,20H,0DBH
        DB       0DCH,0DBH,3 DUP(20H),0DBH,4 DUP(20H),0DBH
        DB       4 DUP(20H),0DBH,0DCH,0DBH,20H,20H,0DBH,0DCH
        DB       0DBH,0DFH,20H,20H,0DBH,0DCH,0DBH,0FFH
;
        DB       20H,0DBH,0DBH,3 DUP(20H),0DBH,20H,20H,0DBH,20H
```

```
        DB      0DBH,3 DUP(20H),0DBH,4 DUP(20H),0DBH,4 DUP(20H)
        DB      0DBH,20H,0DFH,2 DUP(20H),0DBH,20H,0DBH,4 DUP(20H)
        DB      0DBH,0FFH
;
        DB      0DCH,0DBH,4 DUP(0DCH),0DBH,20H,0DCH,0DBH,20H,0DBH
        DB      0DCH,20H,0DCH,0DBH,0DCH,0DBH,20H,0DCH,0DBH,0DCH
        DB      0DBH,20H,0DCH,0DBH,0DCH,0DBH,20H,0DCH,0DBH,20H
        DB      0DBH,0DCH,20H,20H,0DCH,0DBH,0DCH
        DB      00H
;
; Graphics block for the mouse drawing
MOU_MS  DB      4                ; Start row
        DB      58               ; Start column
        DB      10000110B        ; Color
;
; Graphics encoding of a mouse using the IBM character set
        DB      20H,0BFH,5 DUP(20H),0DAH,0FFH
        DB      20H,0B3H,5 DUP(20H),0B3H,0FFH
        DB      0C9H,0D8H,0CDH,0D1H,0CDH,0D1H,0CDH,0D8H,0BBH,0FFH
        DB      0BAH,0B3H,20H,0B3H,20H,0B3H,20H,0B3H,0BAH,0FFH
        DB      0C7H,0C4H,0C4H,0D9H,20H,0C0H,0C4H,0C4H,0B6H,0FFH
        DB      0BAH,7 DUP(20H),0BAH,0FFH
        DB      0BAH,20H,'Mouse',20H,0BAH,0FFH
        DB      0BAH,7 DUP(20H),0BAH,0FFH
        DB      0C8H,7 DUP(0CDH),0BCH,0FFH
        DB      00H
;
; Instruction message displayed at top right of screen
TOP_MS  DB      1                ; Start row
        DB      50               ; Start column
        DB      10000110B        ; Color
;
        DB      'I n s t r u c t i o n s',0FFH
        DB      '     <Esc> to END',0FFH
        DB      'press to        press to',0FFH
        DB      '    FIRE        START GAME',0FFH
        DB      00H
;
; Text message and graphics displayed at the scoreboard area
BOT_MS  DB      15               ; Start row
        DB      22               ; Start column
        DB      10001110B        ; Color
;
        DB      '   *** S C O R E B O A R D ***',0FFH,0FFH
        DB      '  GAME    FIRED    LEFT    SCORE',0FFH
        DB      20H,0C9H,7 DUP(0CDH),0CBH,7 DUP(0CDH),0CBH
```

```
            DB      7 DUP(0CDH),0CBH,9 DUP(0CDH),0BBH,0FFH,0FFH

; Line with variable data is not contained in this block
; but in the DATA_LN block
            DB      20H,0C8H,7 DUP(0CDH),0CAH,7 DUP(0CDH),0CAH
            DB      7 DUP(0CDH),0CAH,9 DUP(0CDH),0BCH,0FFH
            DB      00H
;
DATA_LN DB      19              ; Start row
        DB      22              ; Start column
        DB      10001110B       ; Color
;
        DB      20H,0BAH,20H,20H
GAME    DB      ' 1',3 DUP(020H),0BAH,20H,20H
FIRED   DB      ' 0',3 DUP(020H),0BAH,20H,20H
LEFT    DB      '10',3 DUP(020H),0BAH,3 DUP(020H)
SCORE   DB      ' 0 ',3 DUP(20H),0BAH,00H
;
;*********************|
;   program controls  |
;*********************|
START_COL       DB      0       ; Initial display column used
                                ; by the GRAPHIC_TEXT procedure
GAME_CNT        DB      0       ; Counter for game number
FIRE_CNT        DB      10      ; Counter for rounds fired
SCORE_CNT       DB      0       ; Game score counter
;
;*********************|
;   error message     |
;*********************|
BAD_MOUSE_MS    DB      'Mouse is not operational $'
;
DATA    ENDS
;
;************************** code **************************
;
CODE    SEGMENT BYTE
        ASSUME  CS:CODE
;
START:
;*********************|
;   initialize DS     |
;*********************|
        MOV     AX,DATA         ; AX to program data
        MOV     DS,AX           ; and to DS
        ASSUME  DS:DATA
```

```
; Initialize stack. Note that this instruction is necessary for
; compatibility with non-Microsoft assemblers
        LEA     SP,SS:STACK_TOP ; Stack pointer to top of stack
;**********************|
;   initialize mouse   |
;**********************|
        MOV     AX,0            ; Reset mouse hardware and
                                ; software
        INT     33H             ; Mouse service interrupt
        CMP     AX,0            ; Test for error during reset
        JNZ     OK_MOUSE        ; No problem
;**********************|
; mouse initialization |
;         error        |
;**********************|
; This code executes if there is no mouse installed or no valid
; mouse driver software
        LEA     DX,BAD_MOUSE_MS ; Test message to signal error
        CALL    DOS_STRING_OUT  ; Display error message
        JMP     DOS_EXIT
;**********************|
;   set video mode     |
;**********************|
OK_MOUSE:
        MOV     AH,0            ; BIOS service request code
        MOV     AL,18           ; VGA mode 18. 640 by 480
                                ; pixels in 16 colors
        INT     10H             ; BIOS video interrupt
;****************************************************************
;                  Installation routine for
;                  the vertical retrace interrupt
;****************************************************************
; The following code enables the vertical retrace interrupt on
; a VGA system and intercepts INT 0AH (IRQ2 vector)
; The code assumes a VGA system that supports the vertical
; retrace interrupt. Note that the VGA Adapter Card does not
; support this interrupt
;**********************|
;   save parameters    |
;**********************|
; System port address is saved in CS variables so that they
; can be accessed by the main program and by the service routine
        CLI                     ; Interrupts off
        MOV     AX,0H           ; Clear AX
        MOV     ES,AX           ; and ES
        MOV     DX,ES:[0463H]   ; Get CRT controller base address
```

```
                                       ; from BIOS data area
        MOV       CS:CRT_PORT,DX   ; Save address in memory variable
        MOV       AL,11H           ; Offset of vertical retrace end
                                   ; register in the CRTC
        OUT       DX,AL            ; Select this register
        JMP       SHORT $+2        ; I/O delay
; Value stored in port's data register is also saved
        INC       DX               ; Point to data register
        IN        AL,DX            ; Read default value in register
        JMP       SHORT $+2        ; I/O delay
        MOV       CS:OLD_VRE,AL    ; Save value in variable
;**********************|
;   save old INT 0AH   |
;**********************|
; Uses DOS service 53 of INT 21H to obtain original vector for
; INT 0AH from the vector table
        MOV       AH,53            ; Service request number
        MOV       AL,0AH           ; Code of vector desired
        INT       21H
; ES -> Segment address of installed interrupt handler
; BX -> Offset address of installed interrupt handler
        MOV       SI,OFFSET CS:OLD_VECTOR_0A
; Offset of forward pointer in 16-byte structured table
        MOV       CS:[SI],BX       ; Save offset of original handler
        MOV       CS:[SI+2],ES     ; and segment
;**********************|
; install this INT 0AH |
;        handler       |
;**********************|
; Using DOS service 37 of INT 21H
        MOV       AH,37            ; Service request number
        MOV       AL,0AH           ; Interrupt code
        PUSH      DS               ; Save data segment
        PUSH      CS
        POP       DS               ; Set DS to CS for DOS service
        MOV       DX,OFFSET CS:HEX0A_INT
        INT       21H
        POP       DS               ; Restore local data
;**********************|
;    enable IRQ2       |
;**********************|
; Clear bit 2 of the 8259 mask register
        CLI                        ; Make sure interrupts are off
        MOV       DX,21H           ; Port address of 8259 mask
                                   ; register
        IN        AL,DX            ; Read byte at port
```

```
          JMP       SHORT $+2          ; I/O delay
          AND       AL,11111011B       ; Mask for bit 2
          OUT       DX,AL              ; Back to 8259 port
          JMP       SHORT $+2          ; I/O delay
;*********************|
;  activate vertical  |
;  retrace interrupt  |
;*********************|
          MOV       DX,CS:CRT_PORT     ; Recover CRT base address
          MOV       AL,11H             ; Offset of vertical retrace end
                                       ; register in the CRTC
          MOV       AH,CS:OLD_VRE      ; Default value in vertical
                                       ; retrace end register
          AND       AH,11001111B       ; Clear bits 4 and 5 in VRE
                                       ; register
                                       ; Bit 4 = clear vertical
                                       ; interrupt
                                       ; Bit 5 = enable vertical retrace
          OUT       DX,AX              ; To port
          JMP       SHORT $+2          ; I/O delay
          OR        AH,00010000B       ; Mask to set bit 4 to reenable
          OUT       DX,AX
          JMP       SHORT $+2          ; I/O delay
          STI                          ; Enable interrupts
;*********************|
;   initialize video  |
;     buffer address  |
;*********************|
          MOV       AX,0A000H          ; AX to base address of video
          MOV       ES,AX              ; buffer and to ES
;*********************|
;   set write mode 2  |
;*********************|
; This program uses write mode 2 for graphics display. In this
; write mode the color code is contained in a CPU register
          MOV       AL,2               ; Mode number
          CALL      SET_WRITE_MODE
;*********************|
;   draw color blocks |
;*********************|
; Fill entire screen
          MOV       CH,0               ; Start column
          MOV       CL,0               ; Start row
          MOV       DH,80              ; Horizontal bytes
          MOV       DL,60              ; Vertical bytes
          MOV       AL,00000111B       ; Color = gray
```

```
        CALL    COARSE_FILL
;
; Draw thick gray stripe for duck movements
        MOV     CH,0            ; Start column
        MOV     CL,44           ; Start row
        MOV     DH,80           ; Horizontal bytes
        MOV     DL,16           ; Vertical bytes
        MOV     AL,00001000B    ; Color = gray
        CALL    COARSE_FILL
;
; Draw top vertical line
        MOV     CH,46           ; Start column
        MOV     CL,0            ; Start row
        MOV     DH,1            ; Horizontal bytes
        MOV     DL,29           ; Vertical bytes
        MOV     AL,00000000B    ; Color = black
        CALL    COARSE_FILL
;
; Draw three horizontal lines
        MOV     CH,0            ; Start column
        MOV     CL,29           ; Start row
        MOV     DH,80           ; Horizontal bytes
        MOV     DL,1            ; Vertical bytes
        MOV     AL,00000000B    ; Color = black
        CALL    COARSE_FILL
;
        MOV     CH,0            ; Start column
        MOV     CL,44           ; Start row
        MOV     DH,80           ; Horizontal bytes
        MOV     DL,1            ; Vertical bytes
        MOV     AL,00000100B    ; Color = red
;
        CALL    COARSE_FILL
        MOV     CH,0            ; Start column
        MOV     CL,59           ; Start row
        MOV     DH,80           ; Horizontal bytes
        MOV     DL,1            ; Vertical bytes
        MOV     AL,00000100B    ; Color = red
        CALL    COARSE_FILL
;
; Draw scoreboard framing lines
        MOV     CH,20           ; Start column
        MOV     CL,30           ; Start row
        MOV     DH,1            ; Horizontal bytes
        MOV     DL,14           ; Vertical bytes
        MOV     AL,00000000B    ; Color = black
```

```
        CALL    COARSE_FILL
;
        MOV     CH,60           ; Start column
        MOV     CL,30           ; Start row
        MOV     DH,1            ; Horizontal bytes
        MOV     DL,14           ; Vertical bytes
        MOV     AL,00000000B    ; Color = black
        CALL    COARSE_FILL
; Draw blue scoreboard area
        MOV     CH,21           ; Start column
        MOV     CL,30           ; Start row
        MOV     DH,39           ; Horizontal bytes
        MOV     DL,14           ; Vertical bytes
        MOV     AL,00000001B    ; Blue
        CALL    COARSE_FILL
;**********************|
;   set write mode 0   |
;**********************|
; Write mode 0 is used for text display operations
        MOV     AL,0            ; Write mode
        CALL    SET_WRITE_MODE
;**********************|
; display text messages|
;**********************|
        LEA     DI,GALL_MS      ; Pointer to message text
        CALL    GRAPHIC_TEXT    ; displayed at screen top right
        LEA     DI,MOU_MS       ; Pointer to mouse drawing
        CALL    GRAPHIC_TEXT
        LEA     DI,TOP_MS       ; Instructions text
        CALL    GRAPHIC_TEXT
        LEA     DI,BOT_MS       ; Scoreboard text
        CALL    GRAPHIC_TEXT
        CALL    SCOREBOARD      ; Display variable text line
                                ; and present values
;**********************|
;   set mouse interrupt |
;**********************|
; Set address of interrupt service routine for left mouse button
; pressed (fire gun operation) and for right button pressed
; (start new game operation)
        CLI                     ; Interrupts off
        PUSH    ES              ; Save video buffer segment
        PUSH    CS              ; Program's segment
        POP     ES              ; to ES
        MOV     AX,12           ; Mouse service number 12
; Interrupt mask bit map:
```

```
;   15                    5 4 3 2 1 0
;   |— these bits unused —| | | | | |__ Cursor position changed
;                         | | | |____ Left button pressed
;                         | | |_____ Left button released
;                         | |_____ Right button pressed
;                         |_____ Right button released
        MOV     CH,0              ; Unused bits
        MOV     CL,00001010B      ; Interrupt on left button and
                                  ; right button pressed
        MOV     DX,OFFSET CS:MOUSE_BUT
        INT     33H               ; Mouse interrupt
        POP     ES                ; Restore segment
        STI                       ; Interrupts on
;*********************|
; entry point for new |
;       game          |
;*********************|
START_GAME:
        MOV     FIRE_CNT,10       ; Reset counter for rounds fired
        MOV     CS:GUN_FIRED,0    ; Reset gun fired switch
        MOV     CS:DUCKY_OFF,1    ; Duck no display switch
        MOV     CS:FIRST_DUCK,1   ; First duck in line switch
        MOV     CS:DUCK_X,620     ; Duck and cross-hair coordinates
        MOV     CS:DUCK_Y,410
        MOV     CS:CROSS_X,320
        MOV     CS:CROSS_Y,CUR_LIM_UP
        CALL    XOR_XHAIR         ; Display cross-hair symbol
;*********************|
;    wait for right   |
;    button pressed   |
;*********************|
; This routine allows the player to read last game's score
; until the right mouse button is pressed
; The code also checks for an exit keystroke during this wait
        CALL    KBR_FLUSH         ; Clear old characters from buffer
START_WAIT:
        CALL    KBR_STATUS        ; Carry set if keystroke ready
        JNC     NO_KEY_READY      ; Go check right button if no key
        JMP     READ_KEY          ; Get keystroke
NO_KEY_READY:
        CMP     CS:DUCKY_OFF,0    ; Value set by the right mouse
                                  ; button handler
        JNE     START_WAIT        ; Loop if not changed
;*********************|
;   start a new game  |
;*********************|
```

```
        INC     GAME_CNT        ; Bump counter to next game
        MOV     SCORE_CNT,0     ; Update score count
        CALL    GET_SCORE       ; Calculate score and game number
        CALL    SCOREBOARD      ; Update scoreboard display
;****************************************************************
;                      monitor keyboard,
;                    mouse, and gun fired
;****************************************************************
; The following routine monitors the following user actions
;    1. Mouse movement occurred (MOUSE_MOVE label)
;    2. <Esc> key pressed to end program
;    3. Left mouse button pressed to fire gun
;       Game is over when the 10th shot is fired
;
MONITOR:
        CALL    KBR_FLUSH       ; Clear old characters from
                                ; buffer
GET_STROKE·
        CALL    KBR_STATUS      ; Carry set if keystroke ready
        JC      READ_KEY        ; Get keystroke
;*********************|
;  test for gun fired |
;*********************|
; Update scoreboard if gun fired
        CMP     CS:GUN_FIRED,1  ; Switch is 1 if gun fired
        JNE     MOUSE_MOVE      ; Continue if not fired
;*********************|
;   update scoreboard |
;   and game controls |
;*********************|
        MOV     CS:GUN_FIRED,0  ; Reset switch for gun fired
;*********************|
;  was it hit or miss? |
;*********************|
        CMP     CS:HIT_SW,1     ; Switch set if hit
        JNE     SHOT_MISSED     ; Go if no hit
        ADD     SCORE_CNT,10    ; Update score count
        CALL    GET_SCORE       ; Update scoreboard score area
SHOT_MISSED:
        DEC     FIRE_CNT        ; Counter for rounds fired
        JZ      GAME_OVER       ; Go if ten rounds fired
        CALL    SCOREBOARD      ; Update scoreboard display
        JMP     MOUSE_MOVE
;*********************|
;     game is over    |
;*********************|
```

```
GAME_OVER:
; Erase last duck
        MOV     CS:DUCKY_OFF,1  ; No more ducks displayed
        MOV     SI,OFFSET CS:DUCK_X
        MOV     BX,OFFSET CS:DUCK_COLOR
        CALL    TIME_VRC
        CALL    VARI_PATTERN
; Erase last cross-hair symbol
        CALL    XOR_XHAIR       ; Erase
        CALL    GET_SCORE       ; Calculate score and game number
        CALL    SCOREBOARD      ; Update scoreboard display
        JMP     START_GAME      ; Start new game
;*****************************************************************
;                         mouse movement
;*****************************************************************
; The following routine calls service number 11 of the mouse
; interrupt to detect horizontal or vertical movement. The
; display of the cross-hair symbol is handled by the program
; routine named MOVE_CURSOR
;
MOUSE_MOVE:
        MOV     AX,11           ; Service request to read
                                ; counters
        INT     33H             ; Mouse interrupt
; CX = Horizontal mouse movement from last call to this service
; DX = Vertical mouse movement from last call
        MOV     AL,CL           ; Horizontal counter to AL
        MOV     AH,DL           ; Vertical counter to AH
        CMP     AX,0            ; If AX is 0 then no mouse
                                ; movement
        JE      GET_STROKE      ; Go if no movement
        CALL    MOVE_CURSOR     ; Update cursor position
        JMP     GET_STROKE      ; Wait for keystroke
;*********************|
;    get keystroke    |
;*********************|
READ_KEY:
        CALL    KBR_WAIT        ; Get keystroke in buffer
        CMP     AX,011BH        ; Test for <Esc> key
        JNE     TEST_K2         ; Cascade to other keystrokes
        JMP     PROGRAM_EXIT
TEST_K2:
        JMP     MONITOR
;*****************************************************************
;                          exit program
;*****************************************************************
```

```
; The following code restores normal CRT operation. Processing
; consists of the following steps:
;    1. Restore default value in the vertical retrace end register
;    2. Restore original handler for INT 0AH
;    3. Set default write mode (write mode 0)
;    4. Disable XOR data operation
;    5. Set an alphanumeric video mode
;
PROGRAM_EXIT:
        CLI                         ; Interrupts off
;**********************|
;   disable vertical   |
;       interrupts     |
;**********************|
        MOV     DX,CS:CRT_PORT      ; Recover CRT base address
        MOV     AL,11H              ; Offset of vertical retrace end
                                    ; register in the CRTC
        MOV     AH,CS:OLD_VRE       ; Default value in vertical
                                    ; retrace end register
                                    ; Bit 5 = enable vertical retrace
        OUT     DX,AX               ; To port
        JMP     SHORT $+2           ; I/O delay
;**********************|
;   restore INT 0AH    |
;**********************|
        MOV     SI,OFFSET CS:OLD_VECTOR_0A
; Set DS:DX to original segment and offset of keyboard interrupt
; vector
        MOV     DX,CS:[SI]          ; DX -> offset
        MOV     AX,CS:[SI+2]        ; AX -> segment
        MOV     DS,AX               ; segment to DS
        MOV     AH,25H              ; DOS service request
        MOV     AL,0AH              ; IRQ2
        INT     21H
;**********************|
;   reset video system |
;**********************|
        MOV     AL,0                ; Write mode 0
        CALL    SET_WRITE_MODE
        CALL    DATA_NORMAL         ; Reset normal write mode
        MOV     AL,3                ; Set alphanumeric mode 3
        CALL    BIO_SET_MODE        ; Procedure in SOLUTION.LIB
DOS_EXIT:
        MOV     AH,4CH              ; DOS service request code
        MOV     AL,0                ; No error code returned
        INT     21H                 ; exit to MS DOS
```

```
;******************************************************************
;                          procedures
;******************************************************************
;********************************|
;    cursor movement procedures  |
;********************************|
MOVE_CURSOR      PROC    NEAR
; Erase old cursor and reposition cross hair according to mouse
; movement detected
; Units are in mickeys (1 mickey = 1/200 in)
; If CH high-order bit set then horizontal movement is left
; If DH high-order bit set then vertical movement is up
         CALL    XOR_XHAIR        ; Erase old cross hair
         CMP     CX,0             ; Test for no x-axis movement
         JE      NO_HORZ          ; No horizontal move if CX zero
         CALL    UPDATE_X         ; Update horizontal position
NO_HORZ:
         CMP     DX,0
         JE      NO_VERT          ; Test for vertical movement
         CALL    UPDATE_Y         ; Update vertical position
NO_VERT:
         CALL    XOR_XHAIR        ; Redisplay cursor
         RET
MOVE_CURSOR      ENDP
;******************************************************************
;
UPDATE_X         PROC    NEAR
; Update counter CROSS_X with value in CL testing for limits
; CH high-order bit set if mouse movement was left
         TEST    CH,10000000B     ; Decrement counter if high-order
                                  ; bit set
         JNZ     X_COUNT_DOWN     ; Go if bit set
; Increment counter in loop. Cursor movement is right
X_RIGHT:
         CMP     CS:CROSS_X,CUR_LIM_RIGHT
                                  ; Equate for right-hand limit
         JA      NO_RIGHT_X       ; No right movement
         INC     CS:CROSS_X       ; Bump counter if not at limit
         LOOP    X_RIGHT
NO_RIGHT_X:
         RET
; Decrement horizontal position
X_COUNT_DOWN:
         MOV     CH,0             ; Clear high-order byte of
                                  ; counter
         NOT     CL               ; Convert 2's complement value
```

```
        INC      CL                    ; to unsigned binary
X_LEFT:
        CMP      CS:CROSS_X,CUR_LIM_LEFT
                                       ; Equate for left-hand limit
        JB       NO_LEFT
        DEC      CS:CROSS_X    ; Decrement counter
        LOOP     X_LEFT
NO_LEFT:
        RET
UPDATE_X       ENDP
;****************************************************************
;
UPDATE_Y       PROC    NEAR
; Update counter CROSS_Y with value in DL testing for limits
; CH high-order bit set if mouse movement was up
        XCHG     DX,CX           ; Move value to CX
        TEST     CH,10000000B    ; Decrement counter if high-order
                                 ; bit set
        JNZ      Y_COUNT_DOWN
; Increment counter in loop. Cursor movement is down
Y_DOWN:
        CMP      CS:CROSS_Y,CUR_LIM_DOWN
                                     ; Equate for bottom limit of move
        JA       NO_DOWN_Y       ; No down movement of cursor
        INC      CS:CROSS_Y      ; Bump counter if not at limit
        LOOP     Y_DOWN
NO_DOWN_Y:
        RET
; Decrement counter to move cursor up
Y_COUNT_DOWN:
        MOV      CH,0            ; Clear high-order byte of
                                 ; counter
        NOT      CL              ; Convert 2's complement value
        INC      CL              ; to unsigned binary
Y_UP:
        CMP      CS:CROSS_Y,CUR_LIM_UP
                                 ; Equate for left hand limit
        JB       NO_UP
        DEC      CS:CROSS_Y      ; Decrement counter
        LOOP     Y_UP
NO_UP:
        RET
UPDATE_Y       ENDP
;****************************|
;       general procedures          |
;****************************|
```

```
XOR_XHAIR       PROC    NEAR
; XOR cross-hair symbol. If symbol displayed, erase, and
; vice versa
        CLI                         ; Interrupts off
        PUSH    CX                  ; Save mickey registers
        PUSH    DX
        MOV     SI,OFFSET CS:CROSS_X    ; Offset of display block
        MOV     BX,OFFSET CS:CR_COL     ; Offset of color table
        CALL    TIME_VRC            ; Time display with vertical
                                    ; retrace
        CALL    VARI_PATTERN        ; Display routine
        STI                         ; Interrupts on
        POP     DX                  ; Restore mickey count
        POP     CX
        RET
XOR_XHAIR       ENDP
;****************************************************************
;
SCOREBOARD      PROC    NEAR
; Update program's scoreboard using the values in the variables
; First update rounds left
        MOV     DL,FIRE_CNT         ; Binary count of rounds
                                    ; remaining
        MOV     DH,0                ; Clear high-order byte
        LEA     DI,NUM_BUFFER       ; Buffer for 5 digits
        CALL    BIN_TO_ASC          ; SOLUTION.LIB conversion
                                    ; procedure
; Buffer holds 2 valid ASCII digits. DI -> start of buffer
        XCHG    SI,DI               ; Invert SI and DI
        ADD     SI,3                ; Point to first significant
                                    ; digit
        LEA     DI,LEFT             ; Point to destination
        MOV     CX,2                ; Number of digits to move
        CALL    MOVE_CX_DIGS        ; Auxiliary procedure
; Update rounds fired
        MOV     DL,10               ; Total rounds per game
        SUB     DL,FIRE_CNT         ; Minus rounds fired
        MOV     DH,0                ; Clear high-order byte
        LEA     DI,NUM_BUFFER       ; Buffer for 5 digits
        CALL    BIN_TO_ASC          ; SOLUTION.LIB conversion
                                    ; procedure
; Buffer holds 2 valid ASCII digits. DI -> start of buffer
        XCHG    SI,DI               ; Invert SI and DI
        ADD     SI,3                ; Point to first significant
                                    ; digit
        LEA     DI,FIRED            ; Point to destination
```

```
        MOV     CX,2              ; Number of digits to move
        CALL    MOVE_CX_DIGS      ; Auxiliary procedure
; Update display
        MOV     CS:DUCKY_OFF,1
        CALL    DATA_NORMAL
        MOV     AL,2
        CALL    SET_WRITE_MODE
; Draw blue area for scoreboard
        MOV     CH,21             ; Start column
        MOV     CL,38             ; Start row
        MOV     DH,39             ; Horizontal bytes
        MOV     DL,2              ; Vertical bytes
        MOV     AL,00000001B      ; Blue
        CALL    COARSE_FILL
        MOV     AL,0              ; Write mode 0 for text display
        CALL    SET_WRITE_MODE
        LEA     DI,DATA_LN        ; Scoreboard variable text line
        CALL    GRAPHIC_TEXT
        MOV     AL,2
        CALL    SET_WRITE_MODE    ; Write mode 2 for graphics
                                  ; display
        CALL    DATA_XOR
        MOV     CS:DUCKY_OFF,0
        RET
SCOREBOARD      ENDP
;****************************************************************
;
GET_SCORE       PROC    NEAR
; Calculate game number and score and set in display area
        MOV     DL,GAME_CNT       ; Binary game count
        MOV     DH,0              ; Clear high-order byte
        LEA     DI,NUM_BUFFER     ; Buffer for 5 digits
        CALL    BIN_TO_ASC        ; SOLUTION.LIB conversion
                                  ; procedure
; Buffer holds 2 valid ASCII digits. DI -> start of buffer
        XCHG    SI,DI             ; Invert SI and DI
        ADD     SI,3              ; Point to first significant
                                  ; digit
        LEA     DI,GAME           ; Point to destination
        MOV     CX,2              ; Number of digits to move
        CALL    MOVE_CX_DIGS      ; Auxiliary procedure
        MOV     DL,SCORE_CNT      ; Binary score counter
        MOV     DH,0              ; Clear high-order byte
        LEA     DI,NUM_BUFFER     ; Buffer for 5 digits
        CALL    BIN_TO_ASC        ; SOLUTION.LIB conversion
                                  ; procedure
```

```
; Buffer holds 2 valid ASCII digits. DI -> start of buffer
        XCHG    SI,DI           ; Invert SI and DI
        ADD     SI,2            ; Point to first significant
                                ; digit
        LEA     DI,SCORE        ; Point to destination
        MOV     CX,3            ; Number of digits to move
        CALL    MOVE_CX_DIGS    ; Auxiliary procedure
        RET
GET_SCORE       ENDP
;****************************************************************
;
MOVE_CX_DIGS    PROC    NEAR
; Auxiliary procedure to move a given number of digits into a
; buffer
; On entry:
;         SI -> source holding digits
;         DI -> destination for digits
;         CX = number of digits to move
; Note: A block move is not convenient because ES is used as a
;       video buffer pointer
MOVE_DIGITS:
        MOV     AL,[SI]         ; Get source digit
        MOV     [DI],AL         ; Place in destination
        INC     SI              ; Bump buffer pointers
        INC     DI
        LOOP    MOVE_DIGITS
        RET
MOVE_CX_DIGS    ENDP
;****************************************************************
;*******************************|
;       graphics procedures     |
;*******************************|
TIME_VRC        PROC    NEAR
; Test for start of the vertical retrace cycle of the CRT
; controller Bit 7 of Input Status register 0 is set if a
; vertical cycle is in progress
        MOV     DX,3C2H         ; Input status register 0
                                ; In VGA color modes
VRC_CLEAR:
        IN      AL,DX           ; Read byte at port
        JMP     SHORT $+2       ; I/O delay
        TEST    AL,10000000B    ; Is bit 7 set?
        JNZ     VRC_CLEAR       ; Wait until bit clear
; At this point the vertical retrace ended. Wait for it to
; restart
VRC_START:
```

```
              IN       AL,DX            ; Read byte at port
              JMP      SHORT $+2        ; I/O delay
              TEST     AL,10000000B     ; Is bit 7 set?
              JZ       VRC_START        ; Wait until bit set
              RET
TIME_VRC               ENDP
;****************************************************************
;
VARI_PATTERN    PROC    NEAR
; Display an encoded graphics block
; On entry:
;         CS:SI -> Start of control area of graphics block to be
;                  displayed
;         CS:BX -> Start of block holding color codes
;
; Register setup:
;                  CX = x coordinate of block start
;                  DX = y coordinate of block start
;                  BL = number of rows in block
;                  BH = number of bytes per block row
;                  DI -> start of encoded graphics block
;                  SI -> start of encoded color codes
; Memory:
;                  CS:COUNT_8 ........ Counter for 8 bits
;
; Initialize registers
              PUSH     BX                ; Save pointer in stack
              MOV      CX,WORD PTR CS:[SI]   ; x coordinate
              MOV      CS:X_COORD,CX     ; Store in variable
              ADD      SI,2              ; Bump pointer
              MOV      DX,WORD PTR CS:[SI]   ; y coordinate
              ADD      SI,2              ; Bump pointer
              MOV      BL,BYTE PTR CS:[SI]   ; Number of rows
              INC      SI                ; Bump pointer
              MOV      BH,BYTE PTR CS:[SI]   ; Bytes per block
              MOV      CS:BYTES,BH       ; Store in variable
              INC      SI                ; Bump pointer
              XCHG     SI,DI            ; Buffer start to DI
              POP      SI               ; Color code block pointer
              MOV      CS:COUNT_8,8     ; Prime bit counter
DISPLAY_BYTE:
              MOV      AH,CS:[DI]       ; High-order nibble to AH
TEST_BIT:
              TEST     AH,10000000B     ; Is high-order bit set?
              JZ       NEXT_BIT         ; Bit not set
              MOV      AL,CS:[SI]       ; Get color code
```

```
; Set the pixel
        PUSH    AX              ; Save entry registers
        PUSH    BX
        CALL    PIXEL_ADD
        CALL    WRITE_PIX
        POP     BX              ; Restore registers
        POP     AX
NEXT_BIT:
        SAL     AH,1            ; Shift AH to test next bit
        INC     CX              ; Bump x coordinate counter
        INC     SI              ; Bump color table pointer
        DEC     CS:COUNT_8      ; Bit counter
        JZ      NEXT_BYTE       ; Exit if counter rewound
        JMP     TEST_BIT        ; Continue
; Index to next byte in row, if not at end of row
NEXT_BYTE:
        DEC     BH              ; Bytes per row counter
        JZ      NEXT_ROW        ; End of graphics row
BYTE_ENTRY:
        INC     DI              ; Bump graphics code pointer
        MOV     CS:COUNT_8,8    ; Reset bits counter
        JMP     DISPLAY_BYTE
; Index to next row
NEXT_ROW:
; Test for last graphic row
        DEC     BL              ; Row counter
        JZ      GRAPH_END       ; Done, exit
        MOV     BH,CS:BYTES     ; Reset bytes counter
        INC     DX              ; Bump y coordinate control
        MOV     CX,CS:X_COORD   ; Reset x coordinate control
        JMP     BYTE_ENTRY
GRAPH_END:
        RET
VARI_PATTERN    ENDP
;***************************************************************
;
COARSE_FILL     PROC    NEAR
; Fill a screen area on a byte boundary base
; On entry:
;         CH = Pillar address of start point (range 0 to 79)
;         CL = Rank address of start point (range 0 to 59)
;         DL = Total ranks to fill (1 to 60)
;         DH = Total pillars to fill (1 to 80)
;         AL = I R G B color to use in fill area
;
; Save entry registers
```

```
        PUSH    CX
        PUSH    DX
        PUSH    AX
;
        MOV     AH,0FFH      ; Bit pattern for all bits set
        PUSH    AX
        CALL    COARSE_ADD
; Start address is now set
; Next set up column counter in CX and row counter in DX
        MOV     CL,DH        ; Horizontal fill
        MOV     CH,0         ; CX = horizontal counter
        PUSH    CX           ; Save temporarily
; Row counter = DL * 8
        MOV     AX,DX
        MOV     AH,0         ; Clear high-order byte
        MOV     CL,8         ; Multiplier
        MUL     CL           ; AX = DL * 8
; Set up outer counter in DX
        MOV     DX,AX
        POP     CX           ; Inner loop counter
        POP     AX           ; AL = color
                             ; AH = 11111111B (all bits set)
OUTER:
        PUSH    CX           ; Save inner loop counter
        PUSH    BX           ; Save start address
INNER:
        CALL    WRITE_PIX
        INC     BX           ; Index to next 8-pixel block
        LOOP    INNER
; Index to next column
        POP     BX           ; Restore start of this row
        ADD     BX,80        ; Index to next row start
        POP     CX           ; Restore inner loop counter
        DEC     DX           ; Decrement total rows
        JNZ     OUTER        ; Continue if not end of count
; Restore input registers
        POP     AX
        POP     DX
        POP     CX
        RET
COARSE_FILL     ENDP
;****************************************************************
;
COARSE_ADD      PROC    NEAR
; On entry:
;         CH = pillar number (range 0 to 79) = x coordinate
```

```
;          CL = rank number (range 0 to 59) = y coordinate
; Compute byte address in BX from pillar in CH and the rank in
; CL as follows:
;          byte address =  (CL * 640) + CH
;
; On exit:
;          BX = byte offset into video buffer
;          CX is destroyed
;
        PUSH      AX            ; Save accumulator
        PUSH      DX            ; For word multiply
        PUSH      CX            ; To save CH for addition
        MOV       AX,CX         ; Copy CX in AX
; AL = CL
        MOV       AH,0          ; Clear high-order byte
        MOV       CX,640        ; Multiplier
        MUL       CX            ; AX * CX results in AX
; The multiplier (640) is the product of 80 bytes per pillar
; times 8 vertical pixels in each rank
;
        POP       CX            ; Restore CH
        POP       DX            ; and DX
;
        MOV       CL,CH         ; Prepare to add in CH
        MOV       CH,0
        ADD       AX,CX         ; Add
        MOV       BX,AX         ; Move sum to BX
        POP       AX            ; Restore accumulator
        RET
COARSE_ADD      ENDP
;***************************************************************
;
PIXEL_ADD       PROC    NEAR
; Address computation from x and y pixel coordinates
; On entry:
;              CX = x coordinate of pixel (range 0 to 639)
;              DX = y coordinate of pixel (range 0 to 479)
; On exit:
;              BX = byte offset into video buffer
;              AH = bit mask for the write operation using
;                   VGA write modes 0 or 2
;              AL is preserved
; Save all entry registers
        PUSH      CX
        PUSH      DX
; Compute address
```

```
        PUSH    AX              ; Save accumulator
        PUSH    CX              ; Save x coordinate
        MOV     AX,DX           ; y coordinate to AX
        MOV     CX,80           ; Multiplier (80 bytes per row)
        MUL     CX              ; AX = y times 80
        MOV     BX,AX           ; Free AX and hold in BX
        POP     AX              ; x coordinate from stack
; Prepare for division
        MOV     CL,8            ; Divisor
        DIV     CL              ; AX / CL = quotient in AL and
                                ; remainder in AH
; Add in quotient
        MOV     CL,AH           ; Save remainder in CL
        MOV     AH,0            ; Clear high-order byte
        ADD     BX,AX           ; Offset into buffer to BX
        POP     AX              ; Restore AX
; Compute bit mask from remainder
        MOV     AH,10000000B    ; Unit mask for 0 remainder
        SHR     AH,CL           ; Shift right CL times
; Restore all entry registers
        POP     DX
        POP     CX
        RET
PIXEL_ADD       ENDP
;************************************************************
;
WRITE_PIX       PROC    NEAR
; VGA mode 18 device driver for writing an individual
; pixel or a pixel pattern to the graphics screen
;
; On entry:
;               ES = A000H (or equivalent selector in OS/2)
;               BX = byte offset into the video buffer
;               AL = pixel color in IRGB format
;               AH = bit pattern to set
;
; This routine assumes that write mode 2 has been set
;
; Note: This procedure does not reset the default read or write
; modes or the contents of the Bit Mask register
        PUSH    DX              ; Save outer loop counter
        PUSH    AX              ; Color byte
        PUSH    AX              ; Twice
; Set Bit Mask register according to mask in AH
        MOV     DX,3CEH         ; Graphics controller latch
        MOV     AL,8
```

```
           OUT      DX,AL          ; Select data register 8
           JMP      SHORT $+2
           INC      DX             ; To 3CFH
           POP      AX             ; AX once from stack
           MOV      AL,AH          ; Bit pattern
           OUT      DX,AL          ; Load bit mask
           JMP      SHORT $+2
; Write color code
           MOV      AL,ES:[BX]     ; Dummy read to load latch
                                   ; registers
           POP      AX             ; Restore color code
           MOV      ES:[BX],AL     ; Write the pixel with the
                                   ; color code in AL
           POP      DX             ; Restore outer loop counter
           RET
WRITE_PIX          ENDP
;****************************************************************
;
SET_WRITE_MODE  PROC     NEAR
; Set the Graphics Controller's Graphics Mode register to the
; desired write mode
; On entry:
;          AL = write mode requested
; Also set default bit mask
;
           PUSH     AX             ; Save mode
           MOV      DX,3CEH        ; Graphics Controller Address
                                   ; register
           MOV      AL,5           ; Offset of the Mode register
           OUT      DX,AL          ; Select this register
           JMP      SHORT $+2
           INC      DX             ; Point to data register
           POP      AX             ; Recover mode in AL
           OUT      DX,AL          ; Selected
           JMP      SHORT $+2
; Set Bit Mask register to default setting
           MOV      DX,3CEH        ; Graphics controller latch
           MOV      AL,8
           OUT      DX,AL          ; Select data register 8
           JMP      SHORT $+2
           INC      DX             ; To 3CFH
           MOV      AL,0FFH        ; Default mask
           OUT      DX,AL          ; Load bit mask
           JMP      SHORT $+2
           RET
SET_WRITE_MODE  ENDP
```

```
;****************************************************************
;
DATA_XOR          PROC     NEAR
;
; Set the Graphics Controller Data Rotate register to the XOR
; mode
        MOV     DX,03CEH    ; Graphics controller port address
        MOV     AL,3        ; Select Data Rotate register
        OUT     DX,AL
        JMP     SHORT $+2
        INC     DX          ; 03CFH register
        MOV     AL,00011000B   ; Set bits 3 and 4 for XOR
        OUT     DX,AL
        JMP     SHORT $+2
        RET
DATA_XOR          ENDP
;****************************************************************
;
DATA_NORMAL       PROC     NEAR
; Set the Graphics Controller data rotate register to the normal
; mode
        MOV     DX,03CEH    ; Graphics controller port address
        MOV     AL,3        ; Select Data Rotate register
        OUT     DX,AL
        JMP     SHORT $+2
        INC     DX          ; 03CFH register
        MOV     AL,00000000B   ; Reset bits 3 and 4 for normal
        OUT     DX,AL
        JMP     SHORT $+2
        RET
DATA_NORMAL       ENDP
;
;*******************************|
;    text display procedures    |
;*******************************|
GRAPHIC_TEXT     PROC     NEAR
; Display a message pointed at by DS:DI on the graphics screen
; Message format as follows:
; OFFSET:          CONTENTS:
;       0 —> Screen row
;       1 —> Screen column
;       2 —> Color code
; DISPLAY CODES:
;       00H —> End of message
;       FFH —> End of screen line
; On entry:
```

```
;              DI -> Graphics display block
;
        MOV     DH,[DI]          ; Get row into DH
        INC     DI               ; Bump pointer
        MOV     DL,[DI]          ; And column into DL
        MOV     START_COL,DL     ; Store start column
        CALL    BIO_SET_CUR      ; Library procedure in
                                 ; SOLUTION.LIB
        INC     DI               ; Bump pointer to attribute
        MOV     BL,[DI]          ; Get color code into BL
CHAR_WRITE:
        INC     DI               ; Bump to message start
        MOV     AL,[DI]          ; Get character
        CMP     AL,0FFH          ; End of line ?
        JE      BUMP_ROW         ; Next row
        CMP     AL,0             ; Test for terminator
        JZ      END_TEXT         ; Exit routine
        CALL    SHOW_CHAR
        JMP     CHAR_WRITE
END_TEXT:
        RET
BUMP_ROW:
        INC     DH               ; Row control register
        MOV     DL,START_COL     ; Column control to start column
        CALL    BIO_SET_CUR
        JMP     CHAR_WRITE
GRAPHIC_TEXT    ENDP
;****************************************************************
;
SHOW_CHAR       PROC    NEAR
; Display character in AL and using the color code in BL
        MOV     AH,9             ; BIOS service request number
        MOV     BH,0             ; Page
        MOV     CX,1             ; No repeat
        INT     10H
; Bump cursor
        INC     DL
        CALL    BIO_SET_CUR      ; Library procedure in
                                 ; SOLUTION.LIB
        RET
SHOW_CHAR       ENDP
;
;****************************************************************
;                    INT 0AH handler
;              vertical retrace interrupt
;****************************************************************
```

```
; The following routine moves the duck one step (4 pixels)
; horizontally. The routine executes at every vertical retrace
; cycle of the CRT controller, which is approximately 70 times
; per second
;****************************************************************
HEX0A_INT:
        CLI                       ; Interrupts off
; Save registers
        PUSH    AX                ; Save context at interrupt time
        PUSH    BX
        PUSH    CX
        PUSH    DX
        PUSH    SI
        PUSH    DI
        PUSH    ES
;**********************|
;  test for vertical   |
;  retrace interrupt   |
;**********************|
; Bit 7 of Input Status register 0 is set if a vertical retrace
; interrupt has occurred
        MOV     DX,3C2H           ; Input Status register 0
        IN      AL,DX             ; Read byte at port
        JMP     SHORT $+2         ; I/O delay
        TEST    AL,10000000B      ; Is bit 7 set
        JNE     VRI               ; Go if vertical retrace
;**********************|
; chain to next handler|
;**********************|
        POP     ES                ; Restore context at interrupt
                                  ; time
        POP     DI
        POP     SI
        POP     DX
        POP     CX
        POP     BX
        POP     AX
        STC                       ; Continue processing
        JMP     DWORD PTR CS:OLD_VECTOR_0A
;**********************|
;  activate vertical   |
;  retrace interrupt   |
;**********************|
VRI:
        MOV     DX,CS:CRT_PORT    ; Recover CRT base address
        IN      AL,DX             ; Get value in CRTC address
```

```
                                     ; register
        JMP     SHORT $+2            ; I/O delay
        MOV     CS:AR_BYTE,AL        ; Store value in variable
        MOV     AL,11H              ; Offset of vertical retrace end
                                     ; register in the CRTC
        MOV     AH,CS:OLD_VRE
                                     ; Default value in vertical
                                     ; retrace end register
        AND     AH,11101111B        ; Clear bit 5 in VRE register
                                     ; Bit 5 = enable vertical retrace
        OUT     DX,AX               ; To port
        JMP     SHORT $+2            ; I/O delay
;*********************|
;     test for duck   |
;  display suspended  |
;*********************|
        CMP     CS:DUCKY_OFF,1      ; No duck display
        JNE     SHOW_DUCK           ; Display duck if switch off
        JMP     EXIT_DUCKY
;*********************|
;   ES to video base  |
;*********************|
SHOW_DUCK:
        MOV     AX,0A000H           ; EGA/VGA systems base address
        MOV     ES,AX               ; to ES
; Test for zero x coordinate
        CMP     CS:DUCK_X,0         ; No display if coordinate = 0
        JE      EXIT_DUCKY          ; Exit routine
;*********************|
;     move duck left  |
;*********************|
        CMP     CS:DUCK_X,4         ; Left side limit
        JA      DUCKY_DISPLAY
;*********************|
;   start at new line |
;*********************|
        CALL    XOR_DUCKY           ; Erase duck
        MOV     CS:FIRST_DUCK,1     ; Set first duck displayed switch
        MOV     CS:DUCK_X,620       ; Duck back to right screen side
;*********************|
; get random value for|
;    y coordinate     |
;*********************|
; The duck appears at random between screen pixel rows 362
; and 462
        MOV     BX,100              ; Range of random number is
```

```
                                        ; 0 to 100
            CALL      RANDOM_NUM        ; Generator in SOLUTION.LIB
; DX has random number
            ADD       DX,360            ; Move to screen range
            MOV       CS:DUCK_Y,DX      ; Store in display variable
DUCKY_DISPLAY:
            CMP       CS:FIRST_DUCK,1
            JE        DUCKY_ON          ; Turn on duck
            CALL      XOR_DUCKY
            SUB       CS:DUCK_X,DUCK_SPEED
                                        ; Decrement cursor position
            CALL      XOR_DUCKY         ; Display new cursor
            JMP       EXIT_DUCKY
DUCKY_ON:
            CALL      XOR_DUCKY
            MOV       CS:FIRST_DUCK,0 ; Turn off first iteration switch
;*********************|
; exit service routine |
;*********************|
EXIT_DUCKY:
; Enable 8259 interrupt controller to receive other interrupts
            MOV       AL,20H            ; Port address
            OUT       20H,AL            ; Send EOI code
            JMP       SHORT $+2
;
            MOV       DX,CS:CRT_PORT    ; Recover CRT base address
            MOV       AL,11H            ; Offset of Vertical Retrace End
                                        ; (VRE) register in the CRTC
            MOV       AH,CS:OLD_VRE
                                        ; Default value in VRE
            AND       AH,11011111B      ; Clear bits 4 and 5 in VRE
                                        ; register
                                        ; Bit 4 = clear vertical
                                        ; interrupt
                                        ; Bit 5 = enable vertical retrace
            OR        AH,00010000B      ; Make sure bit 5 is clear
            OUT       DX,AX             ; To port
            JMP       SHORT $+2         ; I/O delay
            MOV       AL,CS:AR_BYTE     ; Recover initial setting
            OUT       DX,AL             ; in address register
            JMP       SHORT $+2
;*********************|
;    restore context   |
;*********************|
            POP       ES
            POP       DI
```

```
        POP     SI
        POP     DX
        POP     CX
        POP     BX
        POP     AX
        STI                     ; Reenable interrupts
        IRET
;
;*********************|
;  display procedure  |
;*********************|
XOR_DUCKY       PROC    NEAR
; This procedure displays and erases the duck
        MOV     SI,OFFSET CS:DUCK_X
        MOV     BX,OFFSET CS:DUCK_COLOR
        CALL    VARI_PATTERN    ; Display procedure
        RET
XOR_DUCKY       ENDP
;
;*****************************************************************
;                       code segment data
;*****************************************************************
;*********************|
;   parameter storage |
;*********************|
OLD_VECTOR_0A   DD      0       ; Pointer to original INT 0AH
                                ; interrupt
CRT_PORT        DW      0       ; Address of CRT controller
AR_BYTE         DB      0       ; Value in CRT address register
OLD_VRE         DB      0
;*********************|
; operational variables|
;*********************|
GUN_FIRED       DB      0       ; Set by gun-fired handler
HIT_SW          DB      0       ; Hit-or-miss switch
                                ; 1 = hit
; Used by the VARI_PATTERN procedure
X_COORD DW      0000H           ; Storage for x coordinate
BYTES   DB      0H              ; Number of bytes per block row
COUNT_8 DB      8               ; Operational bit counter
;
;*********************|
;   graphics blocks   |
;*********************|
; Cross-hair symbol encoded as a graphics block
; Bit pattern for cross-hair:
```

```
; 0 0 0 0 0 w w w | w w w 0 0 0 0 0 ——— 07E0H
; 0 0 0 w 0 0 0 w | 0 0 0 w 0 0 0 0 ——— 1110H
; 0 0 w 0 0 0 0 w | 0 0 0 0 w 0 0 0 ——— 2108H
; 0 w 0 0 0 0 0 w | 0 0 0 0 0 w 0 0 ——— 4104H
; w 0 0 0 0 0 0 r | 0 0 0 0 0 0 w 0 ——— 8102H
; w 0 0 0 0 0 0 r | 0 0 0 0 0 0 w 0 ——— 8102H
; w 0 0 0 0 0 0 r | 0 0 0 0 0 0 w 0 ——— 8102H
; w w w w r r r 0 | r r r w w w w 0 ——— FFFEH
; w 0 0 0 0 0 0 r | 0 0 0 0 0 0 w 0 ——— 8102H
; w 0 0 0 0 0 0 r | 0 0 0 0 0 0 w 0 ——— 8102H
; w 0 0 0 0 0 0 r | 0 0 0 0 0 0 w 0 ——— 8102H
; 0 w 0 0 0 0 0 w | 0 0 0 0 0 w 0 0 ——— 4104H
; 0 0 w 0 0 0 0 w | 0 0 0 0 w 0 0 0 ——— 2108H
; 0 0 0 w 0 0 0 w | 0 0 0 w 0 0 0 0 ——— 1110H
; 0 0 0 0 w w w w | w w w 0 0 0 0 0 ——— 07E0H
;
; COLOR CODES:
; For XORing with 00001000B (GRAY background)
; 0 ——-> 0000B = 0H (pixel is unchanged)
; w ——-> 1111B = FH (pixel is white)
; r ——-> 1100B = CH (pixel is red)
;
; Block control area:                        Displacement ->
CROSS_X DW      320             ; Present x coordinate        0
                                ; range = 0 to 630
CROSS_Y DW      360             ; Present y coordinate        2
                                ; range = 360 to 460
        DB      15              ; Horizontal rows in block    4
        DB      2               ; Number of bytes per row     5
;
; Symbol encoding of cross-hair symbol
        DB      07H,0E0H,11H,10H,21H,08H,41H,04H,81H,02H
        DB      81H,02H,81H,02H,0FFH,0FFH,81H,02H,81H,02H
        DB      81H,02H,41H,04H,21H,08H,11H,10H,07H,0E0H
        DW      0000H           ; Safety padding
;
; Color encoding of cross-hair symbol
CR_COL  DB      0,0,0,0,0,0FH,0FH,0FH,0FH,0FH,0FH,0,0,0,0,0
        DB      0,0,0,0FH,0,0,0,0FH,0,0,0,0FH,0,0,0,0
        DB      0,0,0FH,0,0,0,0,0FH,0,0,0,0,0FH,0,0,0
        DB      0,0FH,0,0,0,0,0,0FH,0,0,0,0,0,0FH,0,0
        DB      0FH,0,0,0,0,0,0,0CH,0,0,0,0,0,0,0FH,0
        DB      0FH,0,0,0,0,0,0,0CH,0,0,0,0,0,0,0FH,0
        DB      0FH,0,0,0,0,0,0,0CH,0,0,0,0,0,0,0FH,0
        DB      4 DUP(0FH),0CH,0CH,0CH,0,0CH,0CH,0CH,4 DUP(0FH),0
        DB      0FH,0,0,0,0,0,0,0CH,0,0,0,0,0,0,0FH,0
```

```
        DB      0FH,0,0,0,0,0,0,0CH,0,0,0,0,0,0,0FH,0
        DB      0FH,0,0,0,0,0,0,0CH,0,0,0,0,0,0,0FH,0
        DB      0,0FH,0,0,0,0,0,0FH,0,0,0,0,0,0FH,0,0
        DB      0,0,0FH,0,0,0,0,0FH,0,0,0,0,0FH,0,0,0
        DB      0,0,0,0FH,0,0,0,0FH,0,0,0,0FH,0,0,0,0
        DB      0,0,0,0,0,0FH,0FH,0FH,0FH,0FH,0FH,0,0,0,0,0
;
; Bit pattern for duck
; 0 0 0 0 w w w 0 | 0 0 0 0 0 0 0 0 ------ 0E00H
; 0 0 0 w w w w w | 0 0 0 0 0 0 w w ------ 1F03H
; 0 0 w w w w w w | 0 0 0 0 0 w w w ------ 3F07H
; 0 w w w w w w w | 0 0 0 0 w w w w ------ 7F0FH
; w w w w w w w w | w w w w w w w w ------ FFFFH
; 0 0 0 w w w w w | w w w w w w w 0 ------ 1FFEH
; 0 0 w w w w w w | w w w w w w w 0 ------ 3FFEH
; 0 w w w w w w w | w w w w w w w w ------ 7FFFH
; 0 w w w w w w w | w w w w w w w w ------ 7FFFH
;
; COLOR CODES:
; For XORing with 00001000B (GRAY background)
; 0 ------> 0000B = 0H (pixel is unchanged)
; w ------> 1111B = FH (pixel is white)
; r ------> 1100B = CH (pixel is red)
;
; Block control area:                        Displacement ->
DUCK_X  DW      620             ; Present x coordinate        0
DUCK_Y  DW      410             ; y coordinate                2
        DB      9               ; Horizontal rows in block    4
        DB      2               ; Number of bytes per row     5
;
; Symbol encoding for duck
        DB      0EH,00H,1FH,03H,3FH,07H,7FH,0FH,0FFH,0FFH
        DB      1FH,0FEH,3FH,0FEH,7FH,0FFH,7FH,0FFH
        DW      0000H
;
; Color encoding of cross-hair symbol
DUCK_COLOR      DB      144 DUP(00FH)
                DB      00H             ; Padding
;
FIRST_DUCK      DB      1       ; Switch for first iteration
DUCKY_OFF       DB      1       ; No duck displayed
;
;****************************************************************
;                   mouse interrupt handler
;                   for left button pressed
;****************************************************************
```

```
; This handler receives control when either mouse button is
; pressed
MOUSE_BUT          PROC      FAR
;
;*********************|
;    test for right   |
;      button pressed |
;*********************|
; The calling routine sets bit 3 if the right button was pressed
         TEST     AL,00001000B     ; Test bit for right button
         JZ       LEFT_BUT         ; Go if bit not set
         JMP      NEW_GAME
;*********************|
; suspend duck display |
;*********************|
LEFT_BUT:
         MOV      CS:DUCKY_OFF,1   ; Set duck-off switch
         MOV      CS:GUN_FIRED,1   ; Set gun-fired switch
;*********************|
;     save context    |
;*********************|
         PUSH     AX               ; Save operational registers
         PUSH     BX
         PUSH     CX
         PUSH     DX
;
;*********************|
;    test x coordinate |
;      for on-target   |
;*********************|
; On-target condition depends on the values assigned to the
; equates ON_Y and ON_X listed at the start of the code
         MOV      AX,CS:CROSS_X    ; Cross hair x coordinate
         MOV      BX,CS:DUCK_X     ; Duck's x coordinate when gun
                                   ; was fired
         SUB      AX,ON_X          ; To make range positive
; On target requires BX - AX < 2*ON_X
         SUB      BX,AX            ; Subtract to get AX - BX
         JNC      TEST_X_TARGET    ; Continue testing if no carry
         JMP      NO_TARGET        ; No target if AX > BX
TEST_X_TARGET:
         MOV      AL,ON_X          ; Load constant into AX
         ADD      AL,AL            ; Double it
         MOV      AH,0             ; Clear high-order element
         CMP      AX,BX            ; AX must be larger
         JC       NO_TARGET
```

```
;**********************|
;   test y coordinate  |
;      for on-target   |
;**********************|
        MOV     AX,CS:CROSS_Y   ; Cross hair y coordinate
        MOV     BX,CS:DUCK_Y    ; Duck's y coordinate when gun
                                ; was fired
        SUB     AX,ON_Y         ; To make range positive
; On target requires BX - AX < 2*ON_Y
        SUB     BX,AX           ; Subtract to get AX - BX
        JNC     TEST_Y_TARGET   ; Continue testing if no carry
        JMP     NO_TARGET       ; No target if AX > BX
TEST_Y_TARGET:
        MOV     AL,ON_Y         ; Load constant into AX
        ADD     AL,AL           ; Double it
        MOV     AH,0            ; Clear high-order element
        CMP     AX,BX           ; AX must be larger
        JC      NO_TARGET
;**********************|
;         hit          |
;**********************|
; Produce high frequency sound to indicate hit
        MOV     BX,3000         ; 3000-Hz frequency
        MOV     CX,100          ; 30 ms duration
        CALL    SOUND           ; Procedure from SOLUTION.LIB
        MOV     CS:HIT_SW,1     ; Set switch for hit
        JMP     EXIT_FIRED
;**********************|
;        miss          |
;**********************|
; Produce a low-frequency, shorter sound to indicate miss
NO_TARGET:
        MOV     BX,600          ; 600-Hz frequency
        MOV     CX,30           ; 30-ms duration
        CALL    SOUND           ; Procedure from SOLUTION.LIB
        MOV     CS:HIT_SW,0     ; Set for missed
EXIT_FIRED:
        MOV     CS:DUCKY_OFF,0
        POP     DX
        POP     CX
        POP     BX
        POP     AX
        RET
;******************************|
;   right mouse button pressed |
;******************************|
```

```
; The only operation performed by the handler is to clear a
; switch
NEW_GAME:
        MOV       CS:DUCKY_OFF,0
        RET
MOUSE_BUT         ENDP
;
CODE    ENDS
        END       START
```

10

Extraordinary Solutions

10.0 Problem Solving

Solution to problems sometimes come in the form of mathematical formulas and equations, or in the form of methods, procedures, and algorithms. Often these solutions are collected in treatises, monographs, handbooks, and reference manuals so that they can be easily consulted and reused. The mechanical engineer, the chemist, the machinist, the physician, and others, frequently consult these books of formulas, methods, and techniques. The book you now read is a solutions manual for programmers of IBM microcomputers. The economics of research and invention dictate that the solution to a problem need be found only once. We humorously characterize the violation of this axiom by saying that someone has "reinvented the wheel."

But in spite of our collections of previously canned solutions we often encounter new or unique problems for which we do not have an exact formula or an applicable precedent. For instance, consider the extreme case of a mechanical engineer who is asked to design a sawmill to make wood products from trees growing in another planet. In this case there would be little use in searching for a similar device or for formulas that apply to materials and conditions that have never been encountered. Nevertheless, our engineer can probably perform tests on these alien trees, compare their physical properties with those of tress growing on earth, and make the necessary adjustments in the design of a sawmill originally developed for our earthly conditions, and thus is not entirely helpless.

This means that in many situations for which we do not have an exact solution we may be able to create one by analogy. A programmer who wants to design a computer game with animated air battles may use as a model the duck shooting gallery game described and listed in Chapter 9. Most of our creative work is not the invention of things entirely new and original, but the modification, revamping, and rehashing of other ideas and conceptions. True originality is indeed rare.

Notice that we have been referring to problems for which there is either an exact solution, an analogous model, or at least a technological or scientific path to follow; problems that we believe are solvable and that we have an idea how to approach analytically. For instance, an IBM microcomputer programmer may be asked to develop a routine to calculate the square root of a number so that the results are valid to 50 significant digits. This may be a task that has never been attempted to this degree of precision, and the programmer charged with its solution may not have the required mathematical skills or programming expertise. But we immediately know, by the nature of the problem, that it is solvable. We may even venture that the solution could be found by following a known method of calculating the square root and continuing the computations until the necessary precision is reached. In computer science this type of solution is often labeled an *algorithmic* solution, although this use of the term is somewhat imprecise.

Not all programming problems have analytical solutions. For example, one might like to have a computer program that will indicate for how long one can continue to drive one's 5-year old car without incurring major repair expenses. A farmer would like a program to plan all farm activities so that next year's winter wheat is planted by October 15. The local merchants would like their computers to forecast whether it will rain during the coming Labor Day weekend and if there will be a white Christmas this year. A local moving company that owns 10 large trucks, 4 pickups, and 7 trailers would like to have software that will schedule tomorrow's contracts so as to have their large equipment travel a minimum number of miles. Most of us would enjoy having a program that will tell us the sequence of bets to place in a roulette game so as to double our original purse in 10 spins of the wheel. Some of these programming problems could have valid solutions, while others certainly will not. One thing is certain: there are no readily available algorithms for any of them.

10.0.1 The Heuristic Method

Whenever an algorithmic solution is unavailable or impractical regarding a problem that cannot be approached analytically, we resort to a technique sometimes called *heuristic programming.* Please note that the word *heuristic* should not be considered as conflicting with *algorithmic*, since it is possible to develop an algorithm by following heuristic methods. In fact, the methods by which algorithms are derived can be classified as analytic and heuristic.

It has never been clearly defined whether heuristics is a science, an art, or both, or whether its study belongs in the field of mathematics, logic, psychology, or philosophy. The purpose of heuristics, in the modern sense, is to investigate the general methods used in problem solving as well as the rules of invention and discovery. Some notable work in this field can be attributed to two great mathematicians and philosophers, Rene Descartes (1596-1650) and Gottfried von Leibnitz (1646-1716). Bernard Bolzano (1781-1848) devoted a considerable portion of his treatise on logic to the subject of heuristics. More recently, Stanford's George Polya revived heuristics in a series of small, entertaining books that are already considered classics on the subject (see Bibliography).

Polya's study of heuristics begins by investigating the mental operations that are used in general problem solving. Polya recommends the following steps and related inquiries:

1. Understand the problem. Ask yourself the following: What is the unknown? What data is available? What are the conditions for the solution? Make drawings and sketches. Try to determine the separate parts in the condition.

2. Devise a plan for solving the problem. Have you seen other versions of the problem? Is there a theorem, formula, or equation that applies to the problem? Can a part of the problem be readily solved?

3. Carry out the plan for solving the problem. Check each step of the solution. Is the step correct? Can you prove that the step is correct?

4. Review the entire process and examine the solution. Can you check the result and the argument? Can the same solution be derived differently? Can the results be used in another problem?

10.0.2 Computers in Problem Solving

The elements of conventional computer problem solving include a set of unambiguous instructions and the input and output of data. The instructions are generally referred to as a *program*, which is based on an algorithmic solution. In a limited sense the computer can be considered a problem-solving device that facilitates, assists, or accelerates conventional calculations; a computational tool much like the abacus, the slide rule, or electric and electronic calculators. The computer's ability to execute instructions (programmability) adds a new dimension of usefulness, convenience, and productivity, but the fact that the program is executed by the machine, instead of by a human operator, does not extend our problem-solving capabilities.

10.1 Solving the Unsolvable

If the computer is considered as a programmable, calculating device, it can be safely stated that no problem solved with the assistance of a computer cannot also be solved without it. Note that this is a statement of possibility, not of practicality. It does not exclude the fact that many technical and scientific problems would take years, or even centuries, of calculation without the computer. The computational speed that computers bring to conventional problem solving is often referred to as *computer power*. In the solution of algorithmic problems we can easily see the advantages of computer power.

On the other hand, we often fail to see how computer power can be used in heuristics. Our minds seem to reject problems of an extremely complicated nature, especially if we fail to see an analytical approach to its solution. We sometimes refer to such situations as *mind-boggling*. Scheduling problems often fall in this category. For instance, in Section 10.0, while listing problems that defy analytical solution, we mentioned the case of a moving company that needs to schedule the activity of various types of equipment in order to minimize the total number of miles traveled by the larger machines.

The factors that boggle our minds in approaching problems of this nature are the absence of an algorithmic method of solution and the abundance of alternatives to test. Suppose that the moving company described in Section 10.0, is equipped with 10 trucks, 4 pickups, and 7 trailers, and has 100 local moving contracts to fulfill on a certain day. Add the complication that the trailers can be attached to 4 of the 10 trucks and to 2 of the 4 pickup trucks. Assume that the 100 daily contracts take place in a 25-mi radius. Some of these moves are so voluminous that they require a truck and a trailer or a truck and a pickup, others require a single truck or two pickup trucks, while others can be performed with a single pickup. The loading and delivery destinations are scrambled throughout this area.

If this moving company had the freedom of scheduling these moves within a 12-h period, in what order and with what equipment should the contracts be executed so as to minimize the miles traveled by the trucks? Some of Polya's methodology (see Section 10.0.1) can be useful in postulating and clarifying the problem, but a concrete method for solving this type of problem is far from evident. Some heuristic rules come to mind, for instance, it could be useful to group the contracts by geographical areas and by the volume of material to be transported. Another variable that could be interesting is finding the closest origin for each destination.

Nevertheless, after forming these groups and calculating all of these connections, it is still not easy to determine the schedule that meets the postulated conditions. It would be even harder to prove that a given schedule, reached analytically, is, in fact, the best option. In the real world the person in charge of such a moving company probably schedules its operation according to experience and to empirical rules that appear effective. The words commonly used to describe this technique are "intuition," "gut feeling," or "managing by the seat of your pants."

10.1.1 Linear Programming

A branch of mathematics called *linear programming* attempts to solve problems that require allocation of resources meeting certain minimization or maximization constraints. Note that the word *programming*, as used in linear programming, is unrelated to the common computer connotation. One particular case considered in linear programming, called the *transportation problem*, attempts a solution to the distribution of products from warehouses to customers in the most efficient manner. This problem is somewhat reminiscent of the scheduling problem of the moving company mentioned in Section 10.1, but on simpler terms. Other solutions attempted through linear programming are related to product blends and mixes and to production planning.

Linear programming solutions are often obtained in the form of a graph in which the intersection of two or more plotted functions represents a minimum or a maximum point. Computer techniques can sometimes be used in a similar manner. A mathematical algorithm known as the *simplex method*, developed in the late 1940s, is also often used in the solution of linear programming problems.

10.1.2 Brute-Force Methods

Linear programming and other analytical methods seem to be of little use in solving a real-life scheduling problem such as the case of the moving company described in Section 10.1. And yet, computer power makes possible an alternative that we often fail to consider: to test all possible options and select the best one. We instinctively shy away from such coarse methods. First, we have been taught to rely on our analytical powers; trying every possible combination does not seem a very refined approach. Second, the number of possible combinations, even in a simple case, can be intimidating.

Computer processing power makes viable methods of problem solving that were impractical or even impossible before this technology. One such scheme, sometimes called a *brute-force* method, is based on the sheer calculating power of a modern digital computer. Brute-force algorithms often work where all others fail. For many scheduling problems and simulations of real-life events there seems to be no other programming approach than the brute-force calculation of all possible options.

10.2 Computer Simulation

A simulation, in computer technology, is the representation in software or hardware of physical or abstract systems or of their behavior. The concept is essentially a mathematical and logical one, and we must resist the temptation of thinking of a simulation as a physical imitation of a system. For instance, a computer simulation of the operation of the moving company described in Section 10.1 does not require the graphics representation of city streets on which the software traces the movements of the company's trucks, pickups, and trailers. This simulation need keep track of the results and interactions of these movements only as they affect scheduling. The graphics could be an attractive feature in the program, but it is not a required element of the simulation. The object of a simulation is the accumulation of data, not the pictorial representation of the system.

Consider the computer simulation of a metalworking lathe. This software would allow the user to input the parameters of a part to be manufactured, and the lathe simulator would follow all the steps necessary in machining this part, keeping track of processing times, energy consumption, tool wear, metal waste, heat generated, or any other necessary variables. After the simulation has concluded, the program would report how much time and energy was spent in manufacturing the part, what tools were used, how much scrap metal was produced, and other information of interest to the user. The most important advantage of the simulation is that it takes place in an accelerated time frame; which means that the simulation of the fabrication of a part that requires 3 h of manufacturing time could take place in less than 1 s of computer time.

Note that the results obtained from a simulation could coincide with those obtained analytically, but that simulated and analytical solutions are obtained by different processes. If a system can be accurately described analytically, through a series of formulas and equations, there is usually little need for a simulated approach. As we have mentioned previously, simulations are most useful in regard to systems that are too complex to be described or reproduced by analytical methods.

The concept of digital simulations in modern computers was first proposed by the mathematician John von Neumann (1903-1957). The first applications were job shop simulations that could be used in manufacturing and development projects. Since then, several general purpose simulation languages have been developed (Simscript, GPSS, Simula, Boss, etc.) and the Society for Computer Simulation was founded.

10.2.1 Computer Modeling

It is generally accepted that for a system to be "simulatable" its state must change in time. The developer of a simulated system must start by determining the *extent* as well as the *detail* required in the model. Most computer simulations are of *discrete-event* systems, that is, systems with states that change in discrete steps. One characteristic of these systems is that they cannot be modeled with a mathematical function such as one or more differential equations.

The typical model of a discrete-event system consists of a series of steps that cause data changes. For example, the computer model of a lathe, described in Section 10.2, could be devised so as to keeps track of tool and part movements, metal chip removal, and energy use, during a series of 1-s time intervals. Several programming languages, called *discrete-event simulation languages*, have been designed to facilitate the modeling of discrete-event systems. The Simscript and GPSS languages are probably the best known. Assembly language can also be used in simulating discrete-event systems. It offers the advantage of greater flexibility and programmer control and the disadvantage of requiring a greater programming effort. The program AGRIMAX, listed later in this chapter, is the simulation of a discrete event system coded in IBM 8086/8088 assembly language.

10.2.2 Time-Lapse Simulations

A time-lapse simulation is a computer program that keeps track of events and data changes in a system during a series of discrete time intervals. The unit of each time lapse depends on the system's activity and on the model's extent and detail. For example, the computer model of a rock formation may use very large time increments to trace geological changes that take place at very slow rates. On the other hand, the model of a nuclear explosion could use very small time increments to keep track of rapid atomic changes at the particle level.

10.2.3 Predictability

In a valid simulation the data changes that take place during each time increment (sometimes called an *iteration*) must be predictable. Note that predictability, in this context, is not synonymous with certainty. The data modifications that result from a modeled event may be statistically predictable, but not certain. For example, the computer model of a metal lathe may take into account that the execution of manufacturing operations to very close tolerances imply a statistically measurable risk of scrapping the part. The simulation would have to include this statistical risk of error in order to maintain its correlation with a real-world device.

This means that the simulation must take into account the statistical risk as a random element in each iteration, if the operation in progress has this burden. More concretely: if in the real world the machining of a cylindrical surface to a tolerance of +/- 0.0001 in implies a 20 percent risk of scrapping the part, the simulated lathe must reflect this risk. If the computer model conforms with the real world device, after a large number of simulations of parts with this error risk, it will show that approximately 20 percent of the manufactured pieces are faulty. It is in this manner that elements or randomness and statistical probability enter into the predictability of an event. These factors are very important in maintaining the validity of many simulations.

10.2.4 Event Interrelation

Many simulations represent the occurrence of several interrelated events. For example, the job shop simulations mentioned in the beginning of Section 10.2 usually include several types of machine tools, such as metal lathes and milling machines. The manufacturing of a certain part could have constraints that determine that the lathe operations must be performed first. This means that for a milling machine to start work, there must be at least one part that has concluded its lathe phase. Other constraints could be that there is a tool at hand and an available machinist. In this manner, events within a simulation could be interrelated and the model must account for these interrelations.

10.2.5 Pools and Queues

In the language of computer modeling and simulations, a pool can be defined as storage for available resources. For example, in the job shop simulation mentioned above, the parts that have had their lathe operations go into a pool of parts that are ready to be milled. As each milling machine starts, the simulation program decrements this pool of mill-ready parts. When the pool empties, one or more milling machines have to wait for the lathes to conclude.

In this same context, a queue is an order of waiting for available resources. In the job shop example mentioned above, the milling machines that do not find parts in the mill-ready pool will form a queue. As parts become available, this queue determines the order in which the milling machines start work.

10.3 Case Study in Event Modeling

The best way to illustrate the programming required for a time-lapse simulation is by developing a specific case. The case selected refers to the scheduling of a generic agricultural harvesting operation. Many of the conditions and details in this example are contrived and will probably not exist in a real-world scenario. We have aimed at creating a generic example that matches or exceeds the complications and constraints of a real situation while avoiding specific and particular details of little general interest.

The program is designed for scheduling the daily operations of an imaginary agricultural harvesting firm. The imaginary company operates agricultural machines of four different types: (1) combines, (2) trailers, (3) tractors, and (4) trucks. Each combine goes into the fields accompanied by a tractor hitched to a trailer. The empty trailers are collected in a staging area. The combines in this case study have no internal storage; therefore, the harvested product must be simultaneously dumped into the trailers. This determines the constraint that, for a combine to work, there must be at least one tractor and one trailer available. Once the trailer is filled by the combine, the tractor takes it to a holding area, where it will be picked up by the first available truck and transported to a permanent storage location. Other constraints become immediately evident: for a tractor to work, there must be at least one empty trailer; for a truck to work, there must be at least one full trailer in the holding area.

The simulation is based on a 10-h workday. The iterations take place at 1-min intervals. The total number of each machine type can vary between a minimum of 1 and a maximum of 20. At the beginning of each simulation the user inputs the total number of machines of each type and their job cycle. The valid job cycle range is 2 to 300 min. The job cycle of a combine is defined as the time necessary to fill one trailer. The tractor job cycle includes the time necessary to move the filled trailer to the holding area. Therefore, since the tractor accompanies the combine while the trailer is filled, the tractor's job cycle will never be less than that of the combines.

The truck's job cycle is the time necessary for transporting the filled trailer to the permanent storage, dumping the product, and returning the empty trailer to the staging area. Since the trailers are the least expensive equipment and do not require an operator, they are considered as auxiliary machines. Trailers have no job cycle of their own, but their availability can determine whether a basic machine (combine, tractor, or truck) can work during an iteration. Job cycles cannot be broken. If the conditions for a machine to start work are present, the machine will start and continue for the duration of its job cycle.

Accidental breakdowns, changes in condition during the workday, and other unforeseen events are not considered in this simulation. However, as mentioned in Section 10.2.3, statistical probabilities and random events can be worked into a computer simulation.

The primary usefulness of this type of program is in scheduling daily operations and predicting machine productivity. The most important element is the machine interrelations, because in this type of operation the variables frequently change from day to day. For example, a combine harvesting a high-yield field could fill a trailer in 30 min. In a low-yield field this same operation could take 100 min. If the trailer's holding area is close to the harvesting area, the tractor can transport a trailer to it within a few minutes. This time increases if the harvesting area is moved to other locations, or if the road conditions deteriorate as a result of bad weather. The same can be said about the operation of the trucks. In a real-world scenario, yields, road conditions, distances, and availability of machines are factors that change quite frequently.

Consider a simple case in which the harvesting company is operating under the following conditions:

Type	Amount	Job cycle, min
Combine	6	60
Tractors	4	70
Trailers	5	
Trucks	6	80

If the combines can harvest at a rate of 1 ton of grain per hour, the company's apparent harvesting potential is of 600 tons for a 10-h workday. However, by running a simulation of these conditions (using the AGRIMAX program listed later in this chapter) we find that, with these job times and support equipment, the combines operate at only 33 percent of the maximum efficiency. This means that the company's daily harvesting potential is inevitably reduced to 200 tons.

Another use of a time-lapse computer simulation is in optimizing the use of resources. For example, let us assume that the harvesting company in this case study would like to schedule their operations so that their critical machines (combines) are used at optimum efficiency. If we accept that this efficiency is inversely proportional to the idle machine time, we can simulate all possible combinations of available machines and select as the best option the one in which idle time is minimized.

Note that the concept of optimization is conventional by nature. Under certain circumstances, the harvesting company in this case study may consider that optimum operation is the one with a minimum idle time for the combines. Under different circumstances, optimum operation could be the option that ensures a maximum production of grain. Still, under other circumstances, optimum operation could be based on the best possible utilization of all machines types — combines, tractors, and trucks.

The AGRIMAX program (see Section 10.4) implements optimization by repeating all possible combinations of auxiliary machines and selecting the best one. The criterion for the best option is chosen by the user from three different options. Option 1 calculates the minimum idle time assuming that all combines must be used. Option 2 calculates the minimum idle time for combines using the minimum number of machines. Optimization option 3 calculates the best utilization of all machine types. In the case mentioned previously in this section, consisting of 6 combines, 4 tractors, 5 trailers, and 6 trucks, with job cycles of 60, 70, and 80 minutes, respectively, AGRIMAX optimization gives the following results:

	Combines	Tractors	Trailers	Trucks
Not optimized	6/33%	4/58%	5	6/42%
Option 1	6/33%	3/76%	5	3/77%
Option 2	3/66%	3/76%	5	3/77%
Option 3	2/81%	2/93%	5	2/87%

Note: Data is machines/utilization.

This means that optimizing for the best utilization and minimum number of combines (option number 2) the program determines that the company can schedule 3 combines, 3 tractors, 5 trailers, and 3 trucks (instead of 6, 4, 5, and 6, respectively), saving considerable resources while maintaining the same daily production.

10.4 The AGRIMAX Program

```
;*****************************************************************
;*****************************************************************
;                        AGRIMAX.ASM
;*****************************************************************
;*****************************************************************
;
; Resource scheduling and optimization program in the form of a
; time-lapse simulation of an agricultural harvesting business
; The program simulates the operation during a 10-h workday of
; the following machines types:
;                         1. combines
;                         2. tractors
;                         3. trailers
;                         4. trucks
; The combines are considered critical machines. Combines,
; tractors, and trucks are considered basic machines because of
; their greater cost and to the fact that they require a human
; operator. The trailers are classified as auxiliary machines.
; Trailers are not taken into account during the optimization
; calculations.
;
; Operating conditions:
; The combines have no internal storage for products. Each
; combine is accompanied by a tractor-trailer, where the product
; is deposited as it is harvested. Once the trailer is filled,
; the tractor moves it to a holding area. The full trailer, in
; the holding area, is then hitched to a truck and moved to a
; permanent storage place. The following conditions derive from
; this description:
; 1. For a combine to work there must be at least one idle
;    tractor and one idle trailer
; 2. For a tractor to work there must be at least one idle
;    combine and one empty trailer
; 3. For a truck to work there must be at least one full trailer
;    in the holding area
; 4. The job cycle of a combine is the time required to harvest
;    sufficient product to fill one trailer
; 5. The job cycle of a tractor is the combine's job cycle plus
;    the time required to move the full trailer to the holding
;    area. The job cycle of a tractor can never be less than the
;    job cycle of a combine
; 6. The job cycle of a truck is the time required to transport
;    a full trailer to the permanent storage and return the
```

```
;    empty trailer to the staging area
; 7. Trailers have no job cycle of their own. The program does
;    not keep track of trailer utilization, but trailer
;    availability can affect the operation of other machines
;
; Variables:
; 1. There can be up to 20 machines of each type (combines,
;    tractors, trailers, and trucks). There must be at least one
;    machine of each type
; 2. The job cycle time for each machine type can range from 2
;    to 300 min
;
; Program operation:
; The simulation of a 10-h workday is performed at 1 min time
; intervals. The program maintains a memory control area for each
; basic machine (combines, tractors, and trucks). The state of
; each machine during each work iteration is bit-mapped as
; follows:
;    1 is stored if the machine was in working state
;    0 is stored if the machine was in idle state
; The iteration counter (ITER_COUNT) is used to calculate the
; address of the current bit in the corresponding machine control
; area. The program maintains one pool for each machine type. The
; pools hold the number of idle machines. Pools are adjusted
; during each iteration. The program also maintains a queue for
; the trailers in the holding area
;
; Optimization:
; Optimization is performed using a brute-force algorithm: all
; possible combinations are tested to select the best one.
; The combinations are based on changing the number of support
; machines. The user can select one of three optimization modes:
; Optimization mode 1 calculates the minimum idle time using all
; combines
; Optimization mode 2 calculates the minimum idle time and
; minimum machines
; Optimization mode 3 calculates the optimum utilization for all
; machine types
; The difference between optimization modes 1 and 2 is that
; mode 2 will eliminate, from the best option, the combines that
; show an idle job cycle. The difference between optimization
; mode 3 and modes 1 and 2 is that 1 and 2 are based on the best
; utilization of the combines and mode 3 is based on the best
; utilization of all basic machines
```

```
;*********************** externals ************************
; Library procedures from SOLUTION.LIB
EXTRN     BIO_CLEAR_SCR:    FAR
EXTRN     BIO_SHOW_BLOK:    FAR
EXTRN     BIO_SET_CUR:      FAR
EXTRN     BIO_CUR_OFF:      FAR
EXTRN     BIO_TTY:          FAR
EXTRN     DOS_KBR_INPUT:    FAR
EXTRN     KBR_WAIT:         FAR
EXTRN     ASC_TO_BIN:       FAR
EXTRN     BIN_TO_ASC:       FAR
;
INCLUDELIB SOLUTION
;*********************** stack ************************
;
STACK     SEGMENT stack
;
          DB        0400H DUP ('?')
STACK     ENDS
;
;*********************** data ************************
;
DATA      SEGMENT
;*********************|
;  iteration values   |
;*********************|
; Total machine values used in last iteration
TOTAL_COMBINES  DB      0       ; Total number of combines
TOTAL_TRACTORS  DB      0       ; Total number of tractors
TOTAL_TRAILERS  DB      0       ; Total number of trailers
TOTAL_TRUCKS    DB      0       ; Total number of trucks
;*********************|
;   program counters  |
;     and variables   |
;*********************|
WORK_COUNT      DW      0       ; Job cycle accumulator
UTIL_PER100     DW      0       ; Percent machine utilization
ITER_COUNT      DW      1       ; Iteration counter. Range 1 to
                                ; 600
MACH_COUNT      DW      0       ; Counter for graphed machines
TOTAL_TIME      DW      0       ; Storage for total machine time
                                ; TOTAL_TIME = 600 * MACH_COUNT
;*********************|
;  work time cycles   |
;*********************|
COMBINE_TIME    DW      0       ; Time cycle for combines
```

```
TRACTOR_TIME    DW      0       ; Time cycle for tractors
TRUCK_TIME      DW      0       ; Time cycle for trucks
;
; Offset and mask for accessing bit-level machine controls
; Byte offset and mask for accessing the individual control bits
; is calculated as follows:
;       BYTE OFFSET = INT(ITER_COUNT / 8)
;             MASK = 1000000B SHIFTED RIGHT BY THE VALUE IN THE
;                    REMAINDER OF ITER_COUNT / 8
ITER_OFFSET     DB      0       ; Range is 0 to 75
ITER_MASK       DB      0
;
;*********************|
;    machine pools    |
;*********************|
; These variables hold a count of the total number of machines in
; the idle state. These values change in the course of a
; simulation
COMBINES_IDLE   DB      0       ; Pool of idle combines
TRACTORS_IDLE   DB      0       ; Pool of idle tractors
TRAILERS_IDLE   DB      0       ; Pool of idle trailers
TRUCKS_IDLE     DB      0       ; Pool of idle trucks
;*********************|
;    machine queues   |
;*********************|
; Full trailers waiting to be trucked to storage
FULL_TRAILERS   DW      0
;
;*********************|
;    machine controls |
;*********************|
; The machine control areas are used to store the state (idle or
; working) in which the machine has been during each iteration of
; the simulation.
; Idle/working data storage area:
; Idle/working machine condition for each iteration is bit-coded
; 0 indicates that the machine was idle during the iteration
; 1 indicates that the machine was working
; The control bit at a certain iteration is accessed using the
; current value of ITER_OFFSET and ITER_MASK
; 75 bytes are necessary to store the machine's idle/working code
; during each of the 600 iterations (75 = 600/8)
; The machine status area:
; In addition to 75 bytes for idle/working state, each machine
; has a 5-byte status area preceding the idle/working data area
; The status area is assigned as follows:
```

```
;                                                 1  2  3  4  5  <- bytes
;                                                 ____  _____
;                                                |     |     |
;   Word status code as follows: _____|        |
;   0000 = machine is idle                       |_____ NOT USED
;   FFFF = machine does not exist
;   other = iteration at which machine started its job cycle
;   Individual machines are located at 80-byte increments within
;   the block that contains all machines of the type. A maximum of
;   20 machines requires 1600 bytes of storage


COMBINE_CTRL       DB      1600 DUP(00H)
                   DW      0FFFFH          ; End of area
TRACTOR_CTRL       DB      1600 DUP(00H)
                   DW      0FFFFH          ; End of area
TRUCK_CTRL         DB      1600 DUP(00H)
                   DW      0FFFFH          ; End of area
;
;*********************|
; optimization controls|
;*********************|
; Storage of parameters for best found option at this point
BEST_COMBINES      DB      0         ; Best number of combines
BEST_TRACTORS      DB      0         ; Best number of tractors
BEST_TRAILERS      DB      0         ; Best number of trailers
BEST_TRUCKS        DB      0         ; Best number of trucks
BEST_COUNT         DW      0         ; Best job cycle
BEST_PER100        DW      0         ; Best percent machine
                                     ; utilization
;
; Maximum number of machines to use during optimization
; These are the original totals installed before optimization
; starts
MAX_COMBINES       DB      0         ; Total number of combines
MAX_TRACTORS       DB      0         ; Total number of tractors
MAX_TRAILERS       DB      0         ; Total number of trailers
MAX_TRUCKS         DB      0         ; Total number of trucks
;
; Variables for optimization option 3
UTIL_SUM3          DW      0         ; Sum machine utilizations
BEST_SUM3          DW      0         ; Best previous sum
;
; Storage of optimization case (stored as ASCII 1, 2, or 3)
OPTI_CASE          DB      '1'       ; Optimization case option
; Counters displayed during optimization
OPTI_ITERS         DW      0         ; Number of total simulations
```

```
OPTI_COUNT       DW      0         ; Number of this simulation
;*****************************|
;          input buffers      |
;*****************************|
INPUT_BUF        DB      4         ; Input maximum is 3 characters
                 DB      0         ; Counter for characters typed
DIGIT_BUF        DB      5 DUP(20H)
;
;*********************************************************************
;                        display messages
;*********************************************************************
GREET_MS         DB      0         ; Row number
                 DB      5         ; Column number
                 DB      07H       ; Normal attribute
        DB       '*******************************************'
        DB       '************************',0FFH
        DB       '  AGRIMAX - A simulator and optimization program'
        DB       ' for an agricultural',0FFH
        DB       '             harvesting operation',0FFH
;
        DB       '*******************************************'
        DB       '************************',00H
COMB_MS          DB      4         ; Row number
                 DB      5         ; Column number
                 DB      07H       ; Normal attribute
        DB       '   MACHINES',0FFH
        DB       '   Enter number of combines: ',0FFH
        DB       00H
;
TRAC_MS          DB      6         ; Row number
                 DB      5         ; Column number
                 DB      07H       ; Normal attribute
        DB       '   Enter number of tractors: ',00H
;
TRAIL_MS         DB      7         ; Row number
                 DB      5         ; Column number
                 DB      07H       ; Normal attribute
        DB       '   Enter number of trailers: ',00H
;
TRUCK_MS         DB      8         ; Row number
                 DB      5         ; Column number
                 DB      07H       ; Normal attribute
        DB       '   Enter number of trucks: ',00H
;
TIMES_MS         DB      10        ; Row number
                 DB      5         ; Column number
```

```
                        DB      07H         ; Normal attribute
            DB          '    TIME CYCLES',0FFH
            DB          '   Enter work time for combines: ',0FFH
            DB          00H
TRAC_TI_MS  DB          12          ; Row number
            DB          5           ; Column number
            DB          07H         ; Normal attribute
            DB          '   Enter work time for tractors: ',00H
;
TRUCK_TI_MS DB          13          ; Row number
            DB          5           ; Column number
            DB          07H         ; Normal attribute
            DB          '   Enter work time for trucks: ',00H
;
GRAPH1_MS   DB          0           ; Start row
            DB          4           ; Start column
            DB          07H         ; Normal attribute
            DB          '       GRAPH AND ANALYSIS OF COMBINE WORKDAY '
            DB          '(* = working and - = idle)',00H
GRAPH2_MS   DB          0           ; Start row
            DB          4           ; Start column
            DB          07H         ; Normal attribute
            DB          '       GRAPH AND ANALYSIS OF TRACTOR WORKDAY '
            DB          '(* = working and - = idle)',00H
GRAPH3_MS   DB          0           ; Start row
            DB          4           ; Start column
            DB          07H         ; Normal attribute
            DB          '       GRAPH AND ANALYSIS OF TRUCK WORKDAY '
            DB          '(* = working and - = idle)',00H
SUMMARY_MS  DB          21          ; Start row
            DB          4           ; Start column
            DB          07H         ; Normal attribute
            DB          '                        MACHINE UTILIZATION ANAL'
            DB          'YSIS',0FFH
            DB          'total machine time (minutes):          total '
            DB          'work time (minutes): ',0FFH
            DB          'percent of ideal utilization: ',0FFH
            DB          '                    ** Press any key to continue'
            DB          ' **',00H
;
MENU_MS DB  10          ; Row
        DB  20          ; Column
        DB  07H         ; Normal attribute
        DB  ' ****************************************',0FFH
        DB  '               S E L E C T',0FFH
        DB  ' 1. Repeat last simulation',0FFH
```

```
            DB      ' 2. Restart (reenter machines and times)',0FFH
            DB      ' 3. Display optimization options',0FFH
            DB      ' 4. EXIT PROGRAM',0FFH
            DB      '          Type option number:  ',0FFH
            DB      ' ****************************************',00H
;
OPTI_MS DB          8       ; Row
            DB      20      ; Column
            DB      07H     ; Normal attribute
            DB      ' ****************************************',0FFH
            DB      '          O P T I M I Z A T I O N',0FFH
            DB      ' ****************************************',0FFH
            DB      '          SELECT OPTIMIZATION MODE',0FFH
            DB      ' 1. Minimum idle time using all combines',0FFH
            DB      ' 2. Minimum idle time and minimum machines',0FFH
            DB      ' 3. Optimum utilization for all machine types '
            DB      0FFH
            DB      ' 4. RETURN TO MAIN MENU',0FFH
            DB      '          Type option number:  ',0FFH
            DB      ' ****************************************',00H
;
OPTI_END_MS     DB      8       ; Row
            DB      20      ; Column
            DB      07H     ; Normal attribute
            DB      '          OPTIMIZATION RESULTS ',0FFH
            DB      '    Number of combines optimized ...',0FFH
            DB      '    Optimum number of tractors .....',0FFH
            DB      '    Optimum number of trailers .....',0FFH
            DB      '    Optimum number of trucks .......',0FFH,0FFH
            DB      '** Press any key to simulate this case **',00H
;
OPTI_CNT_MS     DB      0       ; Row
            DB      0       ; Column
            DB      07H     ; Normal attribute
            DB      'OPTIMIZING',0FFH
            DB      'Simulation No.: ',0FFH
            DB      'Total count is: ',000H
;
DATA    ENDS
;
;
;************************* code *************************
CODE    SEGMENT BYTE
        ASSUME  CS:CODE
;
START:
```

```
;*********************|
; initialize DS and ES |
;*********************|
        MOV     AX,DATA            ; Date segment name
        MOV     DS,AX              ; to DS
        ASSUME  DS:DATA
        MOV     ES,AX              ; and ES
        ASSUME  ES:DATA            ; to allow block operations
;*********************|
;   clear screen and  |
;   display messages  |
;*********************|
RE_START:
        CALL    BIO_CLEAR_SCR      ; Clear screen procedure in
                                   ; SOLUTION.LIB
        LEA     SI,GREET_MS        ; General program greeting
        CALL    BIO_SHOW_BLOK      ; Display procedure in
                                   ; SOLUTION.LIB

;*********************|
;   reset variables   |
;*********************|
; This is required for program restart menu option
        MOV     WORK_COUNT,0       ; Entry values for variables
        MOV     UTIL_PER100,0
        MOV     ITER_COUNT,1
        MOV     MACH_COUNT,0
        MOV     TOTAL_TIME,0
;*********************|
;   input variables   |
;*********************|
; Total combines
        LEA     SI,COMB_MS         ; Pointer to message text
        MOV     DH,5               ; Cursor row
        MOV     DL,34              ; Cursor column
        CALL    MESS_AND_IN        ; Local display and input
                                   ; procedure
        MOV     TOTAL_COMBINES,DL       ; Store input in variable
; Total tractors
        LEA     SI,TRAC_MS         ; Pointer to message text
        MOV     DH,6               ; Cursor row
        MOV     DL,34              ; Cursor column
        CALL    MESS_AND_IN        ; Local display and input
                                   ; procedure
        MOV     TOTAL_TRACTORS,DL       ; Store input in variable
; Total trailers
        LEA     SI,TRAIL_MS        ; Pointer to message text
```

```
        MOV      DH,7              ; Cursor row
        MOV      DL,34             ; Cursor column
        CALL     MESS_AND_IN       ; Local display and input
                                   ; procedure
        MOV      TOTAL_TRAILERS,DL     ; Store input in variable
; Total trucks
        LEA      SI,TRUCK_MS       ; Pointer to message text
        MOV      DH,8              ; Cursor row
        MOV      DL,32             ; Cursor column
        CALL     MESS_AND_IN       ; Local display and input
                                   ; procedure
        MOV      TOTAL_TRUCKS,DL   ; Store input in variable
; Combines job time
        LEA      SI,TIMES_MS       ; Pointer to message text
        MOV      DH,11             ; Cursor row
        MOV      DL,38             ; Cursor column
        CALL     MESS_AND_IN       ; Local display and input
                                   ; procedure
        MOV      COMBINE_TIME,DX   ; Store input in variable
; Tractors job time
        LEA      SI,TRAC_TI_MS     ; Pointer to message text
        MOV      DH,12             ; Cursor row
        MOV      DL,38             ; Cursor column
        CALL     MESS_AND_IN       ; Local display and input
                                   ; procedure
        MOV      TRACTOR_TIME,DX   ; Store input in variable
; Trucks job time
        LEA      SI,TRUCK_TI_MS    ; Pointer to message text
        MOV      DH,13             ; Cursor row
        MOV      DL,36             ; Cursor column
        CALL     MESS_AND_IN       ; Local display and input
                                   ; procedure
        MOV      TRUCK_TIME,DX     ; Store input in variable
;
;****************************************************************
;                        simulation
;****************************************************************
LAST_CASE:
        CALL     ITERATE_600
; Display iteration results for combines
        CALL     BIO_CLEAR_SCR
        LEA      SI,GRAPH1_MS
        CALL     BIO_SHOW_BLOK
        LEA      DI,COMBINE_CTRL
        CALL     GRAPH_MACHINES
        CALL     CALC_STATS
```

```
          CALL      SHOW_STATS
          CALL      KBR_WAIT
; Display iteration results for tractors
          CALL      BIO_CLEAR_SCR
          LEA       SI,GRAPH2_MS
          CALL      BIO_SHOW_BLOK
          LEA       DI,TRACTOR_CTRL
          CALL      GRAPH_MACHINES
          CALL      CALC_STATS
          CALL      SHOW_STATS
          CALL      KBR_WAIT
; Display iteration results for trucks
          CALL      BIO_CLEAR_SCR
          LEA       SI,GRAPH3_MS
          CALL      BIO_SHOW_BLOK
          LEA       DI,TRUCK_CTRL
          CALL      GRAPH_MACHINES
          CALL      CALC_STATS
          CALL      SHOW_STATS
          CALL      KBR_WAIT
;***************************************************************
;                         options menu
;***************************************************************
OPTION_MENU:
          CALL      BIO_CLEAR_SCR
; Display options menu and execute option selected
          LEA       SI,MENU_MS       ; Pointer to message text
          CALL      BIO_SHOW_BLOK    ; Display procedure in
                                     ; SOLUTION.LIB
; Set cursor to input area
GET_OPTION:
          MOV       DH,16            ; Cursor row
          MOV       DL,50            ; Cursor column
          CALL      BIO_SET_CUR      ; Cursor service in SOLUTION.LIB
          CALL      KBR_WAIT         ; Get keystroke
;*********************|
;  process keystroke  |
;*********************|
          CMP       AL,'1'           ; Menu option 1 is repeat last
                                     ; case
          JNE       TRY_2            ; Cascade to next test
          JMP       LAST_CASE        ; Execute option
TRY_2:    CMP       AL,'2'           ; Menu option 2 is restart
                                     ; simulation
          JNE       TRY_3            ; Cascade to next test
          JMP       RE_START         ; Restart program
```

```
TRY_3:
        CMP     AL,'3'              ; Menu option 3 is optimization
        JNE     TRY_4               ; Cascade to next test
        JMP     OPTIMIZE            ; Execute optimization option
TRY_4:
        CMP     AL,'4'              ; Menu option 4 is exit
        JE      EXIT                ; Go if option 4
        JMP     GET_OPTION
;**********************|
;     clean up         |
;**********************|
EXIT:
        CALL    BIO_CLEAR_SCR       ; Video service in SOLUTION.LIB
        MOV     DX,0                ; Reset cursor to screen start
        CALL    BIO_SET_CUR         ; Cursor service in SOLUTION.LIB
;**********************|
;     exit to DOS      |
;**********************|
DOS_EXIT:
        MOV     AH,4CH              ; DOS service request code
        MOV     AL,0                ; No error code returned
        INT     21H                 ; TO DOS
;
;****************************************************************
;                         optimization
;****************************************************************
;
OPTIMIZE:
        CALL    BIO_CLEAR_SCR
; Display options menu and execute option selected
        LEA     SI,OPTI_MS          ; Pointer to message text
        CALL    BIO_SHOW_BLOK       ; Display procedure in
                                    ; SOLUTION.LIB
; Set cursor to input area
GET_OPTI_OPTION:
        MOV     DH,16               ; Cursor row
        MOV     DL,50               ; Cursor column
        CALL    BIO_SET_CUR         ; Cursor service in SOLUTION.LIB
        CALL    KBR_WAIT            ; Get keystroke
;
;**********************|
;  process keystroke   |
;**********************|
        CMP     AL,'1'              ; Menu option 1 is repeat last
                                    ; case
        JNE     OPT_2               ; Cascade to next test
```

```
        JMP     OPTI_CASE123    ; Execute option
OPT_2:  CMP     AL,'2'          ; Menu option 2 is restart
                                ; simulation
        JNE     OPT_3           ; Cascade to next test
        JMP     OPTI_CASE123    ; Restart program
OPT_3:
        CMP     AL,'3'          ; Menu option 3 is optimization
        JNE     OPT_4           ; Cascade to next test
        JMP     OPTI_CASE123    ; Execute optimization option
OPT_4:
        CMP     AL,'4'          ; Menu option 4 is exit
        JNE     GET_OPTI_OPTION ; Repeat input if not 4
        JMP     OPTION_MENU     ; Go to main menu
;****************************************************************
;                       optimization options
;****************************************************************
; Optimization routines use the brute-force method of testing all
; possible combinations of support machines (tractors, trailers,
; and trucks) for the maximum number of combines input by the
; user. The result of each iteration is compared with the
; previous best result to determine the better option
OPTI_CASE123:
; Store optimization case
        MOV     OPTI_CASE,AL    ; Optimization option stored in
                                ; ASCII
;*********************|
; number of simulations|
;*********************|
; Calculate total number of simulations to be performed
; Total simulations is the product of all support machines
; Absolute maximum is 20 * 20 * 20 = 8000
        MOV     AH,0            ; Clear high-order byte
        MOV     AL,TOTAL_TRACTORS    ; First element
        MOV     BL,TOTAL_TRAILERS    ; Second element
        MUL     BL              ; Multiply
        MOV     BL,TOTAL_TRUCKS      ; Third element in total
        MUL     BL
; AX holds total simulations required for this optimization
;*********************|
;   display counter   |
;*********************|
; Store count and initialize current simulation counter
        MOV     OPTI_ITERS,AX   ; From multiplications
        MOV     OPTI_COUNT,0    ; Current simulation counter
; Display counter at left screen top
        LEA     SI,OPTI_CNT_MS  ; Pointer to message block
```

```
        CALL     BIO_SHOW_BLOK     ; Display procedure in
                                   ; SOLUTION.LIB
; Position cursor at display area
        MOV      DH,2              ; Screen row
        MOV      DL,16             ; Screen column
        CALL     BIO_SET_CUR       ; Cursor procedure in
                                   ; SOLUTION.LIB
        MOV      DX,OPTI_ITERS     ; Total simulations
        LEA      DI,DIGIT_BUF      ; Buffer for ASCII digits
        CALL     BIN_TO_ASC        ; Conversion in SOLUTION.LIB
        CALL     DISPLAY_DIGITS    ; Local procedure
;*********************|
; initialize variables |
;*********************|
; Clear 6 words of storage to reset variables
        LEA      DI,BEST_COMBINES     ; Address of first variable
        MOV      CX,6                 ; 6 words to clear
        XOR      AX,AX                ; Clear accumulator
        CLD                           ; Forward direction
        REP      STOSW                ; Store and repeat
; Move installed totals as optimization maximums
        LEA      SI,TOTAL_COMBINES    ; Source
        LEA      DI,MAX_COMBINES      ; Destination
        MOV      CX,4                 ; 4 bytes to move
        CLD                           ; Forward direction
        REP      MOVSB                ; Move and repeat
; Reinitialize machine totals
        MOV      TOTAL_TRACTORS,1        ; One of each to start
        MOV      TOTAL_TRAILERS,1
        MOV      TOTAL_TRUCKS,1
        MOV      UTIL_SUM3,0             ; Variables for option 3
        MOV      BEST_SUM3,0
;********************************|
;        perform simulation     |
;********************************|
SIMULATE_ONE:
        INC      OPTI_COUNT       ; Bump simulations counter
        CALL     UPDATE_CTR       ; Update screen counter display
        CALL     ITERATE_600
; Calculate WORK_COUNT and MACH_COUNT variables for this
; simulation
        LEA      DI,COMBINE_CTRL ; Pointer to control area
        CALL     DUMMY_GRAPH      ; Local procedure to calculate
                                  ; simulation variables
; Calculate TOTAL_TIME and UTIL_PER100 for combines
        LEA      DI,COMBINE_CTRL ; Pointer to control area
```

```
          CALL    CALC_STATS          ; Local procedure
; Test optimization options and branch to routine
          CMP     OPTI_CASE,'3'       ; Test for case 3
          JNE     OPTI_OPTION12       ; Go if not case 3
;**********************|
; optimization option 3|
;**********************|
; In optimization case the criterion is the best total
; utilization. Machine utilization is added for each machine type
          MOV     AX,UTIL_PER100      ; Utilization for combines
          MOV     UTIL_SUM3,AX        ; To performance accumulator
;**********************|
; tractor utilization  |
;**********************|
; Calculate WORK_COUNT and MACH_COUNT variables for tractors
          LEA     DI,TRACTOR_CTRL ; Pointer to control area
          CALL    DUMMY_GRAPH     ; Local procedure to calculate
                                  ; simulation variables
; Calculate TOTAL_TIME and UTIL_PER100 for tractors
          LEA     DI,TRACTOR_CTRL ; Pointer to control area
          CALL    CALC_STATS          ; Local procedure
; Add to previous total
          MOV     AX,UTIL_PER100      ; Utilization for tractors
          ADD     UTIL_SUM3,AX        ; Added to accumulator
;**********************|
;  truck utilization   |
;**********************|
; Calculate WORK_COUNT and MACH_COUNT variables for trucks
          LEA     DI,TRUCK_CTRL   ;  Pointer to control area
          CALL    DUMMY_GRAPH     ; Local procedure to calculate
                                  ; simulation variables
; Calculate TOTAL_TIME and UTIL_PER100 for trucks
          LEA     DI,TRUCK_CTRL   ; Pointer to control area
          CALL    CALC_STATS          ; Local procedure
; Add to previous total
          MOV     AX,UTIL_PER100      ; Utilization for tractors
          ADD     UTIL_SUM3,AX        ; Added to accumulator
; Test if this case is better than best saved case
          MOV     AX,UTIL_SUM3        ; Utilization sum to AX
          CMP     AX,BEST_SUM3        ; Compare with previous best
                                      ; value
          JG      NEW_BEST_SUM        ; Update previous value stored
          JMP     NEW_SIMULATION      ; If not, leave previous best
                                      ; value
NEW_BEST_SUM:
; Move these totals to best values storage area
```

```
        LEA     SI,TOTAL_COMBINES      ; Source
        LEA     DI,BEST_COMBINES       ; Destination area
        MOV     CX,4            ; Save machines and values
        CLD                     ; Forward direction
        REP     MOVSW           ; Move and repeat
; Update best performance sum stored
        MOV     AX,UTIL_SUM3    ; Performance sum for this
                                ; simulation
        MOV     BEST_SUM3,AX    ; Save as best case
        JMP     NEW_SIMULATION  ; Skip over case 1 and 2
;*********************|
; optimization options |
;      1 and 2         |
;*********************|
OPTI_OPTION12:
; UTIL_PER100 holds utilization of combines for this simulation
; BEST_PER100 holds best previous utilization found in
; optimization
        MOV     AX,UTIL_PER100  ; This result to AX
        CMP     AX,BEST_PER100  ; Compare with previous best
                                ; value
        JG      NEW_BEST        ; Update previous value stored
        JMP     NEW_SIMULATION  ; If not, leave previous best
                                ; value
NEW_BEST:
; Move these totals to best values storage area
        LEA     SI,TOTAL_COMBINES      ; Source
        LEA     DI,BEST_COMBINES       ; Destination area
        MOV     CX,4            ; Save machines and values
        CLD                     ; Forward direction
        REP     MOVSW           ; Move and repeat
;*********************|
; get next combination |
;*********************|
; The logic for sequencing all possible combinations is based in
; successively incrementing each machine type
NEW_SIMULATION:
        MOV     AL,TOTAL_TRUCKS ; Count for last simulation
        CMP     AL,MAX_TRUCKS   ; Compare with maximum
        JE      BUMP_TRAILERS   ; Go to next type of machine
        INC     TOTAL_TRUCKS    ; if not, bump this counter
        JMP     SIMULATE_ONE    ; Perform next simulation
BUMP_TRAILERS:
        MOV     TOTAL_TRUCKS,1         ; Rewind machine count
        MOV     AL,TOTAL_TRAILERS      ; Count for last
                                       ; simulation
```

```
        CMP     AL,MAX_TRAILERS ; Compare with maximum
        JE      BUMP_TRACTORS   ; Go to next type of machine
        INC     TOTAL_TRAILERS  ; if not, bump this counter
        JMP     SIMULATE_ONE    ; Perform next simulation
BUMP_TRACTORS:
        MOV     TOTAL_TRAILERS,1        ; Rewind machine count
        MOV     AL,TOTAL_TRACTORS       ; Count for last
                                        ; simulation
        CMP     AL,MAX_TRACTORS ; Compare with maximum
        JE      LAST_COMBINATION        ; No more combinations
        INC     TOTAL_TRACTORS  ; if not, bump this counter
        JMP     SIMULATE_ONE    ; Perform next simulation
;*********************|
;  end of optimization |
;*********************|
LAST_COMBINATION:
        CALL    BIO_CLEAR_SCR   ; Screen service in SOLUTION.LIB
; Move best case found during optimization to simulation
; variables
        LEA     SI,BEST_COMBINES        ; Source of data
        LEA     DI,TOTAL_COMBINES       ; Destination of data
        MOV     CX,4            ; 4 bytes
        CLD                     ; Forward direction
        REP     MOVSB           ; Move byte and repeat
; Simulate best case to load variables
        CALL    ITERATE_600     ; Perform simulation
;*********************|
;  test for option 2   |
;*********************|
; Optimization options 2 and 3 delete combines that have an idle
; job cycle
        CMP     OPTI_CASE,'1'   ; Test for this option
        JE      END_OPTION23    ; Go if option 1
; Check for combines with idle job cycles and remove from total
        LEA     DI,COMBINE_CTRL         ; Pointer to control area
START_OF_ROW:
        MOV     AX,[DI]         ; Get machine's status word
        CMP     AL,0FFFFH       ; Nonimplemented machine
        JE      END_OPTION23    ; Go if no more machines
; Index pointer to data storage area
        PUSH    DI              ; Save machine status pointer
        ADD     DI,5            ; Point to working/idle control
                                ; area
        MOV     CX,75           ; Counter for 75 bytes in data
                                ; area
        MOV     AX,0            ; Clear accumulator
```

```
                MOV     BH,0                    ; Clear high-order byte for word
                                                ; addition
ADD_ROW:
                MOV     BL,BYTE PTR [DI]        ; Get stored value
                ADD     AX,BX                   ; Add to sum in AX
                INC     DI                      ; Bump pointer
                LOOP    ADD_ROW                 ; Continue until end of row
; All bytes in row have been added. Check for zero value
                CMP     AX,0                    ; AX = 0 if no working bits
                JNE     NOT_ALL_IDLE            ; Go if not 0
; Adjust combines
                DEC     TOTAL_COMBINES          ; Counter for combines
NOT_ALL_IDLE:
                POP     DI                      ; Restore start position
                ADD     DI,80                   ; Bump to next row
                JMP     START_OF_ROW
END_OPTION23:
; Display end of optimization message
                LEA     SI,OPTI_END_MS          ; Pointer to block message
                CALL    BIO_SHOW_BLOK           ; Display procedure in
                                                ; SOLUTION.LIB

;*********************|
; display optimization |
;      conclusions     |
;*********************|
; Set cursor to display position in message area for combines
                MOV     DH,9                    ; Cursor row
                MOV     DL,57                   ; Cursor column
                CALL    BIO_SET_CUR             ; Cursor service in
                                                ; SOLUTION.LIB
                MOV     DL,TOTAL_COMBINES        ; Machines
                MOV     DH,0                    ; Clear high-order byte
                LEA     DI,DIGIT_BUF            ; Buffer for ASCII digits
                CALL    BIN_TO_ASC              ; Conversion in SOLUTION.LIB
                CALL    DISPLAY_DIGITS          ; Local procedure
; Set cursor for tractors
                MOV     DH,10                   ; Cursor row
                MOV     DL,57                   ; Cursor column
                CALL    BIO_SET_CUR             ; Cursor service in SOLUTION.LIB
                MOV     DL,TOTAL_TRACTORS        ; Machines
                MOV     DH,0                    ; Clear high-order byte
                LEA     DI,DIGIT_BUF            ; Buffer for ASCII digits
                CALL    BIN_TO_ASC              ; Conversion in SOLUTION.LIB
                CALL    DISPLAY_DIGITS          ; Local procedure
; Set cursor for trailers
                MOV     DH,11                   ; Cursor row
```

```
          MOV       DL,57            ; Cursor column
          CALL      BIO_SET_CUR      ; Cursor service in SOLUTION.LIB
          MOV       DL,TOTAL_TRAILERS       ; Machines
          MOV       DH,0             ; Clear high-order byte
          LEA       DI,DIGIT_BUF     ; Buffer for ASCII digits
          CALL      BIN_TO_ASC       ; Conversion in SOLUTION.LIB
          CALL      DISPLAY_DIGITS   ; Local procedure
; Set cursor for trucks
          MOV       DH,12            ; Cursor row
          MOV       DL,57            ; Cursor column
          CALL      BIO_SET_CUR      ; Cursor service in SOLUTION.LIB
          MOV       DL,TOTAL_TRUCKS  ; Machines
          MOV       DH,0             ; Clear high-order byte
          LEA       DI,DIGIT_BUF     ; Buffer for ASCII digits
          CALL      BIN_TO_ASC       ; Conversion in SOLUTION.LIB
          CALL      DISPLAY_DIGITS   ; Local procedure
;
          CALL      BIO_CUR_OFF      ; Cursor off the screen
          CALL      KBR_WAIT         ; Wait for keystroke
          CALL      BIO_CLEAR_SCR    ; Screen service in SOLUTION.LIB
          JMP       LAST_CASE        ; Execute simulation
;******************************************************************
;                         procedures
;******************************************************************
UPDATE_CTR       PROC     NEAR
; Procedure to update current simulation in screen counter
; Position cursor at display area
          MOV       DH,1             ; Screen row
          MOV       DL,16            ; Screen column
          CALL      BIO_SET_CUR      ; Cursor procedure in
                                     ; SOLUTION.LIB
          MOV       DX,OPTI_COUNT    ; Total simulations
          LEA       DI,DIGIT_BUF     ; Buffer for ASCII digits
          CALL      BIN_TO_ASC       ; Conversion in SOLUTION.LIB
          CALL      DISPLAY_DIGITS   ; Local procedure
          RET
UPDATE_CTR       ENDP
;******************************************************************
;
DUMMY_GRAPH      PROC     NEAR
; Procedure to calculate variables without displaying graph. This
; procedure replaces GRAPH_MACHINES in optimization
; On entry:
;         DI -> control block for machine type to be graphed
; On exit:
;         WORK_COUNT variable has sum of all working iterations
```

```
;         MACH_COUNT variable has total number of graphed machines
;
;**********************|
; initialize variables |
;**********************|
        MOV     MACH_COUNT,1      ; Initialize binary row counter
        MOV     WORK_COUNT,0      ; Counter for working-state bits
;**********************|
;  calculate one row   |
;**********************|
NEW_ROW1:
        MOV     AX,[DI]           ; Get machine's status word
        CMP     AL,0FFFFH         ; Nonimplemented machine
        JE      END_OF_DUMMY      ; Go if no more machines
; At this point there is a machine to graph
        PUSH    DI                ; Save machine status pointer
        ADD     DI,5              ; Point to working/idle control
                                  ; area
        MOV     CX,75             ; Counter for 75 bytes to graph
GRAPH_ROW1:
        MOV     BL,BYTE PTR [DI]       ; Get stored value for 8
                                       ; iterations
;**********************|
;  add-in bits set     |
;**********************|
; Test for bits that are set and accumulate count in variable
        PUSH    CX                ; Save outer loop count
        MOV     CX,8              ; Setup counter for 8 bits
        MOV     BH,BL             ; Bit pattern to BH
        CLC                       ; No carry
ROTATE_BITS1:
        ROL     BH,1              ; Rotate BH bits. Carry set if
                                  ; high-order bit was set
        JNC     UNSET1            ; Go if no carry
        INC     WORK_COUNT        ; Bump counter
UNSET1:
        LOOP    ROTATE_BITS1      ; Continue
        POP     CX                ; Restore outer loop counter
        INC     DI                ; Bump pointer
        LOOP    GRAPH_ROW1        ; Continue until end of row
; Row has been graphed. Index pointer and cursor
        POP     DI                ; Restore start position
        ADD     DI,80             ; Bump to next row
        INC     MACH_COUNT        ; Bump row counter
        JMP     NEW_ROW1
   Adjust row counter and exit
```

```
END_OF_DUMMY:
        DEC       MACH_COUNT        ; Can be used by the caller to
                                    ; get total machines graphed
        RET
DUMMY_GRAPH     ENDP
;****************************************************************
;
CALC_STATS      PROC    NEAR
; Calculate and store iteration statistics
; On exit:
;            TOTAL_TIME = number of machines * 600 min
;            UTIL_PER100 = machine utilization (percent of ideal)
entry:
;            WORK_COUNT variable has sum of all working iterations
;            MACH_COUNT variable has total number of graphed machines
;
;*********************|
;      machine time   |
;*********************|
; Total machine time is the product of the number of machines by
; 600 min in a 10-h workday
        MOV       CX,MACH_COUNT     ; CX holds machines
        MOV       AX,600            ; Total minutes in workday
        MUL       CX                ; AX * CX in DX and AX
; Since product cannot exceed one word, it will be in AX
; Store for use in calculating utilization
        MOV       TOTAL_TIME,AX     ; Store in variable
;
;*********************|
; machine utilization |
;*********************|
; Percent of ideal machine utilization is calculated by dividing
; total work time by total machine time/100
        MOV       BX,100            ; Divisor to BX
        MOV       DX,0              ; Clear high-order word
        MOV       AX,TOTAL_TIME     ; Dividend to AX
        DIV       BX                ; Quotient is in AX
        MOV       BX,AX             ; Move quotient to BX
; Divide total work time by BX
        MOV       AX,WORK_COUNT     ; Dividend to AX
        MOV       DX,0              ; Clear high-order word
        DIV       BX                ; Quotient of this division in AX
        MOV       UTIL_PER100,AX    ; Save utilization in variable
        RET
CALC_STATS      ENDP
;****************************************************************
```

```
MESS_AND_IN     PROC    NEAR
; Display message, input 2-digit number, and convert to binary
; On entry:
;           SI -> message block
;           DH = cursor row for input
;           DL = cursor column for input
; On exit:
;           DX = binary value of ASCII input
;
        PUSH    DX              ; Save cursor position
        CALL    BIO_SHOW_BLOK   ; Display procedure in
                                ; SOLUTION.LIB
; Set cursor to input area
        POP     DX              ; Restore cursor address
        CALL    BIO_SET_CUR     ; Cursor procedure in
                                ; SOLUTION.LIB
; Input 2-digit ASCII number
        LEA     DX,INPUT_BUF    ; Buffer start
        CALL    DOS_KBR_INPUT   ; Keyboard procedure in
                                ; SOLUTION.LIB
; Convert ASCII to binary
        LEA     BX,DIGIT_BUF    ; Pointer to ASCII buffer
        CALL    ASC_TO_BIN      ; ASCII conversion in
                                ; SOLUTION.LIB
        RET
;
MESS_AND_IN     ENDP
;****************************************************************
;
ITERATE_600     PROC    NEAR
; Perform 600 iterations simulating a 10-h workday
; on minute-by-minute time increments
;*********************|
; move totals to pools |
;*********************|
; Machine counts stored in the variables with the prefix TOTAL_
; are moved to the machine pool variables
        LEA     SI,TOTAL_COMBINES       ; First total variable
        LEA     DI,COMBINES_IDLE        ; First pool variable
        MOV     CX,4            ; 4 bytes to move
        CLD                     ; Forward in memory
        REP     MOVSB           ; Move data
;*********************|
; clear trailer queue |
;*********************|
        MOV     FULL_TRAILERS,0
```

```
;**********************|
;    clear machine     |
;    control areas     |
;**********************|
; 4 control areas of 1600 bytes, separated by a 0FFFFH word
        LEA     DI,COMBINE_CTRL ; First control area
        XOR     AX,AX           ; Clear accumulator
        MOV     DX,3            ; 3 areas to clear
CLEAR_1600:
        MOV     CX,1600         ; Counter for bytes to clear
        CLD                     ; Forward direction
        REP     STOSB           ; Store 0 and repeat
        INC     DI              ; Skip area terminator word
        INC     DI
        DEC     DX              ; Test for last area
        JNZ     CLEAR_1600      ; Clear next area
;**********************|
;    first iteration   |
;**********************|
        MOV     ITER_COUNT,1    ; Initialize iteration counter
;**********************|
;     clear control    |
; area for each machine|
;**********************|
        MOV     CL,COMBINES_IDLE        ; Total number of combines
        LEA     DI,COMBINE_CTRL ; Pointer to control area
        CALL    INIT_CONTROLS   ; Local procedure
        MOV     CL,TRACTORS_IDLE
        LEA     DI,TRACTOR_CTRL ; Pointer to control area
        CALL    INIT_CONTROLS   ; Local procedure
        MOV     CL,TRUCKS_IDLE
        LEA     DI,TRUCK_CTRL   ; Pointer to control area
        CALL    INIT_CONTROLS   ; Local procedure
;********************************|
;  entry point for each iteration |
;********************************|
ITERATION_START:
;**********************|
; calculate offset and |
;         mask         |
;**********************|
; Byte offset and mask for accessing the individual control bits
; is calculated as follows:
;        BYTE OFFSET = INT((ITER_COUNT-1) / 8)
;               MASK = 1000000B SHIFTED RIGHT BY THE VALUE IN THE
;                      REMAINDER OF ITER_COUNT / 8
```

```
        MOV     AX,ITER_COUNT    ; Number of this iteration
        DEC     AX               ; Subtract 1
        MOV     CL,8             ; Load divisor
        DIV     CL               ; AX/8. Quotient is in AL and
                                 ; remainder in AH
        MOV     ITER_OFFSET,AL   ; Store offset
; Calculate bit mask from remainder
        MOV     CL,AH            ; Remainder to CL
        MOV     AL,10000000B     ; Unit mask to AL (valid if zero
                                 ; remainder)
        SHR     AL,CL            ; Shift right CL times
        MOV     ITER_MASK,AL     ; Store mask
;**************************************************************
;                       combine processing
;**************************************************************
; Set pointer to combines control area
        LEA     DI,COMBINE_CTRL            ; To first machine
NEXT_COMBINE:
        MOV     AX,WORD PTR [DI]           ; Get machine status
; Test for a nonexistent machine to determine if at end of
; combines
        CMP     AX,0FFFFH        ; Code for nonexistent machine
        JNE     TST_IDLE_COMB    ; Test for idle if not 0FFFFH
        JMP     DO_TRACTORS      ; Tractor routine
; Test for an idle machine
TST_IDLE_COMB:
        CMP     AX,0             ; Code for an idle machine
        JE      COMB_IS_IDLE     ; Go if idle
;*******************|
;   combine working |
;*******************|
        MOV     BX,COMBINE_TIME  ; Job cycle for this machine type
        CALL    WORKING_MACHINE  ; Local procedure to process
                                 ; machine
; Carry set if machine changed status to idle
        JC      NEW_COMB_STATE   ; Go if machine changed state
        JMP     NEW_COMBINE      ; No status change
; Adjust combine pools to reflect this machine's status change
NEW_COMB_STATE:
        INC     COMBINES_IDLE    ; One more idle
        JMP     NEW_COMBINE
;*******************|
;   combine idle    |
;*******************|
; See if idle machine can be changed to working state
; The condition for a combine to work is that there must be at
```

```
; least one idle tractor and one idle trailer
COMB_IS_IDLE:
        CMP     TRACTORS_IDLE,0 ; Test for idle tractors
        JE      NEW_COMBINE     ; Go if no idle tractors
        CMP     TRAILERS_IDLE,0 ; Test for idle trailers
        JE      NEW_COMBINE     ; Go if no idle trailers
;*********************|
;  set combine to work |
;*********************|
; There is at least one idle tractor and trailer
        MOV     AX,ITER_COUNT   ; This iteration number to AX
        MOV     WORD PTR [DI],AX         ; Store in machine status
                                        ; area
;*********************|
;   adjust all pools   |
;*********************|
        DEC     COMBINES_IDLE   ; One less idle combine
        DEC     TRACTORS_IDLE   ; Do the same with the tractor
        DEC     TRAILERS_IDLE
;*********************|
; set tractor to work |
;*********************|
        LEA     BX,TRACTOR_CTRL ; Pointer to machine control area
        CALL    SET_TO_WORK     ; Local procedure first idle
                                ; machine to working state
; Recycle this machine as working
        JMP     NEXT_COMBINE
;*********************|
; index to next combine|
;*********************|
NEW_COMBINE:
        ADD     DI,80           ; Machines are 80 bytes apart
        JMP     NEXT_COMBINE    ; Iterate next machine
;*****************************************************************
;                       tractor processing
;*****************************************************************
; Note that trailers are considered auxiliary machines, therefore
; they do not have a machine control area
DO_TRACTORS:
; Check all tractors in working state and update I/W bit
; Set pointer to tractors control area
        LEA     DI,TRACTOR_CTRL         ; To first machine
NEXT_TRACTOR:
        MOV     AX,WORD PTR [DI]        ; Get machine status
; Test for a nonexistent machine to determine if at end of
; tractors
```

```
        CMP     AX,0FFFFH       ; Code for nonexistent machine
        JNE     TST_IDLE_TRAC   ; Test for idle if not 0FFFFH
        JMP     DO_TRUCKS       ; Truck routine
; Test for an idle machine
TST_IDLE_TRAC:
        CMP     AX,0            ; Code for an idle machine
; Tractors are started by the combine routine. Idle tractors
; cannot start on their own
        JE      NEW_TRACTOR     ; Go if idle
;**********************|
;   tractor working    |
;**********************|
        MOV     BX,TRACTOR_TIME ; Job cycle for this machine type
        CALL    WORKING_MACHINE ; Local procedure to process
                                ; machine
; Carry set if machine changed status to idle
        JC      NEW_TRAC_STATE  ; Go if machine changed state
        JMP     NEW_TRACTOR     ; No status change
; Adjust combine pools to reflect this machine's status change
NEW_TRAC_STATE:
        INC     TRACTORS_IDLE   ; and one more idle
; When a tractor finishes its cycle, it has left the full trailer
; in the holding area. The FULL_TRAILERS queue must be
; incremented. Note that the TRAILERS_IDLE pool does not change
        INC     FULL_TRAILERS   ; Queue or trailers waiting to be
                                ; trucked to storage
NEW_TRACTOR:
        ADD     DI,80           ; Machines are 80 bytes apart
        JMP     NEXT_TRACTOR    ; Iterate next machine
;*****************************************************************
;                        truck processing
;*****************************************************************
; A truck can start work if there is at least one full trailer in
; the holding area
DO_TRUCKS:
; Check all trucks in working state and update I/W bit
; Set pointer to tractors control area
        LEA     DI,TRUCK_CTRL           ; To first machine
NEXT_TRUCK:
        MOV     AX,WORD PTR [DI]        ; Get machine status
; Test for a nonexistent machine to determine if at end of
; tractors
        CMP     AX,0FFFFH       ; Code for nonexistent machine
        JNE     TST_IDLE_TRUK   ; Test for idle if not 0FFFFH
        JMP     NEXT_ITER       ; End of truck processing
; Test for an idle machine
```

```
TST_IDLE_TRUK:
        CMP     AX,0                ; Code for an idle machine
        JE      TRUK_IS_IDLE        ; Go if truck idle
;**********************|
;     truck working    |
;**********************|
        MOV     BX,TRUCK_TIME    ; Job cycle for this machine type
        CALL    WORKING_MACHINE  ; Local procedure to process
                                 ; machine
; Carry set if machine changed status to idle
        JC      NEW_TRUK_STATE   ; Go if machine changed state
        JMP     NEW_TRUCK        ; No status change
; Adjust combine pools to reflect this machine's status change
NEW_TRUK_STATE:
        INC     TRUCKS_IDLE      ; and one more idle
; When a truck finishes its cycle so does one trailer. Therefore
; the trailer pools must be adjusted
        INC     TRAILERS_IDLE    ; and one more idle
        JMP     NEW_TRUCK
;
;**********************|
;     truck idle       |
;**********************|
; See if idle machine can be changed to working state
; The condition for a truck to work is that there must be at
; least one trailer in the holding area
TRUK_IS_IDLE:
        CMP     FULL_TRAILERS,0     ; Test for no trailers ready
                                    ; in holding area
        JE      NEW_TRUCK        ; Go if no trailers to move
;**********************|
;  set truck to work   |
;**********************|
        MOV     AX,ITER_COUNT    ; This iteration number to AX
        MOV     WORD PTR [DI],AX    ; Store in machine status
                                    ; area
;**********************|
;  adjust truck pools  |
;**********************|
        DEC     TRUCKS_IDLE      ; One less idle
;**********************|
; update trailer queue |
;**********************|
        DEC     FULL_TRAILERS    ; Truck takes trailer to storage
; Recycle this machine as working
        JMP     NEXT_TRUCK       ; Recycle this machine as working
```

```
;**********************|
;  index to next truck |
;**********************|
NEW_TRUCK:
        ADD     DI,80           ; Machines are 80 bytes apart
        JMP     NEXT_TRUCK      ; Iterate next machine
;******************************************************************
;                        next iteration
;******************************************************************
NEXT_ITER:
        INC     ITER_COUNT      ; Bump iteration counter
        CMP     ITER_COUNT,601  ; Last iteration executed?
        JNE     OK_2_ITERATE    ; Continue if not
        RET
OK_2_ITERATE:
        JMP     ITERATION_START ; Go to iteration start point
ITERATE_600    ENDP
;******************************************************************
;
GRAPH_MACHINES  PROC    NEAR
; Procedure to generate a screen alphanumeric graph of the
; simulated workday for a machine type. Each machine is graphed
; in one screen row of 75 characters. Each character represents
; 8 min in the workday. The * symbol represents work and the
; - symbol represents idle. Each machine is preceded by its
; number. The routine also counts the number of graphed machines
; and adds the work-state bits
; On entry:
;       DI -> control block for machine type to be graphed
; On exit:
;       Machine graph displayed
;       WORK_COUNT variable has sum of all working iterations
;       MACH_COUNT variable has total number of graphed machines
;
;**********************|
; initialize variables |
;**********************|
        MOV     MACH_COUNT,1    ; Initialize binary row counter
        MOV     WORK_COUNT,0    ; Counter for working state bits
; Set cursor to screen row number 1, column number 4
        MOV     DH,1            ; Row number 1
        MOV     DL,0            ; Column number 4
        CALL    BIO_SET_CUR     ; Cursor service in SOLUTION.LIB
;**********************|
;   display one row    |
;**********************|
```

```
NEW_ROW:
        MOV     AX,[DI]         ; Get machine's status word
        CMP     AL,0FFFFH       ; Non-implemented machine
        JE      END_OF_GRAPH    ; Go if no more machines
; At this point there is a machine to graph
        PUSH    DX              ; Save cursor position at row
                                ; start
        PUSH    DI              ; Save machine status pointer
        PUSH    DI              ; Twice
;*********************|
; display row number  |
;*********************|
        MOV     DX,MACH_COUNT   ; Get binary row counter
        LEA     DI,DIGIT_BUF    ; Buffer for 5 ASCII digits
        CALL    BIN_TO_ASC      ; Convert binary to ASCII
; One or two ASCII digits are now right-justified in DIGIT_BUF
; DI -> start of buffer
        ADD     DI,3            ; Point to first digit
        MOV     CX,2            ; Display 3 characters
DIGITS_2:
        MOV     AL,[DI]         ; ASCII digit to AL
        CALL    BIO_TTY         ; Display and bump cursor
        INC     DI              ; Bump pointer
        LOOP    DIGITS_2        ; Continue
; Insert blank space
        MOV     AL,20H          ; One blank
        CALL    BIO_TTY         ; To display
;*********************|
; display graph codes |
;*********************|
        POP     DI              ; Restore machine status pointer
        ADD     DI,5            ; Point to working/idle control
                                ; area
        MOV     CX,75           ; Counter for 75 bytes to graph
GRAPH_ROW:
        MOV     AL,'*'          ; Assume machine is working
        MOV     BL,BYTE PTR [DI]        ; Get stored value for 8
                                ; iterations
;*********************|
; add-in bits set     |
;*********************|
; Test for bits that are set and accumulate count in variable
        PUSH    CX              ; Save outer loop count
        MOV     CX,8            ; Setup counter for 8 bits
        MOV     BH,BL           ; Bit pattern to BH
        CLC                     ; No carry
```

```
ROTATE_BITS:
        ROL     BH,1             ; Rotate BH bits. Carry set if
                                 ; high bit was set
        JNC     UNSET            ; Go if no carry
        INC     WORK_COUNT       ; Bump counter
UNSET:
        LOOP    ROTATE_BITS      ; Continue
        POP     CX               ; Restore outer loop counter
;*********************|
;    display * or -   |
;*********************|
        TEST    BL,00011000B     ; If these bits set then at least
                                 ; 4 of 8 are working bits
        JNZ     GRAPH_WORK       ; Display the default work symbol
        MOV     AL,'-'           ; Else load an idle symbol
GRAPH_WORK:
        CALL    BIO_TTY          ; Display at cursor and bump
                                 ; cursor
        INC     DI               ; Bump pointer
        LOOP    GRAPH_ROW        ; Continue until end of row
; Row has been graphed. Index pointer and cursor
        POP     DI               ; Restore start position
        ADD     DI,80            ; Bump to next row
        POP     DX               ; Restore cursor at start of row
        INC     DH               ; Bump cursor to next screen row
        CALL    BIO_SET_CUR      ; Cursor service in SOLUTION.LIB
        INC     MACH_COUNT       ; Bump row counter
        JMP     NEW_ROW
; Adjust row counter and exit
END_OF_GRAPH:
        DEC     MACH_COUNT       ; Can be used by the caller to
                                 ; get total machines graphed
        RET
GRAPH_MACHINES  ENDP
;*****************************************************************
;
SHOW_STATS      PROC    NEAR
; Display machine stats text and calculate stats for this
; simulation
; On entry:
;       WORK_COUNT variable has sum of all working iterations
;       MACH_COUNT variable has total number of graphed machines
        LEA     SI,SUMMARY_MS
        CALL    BIO_SHOW_BLOK
; Set cursor to first display area
        MOV     DH,22            ; Row number
```

```
        MOV     DL,34           ; Column number
        CALL    BIO_SET_CUR     ; Set cursor
;*********************|
;     machine time    |
;*********************|
; Total machine time is the product of the number of machines by
; 600 min in a 10-h workday
        MOV     CX,MACH_COUNT   ; CX holds machines
        MOV     AX,600          ; Total minutes in workday
        MUL     CX              ; AX * CX in DX and AX
; Since product cannot exceed one word, it will be in AX
; Store for use in calculating utilization
        MOV     TOTAL_TIME,AX   ; Store in variable
        MOV     DX,AX           ; to DX for conversion routine
        LEA     DI,DIGIT_BUF    ; Buffer for ASCII digits
        CALL    BIN_TO_ASC      ; Conversion routine in
                                ; SOLUTION.LIB
        CALL    DISPLAY_DIGITS
;********************|
;     work time      |
;********************|
; Set cursor to second display area
        MOV     DH,22           ; Row number
        MOV     DL,72           ; Column number
        CALL    BIO_SET_CUR     ; Set cursor
; Machine work time is stored in the variable WORK_COUNT
        MOV     DX,WORK_COUNT   ; Binary value to DX
        LEA     DI,DIGIT_BUF    ; Buffer for ASCII digits
        CALL    BIN_TO_ASC      ; Conversion routine in
                                ; SOLUTION.LIB
        CALL    DISPLAY_DIGITS
;********************|
; machine utilization |
;********************|
; Set cursor to third display area
        MOV     DH,23           ; Row number
        MOV     DL,34           ; Column number
        CALL    BIO_SET_CUR     ; Set cursor
; Percent of ideal machine utilization is calculated by dividing
; total work time by total machine time/100
        MOV     BX,100          ; Divisor to BX
        MOV     DX,0            ; Clear high-order word
        MOV     AX,TOTAL_TIME   ; Dividend to AX
        DIV     BX              ; Quotient is in AX
        MOV     BX,AX           ; Move quotient to BX
; Divide total work time by BX
```

```
        MOV     AX,WORK_COUNT    ; Dividend to AX
        MOV     DX,0             ; Clear high-order word
        DIV     BX               ; Quotient of this division in AX
        MOV     DX,AX            ; Move to DX for conversion
                                 ; routine
        LEA     DI,DIGIT_BUF     ; Buffer for ASCII digits
        CALL    BIN_TO_ASC       ; Conversion routine in
                                 ; SOLUTION.LIB
        CALL    DISPLAY_DIGITS
; Move cursor out of display area
        CALL    BIO_CUR_OFF      ; Cursor off service in
                                 ; SOLUTION.LIB
        RET
SHOW_STATS      ENDP
;*****************************************************************
;
INIT_CONTROLS   PROC    NEAR
; Each machine's control area (80 bytes long) is preceded by a
; 5-byte status area (see data segment). Code FFFFH in this
; header indicates that the machine does not exist
; On entry:
;       CL = total number of machines
;       DI = pointer to machine control area
; Bypass routine if 20 or more machines. FFFFH code is already
; in place in this case
        CMP     CL,20            ; Test for limit
        JGE     EXIT_INIT        ; Go if 20 or larger
; Index to the first nonexistent machine
        MOV     AX,80            ; 80 bytes per machine
        MUL     CL               ; 80 times number of machines
        ADD     DI,AX            ; Add to pointer
; DI -> first machine not in this case (nonexistent)
; Set up counter for number of nonexistent machines (20-CL)
        MOV     AL,20            ; Total machines in control area
        SUB     AL,CL            ; AL = nonexistent machines
        MOV     CL,AL            ; Move to counter
        MOV     CH,0             ; Clear high part of counter
INIT_FFFFH:
        MOV     WORD PTR [DI],0FFFFH    ; Code for no machine
        ADD     DI,80            ; Index to next machine
        LOOP    INIT_FFFFH       ; Continue for count
EXIT_INIT:
        RET
INIT_CONTROLS   ENDP
;*****************************************************************
WORKING_MACHINE PROC    NEAR
```

```
; Procedure to process an iteration for a machine in the working
; state
;
; On entry:
;          DI -> machine status area
;          BX = job cycle for the machine type
; On exit:
;          I/W bit is set for this machine
;          carry set if machine changed status to idle
;          (end of cycle)
;          carry clear if no status change
; Test if machine is at the end of its job cycle
; If the machine status is working, the first status word holds
; the iteration number at which the machine started working
        MOV       AX,[DI]           ; AX = start iteration for job
                                    ; cycle
        MOV       DX,ITER_COUNT     ; This iteration number to DX
        SUB       DX,AX             ; Start iteration minus this one
                                    ; is total iteration in this job
; DX (total iterations in this job cycle) must be smaller than BX
; (job cycle for this machine type)
        CMP       DX,BX             ; Compare to determine end of job
        JGE       JOB_AT_END        ; Go if BX > or =  DX
;*********************|
;  set bit to working |
;*********************|
; Machine is working. Set I/W bit for this iteration
        PUSH      DI                ; Twice
        ADD       DI,5              ; Pointer to I/W storage area
        MOV       AL,ITER_OFFSET    ; Offset to AL
        MOV       AH,0              ; Clear high-order byte for
                                    ; addition
        ADD       DI,AX             ; Add byte offset for this
                                    ; iteration
        MOV       AL,[DI]           ; Read 8 bits into AL
        OR        AL,ITER_MASK      ; Set this bit
        MOV       [DI],AL           ; Replace bit map in memory
        POP       DI                ; Restore status area pointer
        CLC                         ; No status change in this
                                    ; iteration
        RET
;*********************|
;  end of job cycle   |
;*********************|
JOB_AT_END:
        MOV       WORD PTR [DI],0000H      ; Set machine to idle
```

```
            STC                        ; Machine status has changed
            RET                        ; Return to caller
WORKING_MACHINE ENDP
;****************************************************************
;
SET_TO_WORK    PROC    NEAR
; Set first idle machine in the control block to working
; On entry:
;         BX -> start of control block for machine type
; Find first idle machine. Code assumes there is a least one
; idle machine in the control block
TRY_FOR_IDLE:
            MOV     AX,[BX]           ; Status word to AX
            CMP     AX,0              ; 0 is code for idle
            JE      IS_IDLE           ; Go if machine is idle
            ADD     BX,80             ; If not index to next machine
            JMP     TRY_FOR_IDLE      ; and continue search
IS_IDLE:
            MOV     AX,ITER_COUNT     ; Iteration counter
            MOV     WORD PTR [BX],AX        ; Store in machine status
                                            ; area
            RET
SET_TO_WORK    ENDP
;****************************************************************
;
DISPLAY_DIGITS PROC    NEAR
; Display digits in DIGIT_BUF at cursor position, skipping
; leading blanks
            MOV     CX,5              ; Maximum of 5 digits to display
            LEA     SI,DIGIT_BUF      ; Pointer to digits
SHOW_1DIGIT:
            MOV     AL,[SI]           ; Digit to AL
            CMP     AL,' '            ; Is it a blank
            JE      IS_BLANK          ; Go if it is
            CALL    BIO_TTY           ; Display if not blank
IS_BLANK:
            INC     SI                ; Bump digits pointer
            LOOP    SHOW_1DIGIT
            RET
DISPLAY_DIGITS ENDP
;****************************************************************
;
CODE    ENDS
        END     START
```

Bibliography

Angermeyer, John, and Kevin Jaeger. *MS DOS Developer's Guide*. Indianapolis, Ind.: Howard W. Sams, 1986.

Bradley, David J. *Assembly Language Programming for the IBM Personal Computer*. Englewood Cliffs, N.J.: Prentice-Hall, 1984.

Brumm, Peter, and Don Brumm. *80386 A Programming and Design Handbook*. Blue Ridge Summit, Pa.: Tab Books, 1987.

Chien, Chao C. *Programming the IBM Personal Computer: Assembly Language*. New York: CBS College Publishing, 1984.

Conrac Corporation. *Raster Graphics Handbook*. New York: Van Nostrand Reinhold, 1985.

Davis, William S. *Computing Fundamentals—Concepts*. 2d. ed. Reading, Mass.: Addison-Wesley, 1989.

Doty, David B. *Programmer's Guide to the Hercules Graphics Cards*. Reading, Mass.: Addison-Wesley, 1988.

Duncan, Ray. *Advanced MS DOS*. Redmond, Wash.: Microsoft Press, 1986.

——— *Advanced OS/2 Programming*. Redmond, Wash.: Microsoft Press, 1989.

——— *Extending DOS*. Reading, Mass: Addision-Wesley, 1990

——— *The MS DOS Encyclopedia*. Redmond, Wash.: Microsoft Press, 1988.

Franklin, Mark. *Using the IBM PC: Organization and Assembly Language Programming*. New York: CBS College Publishing, 1984.

Gofton, Peter W. *Mastering Serial Communications*. San Francisco: Sybex, 1986.

Halliday, Caroline M., and James A. Shields. *IBM PS/2 Technical Guide*. Indianapolis, Ind.: Howard W. Sams, 1988.

Hogan, Thom. *The Programmer's PC Sourcebook*. Redmond, Wash.: Microsoft Press, 1988.

Iacobucci, Ed. *OS/2 Programmer's Guide*. Berkeley, Calif.: Osborne/McGraw-Hill, 1988.

IBM Corporation. *Technical Reference, Personal Computer*. Boca Raton, Fla.: IBM, 1984.

———*Technical Reference, Personal Computer AT*. Boca Raton, Fla.: IBM, 1984.

——— *Technical Reference, Personal Computer PCjr*. Boca Raton, Fla.: IBM, 1983.

——— *Technical Reference, Personal System/2, Model 30*. Boca Raton, Fla.: IBM, 1987.

——— *Technical Reference, Personal System/2, Model 50 and 60*. Boca Raton, Fla.: IBM, 1987.

—— *Personal System/2 and Personal Computer BIOS Interface Technical Reference*. Boca Raton, Fla.: IBM, 1987.

—— *Technical Reference, Options and Adapters,* vol. 1. Boca Raton, Fla.: IBM, 1986.

—— *Technical Reference, Options and Adapters*, vol. 2. Boca Raton, Fla.: IBM, 1986.

—— *Technical Reference, Options and Adapters*. Boca Raton, Fla.: IBM, 1986.

—— *Technical Reference, Supplements for the PS/2 Model 70, Hardware Interface, and BIOS Interface Technical References*. Boca Raton,Fla.: IBM, 1988.

Intel Corporation, *iAPX 86/88, 186/188 User's Manual* (Programmer's Reference). Santa Clara, Calif.: Reward Books, 1983.

—— *iAPX 86/88, 186/188 User's Manual* (Programmer's Reference). Santa Clara, Calif.: Intel, 1987.

—— *80286 and 80287 Programmer's Reference Manual*. Santa Clara, Calif.: Intel, 1987.

—— *80386 Programmer's Reference Manual*. Santa Clara, Calif.: Intel, 1986.

Jordan., Larry, and Bruce Curchill. *Communications and Networking for the IBM PC and Compatibles*. Reston, Va.: Brady Communications, 1990.

Jourdain, Robert. *Programmer's Problem Solver for the IBM PC, XT & AT*. New York: Brady Communications, 1986.

Jump, Dennis N. *Programmer's Guide to MS DOS for the IBM PC*. Reston, Va.: Brady Communications, 1984.

Kliewer, Bradley Dyck. *EGA/VGA A Programmer's Reference Guide*, 2d ed. New York: McGraw-Hill, 1988.

Liu, Yu-Cheng, and Glenn A. Gibson. *Microcomputer Systems: The 8086/8088 Family*. Englewood Cliffs, N.J.: Prentice-Hall, 1984.

Microsoft Corporation. *Microsoft Mouse Programmer's Reference*. Redmond, Wash.: Microsoft Press, 1989.

Money, Steve A. *Practical Microprocessor Interfacing*. New York: Wiley, 1987.

Morgan, Christopher L. *Bluebook of Assembly Language Routines for the IBM PC & XT*. New York: Waite Group, 1984.

Norton, Peter. *Inside the IBM PC. Access to Advanced Features and Programming*. Bowie, Md: Robert J. Brady Co., 1983.

—— *Peter Norton's Assembly Language Book for the IBM PC*. New York: Prentice-Hall, 1986

—— *The Peter Norton Programmer's Guide to the IBM PC*. Redmond, Wash.: Microsoft Press, 1985.

Palmer, John F., and Stephen P. Morse. *The 8087 Primer*. New York: Wiley, 1984.

Ralston, Anthony, and Chester L. Meek. *Encyclopedia of Computer Science*. New York: Mason and Charter, 1983.

Rogers, David F. *Procedural Elements for Computer Graphics*. New York: McGraw-Hill, 1985.

Rosch, Winn L. *The Winn Rosch Hardware Bible*. New York: Prentice-Hall, 1989.

Royer, Jeffrey P. *Handbook of Software & Hardware Interfacing for the IBM PCs*. Englewood Cliffs, N.J.: Prentice-Hall, 1987.

Runnion, William C. *Structured Programming in Assembly Language for the IBM PC*. Boston: PWS-Kent, 1988.

Sanchez, Julio. Assembly Language Tools and Techniques for the IBM Microcomputers. Englewood Cliffs, N.J.: Prentice-Hall, 1990.

―――― *Graphics Design and Animation on the IBM Microcomputers*. Englewood Cliffs, N.J.: Prentice-Hall, 1990.

Sanchez, Julio, and Maria P. Canton. *IBM Microcomputers: A Programmer's Handbook*. New York: McGraw-Hill, 1990.

Seyer, Martin D. *RS-232 Made Easy*. Englewood Cliffs, N.J.: Prentice-Hall, 1984.

Sargent, Richard, III, and Richard L. Shoemaker. *The IBM Personal Computer from the Inside Out*. Reading, Mass.: Addison-Wesley, 1984.

Scanlon, Leo J. *Assembly Language Subroutines for MS-DOS Computers*. Blue Ridge Summit, Pa.: Tab Books, 1987.

―――― *IBM PC & XT Assembly Language*. Bowie, Md.: Brady Communications, 1983.

Schatt, Stan. *Understanding Local Area Networks*. Indianapolis, Ind.: Howard W. Sams, 1987.

Smith, James T. *The IBM PC AT Programmer' Guide*. New York: Waite Group, 1986.

Smith, Bud E., and Mark T. Johnson. *Programming the Intel 80386*. Glenview, Ill.: Scott, Foresman, 1987.

Stallings, William. *Handbook of Computer Communications Standards*. vols. 1–3. New York: Macmillan, 1988.

Starts, Richard. *8087 Applications and Programming for the IBM PC, XT, and AT*. New York: Brady Communications, 1985.

Vieillefond, C. *Programming the 80286*. San Francisco: Sybex, 1987.

Willen, David C. *IBM PCjr Assembler Language*. Indianapolis, Ind.: Howard W. Sams, 1984.

Willen, David C., and Jeffrey I. Krantz. *8088 Assembler Language Programming: The IBM PC*. Indianapolis, Ind.: Howard W. Sams, 1983.

Wilton, Richard. *Programmer's Guide to PC & PS/2 Video Systems*. Redmond, Wash.: Microsoft Press, 1987.

Woram, John. *The PC Configuration Handbook*. New York: Bantam Books, 1987.

Index

ABOUT THE AUTHORS

Julio Sanchez is a professor of computer science and the author of numerous text and reference books in the field of microcomputers.

Maria P. Canton is vice president of a software development and consulting firm. She serves as documentation consultant to major software firms.

Sanchez and Canton are also the authors of *IBM Microcomputers: A Programmer's Handbook*.

DISK WARRANTY